THE CONTEXT AND CRAFT OF DRAMA

The CONTEXT and CRAFT of DRAMA

Critical Essays on the Nature of Drama and Theatre

Edited by

ROBERT W. CORRIGAN
New York University

and

JAMES L. ROSENBERG
Carnegie Institute of Technology

CHANDLER PUBLISHING COMPANY • SAN FRANCISCO

SUSANNE LANGER, "The Dramatic Illusion," is reprinted with the permission of Charles Scribner's Sons from *Feeling and Form*, pp. 306-325, by Susanne Langer. Copyright 1953 Charles Scribner's Sons.

HENRI GHÉON, "The Conditions of Dramatic Art." From *The Art of the Theatre* by Henri Ghéon. Copyright © 1961 by the Estate of Henri Ghéon. Reprinted by permission of Hill and Wang, Inc.

JEAN-LOUIS BARRAULT, "How Drama Is Born Within Us." From *The Theatre of Jean-Louis Barrault* by Jean-Louis Barrault. First published 1959 by Flammarion, Paris, under the title *Nouvelles réflexions sur le théâtre*. English translation first published and © 1961 by Barrie and Rockliff. Reprinted by permission of Hill and Wang, Inc.

JEAN VILAR, "Secrets," from *The Tradition of the Theatre*, translated by Christopher Kotschnig. First published in *Tulane Drama Review*, Vol. 3, No. 3, 1959, pp. 24-30. Reprinted with permission of the author.

CONOR A. FARRINGTON, "The Importance of Drama." First published in *Tulane Drama Review*, Vol. 5, No. 2, 1960, pp. 65-72. Reprinted by permission.

CHRISTOPHER FRY, "Why Verse?" Copyright © 1955 Christopher Fry. Reprinted by permission of the author.

HAROLD ROSENBERG, "Character Change and the Drama." Reprinted by permission of the publisher Horizon Press, Inc., from *The Tradition of the New* by Harold Rosenberg. Copyright 1959, 1960.

J. L. STYAN, "Manipulating the Characters." Reprinted by permission of the publisher Cambridge University Press from *The Elements of Drama* by J. L. Styan, pp. 163-187. Copyright 1960.

CHARLES MORGAN, "The Nature of Dramatic Illusion." Reprinted from *The Transactions of the Royal Society of Literature*, Vol. 12, 1933. Published with the permission of J. C. Medley, literary executor of Charles Morgan's Estate.

ROBERT W. CORRIGAN, "The Plays of Chekhov." From *Six Plays of Chekhov*, New English Versions and Introduction by Robert W. Corrigan, Rinehart Editions. Copyright © 1962 by Robert W. Corrigan. All rights reserved. Reprinted by permission of Robert W. Corrigan and Holt, Rinehart and Winston, Inc.

JAMES L. ROSENBERG, "Melodrama," revised from a lecture delivered by the author in May, 1962.

RONALD S. CRANE, "The Varieties of Dramatic Criticism." First printed in *Carleton Drama Bulletin*, 1953; reprinted by permission of the author from *Carleton Drama Review*, Vol. 1, No. 2, 1956, pp. 22-38.

NORTHROP FRYE, "Specific Forms of Drama." From *The Anatomy of Criticism* by Northrop Frye, copyright © 1957 by Princeton University Press. Reprinted with permission of the Princeton University Press.

THORNTON WILDER, "Some Thoughts on Playwriting." Published in *The Intent of the Artist*, edited by Augusto Centeno, Princeton University Press, 1941, pp. 83-98. Reprinted with permission of the Princeton University Press.

FRIEDRICH DUERRENMATT, "Problems of the Theatre." First published in *Tulane Drama Review*, Vol. 3, No. 1, 1958, pp. 3-26, in translation by Gerhard Nellhaus. Reprinted with permission of Kurt Hellmer, 52 Vanderbilt Ave., New York 17, N.Y.

EUGÈNE IONESCO, "Experience of the Theatre." From *Notes and Counter Notes: Writings on the Theatre*, by Eugène Ionesco, tr. from the French by Donald Watson. Copyright © 1964 by Grove Press, Inc. Reprinted by permission.

MORRIS CARNOVSKY, "Design for Acting." First published in *Tulane Drama Review*, Vol. 5, No. 3, 1961, pp. 68-85. Reprinted with permission of the author.

PETER SHAFFER, "The Cannibal Theatre." First published and © 1960 in *The Atlantic Monthly*, Vol. 206, October, 1960, pp. 48-50. Reprinted with permission of Greenbaum, Wolff & Ernst.

FREDERIK SCHYBERG, "What Is an Actor?" From *The Art of Acting* by Frederik Schyberg, translated by Harry Carlson, first published in *Tulane Drama Review*, Vol. 5, No. 4, 1961, pp. 56-76. Reprinted with permission of Harry G. Carlson.

HAROLD CLURMAN, "Mistaken Notions." First published in *The New York Times Magazine*, © 1952. Reprinted with permission of the author.

STARK YOUNG, "The Art of the Directing." Used by permission of Charles Scribner's Sons. From *Theatre Practice*, pp. 127-152, by Stark Young. Copyright 1926 Charles Scribner's Sons; renewal copyright 1954 Stark Young.

JEAN VILAR, "Murder of the Director," from *The Tradition of the Theatre*, translated by Christopher Kotschnig. First published in *Tulane Drama Review*, Vol. 3, No. 2, 1958, pp. 3-7. Reprinted with permission of the author.

ROBERT EDMOND JONES, "To a Young Stage Designer." From *The Dramatic Imagination*, copyright 1941 by Robert Edmond Jones. Reprinted with permission of Theatre Arts Books, New York.

SEAN O'CASEY, "Pro-Per Proscenium." Reprinted with the permission of the publisher, George Braziller, Inc., from *The Green Crow* by Sean O'Casey, © 1956 by Sean O'Casey.

GEORGE BERNARD SHAW, reviews of *Hamlet*, from *The Saturday Review* (London). Reprinted with permission of The Society of Authors and the Public Trustee from *Shaw's Dramatic Criticism*, Hill and Wang, Inc., 1959.

STARK YOUNG, "*Hamlet*—1922." Used by permission of Charles Scribner's Sons. From *Immortal Shadows* by Stark Young. Copyright 1948 by Charles Scribner's Sons.

KENNETH TYNAN, review of *Hamlet*. From *Curtains* by Kenneth Tynan. Copyright © 1961 by Kenneth Tynan. Reprinted by permission of Atheneum Publishers.

MELVIN ASKEW, "Duerrenmatt's *The Visit of the Old Lady*." First published in *Tulane Drama Review*, Vol. 5, No. 4, 1961, pp. 89-105. Reprinted with permission of the author.

GORDON ROGOFF, "Mr. Duerrenmatt Buys New Shoes." First published in *Tulane Drama Review*, Vol. 3, No. 1, 1958, pp. 27-34. Reprinted with permission of the author.

Contents

v

THE CRAFT OF DRAMA

Preface

The critic has traditionally and for centuries been the pariah, the uninvited guest at the banquet of the arts, and it has become almost universal in our time to accept Pope's judgment of the critics:

> Some are bewildered in the maze of schools,
> And some made coxcombs Nature meant but fools.
> In search of wit these lose their common sense,
> And then turn Critics in their own defence:
> Each burns alike, who can, or cannot write,
> Or with a Rival's, or an Eunuch's spite.

These are, in many ways, rather attractive sentiments, and most of us—even the poor critics themselves, we suspect—tend to accept them quite (if we may say so) uncritically. But perhaps it is time for a reevaluation of the critic's role—particularly in the field of the theatre, where all too often jollity is regarded as its own excuse for being, and any attempt at intellectual rigor is suspected of being Malvolio-like Puritanism. Certainly there will always be cakes and ale in the parlors of art, but it may not be a bad idea to have an occasional guest who will question their flavor, freshness, and over-all quality.

It is true that the critic is, by and large, not "creative," in the way that the poet and the painter and the composer are, and there may indeed be some critics who, in Pope's brilliant phrase, burn with a eunuch's spite. Periodically, bright young men pop up in the ranks of the critics, seemingly determined to establish a reputation as masters of the witty and destructive insult—whether or not this has any bearing upon the art they are presumably practicing. But, in speaking of criticism, it is obviously not fair to dwell exclusively on bad critics and overlook the clear fact that criticism at its best can be, and often is, an art form in its own right. Granted, the critic is somebody who, in the popular, contemptuous expression, "writes about writing"; but, by the same token, actors and singers are people who simply mouth someone else's words and melodies. The distinction, of course, is between the creative artist and the interpretive artist—one creates something brand-new out of the void; the other takes preexistent material and remolds it. And, though the interpretive artist may well stand on a slightly lower rung of the aesthetic ladder than the creative artist, this relation still does not mean that the practice of his particular skill cannot be raised to the level of art. The ideal critic is someone who tells us about his reactions to a work of art, utilizing all the imagination, perception and passion that is in his power. If he is a great critic, he quite literally remakes the work of art for us. We might add that, in this respect, he is in exactly the same position as the director of a play or the conductor of an orchestra, both of whom are engaged in telling us—imaginatively and powerfully—about their reactions to a drama or a symphony. Where the one artist *verbalizes* his perceptions through words on a page, the other *activates* them by the manipulation of performers.

The critics in this book represent the Critic as Artist; at least, this is the criterion upon which they were chosen. However you may agree or disagree with their opinions, we think you will find throughout their writing the two prime ingredients of fine criticism—intellectual vigor and vitality of expression. (And, again, are these not the hallmarks of almost any work of art?)

It was actually not too difficult to limit our selection to those critics who seemed to us to perform as artists, but we discovered, as we narrowed our selections down, that our artist-critics tended to fall into two categories—those who, to put it very simply, talked about the drama from the outside looking in and those who talked about it from the inside looking out. In other words, what might be called the "theoretical" and the "practical" critics. Had we wished to sound somewhat more scholarly and impressive, we might have labeled the two sections of our book "Theoria" and "Praxis" instead of "Context" and "Craft." In the first section of the book, the critics, many of whom are not active in the field of the drama at all, address themselves to principles, to large and general questions that are rather philosophical in nature: What is a play? How does it work? What is plot? What is the function of language in the drama? What is the role of the audience? The critics in the second section, mainly practitioners of the various arts of the theatre, tend to address themselves to more immediate questions of craftmanship—often speaking autobiographically and drawing on personal experience. Some students, incidentally, may wonder why we bothered with the first section at all, on the assumption that the best critic is the man who has been there, who has done the work himself. Curiously enough, this assumption is by no means true. An author may very well be—indeed, almost invariably is—the worst critic of his own work, and for perfectly obvious reasons. Criticism, after all, if it is an art form, is surely the most objective of the arts, and an artist can no more be truly objective about his creations than can a parent. But to concede this point is not to argue that we should have turned around and eliminated the second section of the book. The artist may not be the best critic of his own work, but at the same time he has things to say about it which nobody else in the world could possibly say—and testimony of this sort is an important part of criticism. If Shakespeare had written any critical essays, he probably could not have improved upon the brilliant work that has been done by generations of subsequent critics, but what we wouldn't give today to have just a preface or two from his own hand!

No, it is clearly not fair to eliminate from the ranks of criticism either the interlopers from other fields or the partial and unreliable artists themselves. We need both. In fact, we need all the good criticism we can get, at all times.

This book is an attempt to provide a little of it. One of us once had a professor who, clapping his hands together in gleeful conviviality, would exclaim: "Art is a banquet!" Well, in many ways, it is. We would like to apply the metaphor to a book of this nature. Here, seated around the long banquet table of time, which is groaning under the weight of the fruits of the harvest, are a group of brilliant conversationalists. The history of criticism, after all, is simply the history of good talk, and criticism itself is to be seen as an unending and uninterrupted conversation involving some of the world's most interesting talkers.

We invite you to listen.

And then, after you have closed the book and put it away, perhaps you yourself will want to join in the conversation. There is always room for a new speaker.

ROBERT W. CORRIGAN
JAMES L. ROSENBERG

PART ONE

THE NATURE OF DRAMA

SUSANNE LANGER

THE DRAMATIC ILLUSION

HENRI GHÉON

THE CONDITIONS OF DRAMATIC ART

JEAN-LOUIS BARRAULT

HOW DRAMA IS BORN WITHIN US

JEAN VILAR

SECRETS

The Dramatic Illusion

Most theoretical treatments of literature draw their material and evidence as much from drama as from lyric and narrative works. A serious analysis of literary art with only an occasional, passing mention of Shakespeare may have seemed to many readers a curious innovation. The reason for it, however, is simple enough, . . . Shakespeare is essentially a dramatist, and drama is not, in the strict sense, "literature."

Yet it is a poetic art, because it creates the primary illusion of all poetry—virtual history. Its substance is an image of human life—ends, means, gains and losses, fulfillment and decline and death. It is a fabric of illusory experience, and it is the essential product of poesis. But drama is not merely a distinct literary form; it is a special poetic mode, as different from genuine literature as sculpture from pictorial art, or either of these from architecture. That is to say, it makes its own basic abstraction, which gives it a way of its own in making the semblance of history.

Literature projects the image of life in the mode of virtual memory; language is its essential material; the sound and meaning of words, their familiar or unusual use and order, even their presentation on the printed page, create the illusion of life as a realm of events—completed, lived, as words formulate

3

them—events that compose a Past. But drama presents the poetic illusion in a different light: not finished realities, or "events," but immediate, visible responses of human beings, make its semblance of life. Its basic abstraction is the act, which springs from the past, but is directed toward the future, and is always great with things to come.

In using common words, such as "event" or "act," as analytic terms, one runs the danger of suggesting far less general concepts, and indeed a variety of them, all equally inadequate to the purpose in hand. "Event," . . . is used in the sense given it by Whitehead, to cover all space-time occurrence, even the persistence of objects, the repetitious rhythms of life, the occasion of a thought as well as of an earthquake. Similarly, by "act" I mean any sort of human response, physical or mental. The word is commonly used, of course, in more specialized senses. It may mean one of the major divisions of a play—Act I, Act II, etc.; or it may refer to overt behavior, rushing about, laying hands on someone, taking or surrendering an object, and so forth; or it may mean a piece of dissembling, as when one says of a person that he feels one way and acts another. In the general sense here employed however, all *reactions* are acts, visible or invisible; so in drama, any illusion of physical or mental activity is here called an "act," and the total structure of acts is *a virtual history in the mode of dramatic action.*

An act, whether instinctive or deliberate, is normally oriented toward the future. Drama, though it implies past actions (the "situation"), moves not toward the present, as narrative does, but toward something beyond; it deals essentially with commitments and consequences. Persons, too, in drama are purely agents—whether consciously or blindly, makers of the future. This future, which is made before our eyes, gives importance to the very beginnings of dramatic acts, i.e. to the motives from which the acts arise, and the situations in which they develop; the making of it is the principle that unifies and organizes the continuum of stage action. It has been said repeatedly that the theater creates a perpetual present moment[1]; but it is only a present filled with its own future that is really dramatic. A sheer immediacy, an imperishable direct experience without the ominous forward movement of consequential action, would not be so. As literature creates a virtual past, drama creates a virtual future. The literary mode is the mode of Memory; the dramatic is the mode of Destiny.

The future, like the past, is a conceptual structure, and expectation, even more obviously than memory, is a product of imagination.[2] The "now" created by poetic composition is always under the aegis of some historical vision which transcends it; and its poignancy derives not from any comparison with actuality, but from the fact that the two great realms of envisagement—past and future—intersect in the present, which consequently has not the pure imaginative form of either memory or prophecy, but a peculiar appearance of its own which we designate as "immediacy" or "now."

In actual life the impending future is very vaguely felt. Each separate act is forward-looking—we put on a kettle expecting it to boil, hand someone a bill and expect to be given change, board a bus with casual confidence that we shall leave it again at an intended point, or board an airplane with somewhat more conscious interest in our prospective exit from its inside. But we do not usually have any idea of the future as a total experience which is coming because of our past and present acts;

[1] For example, R. E. Jones in *The Dramatic Imagination,* p. 40, says: "This is drama; this is theatre—*to be aware of the Now.*" And Thornton Wilder, in "Some Thoughts on Playwriting," lists as one of the "four fundamental conditions of the drama" that "its action takes place in a perpetual present time."—"On the stage it is always now." (*The Intent of the Artist,* p. 83.)

[2] Compare the observations of George Mehlis, . . . Mehlis mistook the nature of the "distancing" effect of memory and expectation, which he thought rested on people's tendency to leave out the unpleasant, and a consequent "aesthetic improvement" of the facts; but despite this error he noted truly the transformational power of both projections.

such a sense of destiny arises only in unusual moments under peculiar emotional stress.

In drama, however, this sense of destiny is paramount. It is what makes the present action seem like an integral part of the future, howbeit that future has not unfolded yet. The reason is that on the stage, every thought expressed in conversation, every feeling betrayed by voice or look, is determined by the total action of which it is a part—perhaps an embryonic part, the first hint of the motive that will soon gather force. Even before one has any idea of what the conflict is to be (i.e. before the "exposition" has been given), one feels the tension developing. This tension between past and future, the theatrical "present moment," is what gives to acts, situations, and even such constituent elements as gestures and attitudes and tones, the peculiar intensity known as "dramatic quality."

In a little-known volume, bearing the modest, impersonal title: *Essays by Divers Hands* (a volume of "Transactions" of the Royal Society of Literature in England),[3] there is a very thoughtful philosophical essay by Charles Morgan, called "The Nature of Dramatic Illusion," in which he seems to me to have both stated and answered the question of what is created in the full-fledged work of dramatic art—the enacted play.

"With every development of dramatic technique," he wrote there, "and every departure from classical structure, the need increases for a new discussion which . . . shall establish for the stage not indeed a formal rule but an aesthetic discipline, elastic, reasoned, and acceptable to it in modern circumstances.

"It is my purpose, then, to discover the principle from which such a discipline might arise. This principle I call the principle of illusion."[4]

"Illusion, as I conceive it, is form in suspense. . . . In a play

[3] N. S. Vol. 12, ed. by R. W. Macan, 1933. The article in question covers pp. 61-77.
[4] Ibid., p. 61.

form is not valuable *in itself*, only the suspense of form has value. In a play, form is not and cannot be valuable in itself, because until the play is over form does not exist. . . .

"A play's performance occupies two or three hours. Until the end its form is latent in it. . . .

"This suspense of form, by which is meant the incompleteness of a known completion, is to be clearly distinguished from common suspense—suspense of plot—the ignorance of what will happen, . . . for suspense of plot is a structural accident, and suspense of form is, as I understand it, essential to the dramatic form itself. . . .

"What form is chosen . . . matters less than that while the drama moves *a* form is being fulfilled."[5]

"Fulfilled" is here the key word to the idea of dramatic form. Everything, of course, has a form of some sort: the famous million monkeys playing a million typewriters for a million years, turning out chance combinations of letters, would be rendering countless phonetic forms (though some of these might not encourage pronunciation); similarly, the most aimless conglomerate of events, acts, utterances, or what not, would *produce* a form when taken together; but before such collections were complete (which would be simply when, for any reason, one stopped collecting), no one could imagine their form. There has to be a sense of the whole, some anticipation of what may or even must come, if the production of new elements is to give the impression that "a form is being fulfilled."

Dramatic action is a semblance of action so constructed that a whole indivisible piece of virtual history is implicit in it, as a yet unrealized form, long before the presentation is completed. This constant illusion of an imminent future, this vivid appearance of a growing situation before anything startling has occurred, is "form in suspense." It is a human destiny that unfolds before us, its unity is apparent from the opening

5 Ibid., pp. 70-72.

words, or even silent action, because on the stage we see acts in their entirety, as we do not see them in the real world except in retrospect, that is, by constructive reflection. In the theatre, they occur in simplified and completed form, with visible motives, directions, and ends. Since stage action is not, like genuine action, embedded in a welter of irrelevant doings and divided interests, and characters on the stage have no unknown complexities (however complex they may be), it is possible there to see a person's feelings grow into passions, and those passions issue in words and deeds.

We know, in fact, so little about the personalities before us at the opening of a play that their every move and word, even their dress and walk, are distinct items for our perception. Because we are not involved with them as with real people, we can view each smallest act in its context, as a symptom of character and condition. We do not have to find what is significant; the selection has been made—whatever is there is significant, and it is not too much to be surveyed *in toto*. A character stands before us as a coherent whole. It is with characters as with their situations: both become visible on the stage, transparent and complete as their analogues in the world are not.[6]

But what really assures the artistic unity Morgan called "form in suspense," is the illusion of Destiny itself that is given in drama, and that arises chiefly from the way the dramatist handles circumstance. Before a play has progressed by many lines,

[6] A German critic, Peter Richard Rohden, saw this difference in our understanding of illusory and actual persons, respectively, as something of a paradox. "What," he wrote, "distinguishes a character on stage from a 'real' person? Obviously the fact that the former stands before us as a fully articulated whole. Our fellowmen we always perceive only in fragmentary fashion, and our power of self-observation is usually reduced, by vanity and cupidity, to zero. What we call 'dramatic illusion' is, therefore, the paradoxical phenomenon that we know more about the mental processes of a Hamlet than about our own inner life. For the poet-actor Shakespeare shows not only the deed, but also its motives, and indeed more perfectly than we ever see them together in actual life." (See "Das Schauspielerische Erlebnis," in Ewald Geissler's collection of essays, *Der Schauspieler*, p. 36.)

one is aware not only of vague conditions of life in general, but of a special situation. Like the distribution of figures on a chess-board, the combination of characters makes a strategic pattern. In actual life we usually recognize a distinct situation only when it is reached, or nearly reached, a crisis; but in the theater we see the whole setup of human relationships and conflicting interests long before any abnormal event has occurred that would, in actual life, have brought it into focus. Where in the real world we would witness some extraordinary act and gradually understand the circumstances that lie behind it, in the theater we perceive an ominous situation and see that some far-reaching action must grow out of it. This creates the peculiar tension between the given present and its yet unrealized consequent, "form in suspense," the essential dramatic illusion. This illusion of a visible future is created in every play—not only in very good plays, but in everything we recognize as a play, and not as dance, pageantry, or other non-dramatic "theater act."[7] It is the primary illusion of poetry, or virtual history, in the mode peculiar to drama. The future appears as already an entity, embryonic in the present. That is Destiny.

Destiny is, of course, always a virtual phenomenon—there is no such thing in cold fact. It is a pure semblance. But what it "resembles" (or, in the Aristotelian language which has been lately revived, what it "imitates") is nonetheless an aspect of real experience, and, indeed, a fundamental one, which distinguishes human life from animal existence: the sense of past and future as parts of one continuum, and therefore of life as a single reality.

This wide awareness, which we owe to our peculiarly human talent of symbolic expression, is rooted, however, in the

[7] On this point Mr. Morgan might not agree with me. Having stated that "form in suspense" is the dramatic illusion itself, and the suspense of form something "without which drama is not," he speaks elsewhere of the dramatic illusion as a rare experience, "the highest reward of playgoing." I do not know whether he uses two concepts or only one, somewhat different from mine.

elementary rhythms which we share with all other organisms,
and the Destiny which dramatic art creates bears the stamp of
organic process—of predeterminate function, tendency, growth,
and completion. . . . In every art [the abstraction of those vital
forms] is differently achieved; but in each one, I think, it is
equally subtle—not a simple reference to natural instances of
that form, but a genuinely abstractive handling of its reflection in non-living or even non-physical structures. Literally "organic process" is a biological concept; "life," "growth," "development," "decline," "death"—all these are strictly biological
terms. They are applicable only to organisms. In art they are
lifted out of their literal context, and forthwith, in place of organic processes, we have dynamic forms: instead of metabo-
lism, rhythmic progression, instead of stimulus and response,
completeness, instead of maturation, fulfillment, instead of
procreation, the repetition of the whole in the parts—what
Henry James calls "reflection" in the parts,[8] and Heinrich
Schenker "diminution,"[9] and Francis Fergusson "analogy."[10] And
in lieu of a law of development, such as biology sets up, in art
we have destiny, the implicit future.

The purpose of abstracting vital forms from their natural
exemplifications is, of course, to make them available for un-
hampered artistic use. The illusion of growth, for instance, may
be made in any medium, and in numberless ways: lengthening
or flowing lines, that represent no live creatures at all; rhythmically rising steps even though they divide or diminish; increasing complexity of musical chords, or insistent repetitions;
a centrifugal dance; poetic lines of gradually deepening seriousness; there is no need of "imitating" anything literally alive
in order to convey the appearance of life. Vital forms may be
reflected in any elements of a work, with or without representation of living things.

[8] *The Art of Fiction,* p. 170.
[9] Cf. Chap. 8, p. 129.
[10] *The Idea of a Theater,* p. 104.

In drama the *situation* has its own "organic" character, that is to say, it develops, or grows, as the play proceeds. That is because all happenings, to be dramatic, must be conceived in terms of acts, and acts belong only to life; they have motives rather than causes, and in turn motivate further and further acts, which compose integrated *actions*. A situation is a complex of impending acts. It changes from moment to moment, or rather, from move to move, as the directly imminent acts are realized and the future beyond them becomes distinct and fraught with excitement. In this way, the *situation* in which characters act differs from their "environment"—a term with which it is sometimes confused, through the influence of the social sciences that invaded the theater a generation ago and bred a teeming, if shortlived progeny of sociological plays, with a few real dramas among them. The environment wherein characters have developed, and whereby they are stunted or hardened, refined or falsely veneered, is almost always implicit (*almost always*, i.e. except where it becomes a conscious factor of interest to someone in the play). The situation, on the other hand, is always explicit. Even in a vague romantic world like that of Pelléas and Mélisande, removed from all actual history, and so ungeographical that the environment is really just castle walls and a forest, without population (the chorus of women in the death-scene simply springs up *ex nihilo*—there were no inhabitants in the background before, as there are in Shakespeare's castles), the situation that elicits the action is clear.

The situation is, indeed, part of the action; it is conceived entirely by the dramatist, and is given by him to the actors to understand and enact, just as he gives them the words to be spoken. The situation is a created element in the play; it grows to its climax, often branching out into elaborate detail in the course of its development, and in the end it is resolved by the closing of the action.

Where "environment" enters into drama at all, it enters as an idea entertained by persons in the play, such as the slum visitors and reformers of the "radical" problem play. They themselves, however, do not appear in an environment, because that sociological abstraction has no meaning for the theater. They appear in a setting. "Environment" is an invisible constant, but "setting" is something immediate, something sensuously or poetically present. The playwright may utilize a setting as Strindberg did in his earlier plays, to establish the feeling of everyday life, or he may put it to the opposite purpose of removing the scene from all familiar associations, as Wagner sought to do by his extravagant stage demands. The setting is a highly variable factor, which the poets of former ages used to entrust to those who put their plays on the boards; a practice which harbors dangers, but also speaks of a healthy faith in the power of the script to guide the theatrical imagination that is to project it. There is a grand freedom given with the simple indication: "Thebes."

Drama is more variable, more tolerant of choices made by performing artists, than any other art and mode. For this reason, the "commanding form," which is established by the playwright, must be clear and powerful. It has to govern the crisscross of many imaginative minds, and hold them all—the director, the actors, the designers of sets and lights and costumes—to one essential conception, an unmistakable "poetic core." But the poet must give his interpreters scope, too; for drama is essentially an enacted poem, and if the acting can only duplicate what the lines already effect, there will be unintended redundancy, and an apparent clutter of superfluous elements that makes the total form impure and opaque (such failures of clear conception, not the use of materials "belonging" to other arts, not bold secondary illusions, are the source of impurity in a work; if the commanding form is organic and its realization economical, the most abnormal materials will be assimilated, the most intense effects of abstracted space, time, or power will become part of the pure dramatic work).

If drama is not made of words as a piece of literature is, how can the poet, who composes only the "lines," be said to create the commanding form? "Lines" in a play are only the stuff of speeches; and speeches are only some of the acts that make drama.

They are, however, acts of a special sort. Speech is a highly specialized activity in human life, and its image in all modes of poetry, therefore, has peculiar and powerful uses. Verbal utterance is the overt issue of a greater emotional, mental, and bodily response, and its preparation in feeling and awareness or in the mounting intensity of thought is implicit in the words spoken. Speech is like a quintessence of action. Edith Wharton described its relation to the rest of our activities very aptly, when she indicated its use in her own poetic medium, prose fiction: "The use of dialogue in fiction . . . should be reserved for the culminating moments, and regarded as the spray into which the great wave of narrative breaks in curving toward the watcher on the shore."[11]

Mrs. Wharton's metaphor of the wave is more apt than her literal statement, because one naturally thinks of "culminating moments" as rare moments, high points of the story, whereas the culmination of thought and feeling in speech is a frequent occurrence, like the culmination and breaking of each wave in a constant surf.

If, moreover, one contemplates the metaphor a little more deeply, it conveys a further relation of speech to the poetic elements that surround it, namely: that it is always of the same nature as they, subject to the basic abstraction of the mode in which it is used. In narrative it is an event, like all the events that compose the virtual Past—the private events that culminate in "direct discourse," the public events that intersect in the speaker's experience, and those which the speech, as a new event, engenders. In drama speech is an act, an utterance, mo-

[11] *The Writing of Fiction*, p. 73.

tivated by visible and invisible other acts, and like them shaping the oncoming Future.

A playwright who writes only the lines uttered in a play marks a long series of culminating moments in the flow of the action. Of course he indicates the major non-verbal acts, but that may be done with the fewest possible words: *enter So-and-so, exit So-and-so,* or such laconic directions as: *dies, they fight, excursions and alarums.* Modern playwrights sometimes write pages of instructions to the actors, even describing the heroine's figure and face, or the style of some character's motions and postures (Strindberg tells the leading actor in *Miss Julia* to look like a half-educated man!). Such "stage directions" are really literary treatments of the story—what Clayton Hamilton called, "the sort of stage directions which, though interesting to the reader, are of no avail whatever to the actor,"[12] because they do not partake of the dramatic form. Ibsen prefaced his opening scenes with minute descriptions of persons and set; but his greatest interpreters have always made free with them. The lines of the play are the only guide a good director or actor needs. What makes the play the author's work is that the lines are really the highlights of a perpetual, progressive action, and determine what can be done with the piece on stage.

Since every utterance is the end of a process which began inside the speaker's body, an enacted utterance is part of a virtual act, apparently springing at the moment from thought and feeling; so the actor has to create the illusion of an inward activity issuing in spontaneous speech, if his words are to make a dramatic and not a rhetorical effect. As a very interesting German writer, Ferdinand Gregori, expressed it, "Gesture is older than words, and in the actor's dramatic creation, too, it must be their herald. Whether it is visible to the audience or not, it must always be the pacemaker. Anyone who starts with

[12] *The Theory of the Theatre,* p. 307. A few paragraphs later he remarked on Granville-Barker's plays: "Barker's printed stage directions are little novels in themselves."

the words and then hunts for the appropriate gesture to accompany them, lies to the face of art and nature both."[13]

The need of preparing every utterance by some elements of expression and bearing that foreshadow it, has led many theorists and almost all naive spectators to the belief that an actor must actually undergo the emotive experiences he renders—that he must "live" his part, and produce speech and gesture from a genuine passion. Of course the stage-occurrence is not his own life, but (according to this view) he must pretend to be the individual he represents, until he actually feels the emotions he is to register. Oddly enough, people who hold this belief do not ask whether the actor must also actually have the motives and desires of his alter ego—that is, whether he must really intend or at least wish to kill his antagonist, or to divulge a secret.

The imputation of bona fide feelings and emotions to the actor on stage would be only a negligible popular error, were it not part and parcel of a broader fallacy—the confusion of theatrical representation with "make-believe," or pretense, which has always led both playwrights and directors to misconceive the relation of the audience to the play, and saddled them with the gratuitous and silly problem of the spectator's credulity. The classic expression of concern is, of course, Castelvetro's warning in his *Poetics,* published in 1570: "The time of the representation and that of the action presented must be exactly coincident. There is no possibility of making the spectators believe that many days and nights have passed, when they themselves obviously know that only a few hours have actually elapsed; they refuse to be so deceived."[14] Corneille, a generation later, still accepted the principle, though he complained that to limit a dramatic action quite strictly to one room and

<hr>

[13] "Die Vorbildung des Schauspielers," in Ewald Geissler's collection *Der Schauspieler.* See p. 46.

[14] Reprinted in *The Great Critics, An Anthology of Literary Criticism,* edited by J. H. Smith and E. W. Parks. See p. 523.

the time span of a theater visit "is so awkward, not to say impossible, that some enlargement of place must of necessity be
found, as also of time."[15]

An art principle that cannot be fully and wholeheartedly
applied, but requires compromises and evasions, should be immediately suspect; yet the principle of making the spectators
believe that they are witnessing actual happenings has been
accepted down to our own day,[16] and though most theorists
have seen its error, it still crops up in contemporary criticism,
and—worse yet—in theater practice. We have fairly well recovered from the epidemic of naturalism, the stagecraft that sought
to dispense with all artifice, and consequently borrowed living
material from the actual world—"drugstore clerks drafted to
impersonate themselves in real drugstores transferred bodily
to the stage," as Robert Edmond Jones described this sort of
dramaturgy. Now it is true that real art *can* be made with such
devices; no device in itself is taboo, not even putting stage-
beggars in clothes begged from real beggars (Edward Woth-
ern, in his autobiography, recalls his acquisition of one such al-
luring treasure). But the theory that a play is a game of "make-
believe" designed by the poet, carried on by actors, and supported by an audience willing to pretend that the stage history
is actual, which still persists, and with it its practical counter-

[15] Ibid., p. 531. From *A Discourse on the Three Unities.*
[16] Strindberg, for instance, was convinced that the spectators in the
theater let themselves be deluded, tricked into believing or making-believe
that what they saw was actual life going on in their presence, and he was
seriously afraid of what popular education, and the general enlightenment
it was expected to bring, would do to people's credulity. In the famous
preface to *Miss Julia* he observes that "the theater has always served as a
grammar school to young people, women, and those who have acquired
a little knowledge, all of whom retain the capacity for deceiving themselves
and being deceived," but that "in our time, when the rudimentary, incomplete thought-processes operating through our fancy seem to be developing
into reflection, research, and analysis, the theater might stand on the verge
of being abandoned as a decaying form, for the enjoyment of which we
lack the requisite conditions."

part—the principle of deluding the audience, aiding the public "make-believe" by making the play seem as real as possible—is another story.

The whole conception of theater as delusion is closely linked with the belief that the audience should be made to share the emotions of the protagonists. The readiest way to effect this is to extend the stage action beyond the stage in the tensest moments, to make the spectators feel themselves actually present as witnesses of the scene. But the result is artistically disastrous, since each person becomes aware not only of his own presence, but of other people's too, and of the house, the stage, the entertainment in progress. Rosamond Gilder reported such an experience in her comment on Orson Welles' staging of *Native Son;* describing the scene wherein Bigger Thomas is cornered by his pursuers, she said: "Here flashing lights, gun-play, shouting and shooting converge on the stage from balcony and boxes. The theatrical illusion, far from being increased, is shattered, and the scene becomes nothing more than a nineteen-forty-one version of Eliza crossing the ice."[17]

I, too, remember vividly to this day the terrible shock of such a recall to actuality: as a young child I saw Maude Adams in *Peter Pan.* It was my first visit to the theater, and the illusion was absolute and overwhelming, like something supernatural. At the highest point of the action (Tinkerbell had drunk Peter's poisoned medicine to save him from doing so, and was dying) Peter turned to the spectators and asked them to attest their belief in fairies. Instantly the illusion was gone; there were hundreds of children, sitting in rows, clapping and even calling, while Miss Adams, dressed up as Peter Pan, spoke to us like a teacher coaching us in a play in which she herself was taking the title role. I did not understand, of course, what had happened; but an acute misery obliterated the rest of the scene, and was not entirely dispelled until the curtain rose on a new set.

[17] "Glamor and Purpose," in *Theatre Arts,* May 1941, pp. 327-335.

The central fallacy in such play production, and in the concept of drama that it assumes, is the total disregard of what Edward Bullough, in an essay that has become deservedly famous,[18] called "psychical Distance." All appreciation of art— painting, architecture, music, dance, whatever the piece may be—requires a certain detachment, which has been variously called the "attitude of contemplation," the "aesthetic attitude," or the "objectivity" of the beholder. As I pointed out in an early chapter of this book,[19] it is part of the artist's business to make his work elicit this attitude instead of requiring the percipient to bring an ideal frame of mind with him. What the artist establishes by deliberate stylistic devices is not really the beholder's attitude—that is a by-product—but a relation between the work and its public (including himself). Bullough terms this relationship "Distance," and points out quite rightly that "objectivity," "detachment," and "attitudes" are complete or incomplete, i.e. perfect or imperfect, but do not admit of degrees. "Distance, on the contrary, admits naturally of degrees, and differs not only according to the nature of the *object*, which may impose a greater or smaller degree of Distance, but varies also according to the *individual's capacity* for maintaining a greater or lesser degree."[20]

He describes (rather than defines) his concept, not without resort to metaphor, yet clearly enough to make it a philosophical asset:

"Distance . . . is obtained by separating the object and its appeal from one's own self, by putting it out of gear with practical needs and ends. . . . But it does not mean that the relation between the self and the object is broken to the extent of becoming 'impersonal'. . . . On the contrary, it describes a *personal* relation, often highly emotionally colored, but *of a peculiar*

---

[18] " 'Psychical Distance' as a Factor in Art and an Aesthetic Principle," *British Journal of Psychology,* June, 1912.

[19] See Chap. 4.

[20] *Op. cit.,* p. 94.

character. Its peculiarity lies in that the personal character of the relation has been, so to speak, filtered. It has been cleared of the practical, concrete nature of its appeal. . . . One of the best-known examples is to be found in our attitude towards the events and characters of the drama. . . ."[21]

This relation "of a peculiar character" is, I believe, our natural relation to a symbol that embodies an idea and presents it for our contemplation, not for practical action, but "cleared of the practical, concrete nature of its appeal." It is for the sake of this remove that art deals entirely in illusions, which, because of their lack of "practical, concrete, nature," are readily distanced as symbolic forms. But delusion—even the quasi-delusion of "make-believe"—aims at the opposite effect, the greatest possible nearness. To seek delusion, belief, and "audience participation" in the theater is to deny that drama is art.

There are those who do deny it. There are very serious critics who see its essential value to society not in the sort of revelation that is proper to art, but in its function as a form of ritual. Francis Fergusson and T. S. Eliot have treated drama in this vein,[22] and several German critics have found in the custom of hand clapping a last vestige of the audience participation that is really the public's lost birthright.[23] There are others who regard the theater not as a temple, but primarily as an amusement hall, and demand of drama that it shall please, delude us for a while, and incidentally teach morals and "knowledge of man." Brander Matthews extended the demand for amuse-

[21] *Op. cit.,* p. 91. The attitude referred to is, of course, the famous "aesthetic attitude," here treated as an index to the proper degree of distance.

[22] Cf. Francis Fergusson, *The Idea of a Theater.* A book so full of ideas, scholarship and discernment that even in taking issue with it I would recommend it to every reader.

T. S. Eliot, in "A Dialogue on Dramatic Poetry" (in *Selected Essays, 1917-1932*), p. 35, lets "E" say, "The only dramatic satisfaction that I find now is in a High Mass well performed."

[23] E.g., Theodor Wiesengrund-Adorno, "Applaus," *Die Musik,* 23 (1930-31), p. 476; also A. E. Gunther, "Der Schauspieler und wir," in Geissler's *Der Schauspieler,* p. 144.

ment—any or every sort of amusement—to all the arts; but as his
renown rests entirely on his dramatic criticism and teaching, his
view of "art" is really a view of the theater casually extended
to all other realms. "The primary purpose of all the arts it to entertain," said Matthews, "even if every art has also to achieve
its own secondary aim. Some of these entertainments make their
appeal to the intellect, some to the emotions, and some only
to the nerves, to our relish for sheer excitement and for brute
sensation; but each of them in its own way seeks, first of all, to
entertain. They are, every one of them, to be included in the
show business."[24]

Here we have certainly two extremes of dramatic theory;
and the theory I hold—that drama is art, a poetic art in a special mode, with its own version of the poetic illusion to govern
every detail of the performed piece—this theory does not lie anywhere between these extremes. Drama is neither ritual nor show
business, though it may occur in the frame of either one; it is
poetry, which is neither a kind of circus nor a kind of church.

Perhaps the greatest snare in the course of our thinking about
theater is its free trafficking with the standard materials of all
the other arts. People are so used to defining each art by its
characteristic medium that when paint is used in the theater
they class the result as "the painter's art," and because the set
requires building, they regard the designer of it as an architect.
Drama, consequently, has so often been described as a synthesis of several or even all arts that its autonomy, its status as a
special mode of a great single art, is always in jeopardy. It has
been treated as essentially dance, by confusion with panto-
mimic dances that have a dramatic plot; it has been conceived
as tableau and pageantry heightened by speech and action
(Gordon Craig held that the designer of its visual aspects was
its real creator), and as poetic recitation accompanied by gestures, sometimes by dance-gestures. This last view is traditional in India, where it is supported by the obvious epic sources

[24] *A Book About the Theater,* p. 6.

of Hindu plays (as usual, finding the source of a phenomenon is supposed to reveal its "real" nature). Hindu aestheticians, therefore, regard drama as literature, and judge it by literary standards.[25] Nietzsche found its origin in "the spirit of music" and consequently regarded its true nature as musical. Thornton Wilder describes it as an exalted form of narrative: "The theater," he writes, "carries the art of narration to a higher power than the novel or the epic poem. . . . The dramatist must be by instinct a story-teller."[26]

But story-telling, narration, is something quite different from story-enactment in a theater. Many first-rate story-tellers cannot make a play, and the highest developments of narration, such as the modern novel and short story, show devices of their own that have no meaning for the stage. They project a history in retrospect, whereas drama is history coming. Even as performed arts, narration and dramatization are distinct. The ancient rhapsodist, for all his gesticulations and inflections, was not an actor, and today, too, people who are known as good readers of poetry or prose need not therefore have any aptitude for the theater.

The concept of drama as literature embellished with concurrent appeals to the sense of sight is belied most convincingly in the very society where it enjoys its traditional vogue; the fact that in India the classic drama survived as a popular art for centuries after both the Sanskrit and the various Prakrits in which it was composed had become dead languages, understood only by scholars, proves that the stage action was no mere ac-

[25] Cf. Sylvain Levi, *Le théâtre indien*, p. 257: 'They [Indian theorists] are wont to consider drama as the juxtaposition of two arts, which simultaneously pursue their respective ends, namely poetry and mimetic dance. . . . Dance and mummery, stagecraft and scenery combine to heighten the illusion and pleasure by appealing to several senses. Representation, therefore, surpasses reading by a quantitative difference of emotion; there is no qualitative difference between them." See also A. B. Smith, *The Sanskrit Drama*, pp. 294-295.

[26] "Some Thoughts on Playwriting," p. 86.

companiment, but was instinctively developed by the actors to
the point of self-sufficiency, making the precise word meanings
of the speeches dispensable; that this drama is, in fact, what
Cocteau called "a poetry of the theater," as well as "poetry in
the theater."

As for dance, though it probably preceded drama on the
boards, and though it uses dramatic plots after its own fashion, it does not give rise to drama, not even to true pantomime.
Any direct dramatic action tends to suspend the balletic illusion. The fact that Greek drama arose amidst ritual dancing has
led several art historians to consider it as a dance episode; but
the dance was, in fact, only a perfect framework for the development of an entirely new art; the minute the two antagonists
stepped out of the choric ensemble and addressed not the deity,
nor the congregation, but each other, they created a poetic illusion, and drama was born in midst of the religious rite. The
choric dance itself was assimilated to the world of the virtual
history they presented.

Once we recognize that drama is neither dance nor literature, nor a democracy of various arts functioning together, but
is poetry in the mode of action, the relations of all its elements
to each other and to the whole work become clear: the primacy
of the script, which furnishes the commanding form; the use of
the stage, with or without representational scenery, to delimit
the "world" in which the virtual action exists; the need of making the scene a "place," so that often the designer produces a
plastic illusion that is secondary here, but primary in the art of
architecture;[27] the use of music and sometimes of dance to keep

---

[27] Cf. Jones, *op. cit.*, p. 75: "The energy of a particular play, its emotional
content, its aura, so to speak, has its own definite physical dimensions. It
extends just so far in space and no farther. The walls of the setting must
be placed at precisely this point."

George Beiswanger, in a little article entitled "Opera for the Eye" (*Theatre
Arts*, January, 1943, p. 59), makes a similar remark: "Each opera has its
own ideal dimensions, and their illusion must be created whether the actual
stage be large or small."

the fictitious history apart from actuality and insure its artistic abstraction;[28] the nature of dramatic time, which is "musical" instead of practical time, and sometimes becomes strikingly evident—another secondary illusion in poetry, but the primary one of music. The guiding principle in the use of so many transient borrowed illusions is the making of an *appearance,* not under normal circumstances, like a pretense or social convention, but under the circumstances of the play. Its total emotional tone is like the "palette" of a picture, and controls the intensity of color and light, the sober or fantastic character of the sets, the requirements such as overture, interludes, and what not.

Above all, that emotional tone guides the style of the actors. The actors are the chief interpreters—normally, the only indispensable ones—of the poet's incomplete but commanding creations. An actor does not undergo and vent emotions; he conceives them, to the smallest detail, and enacts them.

Some of the Hindu critics, although they subordinate and even deprecate dramatic art in favor of the literary elements it involves, understand much better than their Western colleagues the various aspects of emotion in the theater, which our writers so freely and banefully confuse: the feelings experienced by the actor, those experienced by the spectators, those presented as undergone by characters in the play, and finally the feeling that shines through the play itself—the vital feeling of the piece. This last they call *rasa;* it is a state of emotional knowledge, which comes only to those who have long studied and contemplated poetry. It is supposed to be of supernatural origin, because it is not like mundane feeling and emotion, but is detached, more of the spirit than of the viscera, pure and uplifting.[29]

Rasa is, indeed, that comprehension of the directly experi-

---

[28] Schiller, in his famous preface to *Die Braut von Messina,* called the Greek Chorus, which he revived in this play, "a living wall" to preserve the Distance of the work.

[29] Sylvain Levi, *op. cit.,* p. 295.

enced or "inward" life that all art conveys. The supernatural
status attributed to its perception shows the mystification that
beset the ancient theorists when they were confronted with the
power of a symbol which they did not recognize as such. Audiences who can dispense with the helps that the box stage, representational setting and costumes, and sundry stage properties
lend to our poetic imagination have probably a better understanding of drama as art than we who require a potpourri of
means. In Indian, Chinese, and Japanese drama—but most consistently in the Far Eastern—not only events and emotions, but
even *things are* enacted. Stage properties exist, but their use
is symbolic rather than naturalistic. Even the simulation of feeling may be sacrificed to enhance the formal value, the emotional effect of the play as a whole. Objects involved in the
action are simply implied by gesture.[30] In India, some stage
properties do occur—carts, dragons, even elephants—and are
elaborately made of paper, bamboo, lacquer, etc.; others are
left to the imagination. The deciding factor seems to be whether
the action turns on the non-human element, or not. A king who
quite incidentally mounts a chariot merely indicates its existence by an act, but in *The Little Clay Cart* the cart is really put
upon the stage. European spectators at Chinese plays always
find it surprising and offensive that attendants in ordinary dress
come and go on the stage; but to the initiated audience the
stagehand's untheatrical dress seems to be enough to make his
presence as irrelevant as to us the intrusion of an usher who
leads people to a seat in our line of vision.

On the Japanese stage, an actor may step out of his part by
giving a signal and address the audience, then by another formal sign resume his role.

A public that enjoys such pure acting gives itself up to the
dramatic illusion without any need for sensuous delusion. But

[30] See Jack Chen, *The Chinese Theater;* A. E. Zucker, *The Chinese
Theater;* Noel Peri, *Cinq no: Drames lyriques japonais.* The last-named
gives the most detailed account of this technique.

sensuous satisfaction it does want: gorgeous robes and curtains, a rich display of colors, and always music (of a sort that Westerners often find no asset). These elements make the play dramatically convincing precisely by holding it aloof from actuality; they assure the spectator's "psychical Distance" instead of inviting him to consider the action as a piece of natural behavior. For in the theater, where a virtual future unfolds before us, the import of every little act is heightened, because even the smallest act is oriented toward the future. What we see, therefore, is not behavior, but the self-realization of people in action and passion; and as every act has exaggerated importance, so the emotional responses of persons in a play are intensified. Even indifference is a concentrated and significant attitude.

As every act and utterance set down in the poet's script serves to create a perceptible destiny, so all plastic, choreographic, or musical elements that are added to his play in the theater must support and enhance that creation. The dramatic illusion is poetic, and where it is primary—that is to say, where the work is a drama—it transmutes all borrowings from other art into poetic elements. As Mr. Jones says in *The Dramatic Imagination,* "In the last analysis the designing of stage scenery is not the problem of an architect or a painter or a sculptor or even a musician, but of a poet."[31] It is the painter (or architect, or sculptor) turned poet who understands the commanding form which the author has composed by writing the lines of the play, and who carries this form to the further state of visibility, and it is the actor-poet who takes the whole work—words, setting, happenings, all—through the final phase of its creation, where words become utterances and the visible scene is fused into the occurrence of the virtual life.

Histrionic imagination is the same fundamental talent in the playwright, the leading actors, the performers of even the

[31] P. 77.

smallest parts in so far as they are genuine actors, the scene and light designer, the costumer, the light controller, the composer or selector of incidental music, the ballet master, and the director who surveys the whole to his satisfaction or despair. The work on which they are engaged is one thing—an apparition of Destiny.

"From the Greeks to Ibsen the actor has represented, by elocution as well as by movement, human character and human destiny. . . . When drama takes on the abstract character of music or pure dance it ceases to be drama. . . .

"The dramatist . . . is a writer, a poet, before he is a musician or a choreographer. Wagner of course showed that many dramatic elements can be embodied in orchestral music; silent movies showed how much can be done with the visual element alone; but if you add Wagner to Eisenstein and multiply by ten you still do not have a Shakespeare or an Ibsen. This does not say that drama is better than music, dancing, or the visual arts. It is different.

"The defenders of the arts of the theater must be infected by the commodities of the theater if they can forget that all 'theater arts' are means to one end: the correct presentation of a poem."[32]

[32] From E. R. Bentley, "The Drama at Ebb," *Kenyon Review*, VII, 2 (Spring, 1945), 169-184.

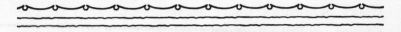

The Conditions of Dramatic Art

HENRI GHÉON

I am going to talk to you about my favorite theories, my own thoughts about the theatre. They won't be anything new; they have grown out of the thoughts of many men. The only value thought has is to belong to the common tradition, to prolong it, to carry on that great spiritual continuity that links us still to our very sources. In all ages the masters were once disciples; receptivity is no hindrance to bold innovation. Good students do not necessarily become great masters, but at least they have the chance.

One reservation: I shall speak of the theatre only as a playwright and a director. My whole life has been dedicated to the writing and production of plays. Aside from my religion, this has been the center of my deepest thought and concern. I shall try now to focus these thoughts for you. The professional critic from his seat on the aisle may well disagree with me. True, he can see what escapes me; but I speak of what I know, and know from experience, as no critic can. If our viewpoints conflict, they may also complement each other.

What is dramatic art in its traditional form? *What* has it become? What *should* it become, what do we hope it may become? I shall speak on these three points. My words may not convince all, but they may perhaps open the way to men of greater genius.

I

Let us first lay down some principles. Today, for lack of guiding principles, much good will, talent, even genius goes to waste; self-flattery, self-conceit, and self-preservation dominate all man's activities and especially literature and the arts. Even if it means being labeled dogmatic or pedantic, we must state boldly any truth we find of value. To drift aimlessly to and fro in the equivocal is the surest way to get nowhere.

Theatre is an *art*. Let us recall briefly the fact that art has two aspects: absolute and relative. It must be absolute: that is demanded by its very nature. An art that does not tend to the absolute, denies itself. Art is born in the mind and nowhere else; it is the ideal, the idea. Yet for all its philosophical and transcendental affinities, art is also relative because it is a technique, a craft that exists only in so far as it is practiced. If the work of art does not emerge from the mind to take perceptible form, it remains unfulfilled. The idea can be judged only by its execution, the genius only by his work. We have all dreamed marvelous poems that will never exist—because they remain a dream. That is the paradox: absolute in theory, art is relative in actuality; execution imposes on it conditions that are inevitably relative—relative to man, to his limitations, to his needs, to his means. That is what the Scholastics teach us, i.e., Aristotle as interpreted by Saint Thomas. It does not seem to me that, in aesthetics at least, we can reject their general conclusions. These conclusions, formulated in a subtle and profound little book, *Art and Scholasticism,* by Jacques Maritain, are exactly what experience teaches; they are not only the wisdom of the ages but also plain common sense.

"All art is free . . . and as art, it is disinterested. . . . The virtue of art looks only at one thing: the goodness to be created, the beauty to shine out from matter, to come into existence according to its own laws, independent of all else." Yet this theoretically pure art must meet something foreign, something opposed to itself, i.e., its instrument, its material. The art is in the artist, the artist in the man. "If there is no man, there is no artist"—and consequently no art. The man who wishes to create will meet a double resistance: the resistance of his own limited nature unable to subject itself wholly to what the mind demands; and the resistance of matter—the indocility of color, marble, sound, or word. He must compromise, he must also use violence; but if he goes too far, forcing the instrument to a note beyond its range, forcing matter into a form alien to its nature, then the instrument, matter itself, will take its own revenge. By all means let art tend to the maximum of freedom, to the absolute; such is its duty. But this maximum has a limit; beyond that limit lie meaninglessness, deformity, cacophony.

In a truly human and therefore relative aesthetic, it would be possible to classify the arts by that degree of the absolute to which they attain, and consequently by the sum of external factors which restrict them. On what level of this hierarchy is dramatic art?

Since Richard Wagner's ambition to restore the Greek tragic poets' concept of drama in "total theatre," such "total theatre" has been exalted as the shrine sacred to the meeting, the marriage, the fusion of all the arts. I do not deny that this point of view has its legitimacy and its grandeur. It is a fact that theatre alone can at one and the same time delight the eye and ear and heart in a balanced harmony of plastic movement, music and poetry.

Does, then, a union of all the arts necessarily produce a super-art? If they are truly united, yes.

Does it produce a purer art? Certainly not.

Each art sharing in this ideal synthesis under an expert hand must look to the other arts for support, inspiration, *élan*, emphasis: gesture must accentuate word, music prolong voice. No-

where else are so many means available . . . not to mention
the chief instrument—the living man, the actor, in whose spirit
and flesh the work is given form and movement. But the more
complex the material, the greater its resistance to one who
seeks to mold it. As the means multiply, so do the servitudes.
The result is that "total dramatic art" just because of its great
resources becomes in fact the most confused, the most contingent of all arts, impeded by the heaviest passive resistance,
balked at every step by massive obstruction.

Does that mean that Aeschylus and Sophocles were not able
to master their material, that their greatest achievements were
perhaps only brilliant compromises? We cannot know: the major part of their performances—the music, the dance—is forever
lost. However, there is no doubt that Wagner in seeking to follow them destroyed all equilibrium of the arts: one art alone,
music, submerges the whole drama. In my opinion there is more
balance in Gluck and Mozart, in Debussy, and Monteverdi. But
that is not our subject here; at the moment I had better not go
into the question of "total drama."

I do not mean that music ought never to be used to illuminate or to emphasize, but that it must always be as accompaniment, as relief or as interlude and no more. However, my subject here is literary drama in the form in which it has come
down to us and is in actual use today: *the spoken drama.*
Does that change the terms of our problem? No, for there is no
theatrical art, however stylistic, abstract, intellectual, that does
not participate in the other arts, that does not speak through
eyes and ears to mind and heart, and that therefore does not
demand of the playwright not only concern for good writing—
a demand made equally on essayist, poet, novelist—but also an
ear for musical order (rhythm, intonation), and an eye for
plastic order (movement, image). We find here, then, the
same contingencies as in "total drama," the same servitudes, the
same "impurity." We must admit this honestly and try to work
out a healthy dramaturgy; but first let us look at the causes for

the sterility of modern theatre; i.e., our book-centered approach to drama.

II

There is some excuse for this long misunderstanding of the first principles of drama. Where could we learn save from books? The works of great playwrights survive only in the writings that record them. And as they come to us in the most abstract form, we are tempted to look on them as we do on masterpieces of poetry and fiction. Are they not only one more literary form among all the others—comedies of Aristophanes and tragedies of Sophocles, blood brothers to the *Eclogues* of Virgil and the *Dialogues* of Plato? Creon speaks to Antigone as Tityrus to Meliboeus, as Socrates to Alcibiades, though with perhaps a little more pathos. As we read, the drama takes shape in our head. But the laws that shape this drama hold good only for production inside our head and not outside it. Such imaginations are as far from the dramatic truth as the inner world is from the outer world. Don't imagine you have been present in spirit at the authentic drama of Aeschylus or of Shakespeare as Aeschylus or Shakespeare conceived it.

For neither Aeschylus nor Shakespeare, nor Sophocles, nor Calderon wrote plays for us *to read;* they wrote plays *to be acted on the stage* and on a *special* stage, plays for an audience and a special audience, plays for immediate production, immediate and evanescent. A few centuries later, even with the most reliable tradition and incontestable documents, we cannot even begin to imagine the way in which Champmeslé or Duparc interpreted Racine. The most skilful revivals are and can be nothing more than adaptations. What relation is there between the original *Antigone* of the theatre of Dionysus and the academic *Antigone* of the Comédie-Française, even when revived by the genius of Mounet-Sully and Julia Bartet? What the true *Antigone* was, we will never know, nor the *Passion* of Gréban, nor *Othello,* nor *Phaedra,* nor *The Misanthrope.* All we have left is a dead book, a text, a skeleton, a blueprint; admirable as this may be, it is not the total living pattern created by those who conceived it and gave it life. The theatre has joined the "classics" in textbooks and lectures, for the esoteric pleasure of a few highbrows: it has become "literature." It is true that the highest form of theatre does deserve a place among literary forms, yet, I repeat, it is a unique literary form that curiously escapes from the printed page. If it does not overflow the page, it does not really exist at all, it has lost its own reason for existence, or if you prefer, has only a semiexistence. Like oratory, it leads a double life, in books and out of books. It would sacrifice the former rather than the latter, give up the library rather than the stage. We may study it in texts, but the text is only a fragment.

I do not deny its importance. It is the kernel, the mother cell, and nothing can replace it. "In the beginning was the Word . . ."—and this has universal validity. When thought renounces the word, it renounces its own definition; and to drive thought from the theatre would be to empty the theatre of substance, to degrade it. But granted that, we must also hold that drama has its own thought which is not that of poetry or of the novel, thought that must escape the written word if it is to have any life or power.

Book-life is enough for a poem, at least as poetry is conceived today—unfortunately perhaps—less and less for recitation and reading aloud, more and more for the silent, intimate joy of a solitary reader, a secret delight and song, murmured deep in the heart. Some even hold that no audience is needed at all, but this is extreme, monstrous—for the *sine qua non* of all art is to be communicable. Without going that far, let us say that, once recorded in a book, a poem can wait for its reader. We all know that Stendhal wrote his novels for readers to come a half-century after his death. Any purely literary work is almost completely achieved in its book, subject only to contingencies of grammar, logic, and, for poetry, of prosody. More or less beautiful typography changes nothing in the intrinsic value of the words as signs of things or of thoughts.

The playwright who thinks only in the written word as does a poet or novelist, who shapes beautiful forms vibrant with book-contained life, runs the risk of creating museum pieces, lifeless and incapable of life, with no momentum beyond the printed page. Of course, there is such a thing as an "armchair theatre" for those with enough imagination, and plays for such readers do exist, though they are really dialogue-novels. This is an essentially falsifying makeshift, one that hampered the career of the most genuine and perhaps the only truly dramatic writer of the nineteenth century, Alfred de Musset.

Another indefensible attitude is that of the playwright who polishes his sentences and hands them over to the director saying: "Here it is—I've done the words, the rest is your job." The words may be there, but they do not yet exist. Could an author who thus abandons his play once written, fancying that the text is enough, ever have put into the text what his art demands? Could he ever have charged the words with the power potential that alone makes them words of drama, dynamic, expressive, explosive? If so, would he not have wanted to make them come to life himself?

The word indeed rules all things, in the theatre as in books; it is the spirit's ambassador. But in the theatre it must be uttered by a human mouth, it must be incarnate in beings of flesh, it must live and move in them; it dictates the act and is the act (the *act* not in a Thomistic sense, but in the mechanical sense of movement). Before it touches and possesses the hearer, it must touch and possess a composite, indocile, and rebellious instrument: the stage, this particular concrete stage, with all its resources and all its resistances. When the playwright has trapped in written words the always relative absolute of his vision, that dream-group of personalities who meet, love, hate, live, and die at his good pleasure—he has as yet done nothing. He owes it to his art and to himself to design a dream that is

realizable, viable, playable, and, if I may coin a pretty poor
word, "exteriorizable." I repeat, he must not say, "Here are
words, give them life, form, gesture, movement, action!" If that
were enough, a scenario would do and drama would amount
to no more than that embryo called *commedia dell'arte*. His
very words must of themselves evoke image, gesture, movement, action, life; to add all this afterward is a poor artifice.
Not that he must calculate them all ahead of time with implacable precision, leaving no room for the actor's imagination:
this would paralyze the play. The life he must infuse is an
appeal to the living actor; it calls out to another life, to life
itself for its own accent and intonation. The playwright impli-
citly suggests to the interpreter a series of possibilities among
which he need only choose. The playwright gives hints, fragments; the interpreter must put them together, give them sense.

But such foresight supposes that the author has complete
grasp of technique. Even if he has an inborn feeling for the
stage—he'll never write a play unless he has that—even so he
must acquire its techniques humbly and perseveringly. Experience is indispensable. The stage offers itself to him as clay to
the potter, stone or wood to the carver. Perhaps he will be
tempted to take a part himself. . . . If he can, he should; then
he truly becomes master craftsman, master of the work. Who
should be that master, if not the one who has conceived it? A
Shakespeare, a Molière—author, director, and actor—that is the
complete playwright.

Here you will quote my own words against me: "That is to
canonize the ephemeral, the impermanent." This is exactly our
difficulty. For posterity, the writer alone survives, as the material conditions of dramatic art are ever changing with the times.
But my point is this: the dramatic writer does not write only
for posterity, and to my way of thinking, he'll never reach it at
all unless he first writes for his own time. I do not say that he
should not seek to be a good writer; I mean that he must accept
and embrace what is most transitory in his art, the only sub-

stances he can grasp, essentially evanescent as they are. I say that it is in them alone that he will make his drama a reality. I say that only in using them, with all their plus and minus qualities, their possibilities and their limitations, will he create a living thing, dramatically speaking. I say it is only at this price that after one century or ten, when nothing remains of his work but the words, those words will still keep a little of the dynamic power proper to drama and to drama alone. For if to-day we cannot revive the original *Antigone,* or the original *Macbeth,* or even the original *Polyeucte,* nevertheless, they still have power to move us, fragmentary and changed though they may be; and they can move us in a way that no *Aeneid* or *Divine Comedy,* no *Don Quixote* or Platonic *Dialogue* can. Had the plays been conceived and executed in the abstract, they would perhaps have beauty, but another kind of beauty. The profound life hidden within them, still welling up within them, springs from their vital origin, for in their own day they were conceived in terms of living elements, they were lived out on a stage by men of flesh and bone. Written words, they were written for men's voices, for their masks and their bodies, and the words are still impregnated with this memory. Given such conditions, the play will be what it should be: a drama. Suppress this need of the playwright for immediate concrete realization and he loses his true being; he had better get another job.

There is nothing equal to the stage as a school for humility. The author is essentially dependent on the possibilities of the actor. In accord with the style, with the laws of the dramatic action (plastic form, movement, development), he must further appeal to the costumer, the set designer, the electrician, the mechanic, the director—if he does not himself direct—above all, to the actors. I should insist here on the harm done to dramatic art when the perilous harmony of these instruments is shattered, when the inadequacy of the play, of the playwright's skill, tempts one or another—director, designer, actor—to work on his own. That is the reason for the too-frequent failures in our contemporary theatre. . . . Do we then conclude that when the spirit of the play has fused author and actors into a living whole and the curtain goes up, then at last the work has come to life? . . . No, not at all—as yet, nothing has been done: there has to be an audience.

For dramatic art is not achieved by an author writing his play in a corner, nor by a group of trained actors giving it life on the stage; it requires also an audience to receive it. It is author, actors, audience. We cannot eliminate any one of these three elements: they are integrally bound together.

You can imagine a picture that an artist paints for himself alone. You can imagine a poem that the poet recites to himself from morning to night but never repeats to other men. You can imagine a novel that has never been read, asleep in a desk drawer. But you cannot imagine a play, written, rehearsed, staged, finally produced, and then acted before empty chairs. At least when this does happen, it is far from pleasing to actors and author; for a play is not an end in itself. I mentioned above the strange liberty of novelist and poet in regard to their public. In our time this has turned into contempt for the public. It is true that to run after the public, to flatter its prejudices and weaknesses, is not the best way for an author to deepen and perfect his art. But it is quite another thing to despise the public, to discourage it, to slam the door in its face and refuse to speak to it. The writer who seeks publication wants to be read, otherwise he would write only to give form to his own ideas, his dreams; no need to go into print. All art is essentially social. But as I have also said, he who writes books is absolutely free to wait for his public. They may come or not, many of them or few, today, tomorrow, in ten years or in a century. It does not matter. The poem, novel, essay, remains printed on the pages of its book; it exists now and will not exist with any more reality on the day when it has ten thousand, twenty thousand, a hundred thousand readers. It is not influenced by the eventual reader; he cannot change it either before or after (I am not speaking of commercial literature); it is the reader alone who is influenced, more or less deeply, sooner or later. Great writers, like our classic writers, will show a certain elementary and courteous consideration for their public, being careful in grammar, syntax, logic, using language not too remote from common speech. But they know too that a book can be reread, picked up when one wishes, put aside again, returned to, opened and closed again; hence they will not dilute their thought because it is difficult, nor their style because it is elliptical. If the reader complains, so much the worse for him—he is not worthy to understand! No poem or novel or essay need be popular.

The case is quite different with dramatic work. It is like a book that is being read aloud, its pages turned remorselessly from the first to the last chapter. When a word has been spoken, it has been spoken; you cannot ask the actor to repeat it. That certainly would be a rich comedy, if you could imagine a difficult play punctuated by spectators rising in turn, demanding a replay of some fragment of the first act, a monologue in the third—they had missed the point at the time. The more intelligent—and those longing to seem intelligent—would protest with indignant "shushes!" Altercations, disorder, fist-fights! The drama would move off the stage into the house: action on the stage would stop. I am not fooling. Whether he pays for his seat or not, the spectator wants to understand, right on the spot, what the actor is saying. Hence the need of clarity, of intelligibility. The theatre is the very shrine of the manifest. This is the first servitude that the playwright must accept, willingly or not: no matter how exquisite, stylized, erudite, significant, image-flowered it may be, the language he uses must be understandable by all.

A second servitude is no less rigorous. We must go beyond the letter and the word to the object which they signify. It is no use for the words to be exact, the sentences well constructed, the ideas logically and clearly developed, if the thought or feeling touches no chord in the minds and hearts of the audience and calls forth not even a faint echo of that feeling and that thought! Still worse if they call out a contrary reaction. That can happen; in fact it happens frequently. Some weep, and others laugh at the same thing; two plays are being performed at the same time, one comic, one pathetic. Which is the true play, tell me? The one the author intended? In that case, let him keep it to himself. He is expressing feeling and thoughts to his contemporaries that they do not share. "Excuse me," you may object, "do any two men ever have even one emotion or one idea exactly alike?" Certainly not, in details. But in general, yes. For there are certain intellectual and moral values on which the majority agree in any real society: good and evil, true and false (I do not say beauty and ugliness; these are aesthetic values, and as such are subject to variation in the best of societies; let us not get involved in pure aesthetics, please). Agreement on what is good, agreement on what is true: the man who writes for the theatre must create at least that minimum of communion between his work and his audience. Only then will he touch feelings and win the assent he desires. A play really exists, lives and really lives, only when its life-spark leaps from the stage and from the playwright's soul across to the audience in a moment of vital contact. That is why Jaques Copeau said in a phrase I love to quote:

There will never be a new theatre (meaning a reaction against today's falsified theatre in a return to tradition) until the day comes when the man in the audience murmurs in his heart and with his heart the same words spoken by the man on the stage.

Yes, the day when author and spectator—and I may add, actor also, for he is the hyphen between them—are one, and stand together on the same intellectual and moral ground. For communion we need such ground. But it can exist only in a truly organic society, by which I mean a society that has a center, a coherence and unanimity: it recognizes one good as *good* and one truth as *true*.

But if society is not organic, or if there is no society at all—what happens? Well, there will not be any theatre, or at the most a fragmentary, stammering, time-serving theatre. There will be no understanding, no communication, no communion. The play will have to crawl into the book, and wait for better days.

It cannot wait too long; for in the theatre, too long a delay in realization alters the concept itself. While the author is working on his play, unless he has at hand and under his control all the elements of language and technique as well as actors and audience, the validity of his "creative activity," as Maritain says, will be hopelessly falsified. He is not one, but two, or rather three; what matters is not only that many speak his name, but that all should answer him.

There is a school that conceives the stage as a room with one wall removed where something happens. I imagine it more as a platform set up in the midst of a crowd, a place of perpetual barter. A dramatic author must make a practical study of the conditions of that barter, discover its laws, make sure that it is possible, that he is not speaking a tongue alien to his public.

Thus dramatic art presupposes both in theory and in fact the existence of a homogeneous society, a "people" in the noblest meaning of the word. It is not a closed art, nor a long-range art, but an open, immediate art. Pity the author who feels within himself power to give substance to a dream that haunts him, yet who can find nothing outside to help him. It would be a miracle if he could create life in the present only by his hope for the future. True, there are certain great works that for special reasons did not succeed in their author's lifetime, even though they were essentially in accord with their age; their dramatic success was only a little deferred. But no plays of real vitality were misunderstood and rejected in their own day only to grip the emotions of an audience centuries later. Plays that survive or revive, as I have said, are plays that have once been alive.

Such are the essential conditions for drama. It depends on its own lifetime to exist or not. No talent, not even genius is enough: good luck is needed too.

You understand that all these principles call for qualification. There are special cases that escape the general rule and to which I shall return. The important thing is that the problem be established on solid ground. I take back nothing essential. The born dramatist may also be a great poet or a great creator of characters; his art may embrace beauties that poetry and novels can possess only fragmentarily, for being neither poet nor novelist, he can call a whole world into life and movement. Yet by this very fact he must work in a relative medium with substance that is in part perishable. No withdrawal to his tower will safeguard purity. Unless he comes down again, the work will not be a play. The dramatist is imprisoned in the contingencies of theatre and of society; the character of his art is essentially social.

[Translated by Adele M. Fiske]

How Drama Is Born within Us

JEAN-LOUIS BARRAULT

Drama is as old as man; it is as closely linked to him as his double for the theatrical game is inherent in the existence of any living being. Man has invented fire, together with Dionysian and Apollonian arts, and that is what makes him different from the animal, but man and animals have one thing in common, they both love playing. Animals, like men, know how to play, and as soon as they begin to do so they display a kind of imagination which one would not credit them with. A dog does not know how to draw, a horse cannot sculpt, a cat does not show any sign of deep delight when the radio plays Bach, and a beaver will not think of adding decorations to the house which it builds, but when it comes to dancing, singing, or to mimicking a fright or enjoyment, all the animals can do that.

Observe a dog playing with a ball or a cat playing with a piece of paper held by a thread, and see how it enjoys the merry-go-round of faked fears, feints, pseudo panics and wild excitements. Suddenly in the middle of all that, an abrupt stop! An imaginary enemy has been seen, and one has to crawl,

41

hold one's breath, and approach it with precaution. This is a tense moment! The climax is near, the price of it may be life itself! Ready: the enemy is now within reach! One, two, three, and the dog makes a sudden pounce on the deadly enemy represented by the ball with which he was playing. He catches it, holds it prisoner, he bites but without killing it, he throws it in the air, barks with joy and performs a swift victory dance around it. Five minutes later, this very same dog will come to you pretending to be in agony because of an imaginary thorn in his paw, or adopt an attitude of perfect indifference if he sees you with a suitcase in your hand. To superimpose an imaginary reality upon actual reality is a tendency shared by all living beings—whether men or animals. What's the cause of it? Does the reason for it lie in the desire to live imaginatively a story which could not be lived if this story were true? One has all kinds of courage in imaginary situations. It is pleasant to play with the notion of fear when there is no real cause for fear. This desire for 'acting' comes perhaps from the urge to get a full grasp of real life and its problems through an artificial re-creation of life, something which is really 'filtered' life, or life at one remove. This is something in which attitudes and behaviour are more clearly outlined and lucidity is not blinded by the urgency of decision. It is therefore a training ground for virtual actions which can be beneficial in cases of incapacity to act; it is a school of energy, a place where one recharges one's batteries.

All men are double, that is a well-known fact, and one would not be surprised to hear that men are multiple: 'there are many men in one man.' Yet if each of us is a compound of many personalities, the fact that another self seems to be always present in us, makes us say that we are double. Our double has its own individual life; it is he who at night lives our dreams. Life on the stage is a dream dreamt when one is awake. There has been in recent years a good deal of talk about the lie of the theatre. It is frequently said that the actor when act-

ing deludes himself and lies, and the spectator does the same
and lies when he believes what he sees. Diderot's famous paradox of the comedian or of the spectator is supposed to be the
result of a connivance between two liars. That is very possible;
but what of it? Dreams also are supposed to be lies but in fact
nobody knows anything about it. Let us content ourselves with
saying that the theatre, like life, is a dream, without caring too
much about the question of lie.

The whole history of the theatre shows us that it has its
source in imitation, which of course is not the lifeless copying
of nature, but the re-creating of life through artificial means.
The artist gives life to a kind of magic object which has more
life than any ordinary object. A picture, a bust, a symphony,
ought in fact to belong to the living world. 'Creation' is for the
artist a kind of sexual action at the end of which he gives life
to something. If life is a symphony of colours it is normal to invent the painter; if it is a dance of forms then a sculptor must
be born; and if it is a pattern of sounds then it is clear that music
exists as well as man. What appearances will life take in order
to justify the invention of an 'imitator'? Painting, sculpture, architecture, music, poetry, are historically valid; can we also
say that the art of the 'imitator' deserves a history? Our friend
Fluchère in a fascinating study of Shakespeare and the Elizabethan theatre said two things which deeply impressed me:
'The theatre which interests us,' he said, 'is the spoken theatre,
the theatre which belongs to literature,' and he added: 'the
theatre is above all an experimental art of language whose primary mission of entertaining and instructing rests on the success of the ceaseless verbal experiments and on the actor who
endeavours to convey these experiments to the public.' From
these two sentences, I retain two points:

1. The 'spoken' theatre, considered as 'an experimental art of
   language,' deserves its history which will be a branch of the
   history of literature.
2. The author, bent upon his primary task of entertaining and

instructing, will adopt as a means of expression, that is to say of creation or procreation—speech, that is to say language with which he will experiment ceaselessly.

These two points imply that the history of the theatre does not date from the origins of man. Man in his struggle for life began with dances, shouts, songs, incantations and warlike mimes meant to bring to him the strength of his ancestors and power over his enemies. These manifestations do not belong to art, which implies gratuitousness, but to the world of magic; they were part of a profound, mysterious and metaphysical reality which was at one with life. When men began to trace graffiti of animals on walls, it was in order to protect themselves from animals, to master them in order to eat them or to make use of them. It was therefore a form of magic. When men sculpted their first masks, they aimed at giving form to their inner face or to the traits of their assumed role; they were trying to bring to light the appearances of their most mysterious instincts. The primary aim of these attempts was not art but efficacy. Whatever art there was lay in the technical perfection of these magic acts (the drawings made with powders, upon the earth, during voodoo ceremonies in Haiti have a kind of perfection which is due not to their beauty, but to their efficacy; yet it just happens that one serves the other).

Human behaviour is made of gestures, songs, dances, drawings, masks, sculptures, choices of perfumes, incantations accompanied with drum and bells, or simply of human bodies clashing one against the other in frenzies, of trances or possessions, which have nothing to do with literature but have everything to do with man. The origin of the theatre lies in the attempt to imitate and to re-create these forms of human behaviour. If we ask ourselves how the theatre is born in us and what it endeavours to re-create, I should be inclined to answer instinctively—a certain silence. Let us see what this means. When the arts reach our senses, they satisfy them one by one. For instance, we might be deaf and appreciate painting, we might be blind and appreciate music, and sometimes we even shut our eyes in order to hear better. Life, when re-created by the artist, reaches us in a kind of 'specialized' form, and only through one sense at a time. In normal life, on the contrary, we absorb the outside world simultaneously through all the senses and pores of our body; there is not a single nerve in us which does not record some kind of contact. While the outside world is thus impinging on us, we perceive at the same time all the various aspects of an internal life—memories from our past, the industrious agitation of our blood, the noise of saliva in our mouths, the crackings of our joints, the bellows of our breathing, etc. etc. . . . If we concentrate our attention on any one of these moments in the present when the outside world continuously impinges on our internal world, we soon perceive beyond that medley of noises and distant sights and sounds a kind of faint murmur which is caused by the slight and surreptitious breeze of the present-on-the-move upon silence. Claudel used to say that the stars make a noise, and he used to call the sky the celestial kettle. The present causes silence to vibrate. Time flows, the present moves on, life passes, silence trembles, and we do the same, we tremble with anguish at the continuous movement, flow and vibration, which is irrevocable and which terminates in death. Consciousness of the tragic rolling carpet condemned to end in the dark abyss, tightens up the throat, and sends the blood buzzing to our head; one has at once a feeling of claustrophobia and of being stifled under blankets, yet the machine has been set in motion and cannot be stopped. Silence, the present, and all the perceptions which reach us, plunge us into a panic; anxiety nearly chokes us, and there is only one way of getting out of this terrifying state, it is by breaking this silence and making the present inaudible, so we plunge into talk, noise, whirls of ideas and discussions of all kinds. We try to become conscious of life in order to do away with the consciousness of death. Action is not enough, we plunge into agitation, we think of the future, and of the past, but we no more mention the word present than we would mention the word rope in the house of a man who has been hanged. We prefer to live in a world drowned in noise than in the real world where a kind of silence unavoidably leads to Nothingness . . . or to God . . . two notions equally terrifying. To become conscious of the present is to become conscious of death, for the present is continuous death. The only real and concrete thing in life is the present, yet as if to torment us, the present is impossible to grasp and to hold. The present ever lies between something which is not yet, and something which has already been, and it changes ceaselessly. Nothing can hold this march towards death, and what is more, everything truly real in life takes place at that very moment which, so to speak, is nothing, and outside such a moment nothing is real. This is a terrifying enough statement and it is not surprising that we whistle with bravado in order to hide our fear. To re-create life, seen from this angle, is to go back to the source of the theatre.

Theatre is basically the art which takes place in the present and appeals simultaneously to all the senses, all the nerves, all the instincts, all at the same time. It is essentially the art of sensation, the art of the present, therefore of reality in all its aspects, from hell to heaven, as they would have said in the Middle Ages. It is also the art of putting to death, that is why there is a bull's head on our emblem. Recently Montherlant told me, 'I have understood at last the deep meaning of bull fights! They represent the history of man, the bull plays the part of man, and it is the very art of Life.' The actor receives life through the present, which is simultaneity and a 'kind of silence,' from that he decomposes life and re-creates it. How does he decompose it? The present is the ephemeral spark of which we are the image; through its continuous births and deaths it is ceaseless movement of exchanges, rejections and absorptions according to an implacable pattern which cannot alter its rhythm. The actor who observes life is struck by whatever is movement and exchanges and by whatever transports itself into a rhythm. He is so close to real and complete life and to the life of sensations that he cannot use for his creations media so remote as abstract writing, two-dimensional painting or the massiveness of stone. Music is what is closest to him, but even music cannot convey the impression of physical reality which he obtains from the contact of the present.

If man could truly become an instrument worthy of art, he would be the ideal artificial means of recreating the life of the present. That should be possible, for man has in his body the seat of movement (which is his spine, pliable as a whip), the centre of exchange (which is his respiratory apparatus and the continuous comings and goings of appetites and refusals) and the seat of rhythm (his heart which is also his magician). In order to translate the intoxicating sensation of man caught in the life of the universe, one has only to plunge man into space, the individual into the world, the one into the infinite and the being into the whole. That is why drama is essentially the conflict between the individual and the collective, between inner and external forces. Whenever the 'chosen' man or the ideal actor becomes conscious of the silent murmurs of his space-present, he will, as we suggested, first feel anguish, then, according to his temperament or his humour, he will either turn his anguish into metaphysical or divine drama attuned to esoteric liturgy, or in order to reassure himself he will take to whistling, telling stories or dancing 'in order to forget his fright.' Then his theatre adopts the free forms which one finds in farce, satyric drama and Bacchic ceremonies. Confronted with the type of life which strikes us as if it were an apparition, we adopt two lines of behaviour, both dictated by our emotions. We either transform it into something divine which we can face and which is tragedy, or we pretend to ignore it, and we can then indulge in all types of merriment, and that is comedy. In the first case we trust life, and in the second case we rather fly away from it. That is why tragedy is exalting while comedy is not so gay after all.

Honorius said: 'The priest is a tragic actor who re-enacts in front of his Christian audience in the theatre of the church, the struggles of Christ and the victory of Redemption.' This is all the more striking in that it was said in the twelfth century. Mass can be divided into three acts which are:

1. The proclamation of the Faith;
2. The tragedy of the order of the Mass;
3. Communion and joy.

The order of the Mass follows the pattern of a symphony: there is the first movement which is rapid, there is the anguish-laden and opaque andante and there is the joy of the third movement. Bearing in mind Menander's sayings in one of his comedies: 'Joy prevents me from knowing where I am,' one could conclude that tragedy and comedy are the two faces of this very same thing which is precisely the 'kind of silence' which only appears in the present. Tragedy and comedy are the two opposite faces of terror or sterile anguish: 'Gods, free me from my sterile anguish,' says Aeschylus in the *Oresteia*. In fact, until Aeschylus, every poet ended his tragic trilogies with a satyric drama which dealt with the same subject. We there-fore had the face and the obverse of the same medal. *Proteus* was a kind of farce which went with the *Oresteia,* and it de-scribed Menelaus's return with Helen, it was a burlesque song accompanying the funeral of a whole race. When, after Sopho-cles, poets began writing satyrical dramas which were unre-lated to the tragic themes of their trilogies, comedy and trag-edy ceased to be connected one with the other, and they were uprooted. The single cell which they formed originally was di-vided into two which assumed independent lives from then on. When they were one, they were connected by a religious atti-tude. If art blossoms as soon as the profane is separated from the sacred, its decadence is not very far. This is true of all ages and of all countries. When the religious spirit disinte-grates, art for art's sake appears and flourishes. A whole heritage, a golden age, is squandered and replaced by a slow period of decadence. 'We have kissed away kingdoms and provinces,' says Shakespeare in *Antony and Cleopatra*. Like life the theatre evolves in cycles. A new religion born from a period of dark depression revives existence and gives rise to a new civilization. For a while, the theatre which had decayed during the period of decadence, is rejected and condemned to go through its 'purgatory.'

But the theatre does not die easily, and it leaves its prison for a clandestine existence: peripatetic comedians, minstrels and tumblers keep the flame alive in inns and pub courtyards. Once the new religion is well established it feels the need to re-create the theatre which finds its place again in liturgical ceremonies. It begins with a voice and a chorus, then 'imitation' progresses, the acting is perfected, and one day dialogue is invented. The theatrical ceremony moves away from the altar, passes into the nave, comes out in front of the church, and in no time it is again in the public square. The theatre becomes a social art; it is the acme of collective art; all the various corporations take part in it. The gods and the city enter the dance, and politics bring a new life to it. The priests are overtaken by events and satyrical farce and carnivals are an excellent means of letting out human exuberance. Tragedy becomes more and more refined and comedy more and more teeming with life. Meanwhile religion keeps growing and getting old, and people become more educated and tend towards emancipation. One day, comedy goes off to live its own life, leaving tragedy on its own. Civilization becomes more refined, and people tire of holy wars. Politics corrupt everything and sow confusion everywhere. The more taste develops, the more the revolt towards the collective and the social element increases. Then the theatre concentrates on domestic dramas. Psychology makes its appearance, drama loses its violence and becomes 'bourgeois.' The people try to react but unfortunately they, too, have lost their religious feelings, so drama decays. In the early religious phase, while drama was still connected with magic, the Dionysian element was called eroticism, and phallic art was part of religious life; they were in fact two aspects of the same physical rite.

Now that religion is no longer part of life, and the profane is independent of the sacred which has become an abstraction, eroticism becomes obscurity and corruption spreads like a disease. The day is not far off when a new religion will appear and the theatre will be again banned, excommunicated and condemned to take to clandestine living. Whether religion is called Christianity, Buddhism, or otherwise, the cycles and the fate of the theatre are the same and they belong to the phases of life. One might sum up by saying that the theatre is the first serum that man invented in order to protect himself against anxiety. In order to combat solitude, men come together and sometimes form the magnetic gathering called the public; they gather in order to live together dramas of life which have been rendered 'harmless' through imagination. In the course of the performance everyone is injected with the serum of the disease which is anguish. Art consists in transforming the disease into a serum, otherwise the injection communicates the disease. Naturalism is the disease which propagates itself by contagion. The poetic theatre is on the contrary the beneficent serum which brings health to man. The art of the theatre has therefore since the beginning been a means of defence and not a gratuitous or debased form of entertainment. Since man has existed the theatre has always been something of public utility. In order to preserve life, man sleeps, eats, procreates (so as to maintain the race alive) and plays. To play is to struggle against anguish and to invent happiness which suppresses it. In order to play, man has since the beginning, relied upon himself.

[*Translated by Joseph Chiari*]

Secrets

JEAN VILAR

The art of theatre was not born one day in the heart of that drunken fellow who, at a Greek crossroads, sang his joys and sufferings. The art of theatre is also the product of the passion (serene or driven, depending on the individual) for knowledge.

Bacchus, I know, is often the boon companion of actors and playwrights. Dramatic creation remains, nonetheless, a matter of control, for actor as well as playwright. Wilde's stricture is law in this craft: "Only the critical spirit is creative." No work of art (and no acting or direction) can depend on inspiration alone without damage to itself. Inspiration, a necessary evil, provides, in theatre as in architecture, only a rough sketch for a masterpiece which must be *built*.

Playwright! You cannot employ the novelist's resource of description and explanation; and what real good would his palette of true details from life be to you? Your characters must talk, whether in prose or verse, and you know that you have only one effective weapon: the spoken word.

The dialogue of Dostoyevsky's characters has but one accent, a common identity. Balzac sought to differentiate the speaking styles of his characters—was it necessary? Stendhal cared not a fig for such idle foolery.

The speaking style of Alceste, however, is not like that of

51

Dandin; Hamlet's cadences are not those of Macbeth. And the basic reproach that may be levelled against Racine is that the language of his heroes and heroines is too absolutely controlled by the master prosodist: Hermione's cry is that of Phaedra; Antiochus' lament is echoed in Titus'. Prosody, prosody above all, alas! We admire and are astonished by the spareness of this perfect Hellenist's vocabulary: let us not praise him for having so little variety in the range of his cadences, for having compelled all his powdered monsters to employ an identical syntax. A dramatist is not only a poet.

The stage accommodates itself with difficulty to the overstrict rules of the perfect stylist. Character must always remain free with respect to the dramatist's prosody.

❉   ❉   ❉

Back to our subject.

The art of theatre, then, is ruled by the passion for knowing. Granted, playwright and actor are not Cuvier and Socrates. Neither ever frees himself from the demands of his imagination or from the mythomaniac demons who possess him. Which is to say that the speculative bent of the philosopher or the laboratory researcher are never to be found in him. Illusion, if not lies, rules his professional life.

Actors spend their time in pursuits filled with obsessions and hallucinations regulated by an often less than blithe mythomania. Malraux spoke truly when he said: "Theatre is not serious; mythomania is." And Talma, following his son's corpse to the cemetery, realized at the graveside that he had been *observing* the behavior of a bereaved father all the way.

I know that this is not exactly mythomania. It is more, really: the professional imaginer at his exercises. The pathological liar is the actor's innocent brother; true mythomania is only a risky game compared with the psychic life of the actor. There are many actors—more than one would think—who in the course of time lose their grasp on reality. Some end their days in asylums, victims of their own fantasies.

The spectator, too, is a mythomaniac. The movies have made clear the nature of his myth. The little hunchback, coming out of his neighborhood theatre, feels in his body the easy grace of Gary Cooper. And his wife, when he becomes enterprising in the night, first refuses him, then sighs, when he insists: "Put out the light, then." A story by Carette.

Smile, if you will. But don't forget that the art of theatre attracts and seduces to the extent that it pictures to man and woman a momentary vitality from which the imagination derives a pleasure often more durable than that of sex.

Vitality and pleasure; and, just as for the mythomaniac, an all-embracing, constant, daily need for untruth. The spectator who fails to yield to these understandable follies is rare: Let's face it, he's a theatre professional.

Yes, the deception of ourselves by others and of others by ourselves is that natural demon in us which leads to theatre, calm or hectic, no matter. For creatures and things deceive us constantly, even the most faithful and sure. Few, if any, of our admirations and loves are free of illusion; that is, of errors of judgment, if not of outright lies. Everything in the realm of the senses and imagination (hence, of artistic creation) is subject to vagaries, hesitations, instability. There is no human work or creature which, in the light of some revealing happening, is not finally seen in its true contradictions. And there is no art which more necessarily unites illusions and reality than theatre; a fact unknown to the public though plain to see. Accomplices?

Truth and lies. Secrets and exposure. Theatre, in its essence, is made of our essence. It will never die.

❋ ❋ ❋

As often as we disguise our thoughts and actions, so often are we caught by the obsession to know and to see the truth. This is the cruel, incisive weapon of genius. Truth is often inhuman for those who lack the courage or passion to confront it. All of us flee it, often.

The search for truth, however, this insatiable need to penetrate to the very depths of the hidden existence of all beings, is at once poison and antidote to us. Oh, you can be a good actor without these preoccupations; but I don't believe there are any great actors who are not forced by the demands of their art to pursue this quest, this frequently painful interrogation of oneself in relation to others, of the masks of others in relation to oneself.

Are the distorting mirror and the mask the only human states reflected in the theatre's inner secrets? No, another mode of theatre exists in us all: the desire to reveal. Who has not thrilled to the strong, pure emotion of confession, the more so when confession must bring catastrophe. "The players tell all," Hamlet assures us. Drama above all, when it is conceived by Shakespeare.

*   *   *

Let's talk about the spectator.

It is by searching for truth and, along the way, learning the realities of others, their motives and individual passions, that we create ourselves. To know the truth at last strengthens our confidence in ourselves, in the validity of our experience, in the soundness of our judgment; in a word, in our understanding of creatures and things. It seems to me, too—fortunately for the continuance of our art—that this knowledge is the most common there is, acquired by everyone who has passed beyond adolescence. It is our common property, not the special gift of the exceptionally intelligent.

Which is why we must never despair of the natural genius of the audience. Why, also, we need not despair of the quality of their judgment, since we may be sure of the existence of private, often remarkable dramas in the life of every man and woman.

*   *   *

And understanding. Yes, understanding, too. For the theatre, in its masterpieces, is not only the enchanted circle of poetry, cruelty and beauty of gesture. Intellectual understanding; for a genius always distills a meaning comprehensible to all from the stories—exceptional as they are in themselves—of his heroes. If this meaning is not clear, don't try to tell me, "But he has genius." All men and women understand the universal joys and sufferings. Everything else is argumentation, academic fustian, manifestoes, quibbles, dust in the eyes. For men and women come to the theatre prepared, whoever they are, and their private world is a richer soil than even Aeschylus' and Shakespeare's naked monsters. Life, their life, has forced them to understand; not just to hate remorselessly or forgive at once, but to understand. It has bound them to suffering, to chastisement, to cowardice, to what you will, and we have in us a memory that retains it all. We are the sum of those memories, and our memory prepares us and compels us to accept the masterpiece.

The theatre, like our passions, is illusion. It is also action.

If there are no pathetic plays that are not first plays of action, there are equally no verisimilar plays which are not in fact illusory, dead with the last word set down by the poet. A play must be neither all action, nor all imagination. A masterpiece must have reality.

> Let [me] command a mirror hither straight,
> That it may show me what a face I have. . .
> —(Shakespeare, *Richard II*, IV, i.)

The theatre is that mirror. It reflects, in its masterpieces as well as in its plays of a day, our innermost life. A woman, however calm in appearance, in whom are passions of the heart and senses, discovers in the theatre a part of what she knows herself to be and cannot suppress, and feels the weight of another. Such honorable adultery is committed by our most faithful companions: They love, enduringly, a Romeo or a Chimène; not necessarily the actual person of the actor or actress who plays Romeo or Chimène.

Truth and phantom—a mirror, that is theatre.

❖   ❖   ❖

Projects, yet realization; reflection, yet action; dreaming in the chimney-corner, yet struggle for life—that is our lot in the theatre. By unremitting effort, we have to resist the charms of illusion, which draws us like a vacuum; we have to wed it to the sun of everyday.

Oh, I know! illusion is not dreaming, for the level head. Napoleon reminds us that, where the destiny is great, calculation enters the world of imagination and is not far from dreams. Imagination is not only the artist's tool. At night, at least, the realistic mind drowses in its meditation.

At home, I repair more often to my library. . . . It is on the third floor of a tower. . . . That is my castle. I try to keep it for my sole empery and to remove this only corner from the conjugal, filial and civil community. Unhappy he! to my view, who has not in his home a private home, where he may woo his solitary self, and hide.— (Montaigne)

If imagination is "mistress of error," it is nonetheless necessary before, after, and during action. As de Retz said, it is incumbent on us then to distinguish between the "unusual and the impossible"; a dilemma more refined than Hamlet's "To be or not to be."

      ❋   ❋   ❋

Imagination, tool of man and artist's world, is that boundless realm which the stage, and only the stage, can represent. And that is why (this is my conclusion from the preceding lines), just as imagination is abstract and unlimited, even so the stage must be unlimited, unconfined and, if possible, bare. Then the imagination delights and rejoices: the playwright's, the spectator's, the actor's.

That is, is it not, the lesson taught by those masterpieces which are not purely literary? It is the lesson taught by the Greek amphitheatre, the trestle-boards of Spain, the Elizabethan platform and the French tennis court. It is also the example given, in its own way, by that new art of our times, the delight of our

fellow-creatures of today—the cinema, with its boundless freedom of montage and fields of vision.

> Give me the glass, and therein will I read.
> No deeper wrinkles yet? hath sorrow struck
> So many blows upon this face of mine,
> And made no deeper wounds? O flattering glass,
> Thou dost beguile me!—(Shakespeare, *Richard II,* IV, i.)

And how marvelously skillfully this mirror of man, the theatre, beguiles us! It must beguile us, and it must *flatter* us. It
is not for nothing that the great poetic works of the stage end
with a transfigured image of the hero, be he a devil.

The hero is, in truth, always a monster. The laws of the stage
require it which, among others, require unity of thought in function of the unity of character: that is, the unity of *obsession.*
Chimène is as monstrous as Shylock.

    ❋   ❋   ❋

Let's get back to our beguilements.

Is there any more perfect example of our imaginative self-
deception than Richard II's coffin brought onto the stage and
opened? Then the spectator indeed fools himself. Illusion calls
the tune; *imaginatio generat casum.* No need for the actor. And
let the corpse not show his face! After three hours of the play,
the hero is so completely become myth that there is, God
knows! no need for his physical presence. Basta! The actor who
played Richard can go smoke his first cigarette of the evening in his dressing room and return to his private life. And
yet, out on the stage, the hero continues. No need, at the final
and culminating point of this masterpiece, for the actor's voice,
or mask, or presence. The symbol alone suffices. The coffin alone
is enough—the empty coffin.

    ❋   ❋   ❋

I was working on this essay when I had occasion to view an
actor's face in the final petrifaction of its mask.

A hospital room. The bare walls whitewashed. Naked. Real.

Aggressive. Flowers around the well-loved dead preserved something of our tenderness, something of the life of our sorrowing hearts. He lay with his upper body raised up, chin lifted, the hair still black and plentiful, the lips thinner than ever, dressed in an ordinary suit, without collar, tie or shirt, the undershirt high at the neck. His hands were folded on his stomach, holding a bunch of violets.

He was unrecognizable.

Yet those were his body and hands and face; his nose, his mouth, his angular bones. The lids were lowered over the eyes which had reflected his heart. No smile animated his face. We were looking at a mannequin.

Death does not magnify actors.

Our art is movement; death freezes us. We are incarnation; it destroys our flesh. We attempt to grasp the soul of a character; it takes our own. More eloquently, often, than words, our eyes express suffering and joy; the lids close. Moving and at rest, our hands on stage live with the life of the character; they are forever immobile. We are supple, expansive, sensitive; we become stiff and aloof.

If death claps on the actor's face the mask of a reality without illusion, without flattery; if this cruel, truthful visage belies our dreams; just so does crude reality in theatre plant a desert in our hearts. It affronts our need for flattering illusion, our light-hearted desire to see ourselves other than we are. For theatre, I believe, is unreality, dreams, psychic magic, mythomania. And if it is also reality, at least it must drug and intoxicate us, speed us from the theatre with a heart quickened, the mind full of wonders, and life strong within us.

Cover the dead actor's face.

* * *

Hamlet deceives himself. He is a big boy ashamed of his solitude. Hamlet has difficulty convincing us of the tragedy of his situation; of the tragic-ness of his tragedies. His personal drama is too vast—or too simple. Fresnay has said: "I don't know why he comes on the stage, nor why he leaves it." It is the most obscure of all the great roles.

So Hamlet deceives us.

The play's the thing to confound the guilty? To make him confess? No, Your Highness; the culprit is too much a realist and too familiar with the very particular circumstances of his crime to betray himself at its parody. No, my Prince, it is the honest man—if such there be—who trembles before the parable of a fault or a criminal life. Neither perfectly good, nor wholly evil, the honest man alone is capable of betraying himself. As for the remorse aroused in the criminal's bosom by the spectacle of his crime, let's have no illusions. Don't flatter the actor, please! We aren't all conceited fools. Macbeth would have bored Weidmann or Landru, you may be sure. Nor do they put on plays in the *rue des Saussaies*. And don't try to tell me that the re-enactment of the crime is theatre; the murderer may be upset by it, but he doesn't confess.

Let me assure you, my Prince, Himmler cared little enough for our gestures and paint, for our eyes dilated by passion or lining color. He wasn't fond of Shakespeare: found him too gory, or too wordy. He wept tenderly over the death of a canary. These are not like Macbeth-like niceties of feeling.

It is the honest men and women, those in whom the sense of guilt is not worn out, who follow with feverish attention the destinies of our bloody heroes. We know they always have some faults to expiate, and they hear in the masterpieces the faint echo of their vices, their faults, their secret lives.

Stage illusion is the reality of their dreams.

[Translated by Christopher Kotschnig]

PART TWO

THE LANGUAGE OF DRAMA

CONOR A. FARRINGTON

THE LANGUAGE OF DRAMA

CHRISTOPHER FRY

WHY VERSE?

The Language of Drama

CONOR A. FARRINGTON

When one rides out to do battle with the ogre of Realism it is at first dismaying to see how many noble shields and lances already litter the field. Rostand, Maeterlinck, Hofmannsthal, Yeats, Lorca, Claudel, Auden, Eliot, Fry . . . one had not thought there were so many. Not that they were all dishonorably unhorsed, but—the ogre still rules. And there are the critics too, like captured squires, bending to serve the one in power, always wistful and alert for liberation, it is true, but not actively encouraging to further challengers. And they have good reason for their hesitation since some who came to set them free are now among their persecutors.

A recent challenger, T. S. Eliot, has summed up his aims with regard to the drama, in several critical essays, notably one entitled "Poetry and Drama" and his statements can be taken as fairly representative and indeed more clearly, though modestly, expressed than most. "What we have to do," he says, "is to bring poetry into the world in which the audience lives and to which it returns when it leaves the theatre." "Audiences should be made to hear verse from people dressed like ourselves, living in houses and apartments like ours and using telephones and motor cars and radio sets."

One is conscious of two things on reading these sentences;

firstly that the author has a somewhat chemical attitude to the problem. Audiences should be "made to hear verse," poetry is to be "brought into the world in which the audience lives." The essay indeed might be subtitled "How to Introduce Poetry into the Drama without Coloring the Liquid or Producing a Taste." Even the title as it stands, "Poetry and Drama" hints at the way the author's mind works; there they are, detached as if they could be considered wholly separately and also could be, with great tact and ingenuity, rewed. It is doubtful, however, if the robust drama of the past will be reborn from such an artificial union.

The second thing one notices is how close the poetic dramatist has come to the Ibsenite commandment to use "the genuine language spoken in real life." Eliot, however, is not the only poetic playwright to have been hypnotized, as it were, by this commandment; others, too, have tended to tone down their poetry progressively, to beat their lances into teaspoons; it is true of Lorca, Fry, even of Yeats to some degree. We are faced with the paradox that Eliot is less poetic in *The Confidential Clerk* than Ibsen in *The Wild Duck*, Lorca less poetic in *The House of Bernarda Alba* than Chekhov in *The Three Sisters*.

When we look back at Ibsen and Chekhov, who were themselves the spearheads of the last successful revolution in dramatic language, we find they wrote as they did not because they had aesthetic theories about the language most suitable for their art; they wrote realistic dialogue simply because they had certain characters in mind who could not express themselves in the idiom audiences currently accepted in the theatre. Eliot recommended that drama should be written in the idiom of the audience: Ibsen and Chekhov, like all true dramatists, wrote in the idiom of their characters. The distinction is crucial.

It was an instinctive striving towards a fitter means of expression that brought realistic dialogue into the theatre and it will be a similar striving that will bring in its overdue successor, not willed attempts to create a poetic theatre by administering verse like vitamins, specially made up in a palatable form. This last is what Eliot recommends, he proposes to lower his language to the audience's idiom rather than draw up the audience to his own. It may be pointed out that he lowers his language in order later to draw up his audience with it. I can only say this reminds me of those clergymen who spend a great part of their time ingratiating themselves by playing football with the boys, golf with the men, having cocktails with the women, exhibiting to all their manly laugh and occasional studied swearword, to gain indulgence for the inevitable talk of Higher Things. The procedure is somehow faithless and undignified in man of God or dramatist and audiences will not be moved by it, nor souls be won.

The truth is that if any of the modern literary dramatists had one half of the broad human concern and the urgency to express it that Ibsen or even Zola had, realism would have been driven out long ago, and driven out with the same words that Zola used proclaiming of the drama of his day, "It is dying of extravagances, lies and platitudes."

Before we leave the realists it is worth noting that the poignancy of effect they undoubtedly achieved quite often was achieved by a process of reaction and contrast. They had said to poetry "Get thee behind me," and poetry did just that. It follows all their characters about like shadows and speaks in overtones through every shrug and sigh. Firs' weary speech at the end of *The Cherry Orchard* derives its poignancy from the contrast between its subject, the apparent inconsequence of living, and its manner, a semi-incoherent murmur. The contrast between what the realists wrote and what their more explicit, not to say verbose, predecessors might have written, also lends freshness to their dialogue. This was a time when reticence itself was a convention, when implicitness and inarticulacy were dramatically significant. Shakespeare of course knew all about the value of homely idiom, of contrast between mood and utterance; Lear's "Pray you, undo this button" in his dying speech is perhaps the most poignant line in the play, but Shakespeare also knew better than to write the whole play in that tone and idiom.

Unfortunately, however, recent realists have not been so sensible. Reticence, inarticulacy, homely idiom and, so to speak, the undoing of buttons have been elevated into articles of the current dramatic creed—a reticence which is no longer a healthy reaction but a lazy abdication, an inarticulacy which is not dramatically significant but is the inarticulacy of characters who have nothing to say. In so far as it can be held responsible for the one-dimensional banality that now passes for dramatic language Ibsen's demand for "the genuine language spoken in real life" is the most stultifying injunction ever to rule in the theatre.

There is one dramatist, Synge, whom Eliot discusses briefly in his essay and dismisses as a special case since Synge's plays are "based upon the idiom of a rural people whose speech is naturally poetic." This will not quite do; it might have been a valid dismissal if Synge had been writing for a closed society, if his audience had also been that rural people. But the people of Galway, Mayo, and the Western Islands are not and were not his audience. His audience was first the Dublin public— complete with houses, motor cars, and telephones, to whom the idiom was comparatively strange—and later the public of most civilized cities of the world. Synge succeeded not because he wrote in a style attuned to the ear of his audience, but because the rural idiom provided a convention within which they could accept language more expressive than their own.

It is worth noting too that Synge is the only modern poetic dramatist whose style grows richer and more highly wrought from play to play. Unfortunately this rural idiom, together with Synge's own defensive modesty, has obscured the significance of his development to the extent that critics can say, like Ronald Peacock, that he is an isolated figure of no universal significance. At the risk of seeming chauvinist, I suggest his example is of great significance indeed. True, in his first play *The*

Shadow of the Glen he could write sentences like: "It's proud and happy you'd be if I was getting my death the day I was shut of yourself." Now this is almost a word for word transliteration from Gaelic; in writing thus he was awkwardly following rural idiom, the slave of dialect. But soon, in *The Playboy of the Western World* his speech has developed the carriage of a thoroughbred wherever we sample it; for instance, "He'd beat Dan Davies' circus, or the holy missioners making sermons on the villainy of man!" Already the specifically native idiom is fading, and in the tragic peak of his last play *Deirdre of the Sorrows* it is barely perceptible:

I see the flames of Emain starting upward in the dark night and because of me there will be weasels and wild cats crying on a lonely wall where there were queens and armies and red gold, the way there will be a story told of a ruined city and a raving king and a woman will be young for ever.

This is not local speech at all but universal. This "idiom of a rural people" was nothing more than a liberating convention. It is interesting to observe, too, that in this last play Synge combined it with another time-honored convention, that of the historical or legendary play, a mode Eliot employed in what many, including myself, consider his most successful venture into the theatre, *Murder in the Cathedral*.

There is one place, even today, where that poised unification of an audience, which is what all drama is bent upon achieving, still regularly occurs and that is the opera house. It is no coincidence either that the opera house is the place where dramatic convention most robustly survives. Opera, fortunately, cannot exist without it; whatever new developments in *sprechgesang* are introduced singing will never sound plausibly like the chatter we have just heard in the foyer. As it is, Wolfram, Fiordiligi, or Radames finish a passage and stand transmogrified against a gale of cheers, or perhaps they even take a bow; but when the conductor raises his baton they step back into the world of illusion and the audience, without the slightest diffi-

culty, follows them. Perhaps we smile a little scornfully at this
procedure, but it is a tribute to the robustness of an embracing
convention and we should rather be full of envy.

For dramatic conventions are not a limiting but a liberating
factor in the drama. They liberate because they permit selection of manner and matter to suit the characters and issues of
the play. The conventions of the Elizabethan theatre in particular permitted the use of all kinds of dramatic shorthand which
enable playwrights to encompass vast areas of action and depths
of expression not only by obvious means like soliloquies and
asides, but also by scenes like that between Beatrice and Alse-
mero in Middleton's *Changeling* or that between Gloucester
and Lady Anne in *Richard III*, each of which is more a concentrated résumé of a process of wooing than a single occasion.

The dramatist attempting a representation of contemporary
life and language is, on the other hand, rigidly limited. Eliot
himself confesses that in writing *The Family Reunion*, he spent
far too much time establishing a situation. This is a typical drawback in the representational play. Not only does the stage have
to be dressed but the action and the conversation have to be
dressed too; people have to greet each other, thank each
other, inquire after each other, offer each other cigarettes and
matches, be plausibly occupied both on stage and off it; they
have to observe all the formalities of ordinary life which are
quite inessential to anything except the irrelevant game of making what is going on seem "real." So much time has to be spent
on superficial plausibility that it drastically reduces the time
for presenting the real issues of the play. Your Elizabethan has
gaily swallowed several camels before your modern has even
begun to strain at his gnat.

It is clear then that the remedies of most modern poetic dramatists have been too superficial. As John Gassner says, "modern verse drama has been limited in power by the fact that it has
been a more or less artificial graft on our stage"—and one might
add that in many cases the stock has sent up sap that withered

the shoot. The whole stock of realistic-language drama must be chopped away from that plot reserved for serious drama, and the plant regrown from seed, for three reasons.

The first is the audience's reason. I am convinced that people will not much longer continue to visit the theatre merely to listen to representations of their own inarticulacy. They come, rather, to hear expressed what they cannot express themselves, to have crystallized for them emotions that they bear about within them in solution; to escape—out of themselves, yes, but also into themselves, all by sharing emotionally in the life of the characters portrayed, which is impossible unless the language, the basic plasma of the theatre, is capable of supporting and communicating life. It is not too far-fetched to suggest that the current popularity on the stage of adaptations of radio scripts like *Under Milk Wood,* poems like *John Brown's Body,* autobiography like *Pictures in the Hallway,* novels like *Ulysses, Finnegans Wake,* and Dos Passos' *U. S. A.,* readings from Dickens, Mark Twain, Shaw, Edna Millay are all signs of the thirst of audiences for matter richer and more expressive than the contemporary drama, to its discredit, is able to provide.

The second reason is the actor's reason. He cannot bring to life characters which have no intrinsic life of their own. He is being handed the unconvertible coin of platitude, verbal and psychological, and can do no more than pass it on; he may proffer it humbly or fling it in the audience's face, it will purchase little response anyway. For poetry, in the broad sense, is the means whereby the dramatist communicates with the actor, it is the capsule in which the character the actor must embody comes to him; nothing else will survive the often arduous and changeable journey and still contain that essential variety of vitality which it is his art to embody.

Moreover, only poetry whose faculty is to say three things at once, gives him that creative opportunity of manipulating the various strands of meaning in his own way to make something that is all the more compelling for being peculiarly his own.

The reproduction and illumination of the word is the center of the actor's art. It is a serious reflection that in America, where the standard of acting is generally high, the vocal tones of actors are flat and lacking in variety; the actor's principal instrument is incapable because unexercised, and most attention is devoted to the periphery of his art.

It might be added here that American critics and writers on the drama, though the most penetrating and illuminating anywhere, are singularly uncertain in their "ear." For instance, they can speak of O'Casey's style, which is rarely more than a heap of alliterative and often inapposite adjectives, in the same breath as Synge's; they can praise the cheap chintzy speeches of Marchbanks in Shaw's *Candida,* they can accept the inert, near-fetched sentimentality of Saint Joan's crucial speeches as worthy of a saint of God. These are all failures of critical "ear."

With regard to verse in the theatre, the actor should be the warmest pleader in its favor. If he speaks in prose, the ear of the audience is trained basically on the meaning, the grammar of his speech; the liberties he can take to color or emphasize anything are strictly limited. But when he is speaking verse he imposes a rhythm on the ear of the audience which, though it does not free him from conveying the sense, sets up a tension, permits an interplay of loyalty between sense and rhythm that makes his speech far more telling. Words can be given much more "air" within the binding matrix of rhythm, a sense of onward motion is established, changes of speed are more keenly felt, pauses are tauter, all kinds of subtle emphases are available which unpatterned prose cannot provide.

It follows from this that a regular and perceptibly stressed verse is the most useful in the theatre. Eliot has evolved a line, he tells us, with a varying number of syllables and three stresses divided irregularly by a caesura. It is as well he told us; one critic writing on him refers repeatedly to his "pentameter"; an actor of unusual sensitivity, known to me, played the title role in *The Elder Statesman* taking the line as a four stress one, perfectly plausibly. If the skilled go astray, how will the unskilled audience pick up the pattern? Eliot's verse form, and Fry's both miss the primary theatrical point of verse, that of imposing a ground swell, a basic rhythm.

I am far from suggesting that verse is essential to the drama. Let the practical requirements of the matter dictate the manner. The theatre has not been greatly enriched by the "I-will-now-sit-down-and-write-a-tragedy-in-terza-rima-on-some-subject-imitated-from-the-Greek" attitude. Synge's work again is adequate proof of what can be achieved without verse. Synge, however, had an uncannily perfect ear for athletic prose rhythms, some of which, elaborately formal, are worth studying. Eliot's deprecation of verse mixed with prose is once again rather aesthetic than practical; there are circumstances where a step from prose into verse may be dramatically striking. After all, the Spanish classical dramatists who used half a dozen metres in one play often achieved notable effects with changes of metre. The essential thing is the cultivation of the dramatist's ear and its unprejudiced application to his material.

This brings us to the third reason for a radical alteration in the language of drama, which is the dramatist's reason. For the language of drama is the means of communication not only between actor and audience and between dramatist and actor but between the dramatist and his characters. We are not to presume he has an absolutely clear idea of the character he is attempting to delineate, that he writes down a cold summary of what his character should say, and then whittles it into dialogue. The dramatist is like, rather, a dedicated Ahab, whose instinct it is to sense the presence of his quarry, whose skill it is to throw phrase upon phrase like harpoons after him, which plunge down slack and lifeless in the dark till at last one strikes, then another and another until the lines contain the whole strength of the prey. It is actually by means of particular words and phrases that he discovers the character, it is the authentic excitement of discovery that makes dramatic literature, and it is the embodied re-

enactment of that discovery that makes drama. It is not enough
to throw, as it were, a whole sea onto the stage, as O'Neill does,
and tell us to find our own whale. Nor is it enough to pick up
scraps of what other men have already killed and cured, like all
the playwrights of the cliché, who go dressed like whalers to
the supermarket and come home with a ton of tins. I have spoken
of the authenticity and excitement of discovery; Synge was referring to the same thing when he wrote, "On the stage one must
have reality and one must have joy." Reality, or authenticity;
joy, or excitement. The individual origin of every drama is a
verbal process which probes, discovers, celebrates, and preserves
in one action, and any theory of drama that does not look back
to this origin is no more than the chattering of teeth.

Everyone in the theatre is a sharer in the same experience
from dramatist to audience-member. What is it about Hamlet,
Oedipus, Phèdre that grips us? It is because they are discoveries,
not revelations; because Shakespeare, Sophocles, Racine wrote
not merely to show us what these souls were like, but to find
out.

Hence, merely external and aesthetic theories of language
are not relevant or helpful. Eliot, having praised Yeats for his
"purging out of poetical ornament" in his later plays, goes on
to say, severely, "the course of improvement is toward greater
and greater starkness." Why? Have souls all grown starker since
Shakespeare's day that we need greater starkness to comprehend them? This is the realist heresy all over again. However,
Hamlet, in his dying breath, indulges in poetical ornament
when he says, "this fell sergeant Death is strict in his arrest." This
wry, military metaphor conveys more than any starkness could,
this ornament could not be purged out without purging out a
part of Hamlet himself. Again, what does Shakespeare do at
the peak of one of his most intense scenes, where Othello has
been wrought to the desire for revenge—how does he describe
the strength of that desire but in an elaborate poetical ornament:

> Like to the Pontic sea
> Whose icy current and compulsive course
> Ne'er feels retiring ebb but keeps due on
> To the Propontic and the Hellespont.

Could starkness do what this does so overwhelmingly well? Firstly, in conveying the headlong impetuosity of his desire, particularly by means of the jostling consonants in the second line; secondly, the fateful double repetition of that single syllable in the proper names; thirdly, the perspective of character it gives, sending our minds reaching back to his "travel's history," reminding us of the dimensions of that life now so fatally narrowed to revenge. If such characters are to be made known to us, it simply cannot be done by "starkness." And it is fatuous to say that people don't talk like that nowadays. Did Venetian Moors talk like that? Did Elizabethan vintners and scriveners? No, but Othello suffered like that, and people do still suffer like that and must be given voice.

Man has not changed in essence since these plays were written. Drama, however, which went indoors during the nineteenth century, has now largely descended to the cellars, while outside man is reaching for the stars. That we live in a dramatic age is obvious everywhere, except in the theatre. I suggest that the protagonists of Drama need to study again the basis of their art, which is the living word. And it is no use proclaiming "We are not Shakespeares" till we have tried and failed to be.

Tyrone Guthrie, at the end of his book, *A Life in The Theatre*, declares that drama is primarily a ritual, and likens it to Holy Communion. If that is valid then the language is the wine by which we are unified and nourished. To the outward eye today the ritual may seem complete, but what we pass about is an empty cup, a dry, unconsecrated chalice. Only when the cup is filled again will communion, communication, once more be made.

Why Verse?

CHRISTOPHER FRY

There are many people to whom verse in the theatre is an irritating, or boring, or distracting, or pretentious flight of fashion; and in certain moods I can pish and tush with the best of them. This point is not held so strongly about literature in general. It isn't often said that there should be no such thing as poetry at all. When Wordsworth writes:

> Felt in the blood, and felt along the heart

we should think twice, perhaps, before we asked him why he didn't write the passage in prose. "Felt in the blood, and felt along the heart" is a good example, by the way, of the speed and economy with which poetry can express what would take prose far longer.

What reason is there for limiting the theatre to one form of communication? It is even believed that the prose play and the verse play are in opposition, or that the one precludes the other; there appears to be a kind of color bar in the matter. Such rivalry is nonsense. Indeed, prose and verse existing side by side counter each other's dangers. If they pass altogether out of each other's reach they cease to be themselves, becoming on the one hand journalese, official cant, or any other string of sentences; and on the other a vagueness, an abstraction, a preciousness. This interplay of difference, one touching the hand of the other as it separates, like men and women dancing the Grand Chain, is what keeps each in its own state of grace.

One explanation of our impatience with a verse play is that the spring of theatre is action, and any insistence upon words is felt to hang like heavy clothes on the body of an athlete. When we go to the theatre we go to be interested by a story of lives living out their conflicts in a concentration of time. We do not go to hear them discuss the matter; we go to see and hear them live it.

But we know that words and actions are not unrelated. One illuminates the other; and the full significance of action can be explored only by words. If we compare the murder of Maria Marten in the Red Barn, with the murder of Duncan in Macbeth's castle, we see that in each the physical action is roughly the same, but the significance of the action is entirely different. The one is merely done, the other is experience, and the experience is in the words. What is more, the experience is the true nature of the action. The experience ultimately is the action. The action is not the dagger in Duncan's breast, or the blood on Macbeth's hand, but rather the limitless experience of the words arising out of them: the experience of:

> Macbeth does murder sleep!

of:

> ... this my hand will rather
> The multitudinous seas incarnadine,
> Making the green one red.

The three words "this my hand," in the context, so deepen our thoughts about the human hand and what it performs, that the action is not only true of this one human, and this one deed; it becomes also an elemental action, done in the beginning of the fallen world. In sounds alone, "multitudinous," which heaves like a wilderness of molten lava, set against the three monosyllables "this my hand," gives us, or should give us, an experience of being. We begin to feel there is not one action, but two, not two, but twenty in the course of a speech.

You may be prepared to agree with me that words give us a larger, or deeper, experience of action, but still you may say, "Why verse? Why this formality of syllables? Why this unnatural division of sentences into lines?"

I suggest we forget the questions, and go on as though verse plays, like wasps, are apparently with us for some reason which they don't reveal. I only ask you to allow me to suppose an organic discipline, pattern, or proportion in the universe, evident in all that we see, which is a government uniting the greatest with the least, form with behavior, natural event with historic event, which stamps its mark through us and through our perceptions, as the name of Brighton is marked through a stick of rock candy. When Milton says: "Elephants endors'd with towers," or when Wordsworth says: "A noticeable man with large gray eyes," they are not being so true to that organic discipline as, for instance, Chaucer, when he says:

> Now with his love, now in the colde grave
> Allone, withouten any companye.

I ask you to allow me to suppose a shaping but undogmatical presence "felt in the blood, and felt along the heart," which is of a kind with the law of gravity, and the moral law, and the law which gives us two legs and not six.

From the way I am going on you would think I was talking about the Eleusinian mysteries, not about a theatre in which you propose to spend an entertaining evening. It is the fault of the question "Why verse?" I should really write a play which would be so good that the question would never arise, a play which would please not some of the people some of the time, but all of the people all of the time, which would be both the immediate appearance of things and the eternal nature of things, combined with felicity.

I wish I could promise any such thing. Every few generations have to shape afresh the language which will express both these things together; and some of us find, like the donkey, that communication with our fellow being is something not easily achieved. We may think we have avoided all misconception, and then overhear a member of the audience making his comment, as after a performance of *The Dark Is Light Enough* (a play about the Austro-Hungarian war, taking place near Vienna) when a gentleman said with charitable resignation, "I never can understand these Russian plays."

It is no good asking poetry to tell us what it says; it simply *is* what it says. In the theatre it must have a direct surface meaning, an immediate impact of sense, but half its work should be going on below that meaning, drawing the ear, consciously or unconsciously, into a certain experience of being.

This has been an age of signposts, of ideologies, of patent cures, of battle cries; we must take up our positions, draw clear lines between this or that, label, analyze, dissect; we must live the letter, for the letter is the law. But we have been looking at the possibility that poetry has another, deeper law. The truth of poetry deepens under your eye. It is never absolute. There is no moment when we can trumpet it abroad as finally understood.

In a play I wrote called *A Sleep of Prisoners*, Cain and Abel throw dice together, and Abel prays as he shakes the dice:

> Deal me high, deal me low.
> Make my deeds
> My nameless needs.
> I know I do not know.

In our anxiety to be in the know we defend our scraps of knowledge and decision so passionately that over the centuries we have burned, tortured, imprisoned, shot, and blown up those who contradicted or doubted us. But the spirit of our scrap of knowledge was in the contradiction and doubt, as much as in the belief. What we were torturing and blowing up was the spirit of truth.

Poetry in the theatre is the action of listening. It is an unrolling exploration, following your nose, or it would be better to say following your ear, for sound itself, pure sound, has logic, as we know in music, and what does that logic accord to if not the universal discipline felt along the heart? What part this logic plays in our life here on the earth is beyond calculation. If it wakens harmony, modulation, and the resolving discord in us, we are nearer to our proper natures.

> The man that hath no music in himself,
> Nor is not moved with concord of sweet sounds,
> Is fit for treasons, stratagems and spoils;
> The motions of his spirit are dull as night,
> And his affections dark as Erebus:
> Let no such man be trusted.
> Mark the music.

Mark the music. Even in the broad give-and-take of the theatre our ears should be able to accept the interplay of the vowel sounds of a line of poetry, and know them as indications of the universal discipline, and consider the comma in the line with almost as much purpose as the comma on the underwing of the butterfly. But this precision has to exist within the broad and tough character of the theatre; it has to hold its own against distractions of many kinds: against coughs in the auditorium, failings in the author, even—on rare occasions—against irregularities of the actor's memory; just as in life our awareness of our larger natures has to hold its own against a host of distractions within and without.

So the general lines of the play, the shape of the story, the disposition of the characters, should point and implicate by their actions and their wider uses the texture of the poetry. The large pattern of the action should have a meaning in itself, above and beyond the story; the kind of meaning which gives everlasting truth to myths and legends, and makes the fairy story into a sober fact; a meaning not so conscious as a parable or so contrived as an allegory, but as it were tracing a figure which the poetry can naturally and inevitably fill.

This is all very well, you may now say, this fine theory; but we have to put up with verse plays as they are, not as ideally they should be; it seems to us that a good deal of these plays could be written at least as well, and more honestly, in prose. Why, for instance, should you present to us as verse a speech such as this:

> I sometimes think
> His critical judgement is so exquisite
> It leaves us nothing to admire except his opinion.
> He should take into account
> The creative value of the fault.

I have no answer to satisfy you if you believe that human nature, or human personality, is divided into two parts, of whatever proportion, the prosaic and the poetic. I think we live always with a foot in each camp, or rather, that there is no moment when we can safely say that we belong entirely to one or the other. There is no moment when we can certainly say that even our apparently most insignificant actions have not a significance greatly beyond ourselves.

It is this tension between two meanings which verse conveys, favoring sometimes one, sometimes the other. The prosaic or colloquial can be rhythmically just sufficiently charged to resolve into the implication of verse at a moment's notice, even halfway through a sentence, and back again, without disturbing the unity of the speech, in the way that the spirit and the flesh work in ourselves without noticeably sawing us in half. The writer's responsibility is to know when he can safely break free of this, and relax for contrast into the rhythms of prose.

In *The Dark Is Light Enough* there comes a moment when the situation reduces everyone to silence; when there seems no way of the scene going on without bringing the curtain down. And then the Countess begins to speak. I will tell you what she says, not because the verse does what I want it to do, but it says something to our purpose.

How shall we manage, with time at a standstill?
We can't go back to where nothing has been said;
And no heart is served, caught in a moment
Which has frozen. Since no words will set us free—
Not at least now, until we can persuade
Our thoughts to move—
Music would unground us best,
As a tide in the dark comes to boats at anchor
And they begin to dance. My father told me
How he went late one night, a night
Of some Hungarian anxiety,
To the Golden Bull at Buda, and there he found
The President of your House of Deputies
Alone and dancing in his shirtsleeves
To the music of the band, himself
Put far away, bewitched completely
By the dance's custom; and so it went on,
While my father drank and talked with friends,
Three or four hours without a pause:
The weighty man of seventy, whose whole
Recognition of the world about him
During those hours, was when occasionally
He turned his eyes to the gipsy leader
And the music changed, out of a comprehension
As wordless as the music.
It was dancing that came up out of the earth
To take the old man's part against anxiety.

A comprehension as wordless as the music. It is this comprehension which poetry tries to speak, this revelation of discipline that comes up out of the earth, or is felt along the heart;
it is this which verse has to offer.

PART THREE

THE CHARACTERS OF DRAMA

HAROLD ROSENBERG

CHARACTER CHANGE AND THE DRAMA

J. L. STYAN

MANIPULATING THE CHARACTERS

Character Change
and the Drama

HAROLD ROSENBERG

"We have already seen Bernard change; passions may come that will modify him still more."—ANDRÉ GIDE, *The Counterfeiters*

I

An egg with an ancestry, developing, changing its form, maturing; later, degenerating, dying, decaying, again changing its form; always in a slow gradual way except for the shocks of birth and death—such is the broadest metaphor of the human personality developed by the organic point of view and expressed in such studies of mutation as biology, biography, history, psychology. Whatever unity an organism maintains at the base of its transformations is something mysterious: the single being may be compared with other organisms which it resembles, it may be classified, accounted for statistically, subsumed under a type; but its individuality can only be "felt." To the human person himself his own coherence is, as Herbert Read once put it, "an organic coherence intuitively based on the real world of sensation."

On the other hand, the concepts of morality or social law, applying exclusively to human beings and ignoring possible analogies with other living creatures, tend to define the individual not as an entity enduring in time but by what he has done in particular instances. A given sequence of acts provokes a judgment, and this judgment is an inseparable part of the recognition of the individual. Here too there is no final comprehension of the single person; but whereas the organic approach points towards the existence of individuals, each of whom can be grasped only by a nonrational operation, social legality operates as if it were unaware of them altogether, except as they are totally defined by their "overt acts." If the law is not always satisfied with itself, it is not because it feels the need at any time to discover more about the nature of individuals, but for the reason that it realizes all at once that acts are being performed for which it has no means of holding them responsible.

The law is not a recognizer of persons; its judgments are applied at the end of a series of acts. With regard to individuals the law thus creates a fiction, that of a person who is identified by the coherence of his acts with a fact in which they have terminated (the crime or the contract) and by nothing else. The judgment is the resolution of these acts.[1] The law visualizes the individual as a kind of actor with a role whom the court has located in the situational system of the legal code.

In contrast with the person recognized by the continuity of his being, we may designate the character defined by the coherence of his acts as an "identity." Representing the human individual as an actor, the term stands against the biological or historical organism-concept, which visualizes action as a mere attribute of, and clue to, a being who can be known only through an intuition.

The modern novel has more in common with the biological or historical view of character than with the legal. *Remembrance of Things Past* and *The Magic Mountain* are models of a literature of character metamorphosis, *Finnegans Wake* a high point in the rendering of organic texture.

---

[1] Raskolnikov, for example, in *Crime and Punishment* sought judgment so that his act would be completed and he could take on a new existence.

As for the legal definition, its way of shaping personae with a hatchet causes it to seem at first glance far removed from the needs of imaginative writing. Without considering the symbolic, collective or residual ingredients of feeling or motive, the law comprehends its "characters" in terms of the most commonly ascertainable elements of their acts. Only information relevant and material to the legal "cause of action" may be introduced as bearing on the parties and their transactions. The law is forever fixed to that edge of individuality where particulars are caught in the machinery of the abstract and pulled into an alien orbit. Yet in the old tragedy, the individual was similarly torn away from himself by the force of an impersonal system.

There too, however, distinctions must be made: social law is not dramatic law. That the persons who stand before the bar of justice are identities, that they appear to be personifications of, and completely explainable by, the logic of their crimes, is the effect of a visible artifice of judicial thinking. In fact, of course, a man who has committed a murder may not have acted in a manner recognizable as murderous until that last instant when he pulled the trigger. That he meant to kill at that moment satisfies the law's demand for premeditation and homicidal malice; but since all the acts of the criminal were not of a criminal quality, there is forced upon our consciousness a lifetime of extenuating circumstances. All those common details of existence, gestures in every way resembling our own, even including those preceding the murder—entering an automobile, stepping on the gas, obeying the traffic lights—to say nothing of receiving certain influences, being molded by certain values, which go more to form part of the criminal in the innocence or "alegality" of his animal duration than of the relevant *res gestae* of his crime, the law takes into account only to fill in the scenic accompaniments of the last act and the rationale of its intent. So that dealing with identities rather than with personalities, the law is enabled to do so only by willfully converting persons with histories into emblems of unified actions of a given order. In other words, the law, like its victims, suffers from the discrepancy between being and action, the failure of the individual to conform in every respect to his role. Were this not so, law and justice could be synonymous.

If, however, the old drama, as contrasted with biographies of actual or of fictitious persons, succeeded, as has been asserted by ethical critics, in supplying a picture of action in which a kind of justice and a kind of law conform to each other, it must be because the dramatist started with identities. Like the judge he left aside personalities, their growth, their structural peculiarities; like the judge he established the particularity of a character only on the basis of the coherence of his acts with a chosen fact; like the judge he was interested in psychological phenomena not for themselves but only as bearing on the plausibility of the judgment with which he terminated the action. But unlike that of the judge, the dramatist's definition of the character was not an arbitrary superimposition that exchanged the emotional, intellectual and mechanical characteristics of a biological and social organism for some one deed that concerned the court; it constituted instead the entire reality of the character, avoiding the ruinous abstractness of the law by determining in advance that his emotions, his thoughts and his gestures should correspond with and earn in every respect the fate prepared for him . . . In short, because the dramatist had created his characters he could maintain the relation between their emotions, their thoughts and their destinies; while those who confront the judge on his dais were, unfortunately, born.

Its distinction between personality and identity, quietly implied by its mode of defining the individual as an identity, is what dramatic thought has in common with the legal. The characters of biography and the novel are persons with histories, but in the drama the characters are identities with roles. The distinction relates to a difference in purpose of biography and tragedy. Biography aims to picture a life as fully and precisely as possible with the type of exactness which is proper to history, that is to events visualized as successive in time. But drama, as a "poetical picture of life," is composed of events which, though seemingly related sequentially and causally, are chosen with reference to the application of specific laws leading to a judgment: the conventional coherence of these events, the suggestion to the spectator that they have actually happened or are at least within the range of probability, is superficial, and far from determining the outcome of the action serves only to connect in the mind of the audience the natural world of causal determination with the dramatic world of judgment. Those psychological explanations of the motivations of dramatic figures which form so large a part of criticism apply to this layer of causality which is the outer form of dramatic movement; they do not touch on the dramatist's act of judging,[2] derived from his conception of how the world is ordered, by which his characters are moved. Psychology can establish the plausibility of Macbeth's or Lear's behavior, but for the sufficiency of his motivation we must refer not to a possible Macbeth or Lear in "real life" but to the laws of the Shakespearean universe.

It is with respect to these laws that drama reaches objectivity, that the dramatist's image mirrors the lives of actual people. In "nature" individuals may evade any system of ends; but a dramatic identity is a creature in whom a judgment is involved at birth, a judgment which delivers him to pathos and gives meaning to it. In thus substituting identities, whose motor organs are judgments,[3] for personalities who live erratically within the

[2] Instead of the "dramatist's act of judging" we might refer to the "dramatist's act of seeing judgment as involved in and carried out by action." From the naturalistic point of view, there is no judgment impressed upon action, and the presence of judgment in the drama must therefore be attributed to an act of the dramatist; but from the "dramatic viewpoint" there is no action that is not an effect of judgment, whether of the gods, the fates or history, and the judgment is therefore seen as present in the real formula of the action, is said to be discovered by the dramatist, and not to be the result of his act.

[3] The moral judgments of drama may, of course, not seem moral at all in the conventional sense; the dramatist may choose to execute a character because he is powerful rather than because he is wicked.

freedom and hazard of moral laws not yet discovered, drama brings into being figures who are at once particular and general and its account of events appears as "more philosophical than history."

II

Religious thought also interprets the individual as an identity; it looks to the judgment that will establish his eternal role. To it the pyschology of personality-development is irrelevant; for upon the fixed situation of an identity, mutations of the personality have no bearing. As in the bloody book of the law, there are in religion stirring examples of this division between identity and personality. For instance, in demoniacal possession identities usurped personalities: the demon, in all respects a new being controlled by the conditions of a supernatural world, subjected the individual to its own will.[4] The personality of the possessed remained intact. The demon was a character with a name of his own. His voice was heard from the mouth of a man—but he was not that man, any more than Hamlet was Barrymore. And he could be influenced only by means fundamentally identical in all contemporaneous cases of possession —there was one law for demons belonging to the same system. Exorcism was a contest between powers of a purely religious cosmos. The exorcist addressed the demon directly; no attempt was made to affect the psychological structure of the possessed. As we have said, it was irrelevant.

An identity is constant. In the worlds which give rise to identities, growth is excluded and change of character occurs above the rigid substratum of the identifying fact: whatever happens to the murderer, the murder still stands as his sign. Dramatic reversal of situation derives its overwhelming effect from this persistence of identity. Everything has turned inside out, yet the actor goes on doing the same thing. Were psycho-

---

[4] . . . The cases reported in the Middle Ages, including the epidemic outbreaks of possession, are perhaps the most striking.

logical adjustment to the new position possible, it would destroy the tragic irony and disperse the pathos.

Identity may be revealed more fully as a drama progresses. In such so-called character development, behavior rises or declines on the moral plane without, however, altering the fact by which the character is identified; we simply see a second side of the same character: e.g., the idling Prince Hal's "Well, thus we play the fools with the time" belongs to the same royal identity as Henry V's conscientious "Our bad neighbor makes us early stirrers, / Which is both healthful and good husbandry." Unchanging identity may also be present in the sudden reversals of moral direction that occur in *crise de conscience* episodes of novels and plays, moral reversal being merely a species of character development carried on at quick-time.

Yet identity itself may change in a drama, not through moral or psychological development, but through a process that causes the central fact which identifies the character to give place to one belonging to a different constellation of values. When such a shift of centers occurs, the fact to which the character's action was previously attached loses its power to move him. His moral nature may remain substantially the same, but his acts crystallize differently; he is a different dramatic individual; all his likelihoods have been recast.

It is especially in the substitution of one identity for another, or for a personality, that the type of coherence which marks the identity is clarified, since change of identity takes place, as we shall see, all at once, in a leap, and not as in personality through a continual transformation of elements.

To begin with the legal instance: the fact of the crime organized (by determining their relevance) the acts of the criminal and interpreted them. For the law he lived by that fact alone. Were it suddenly discovered that no crime had been committed, the coherence of his action would collapse and the prisoner, having been converted in an instant into the hypothetical and undefined figure of an innocent man, would no longer exist under the eye of the court. If thereafter he were charged with a different crime, his legal identity would depend upon this new fact and would be entirely unrelated to the one he had lost; he would emerge out of the void as a "new man."

In religion identity and change of identity have been, one may say, the dominant interest of the most significant and important ceremonies. Professor Guignbert writes in *Christianity*:

In the Phrygian cult of Cybele and Attis, but not in that alone, for we find it in various other Asiatic cults and in that of Mithra, a singular ceremony, called the *taurobolium,* took place. It formed part of the mysterious initiatory rites exclusively reserved for believers.

Having given an account of the rites, Guignbert explains their transforming function:

The pit signifies the kingdom of the dead, and the mystic, in descending into it, is thought to die; the bull is Attis, and the blood that is shed is the divine life principle that issues from him; the initiate receives it and, as it were, absorbs it; when he leaves the pit he is said to be "born again" and milk, as in the case of a newborn infant, is given him to drink. But he is not born the mere man again he was before; he has absorbed the very essence of the god and, if we understand the mystery aright, he is in his turn become an Attis and is saluted as one.

Guignbert then draws attention to the resemblance between these rites and the Christian baptism and eucharist.

The change consists then in both the legal and religious instances in (1) the dissolution or death of the previous identity through cancellation of its central fact[5]—this may involve the physical death of the individual (as with Ivan Ilych, whom Tol-

---

[5] That the purpose of the law in executing a criminal is to avenge itself upon him or to deter others has long been denied by philosophers of the law. The logic of the execution becomes clear when we understand it as an attempt to eliminate the criminal identity and thus to cancel the crime itself which that identity personifies. The death of the criminal is incidental to this aim of cleansing the past. Any other means equally certain of accomplishing the dissolution of the criminal identity would be, theoretically, as satisfactory.

stoy abandoned on the threshold of change) or his symbolic
death; and (2) a reidentification, wherein the individual is
placed in a new status, is "reborn," so to say, and given a new
character and perhaps a new name.

Drama is no more religion than it is law. But the fact that
the phenomenon of religious conversion is the only one which
actually[6] effects a change of identity in the living person, in
which through the touch of death a course of living is annulled
and another substituted without rupturing the organic continuity of the individual, relates religion and drama in a peculiar
way. To present identity-replacement in a credible manner the
dramatist must imitate the experience of religion and subject
his character to the ordeal of death. But he may do so in terms
of action alone and without adopting any metaphysical supposition as to the cause of the change. In a word, dramatic death
and regeneration need not be involved in faith:[7] there is the
death-laden incident; then occurs a transfer of identities within
the single figure, a change of faces behind the mask.

The process appears with characteristic modifications in different literatures. A very early account of identity-change is the
life story of the Biblical Jacob, whose character is built out of
connotations of the word from which his name was derived, as
when Esau complains in the Hebrew pun that he was "Jacobed"
twice. A self-reliant trickster, he wins his way through ruses and
negotiations until the threat of death descends upon him in the
approach of the avenging Esau. Then "greatly afraid and distressed" he calls on God to save him and schemes to be the last
of his company to die. Alone behind the encampment, however,
he is met by the angel and wrestles with him until dawn. During this contest he receives the sign of the dislocated thigh and

[6] The legal change is of course a purely formal one.
[7] Death in the drama means only cessation of the character's action and
the impossibility of his taking it up again. This stoppage may mirror natural
death—the character has died or been killed; or, as in the impostor type of
comedy, the death may apply to a fictitious identity—the individual continues to be present but through having been exposed as a fraud cannot go
on with his old act.

his name is changed to Wrestler-With-God. In the morning he advances to meet his brother, whose fury has been unaccountably—psychologically, that is, though enforcing the point of Jacob's new identity—transformed to love.

From that time the lone adventurer, gainer of property and wives, has disappeared; in his place sits the patriarch, and interest shifts to his children. In the next episode, the seduction of Dinah, it is his sons who plot and carry out the treacherous revenge. The transformed Jacob, Isra-el, his character "deducible" from his wrestle with God, is busy with the erection of altars.

This is an extremely simple picture of the process of identity-change. There is a minimum of action-detail, only the death threat and alteration by contact with the divine over-plot and by renaming.

In the next example, a personality is transformed into a dramatic identity. In it, the action of a person, which is the expression of a psychological condition, is contrasted with that of an identity, which always takes place in response to his role— which he performs as required of him by the plot, by the whole in which he is located. That this hero is a person at the outset means that the work begins as a species of biography; that he changes into an identity means that from that point on the biography-drama becomes a true drama.

In *Hamlet* there is a fusion of two forms of interpretation, the naturalistic and the dramatic. The argumentative, self-analytical Hamlet of "nonaction," describing himself in every speech, and using speech as a substitute for deed, is very much the figure of a personality, of a being insufficient for, *because irrelevant to,* the dramatic role offered to him.[8] Hamlet has all

---

[8] Psychological criticism lays Hamlet's failure to act to the preponderance of one trait, usually the reflective one. Interpreting his character in terms of dramatic identity, we relate his incapacity to a structural insufficiency, that is, to his failure to be part of an action-system, a defect for which there is no psychological remedy.

> I do not know
> Why yet I live to say 'this thing's to do,'
> Sith I have cause and will and strength and means
> To do 't.

the qualities required for action; what he lacks is the identity structure which would fit him to be a character in a drama, a one-ness with his role originating in and responding to the laws of his dramatic world. Thus he is contrasted or "paralleled"[9] with Laertes whose situation is similar to his, "For by the image of my cause, I see / The portraiture of his," but who is characterized as an identity by his readiness to act; and the point is repeated in setting off his psychological diffusion against the acting-craft of the visiting players. It is not a weakness of personality that impedes his action but the fact that he is a personality. The revolving sword of judgment cuts him off at that point where he would force an entry into the dramatic cosmos. He has been exiled to a middle ground between the natural world and the dramatic; governed by contradictory laws, it is a playground of somewhat insane fantasies. Hamlet is inadequate to carry out the Orestean judgment because he has been permitted to retain a portion of himself. As a new kind of hero, the person who matches his self against his part, he thinks too much not because he is an intellectual but because it is impossible for him to do anything else. The mystery which surrounds him consists in that he is neither an identity nor a personality wholly but a combination of both, an hypothetical actor who has wandered by accident upon a stage.[10]

Clearly, then, this character must be changed if the play is to become a tragedy, if the action is to resolve itself and not to break down into a series of episodes exposing psychological layers. To arrive at a pathos, Hamlet must be given an identity which will alter his relation to the action and fit him into the drama. But there is only one way to represent such a change dramatically.

Until we meet Hamlet on his return from the voyage to England, where he had been sent to his death and narrowly escaped in the grapple with the pirates, we have to do with the standard figure of Hamlet-criticism. But after this immersion

[9] "Save yourself, my lord." etc. The scene belongs in all respects to the rôle of Hamlet.

[10] "For he was likely, had he been put on, / To have proved most royally.'

in symbolic death,[11] we encounter a new character, a regener-
ated man. In his next appearance on the stage, Hamlet takes
death as his subject and discourses on it as an insider. More to
the point, he has acquired a certainty with respect to his feelings and a capacity for action. "This is I," he announces, as he
leaps into the grave of Ophelia, "Hamlet the Dane!" Having
named himself he is at once attacked by Laertes but with unexpected firmness proclaims his dramatic equality.

> I prithee, take thy fingers from my throat;
> For, though I am not splenetive and rash,
> Yet have I something in me dangerous,
> Which let thy wisdom fear. Hold off thy hand!

With this "dangerous" new ability to act, he is no longer troubled by ambiguity of feeling: "Why, I will fight with him upon
this theme. . . . / I loved Ophelia . . ." To his mother Hamlet's
self-assured identity is unrecognizable; she sees him as he was
before the change:

> This is mere madness,
> And thus a while the fit will work in him.
> Anon, as patient as the female dove
> When that her golden couplets are disclosed,
> His silence will sit drooping.

But Gertrude is mistaken. For Hamlet has commenced to act
his role of self-purifying vengeance, had assumed immutably his
dramatic being, at that moment when aboard the ship bound
for England he had read his death-warrant. Then for the first
time his mind had responded with the immediacy of the actor:

> Being thus be-netted round with villainies—
> Ere I could make a prologue to my brains,
> They had begun the play—

And now this hero who had looked with such passionate envy
upon passion is "constant in his purposes" towards the King. The

---

[11] "High and mighty," he writes to Claudius without apparent reason, "You
shall know I am set naked in your kingdom."

magical event barely indicated ("Had I but time, O, I could tell you") has released his forces. His action hustles the play to its tragic close and the apparently accidental character of his revenge serves to emphasize that he is controlled at the end not by the conflicting intentions of a self but by the impulsions of the plot. Transformed from the image of a personality into that of a dramatic identity, he has found at last his place in the play.

Our third example is from Dostoevsky's *The Brothers Karamazov*. This author's handling of change of identity follows more literally experience of typically religious conversion than does either that of the Old Testament or of Shakespeare; it is related directly to Christian beliefs and emotions.

The "Biographical Notes" of Father Zossima set out two parallel cases of identity-change. First there is Markel, Zossima's brother, whose conversion is briefly sketched to furnish a ground for Zossima's own conversion which comes later and is developed in greater detail. After his brother's death Zossima was sent to Petersburg to enter the Imperial Guard. From the house of his childhood, he records, he had brought none but precious memories of a religious import, but these grew dimmer in the cadet school and he became a "cruel, absurd, almost savage creature." . . . A disappointing love affair, an insult, and a challenge to a duel . . . "and then something happened that in very truth was the turning point of my life." The evening preceding the duel, he flew into a rage and struck his orderly so violently that his face was covered with blood. When Zossima awoke the following morning he went to the window and looked out upon the garden. The sun was rising. "It was warm and beautiful, the birds were singing." At that point the conversion began.

What's the meaning of it, I thought, I feel in my heart as it were something vile and shameful? Is it because I am going to shed blood? No, I thought, I feel it's not that. Can it be that I am afraid of death, afraid of being killed? No, that's not it at all . . . And all at once, I knew what it was; it was because I had beaten Afanasy the evening before!

Then Zossima recalls his converted brother, the deceased Markel. On the field of honor, risking his companion's contempt, he halts the duel after his adversary has fired. A short time later he becomes a monk.

This incident, turning on danger of death though fear of death is denied, stages the typical antecedent conditions listed by psychologists for cases of religious conversion; it may be assumed that, apart from his own experience after being threatened by the Czar's firing squad, Dostoevsky was familiar with the subject through books on the psychology of conversion. Yet Zossima's transformation arouses no suspicion that it is an ideological fable of the descent of Grace rather than a genuine dramatic happening. The change takes place through events which, for all their realism, are the equivalent of the legendary and picaresque circumstances of the Bible and *Hamlet*. In all three examples, the process underlying the character's change is the same, although the nature of the action accompanying it is different in each instance and explanations vary from angelic intervention to terror and remorse. In all three an identical anxiety is present. In the terse account of Jacob's transformation he is described as "greatly afraid and distressed," Hamlet recalls that ". . . in my heart there was a kind of fighting, / That would not let me sleep," while Zossima feels "something vile and shameful."

The so-called psychic states preceding conversion seem all to have this in common, that they dissolve the economy of the individual, and excite the soul, but cannot satisfy it or allay its disturbance. They are psychic states which propound questions, but do not answer them; they initiate, but do not complete. They provoke a suspension of the soul in which they are being experienced.—*Religious Conversion*, Sante de Sanctos

III

Individuals are conceived as identities in systems whose subject matter is action and the judgment of actions. In this realm the multiple incidents in the life of an individual may be synthesized, by the choice of the individual himself or by the decision of others, into a scheme that pivots on a single fact central to the individual's existence and which, controlling his behavior and deciding his fate, becomes his visible definition. Here unity of the "plot" becomes one with unity of being and through the fixity of identity change becomes synonymous with revolution.

Of this dramatic integration religious conversion, of all human conditions, supplies the most complete example, although only an example. Through conversion the individual gains an identity which revolves upon a fact that is subjective in its unifying effect upon him yet extra-personal in its relation to his world. In all converts, regardless of what they are converted to, there comes into being that surface coherence which is the sign of the dramatic character. To other individuals unity of action may be *attributed;*[12] the convert claims his one-ness to be himself and compels his life to conform to his interpretation.

It is recognition of the individual as an identity that establishes the fundamental connection between religious and dramatic thought. In both, the actor does not obey his own will but the rules of the situation in which he finds himself. In both, change (and escape from the plot) can be accomplished through one means alone, the dissolution of identity and the reappearance of the individual in a "reborn" state. In thus reflecting the limits imposed by action, the "unnatural" processes of religion and drama correspond to those of actual life.

[12] This is rarely done by biographers, who stress the "human" aspects of a character. But contrast Prince Mirsky's biography of Lenin as a man who had almost no personal life.

Manipulating the Characters

J. L. STYAN

In drama 'character' is not an author's raw material: it is his product. It emerges from the play; it is not put into it. It has an infinity of subtle uses, but they all serve in the orchestration of the play as a whole; and so character finds this place in the scheme. But we face probably the most difficult and confused problem, a real stumbling-block, in dramatic appreciation, and the most I can do is to offer some pointers to what seem to be the real issues for the playgoer.

Some of the dangers of falsely assessing character are obvious, but none the less awkward to avoid. We set up our own barriers to full appreciation if we take a misplaced interest in a fictional character for its own sake and out of context. Because of the peculiar sympathies a writer calls upon through character, we have a natural urge to talk about, say, Cordelia as a daughter or Edgar as a son. Because the figures do have human aspects in the play, we are encouraged to that extent to talk even of Strindberg's ghosts, Pirandello's fantasies or Yeats' masked symbols in terms of individual thoughts and feelings. We talk about what we are more sure of: human qualities and attributes.

It may be that in the frustrating task of defining a play for ourselves after seeing a performance, we take the easy way and search for a character as an absolute: we define the play *Hedda Gabler* by the qualities in Hedda the woman, *Macbeth* by qualities in the man. Perhaps we go so far as to assume it a mark of indifferent playwriting if we cannot do this. Perhaps up to a point Ibsen and Shakespeare ask us to do so: a dramatist who works with human nature as his material is surely interested in character? Yet every time we look for character as something which can be neat and complete and satisfyingly objective, we are liable to blind ourselves, and judge the play by character alone, perhaps by a self-created thing. Since Aristotle, the student of drama has been led into considering character as a separate entity, without full regard for its being cause or effect.

Natural as this is, at its best it represents a slacker criticism, something of a failure to envisage the broad complexity of a character's function in a play. At its worst, for an audience to grow to love a character as if it were an old friend is to reduce interest in the actor as a person. We have to beware lest any one element like character, whether because it is a particularly striking element, or because an actor's performance has been out of proportion to his part, becomes the false centre of attention, prompting us to garner illegitimate impressions. It might lead us away from the play; it might become the play itself.

In recent years the warnings against this habit have perhaps been rather too loud. Professor Wilson Knight offered a seminal concept about Shakespeare's characters, stating that 'the persons, ultimately, are not human at all, but purely symbols of a poetic vision.' But in some sense we *must* feel Lear, Macbeth, Hamlet are human. We pity or admire because we are throughout the performance in contact with humanity in human situations: the figures in the pattern are, after all, human figures in a human pattern. Lear, Macbeth, Hamlet speak for human beings; they speak for us—or what value is there in the play.

Professor L. C. Knights pursued this topic, and suggested

that character was 'merely an abstraction from the total response in the mind of the reader or spectator.' He was rightly concerned that our proper interest in a play should not be deflected, lest we should 'impoverish the total response'; his words were more guarded. But it was noticeable that in his analysis of a play that followed this statement, he made no reference to a physical stage or to a live actor embodying a character. He demolished actor with character and substituted another abstraction in its place. When he suggested that *Macbeth* had a greater affinity with *The Waste Land* than with *A Doll's House,* it was almost a case of throwing the baby out with the bath water.

Common sense cannot accept that a character is no more than a mouth for an arrangement of words. We are bound to examine the fuller contribution we know to exist. It would be irresponsible to ignore its strangely binding quality in commanding an audience's response. And that quality is tied up with the presence of the actor on the stage.

To solve these problems we appeal to experience. The unique contribution of the living actor is his ability to fill in the author's outline, retaining whatever symbolic and universal suggestion that outline carries while representing it to an audience as alive and urgent. The key-word here is *alive.* All values in art depend upon the power of communicating them, making them a wholly felt, breathing force to the recipient. This is the limitation on the symbol: the character must be sufficiently human for the actor congruously to present it in his own person and for the spectator to recognize it. It is the test of a good morality play that it should make human where its lesson is most abstract. Tragedy depends for its intrinsic effect on keeping its hero mortal. If the gods are called in, whether in Aeschylus's *The Eumenides* or in Giraudoux's *Amphitryon 38,* they must think like people, as must ghosts and apparitions. And the test of the modern symbolic melodrama, say Betti's *The Queen and the Rebels,* like the test of classical tragedy, is whether the character can remain living while carrying an exceptional load

of wide meanings. In this play, can Argia the self-seeking
prostitute support a queenly martyrdom? The author's choice of
such extremities is partly to offer unexpected hope for an abiding Christian dignity in life. To this we may wish to give consent, but not unless the character in the person of the actress can
convince us of the truth in this particular human transformation.
Living symbols will be judged by life.

But here is new danger. 'Judged by life': does this mean the
characters must be lifelike? Is it implied that our circumspect
modern audiences will not find a character adequate if they cannot find a parallel within their own experience? In the words of
Mr. Raymond Williams, 'we must be careful that our judgement
depends not on whether the characters are lifelike, but on
whether they serve to embody experience which the actor has
shown to be true.' It is a safer approach that does not bring
preconceived, external and invalid standards from real life
to the judgement of an artificial arrangement like a play. But
we do.

As before, it is easy to see why we do. We find differences
between speakers labelled in the way they speak: idioms, in-
flexions, sometimes tricks of speech distinguish them. But whether
this is for the purpose of identifying the speaker in the mind of
the actor as he acts, or at the other extreme, of the reader as he
reads, is irrelevant: representation of life is not an end in itself. The relevant question is to ask *why* Shakespeare makes
recognizable in this or that form Beatrice or Mercutio or Juliet's
Nurse or Shylock, naming some most commonly discussed as
'living' individuals. Once such a question is asked, character slips
into its proper place.

Another side of the same fallacy is the belief that the author
who can convince the playgoer that a character has a life of
its own has fulfilled a proper end of drama. The playgoer's
conviction is held to be the mark of a good play. Such a theory
must be to the detriment of all the plays not written in the realistic convention—the bulk of the world's output—if the nature

of the conviction is not more closely specified. Different kinds of
play anticipate different kinds of conviction. We are not asked
to believe, for example, that Shaw's Joan or Anouilh's Antigone
or Giraudoux's Hector in *Tiger at the Gates* would have been so
up-to-the-minute in their thinking. Anachronisms have always
been part of the stock-in-trade of a dramatist trying to impress
timeless values on a contemporary audience. Such characters
convince because they are *consistent* within the little world built
for them, which may be fantastic or distorted, very wide or very
narrow. Theirs is a truth probable to their own world. Conviction may be important to the success of a play, but it will be
determined by the organization of all the elements within it
and may not be directly related to character at all.

This is not to deny that realistic characterization may be important in itself if it suggests, like the iceberg, a depth not visible on the surface. Human psychology can itself constitute a
theme. Provided this depth of characterization is relevant, that
is provided the theme is dependent on this sort of conviction,
common-sense would not deny it. In such a case the psychological overtones of the play may be one source for the theatre
experience, and must be valued as such. Thus Strindberg in his
Preface to *Miss Julie* can justifiably write,

An event in real life—and this discovery is quite recent—springs generally from a whole series of more or less deep-lying motives . . .
In explanation of Miss Julie's sad fate I have suggested many factors:
her mother's fundamental instincts; her father's mistaken upbringing
of the girl; her own nature; the suggestive influence of her fiancé on
a weak and degenerate brain; furthermore, and more directly: the
festive mood of the Midsummer Eve; the absence of her father; her
physical condition; her preoccupation with animals; the excitation of
the dance; the dusk of the night; the strongly aphrodisiacal influence
of the flowers; and lastly the chance of the two of them together in a
secluded room, to which must be added the aggressiveness of the
excited man.
Thus I have neither been one-sidedly physiological nor one-sidedly
psychological in my procedure.

In this play Strindberg wishes to stage a tragic struggle between heredity and environment. To do it he uses as a common point of reference modern understanding of psychology. In this struggle, Julie, carefully circumscribed by her background, is the author's realistic symbol for his purpose. Nevertheless, each of the factors Strindberg enumerates in explanation of Julie's behaviour plays a double part, for in addition to making this character in this situation credibly 'real,' each also represents a factor in the struggle. Thus each also represents a facet of the theme. It is unwise, even in realistic drama of the best sort, to separate the character from the play, the psychology from the theme.

We must avoid begging essential questions about the source of the experience. There is a distinction to be made between the *dramatis persona* of the scene and the personality which emerges as part of the impression we derive. Character in the usual sense of 'personality' is not an agency for the writer as speech is. Even in a leading part it may indeed not exist, as many expressionistic dramas have shown; in the minor parts of even realistic drama we may not expect it. An impression of personality is more truly a by-product, a facet of the image, sometimes only an accident that happens because of the occasionally narrative turn of a play. In the weak play, we may be kept happy by the presence of personality when what that stands for cannot engross us. The author who is a cheat will tap associations from our own or typical acquaintance, till we give body to the pale shadow the author has made of his character. On the other hand, tapping our preconceived notions of character can be legitimate procedure, as in a play planned to upset those notions (we think of conventional Parson Manders in Ibsen's *Ghosts*), or in the modern play using old legend (the heroes in *Tiger at the Gates*). In the latter case, Giraudoux expects us to make his Helen and his Hector familiar figures, the better to remind us of their eternal existence. Yet even here the characters remain primarily *dramatis personae*.

A rule for one type of play may not apply to another. The real test is whether a character can do what the play requires of it. The type of play that designedly breaks realistic rules thus presents a set of special problems. How do we judge a character in a farce or an extravagant comedy? Standards from life can only distract. We agree to allow half-people like Sergius and Raina from *Arms and the Man* to be the head and tail of a pantomime donkey if together they serve their purpose. The mouthpieces of a Shavian discussion-drama may be rare folk among our drawing-room acquaintance, but may be valid on Shaw's stage. What place are we to allow for the masked characters of Greek or Roman drama or of the *commedia dell'arte?* Do we think less of majestic, unearthly Electra or of fragile insubstantial Millamant or of one-track, head-on-legs Jack Tanner because they do not display the same three-dimensional qualities of realism as Falstaff and Madame Ranevsky? We measure the adequacy of a character by the unity and completeness of the dramatic impression to which it contributes: if we can add nothing, nor wish to take anything away, the character has served.

The concept of character derives from the mask. The mask imposes a tight control upon one aspect of reality to present it simply. Basically, it dispenses with the need to 'act'; for two antithetic masks juxtaposed upon one stage provide the substance of a situation and the plan for a play. The development of drama, as Archer might have maintained, seems to have been the gradual freeing of the actor from the restrictions of the mask, but as long as the author was still writing for an actor on a stage, neither has been totally free. Always the basic premise of theatre has remained, that a play must concentrate and confine life within fixed limits. An author happily acknowledges these limits—even today. One can understand the usefulness to authors of what, in the jargon, are called 'types,' especially in radio drama where distinctions of voice are essential to recognition by ear alone. An author frequently welcomes the readiness

of a preconditioned audience to supply for him the villainy behind a pair of cruelly curling moustaches, or the innocence behind a bonnet and shawl. Moustaches may have been replaced
by cleaner upper lips, bonnets and shawls by more fashionable frills, but in the eyes the seediness or the sweetness, as the
case may be, is the same. The author relies upon a character to
serve as a known quantity: if the audience will not furnish it,
the author must establish it. From another point of view, there
probably remains a preference among the acting profession for
'character' parts, because, in one way, less effort is needed to
satisfy the requirements of a character with definite, that is, more
limited, life.

A sequence from *Arms and the M 'n* may help us rethink the
nature of characterization, in particular in artificial comedy. This
kind of play falsifies and overstresses some aspect of human
nature so that its absurdities are thrown up and tested. So in
Shakespearian comedy we are encouraged to laugh at and judge
the romantic excesses of Hermia and Helena, or in Restoration
comedy the affectations of Lord Foppington and the mock de-
corums of Lady Wishfort. Sergius and Raina in this passage are
of a rather more complex order:

RAINA, *very solemnly.*   Sergius: I think we two have found the higher
love. When I think of you, I feel that I could never do a base deed,
or think an ignoble thought.

SERGIUS.   *My lady and my saint! He clasps her reverently.*

RAINA, *returning his embrace.*   My lord and my—

SERGIUS.   Sh—sh! Let me be the worshipper, dear. You little know
how unworthy the best man is of a girl's pure passion!

RAINA.   I trust you, I love you. You will never disappoint me, Sergius.
LOUKA *is heard singing within the house. They quickly release each
other.* I cant pretend to talk indifferently before her: my heart is
too full. LOUKA *comes from the house.* . . . I will get my hat; and
then we can go out until lunch time. Wouldnt you like that?

SERGIUS.   Be quick. If you are away five minutes, it will seem five
hours. RAINA *runs to the top of the steps, and turns there to ex-*

*change looks with him and wave him a kiss with both hands. He
looks after her with emotion for a moment; then turns slowly away,
his face radiant with the loftiest exaltation. The movement shifts
his field of vision, into the corner of which there now comes the
tail of* LOUKA's *double apron. His attention is arrested at once. He
takes a stealthy look at her, and begins to twirl his moustache
mischievously, with his left hand akimbo on his hip. Finally, striking the ground with his heels in something of a cavalry swagger,
he strolls over to the other side of the table, opposite her, and says*
Louka, do you know what the higher love is?

LOUKA, *astonished.* No, sir.

SERGIUS. Very fatiguing thing to keep up for any length of time,
Louka. One feels the need of some relief after it.

In the words and actions of Shaw's puppets, every detail exemplifies his efficiency and economy in caricaturing human behaviour.

An audience seeing these words enacted does not trouble itself to entertain doubts about verisimilitude: in the theatre such
a question does not arise. What then are we concerned about?
Perhaps the manner in which their speech and gesture burlesque our own? This is a sophisticated reaction, which if it occurs at all, probably does not do so during the performance.
The immediate wish of the audience is to follow the 'logic' of the
action, to guess by its own knowledge of human behaviour what
prompts Raina or Sergius to say or do what Shaw makes them,
to follow the play's general line of intention. Sergius and Raina
have been so excessively applauding each other with a pleth-
ora of clichés,

You have been out in the world, on the field of battle, able to prove
yourself there worthy of any woman in the world . . . ,

Dearest: all my deeds have been yours . . . ,

that it is almost impossible for the actors to do anything less
than 'ham' their lines. Their activity of gesture and movement
—they greet each other impetuously, Raina suddenly sits de-
murely, Sergius kneels impulsively—suggests self-consciousness,

because true emotions do not fluctuate so rapidly. Even if this means the audience is not aware of the false romanticism that marks these characters, the downright lie from Raina, 'And you have never been absent from my thoughts for a moment,' will convince it that one at least is posing. Such easy ironies are at work quite without conscious effort of thought on our part. We come prepared to enjoy the insincerities of characters presented as distortions of human beings, misrepresentations of life.

They proceed to the limits of the line they have begun to pursue, while we know instinctively that they have forced themselves into an impossible position from which the only return must be anticlimax. We are delighted when Raina, dropping her voice and her eyes, brings to the surface the thought that she has long been privately caressing: 'I think we two have found the higher love.' It is part of the Shavian method to have a character say, not what is likely to be said in life, but what is preposterously representative of its type of mind. 'Higher love' implies a divinity which *this* representation cannot in any world exemplify. It is immediately belied by the next half-truth she utters: 'When I think of you, I feel that I could never do a base deed, or think an ignoble thought.' We are not to forget Raina's 'poor darling' of the final moment in Act I as she protects Bluntschli from Catherine, nor her tell-tale dissimulation in front of Sergius and her father a moment before in Act II.

With the mention of 'the higher love,' a key has been struck, and Sergius takes the note from her in an effort to render feelings reverently in keeping with the style she has set: 'My lady and my saint!' So they vie with each other to adopt the appropriate spirit for a heavenly occasion, the romantic debauch for which their sort of love stands. Unfortunately they have trouble in deciding who is saint and who is pilgrim. Their exchange grows to a stagey crescendo too embarrassing to sustain, and Shaw relieves them by the timely-untimely entrance of Louka. Divinity disperses in a flash: even the higher love must sometimes be aware of what the servants think. Raina, however, does not neglect to recover her poise with a satisfying excuse and a mollifying cliché: 'I cant pretend to talk indifferently before her: my heart is too full.' They part with gestures derived from their childhood story-books, to all appearances convinced that this is the correct behaviour.

The audience does not care whether Raina and Sergius are deceiving themselves or each other. But we are concerned to deduce, if there is to be any continuity of interest in the scene, that their little world is a false and fickle one. As such it must be clear, for our critical pleasure, that it will rapidly become too prickly to live in. That Sergius, released from the obligation of Raina's presence, reassumes what we take to be his normal manner of treating the opposite sex when he turns to Louka, is pleasing because it satisfies half-held expectations. In addition, it comments on his behaviour with Raina, revealing him as a *poseur* and in part explaining the exaggeration of his speech and gesture. With but a little pin he is deflated. And yet our hearts are oddly warmed towards him at the same time, both because Raina deserves the treatment she gets, and because Sergius suddenly becomes understandable within his own rules of conduct. One might almost have said he becomes human. His move to flirt with Louka effectively brings down the flimsy pack of cards he and Raina have been assiduously piling up. It does not worry us that he descends so hastily from the refinement of the higher love to the crudity of his addresses to a servant: we are content to feel, in the play's own bold terms, that this gesture might fairly represent a certain attitude of mind, itself not unfamiliar.

To some extent this excerpt exemplifies the function of character in any play. Sergius and Raina are consistent within themselves. We give Shaw the licence, and he makes use of it to manipulate his characters for particular ends. When he has established the quality for which each stands, we look to it for confirmation of our earlier impression; but what, ironically, we see, is that quality being exposed. The continuity of the character is all-important to the author if he is to communicate with us. The gross statement of Shaw's crashing anticlimax depends for its effectiveness upon our seeing the same Sergius who talked before with Raina talking now to Louka.

It is no great step from saying that characters have only that limited existence the play requires of them to saying that character is dependent upon the action it exists to enact. The only satisfactory way to understand character is thus to see it as a way of defining a dramatic impression. Our ultimate interest should not be in the character itself, though this may be a way of starting interest, of separating particular impressions, often of providing a continuity of an idea through the person of one actor. But the fastidious playgoer returns to the play. D. H. Lawrence's celebrated statement belongs to drama too:

Again I say, don't look for the development of the novel to follow the lines of certain characters: the characters fall into the form of some other rhythmic form, as when one draws a fiddle-bow across a fine tray delicately sanded, the sand takes lines unknown.

As in the novel, so in the play. The form of the impressions determines and deploys the detail of characterization, shows us the perspective of the character. So before we look for consistency in a character, we look for consistency in the relationship between one and another. Just as two contiguous speeches project an image, so two characters contribute to its formation. Hamlet is not Hamlet without Claudius, without Gertrude or without Ophelia. He discharges his meaning in the context of a scene.

It is true that character *discloses* itself by physical appearance, by self-exposition (if we take it at face value) and by what others think. So in Chekhov's straightforward one-act farce *The Bear*, first we see Grigory Stepanovitch Smirnov as an overbearing, middle-aged landowner. Second, he talks about himself:

Brr! How mad I feel today, how furious! I'm positively shaking with rage. I can hardly breathe. . . . Ugh! my God! I'm almost fainting!

Third, Elena Ivanovna Popova says of him: 'You're a coarse, ill-mannered fellow! Respectable people don't talk like this to a lady.' But these technical aids offer no positive meaning apart from the particular presence of the other character—the widow with the dimples on her cheeks, Madame Popova, who resists his intrusion and makes him forget his pomposity, his misogyny and his anger, who challenges him with her husband's pistols and her charm. The play creates the simplest of impressions, constructed on the 'before-and-after' pattern. It reaches a ludicrous climax:

A duel! Yes, that's equality of rights, that's emancipation! There's equality of sexes for you! I'll pop her off just as a matter of principle!

All the processes of the play have gone to force this crisis, and reality has been left far behind. But in a moment a touch of reality is introduced, and we recognize an affectation familiar to us. The pace halts, Smirnov pauses, and the anticlimax arrives: 'But what a woman! . . . I'm almost sorry to have to kill her!' He capitulates. Her capitulation will follow, and, to our joy, her initial pose,

I will never go out. . . . Why should I? My life is over. He lies in his grave—I have buried myself in these four walls. . . . We are both dead,

is equally shattered. We do not think chiefly of Smirnov, nor of Popova, but of the sparks flying between them. Character discharges its meaning in friction and reaction.

The reader may argue that character *develops,* which is not, he may say, something a mere 'mask' allows. But the development of character is in fact nothing but a finer definition of the features of the mask. It is properly the development of the image that deludes us into seeing a development in the character. In some plays, like *King Lear* or *A Doll's House,* the idea of change in the character can itself be a central impression, but we must not receive an effect and take it to be a cause. We oblige the author by consistently linking together this aspect and that of the mask as it appears to us. This is facilitated by the continuous presence of the actor, and we are likely to go astray only if the author has not sufficiently provided for our natural desire to complete half-formed images, or if he has left the actor with words so empty that he must fill them out from his own resources, perhaps from his own personality: the abuse of a playwright's work may be due to a fault in the play itself.

Four consecutive speeches from the beginning of Strindberg's exceptionally closely knit play *Miss Julie* suggest in little how character is created and how it develops:

JULIE. Thank you. Don't you want some yourself?

JEAN. I don't care very much for beer, but if it is a command, of course—

JULIE. Command?—I should think a polite gentleman might keep his lady company.

JEAN. Yes, that's the way it should be.

Miss Julie is virtually alone with Jean her footman for the first time, since Christine the cook has fallen asleep. Thus anything said between them now takes on a meaning arising from a dramatic counterpoint: what these particular people say in private works against what a lady and her servant should say in public. Character emerges less from the seductive coyness of Julie's remarks and from Jean's reticence and embarrassment (secondary symptoms) than from the fact that this remark is made to this person in this circumstance.

Julie had asked for beer: 'My taste is so simple that I prefer it to wine.' She first slyly invites Jean to join her in drinking it. The seeming quibble about the social standing of beer or wine and the appropriateness of the drink to the drinker hints at the change in their relationship to come and partly prepares us to accept their perverse states of mind. Jean's reply is double-edged. He is unwilling to abandon his position of the man in the relationship, although he is still aware of his social inferiority. In the audience we await his reaction: had he replied 'Yes,' we should have assumed he was asserting his masculin-

ity; had he replied 'No,' he would have been accepting his
menial position. His actual reply, enhanced for us by the actor's momentary hesitation, establishes his indecision at this
stage of his 'development.' But will she reduce him again to servant, or raise him to an open equality as between man and
woman? Her words tell us she takes the second course: 'I should
think a polite gentleman might keep his lady company.' By her
voice, softer and more insinuating, she raises him to her level.
They are now 'lady' and 'gentleman.' Will Jean accept this ad-
vancement? Yes, but with a degree of reluctance in the implied
conditional: 'that's the way it should be.' This last remark of his
is potent with a sudden new regard he has for himself. It pre-
cipitates a vision of him as the dominant partner in a sexual relationship, but one with latent abnormalities.

Character implies relationship, and development of character suggests growth towards a more precise, evolving relationship, our guided deduction. It should not confuse the argument
to call this relationship the situation. Both Jean and Julie seem
to develop, more especially Jean in these lines, but it is properly the situation that has meaningfully progressed. Situation is
manipulated by the author; character, involved by it, appears
to grow. As character grows, in turn it reveals relationship.

'Relationship' is not being used here in the limited sense of
a personal connection between people, but in the dramatic
sense of a relative connection between characters, which can of
course include a personal connection. We are asking not how
characters affect one another, but how they affect the action.
Once this is done, relationship between characters can be seen
to exist even where they do not meet, as Falstaff, for example,
does not meet King Henry but must by his behaviour put a construction upon what the King stands for. Neither does Macbeth
'meet' his Porter; nor the Dauphin Baudricourt's Steward. But
all have their place in the pattern.

A useful concept of recent coinage is that discussed by Dr.
E. M. W. Tillyard as differing 'planes of reality.' One charac-

ter can bear relationship to another even when it is presented at a lower or higher 'level' within the play, not necessarily a social level, but an imaginative one. We respond to a similarity or to a contrast by making the association in the sequence of impressions: so Sir Toby is imaginatively linked with Orsino, Touchstone with Jaques. Looking for so-called 'sub-plots' misleads us into falsely anatomizing a play's unity of feeling. Degrees of fiction in the shape of actors are set on the same stage and related dramatically, especially in the fantasies of artificial comedy. *A Midsummer Night's Dream* uses this freedom extravagantly.

Within the magic of the moonlit wood near Athens, Shakespeare is at liberty to play dramatic variations upon his motifs of love-sickness. In the first scene the varieties of moon imagery paint the thematic setting for this wedding play: it is the moon that 'lingers desires,' 'the cold fruitless moon of chastity,' which is opposed to the romantic moon that,

> Like to a silver bow
> New-bent in heaven, shall behold the night
> Of our solemnities.

This moon in turn weaves the spell that 'hath witched the bosom' of Hermia. The world of *fancy* shall merge into the world of *fantasy*. Within this web of charmed love and fairy moon-madness, within this loose dialectic of verbal imagery, Shakespeare symbolizes his lovers and his fairies in the forms we know. Bottom and the mechanicals with their burlesque of Pyramus and Thisbe supply mongrel and preposterous elements that are caught up in the pattern and used to balance, criticize and complicate the luxury of sentiment the others display.

The theme is the irrationality of love, explored in the comic licence of the moonlit wood. There are five worlds of potential and actual lovers, and the formal illusion of the play is to make us wonder in which world we stand ourselves. Not in the

literary world of Pyramus and Thisbe, nor in the regions of the
supernatural of Titania and Oberon, nor in the grotesque circle
of Bottom and his friends, nor among the tinsel passions of Ly-
sander, Demetrius, Helena and Hermia. We can identify ourselves only with the rational onlookers Theseus and Hippolyta,
who prompt us to look with the eyes of the newly-married couple for whom the play was possibly written. With their anticipation we shall speculate about romantic beliefs. Through the
agency of Puck, all lovers' sincerities are forsworn, and all their
protestations of faithfulness are disputed and denied; the delicate purity of ideal fairy love is repudiated by Titania's sophisticated relationship with Oberon, and coarsely soiled by Bottom the worldly lover; and Ovid's noble story of the perfect
love of Pyramus and Thisbe performed by the ignoble cannot
be other than burlesqued. No sentimental sweet assumption we
have had is allowed to rest. With what quizzical judgement
Theseus concludes,

> Lovers and madmen have such seething brains,
> Such shaping fantasies, that apprehend
> More than cool reason ever comprehends!

Shakespeare is ironically asking whether we are prepared to
acknowledge with 'cool reason' the validity of all the fancies
with which unreason comforts itself.

This is the disquieting virtue of the play, to allow us no
moment of easy sympathy with any kind or degree of love. We
can only detach ourselves with Theseus and Hipployta. By
travesty and burlesque, all pleasing preconceptions and mis-
conceptions are fretted and disparaged. We are quietly told of
our inadequacies—'But, howsoever, strange and admirable.' This
line from Theseus's lady suggests the lightness in the tone of
Shakespeare's reprimand and the gentleness in the touch of his
punishment.

This complexity could not have been secured had not the
author felt himself free to caricature the lovers, the fairies and

the clowns, free to colour each set of characters to clash with another. Laughter follows the shocks of the feather-weight irony. As each group, acting on its own plane of reality, taking its own standards of conduct so seriously, is juggled by the conjuror, romance is made an object of fun. When we examine the mechanism by which two of these caricatures, Bottom and Titania, are, at the master-stroke of Act III, scene i, thrown together, animal disporting with angel, fairy in love with ass, character has become a critical term of strictly limited usefulness, or else one so wide in its application that it must embrace the whole structure of the scene. In Shakespeare's romantic comedies, like *A Midsummer Night's Dream, As You Like It* and *Twelfth Night,* character is more structural than individual, more general and formal than personal.

Pirandello manipulates character in a highly original way, daringly asserting the freedom of the stage. *Six Characters in Search of an Author* provides a brilliant example. 'What is true?' is Pirandello's basic question, and his play is a complex task for the analyst, especially since breaking down the play's objects into neat compartments, for example (i) how an artist creates, (ii) what reality there is in art, (iii) what reality there is in life, does not help, since these three and other problems are being dramatized simultaneously. In reading the play, one may find it jerky, without an organic centre and therefore unconvincing. This, I believe, is because one tends to tease out the separate strands of the theme from without. In performance, the play is smooth and interlocking, and the ideas move centripetally by the powerful magnetism of the play's emotion. Characters that in the text seem to divide the play, in performance bind it by being precisely placed in the structural relationships enacted.

See this play as one composed of dramatized, implicit discussions between characters, some of whom have the ability to speak with more than one voice. Two of the Six Characters in particular, both by being the centre of interest and by moving freely between all the worlds of imagination the play defines, encourage us to feel the meaning of the play as a unity. The Stepdaughter and the Father speak as characters in the absent author's play, while at the same time they imply what the absent author would have said in his own defence; so the relationship author-character is demonstrated and the processes of creative art are argued. When the Stepdaughter and the Father are seen as characters with more life than the actors who are to play, actor criticizes character and character criticizes actor, and the relationship character-actor is argued. Pirandello reserves his final cumulative shock when we are persuaded that the actors are but characters, that, in the final chaos of the play when the Stepdaughter goes laughing hysterically through the auditorium, the characters are but actors, and that we are but an audience, susceptible to anything we take for granted in the theatre or in life. This hits us with the horror of a blow in one's sleep. The game is one of trying to find the 'right' viewpoint, the 'comfortable' attitude towards any given idea. Are we in the play or in reality? Are we looking with the eyes of the author or the character or the actor or the audience? The play does not leave us with any consolatory answer. Our final queries are about life, not about art, and Pirandello's skill is positive by being negative, serving to enlighten us by confounding us.

A particular piece of analysis will indicate the variety of forces working upon the imagination at the same time. In the following scene, Madame Pace, the repulsive milliner brothelkeeper, remaining completely the character of the absent author's fiction, speaks a broken English, which amuses the watching group of actors and actresses and pleases the Director:

DIRECTOR: . . . Yes, speak like that, Madame! It'll bring the house down! We couldn't ask for anything better. It'll bring a little comic relief into the crudity of the situation. Yes, you talk like that! It's absolutely wonderful!

STEPDAUGHTER. Wonderful! And why not? When you hear a certain sort of suggestion made to you in a lingo like that. . . . There's

not much doubt about what your answer's going to be . . . Because
it almost seems like a joke. You feel inclined to laugh when you
hear there's an 'old señor' who wants to 'amuse himself with me.'
An 'old señor', eh, Madame?

MADAME PACE. Not so very old . . . Not quite so young, yes? And
if he does not please you . . . Well, he has . . . *prudencia.*

MOTHER. *Absorbed as they are in the scene the Actors have been
paying no attention to her. Now, to their amazement and con-
sternation, she leaps up and attacks* MADAME PACE. *At her cry
they jump, then hasten smilingly to restrain her, for she, meanwhile has snatched off* MADAME PACE's *wig and thrown it to the
ground.* You old devil! You old witch! You murderess! Oh, my
daughter!

STEPDAUGHTER, *rushing over to restrain her Mother.* No, Mummy,
no! Please!

What is the audience thinking as it listens to this? To make
each remark carry meaning, it must first have decided where
the character speaking stands in relation to the character com-
mented upon. The spectator will also be trying to assess where
the character stands in relation to himself. When the Director
says, 'Yes, speak like that, Madame! It'll bring the house down!
We couldn't ask for anything better,' we know he is speaking
from a position *outside* the play-within-the-play in which we
take Madame Pace to be, and in part speaking for us in the audience, since, like the choric group of actors and actresses on
the stage, we are also watching the rehearsal he is conducting.
But when he adds, 'Yes, you talk like that! It's absolutely wonderful!' there is a shift of understanding and we take up a position outside *him,* because now he has started talking to a 'character' as if she were an 'actress,' and we recognize that he is being deluded by the degree of reality Madame Pace possesses.
From our superior position we criticize the inadequacy of his
vision, and reflect momentarily upon our former limitation when
we joined him in his approval of the cheap theatrical titillation
of the broken English. The art of the theatre is under the mi-

croscope whenever the Director speaks. Nor is the Director's
shortsightedness allowed to appear a human shortcoming, an
understandable weakness. Because the situation of Madame
Pace and the Stepdaughter is melodramatically emotional, it
colours all attitudes not in keeping with melodramatic feeling,
and we involuntarily condemn the Director and his company
as culpable monsters whenever they speak for the theatrical
profession.

We are thus prepared for the Stepdaughter's criticism of the
Director, 'Wonderful! And why not?' with which we now agree.
We assume she is with us *outside* the rehearsal, as if in the audience looking on. We quite forget that the passion with which
she turns on the Director, comes not wholly of a desire to criticize the ways of the theatre, but more of her own passionate
concern with the part she must perform in the play-within-the-
play, whose reality she never questions. The venom of her
sarcasms should have passed the warning that she is only half
outside the rehearsal. In giving her our sympathy we find ourselves making the mistake we have made already many times,
as the author intends: the mistake of taking the Six Characters
as real and the Director and his company as unreal. The emotions of the play-within-the-play are again made deliberately
harrowing by the ugly euphemisms in the Stepdaughter's mimicry of Madam Pace. As soon as the Stepdaughter recreates the
scene in her mind, her position shifts as if by the impulsion of
her bitter thoughts. She addresses Madame Pace directly: 'An
"old señor," eh Madame?' Immediately we recognize that she
is *inside* the play again, suffering in a second capacity.

When Madame Pace replies, her callous 'Not so very old . . .
Not quite so young, yes?' can only be spoken completely 'in
character.' It is spoken directly to the Stepdaughter, showing
she is quite oblivious of the critics around her in the persons of
the actors and the characters and of us, the true audience. By
her very obliviousness Madame Pace's reality comes in question.
Yet because of the sincerity of the scene she is enacting, against

which the Director and his actors seem petty, we tend unconsciously to question the substantiality of the others too. The
play modulates through a discussion of the shams of the theatre to one of the relationship between character and reality.

The Mother, who has been looking at the scene as if it were
the past resurrected, suddenly by the force of her emotion takes
the past to be the present and the play to be reality. In a flash
we are startled, as we were when Madame Pace made her supernatural entrance, into the illusion that the exchange between
the Mother and Madame Pace is the only truth. This effect is
enhanced by the credibility of Madam Pace's horror when her
wig is thrown off. The Stepdaughter, deceiving us by her double role inside and outside the play-within-the-play, for a
space suggests that her attempts to calm her mother are the attempts of a child to appease a parent, until we reflect this might
also be the behaviour of a daughter conscious of her mother's
making a *faux pas* in public, the public being the Producer and
his company. This impression, that the Stepdaughter is farther
outside the play than the Mother, is stressed when the Father's
advice to the Mother follows: 'Calm yourself, my dear!' This re-
affirms that she is moved by the presence of Madame Pace to
the exclusion of all else. In performance, the half-existence
of the Mother by contrast makes the Stepdaughter more 'alive'
than the play's structure would suggest.

The modulations of the action are easy. The audience turns
its feeling and its critical intelligence elastically on this, then
on that, aspect of the subject, because it is led through the
play uncertain of the level at which it must feel and of what
it is free to criticize. Through the vacillation of response to this
or that character Pirandello is able to dramatize his abstract
discussions.

The complexity of the play's suggestions increases rapidly.
The ambiguities become bewildering in the scene of Madame
Pace's shop which the Stepdaughter and the Father enact for
the Director:

FATHER, *coming forward, a new note in his voice.* Good afternoon, Miss.

STEPDAUGHTER, *her head bowed, speaking with restrained disgust.* Good afternoon!

How are we to see these characters now? Are they merely representing the spectator's point of view, criticizing the professionals and showing them how it should be done? If this make-believe is a further comment on theatrecraft, then they are acting acting. But Pirandello means us to accept their performance as truth, for his direction to the Father is that he must at first look troubled and very pale,

But as he approaches from the back of the stage he smiles, already absorbed in the reality of his created life. He smiles as if the drama which is about to break upon him is as yet unknown to him.

As the sequence develops, we are to be moved by a more realistic style of acting: actors of Pirandello must be 'plastic' according to the distance of their speech and movement from the author's conception of the 'true' reality. In 1925, the author wrote:

The six characters must not appear as phantoms, but as 'created realities', immutable creatures of fantasy. They are more real and consistent than the voluble actors.

And the play itself has provided for a subtle changeover by which the Stepdaughter and the Father are more convincing than the actors. We are to take the brothel scene as reality, so that when the Ingénue interrupts with 'Oh, I say! Those are *our* hats!' we are shocked into recognizing that we are being deluded, and the discussion of our awareness of degree of reality is successfully dramatized. This aspect of the play is later emphasized when the Stepdaughter criticizes the Father's *performance:* and then again when the Leading Man and the Leading Lady attempt to re-enact the performance they have seen. They act now with a lesser realism, though Pirandello makes

it clear that their acting must be near enough to accepted standards to make us consider it seriously as a possible interpretation:

The playing of this scene by the Actors will appear from the very
first words as something completely different from what was played
before, without its having, even in the slightest degree, the air of a
parody.

The Father's immediate reaction is to cry, 'No!', and the Stepdaughter cannot restrain a burst of laughter. By this process of
refining our standards of reality in dramatic statement and
counter-statement, we are forced to argue about probability and
credibility. Our thoughts are set wrangling with our feelings.

It would be unlike Pirandello to leave us complacent. Before we are allowed to go, he arranges it that the climax of the
play-within-the-play coincides with the climax of our experience, and that the fictional reality of the characters becomes
inextricably confused with the comparative reality of the Producer and the Actors. The end of the play introduces a revol-
ver shot which is perhaps the most effective shot in drama. It
effects a conjunction of the real and the unreal, hits off the
climax of our emotions and sums up the play's puzzle. By this
shot, shadow is made solid, and the spectator dizzy with a terror of the unknown.

Then first from one side, then from the other, the Actors re-enter.

LEADING LADY, *re-entering right, very much moved.* He's dead. Poor
boy! He's dead! Oh what a terrible thing to happen!

LEADING MAN, *re-entering left, laughing.* What do you mean, dead?
It's all make-believe! It's all just a pretence! Don't get taken in
by it!

OTHER ACTORS, *entering from the right.* Make-believe? Pretence?
Reality! Reality! He's dead!

OTHERS, *from the left.* No! Make-believe! It's all a pretence!

These contradictory extremes compel our silence, not our
laughter: they mark the subtlety with which the characters have
been manipulated, and our absorption in the play.

To stifle *Six Characters in Search of an Author* with preconceived notions of what character may do in a play, or what degree of conviction it must carry, is to treat character as something external, hopelessly making nonsense of the experience. The playgoer can finally admit character only as a mask in its meaning and a puppet in its action, and judge it only by standards of reality and conviction which the orchestration and total purpose of the play demand.

PART FOUR

THE STRUCTURE OF DRAMA

CHARLES MORGAN

THE NATURE OF DRAMATIC ILLUSION

ROBERT W. CORRIGAN

THE PLAYS OF CHEKHOV

JAMES L. ROSENBERG

MELODRAMA

The Nature of
Dramatic Illusion

CHARLES MORGAN

Whoever traces the rather meagre history of dramatic criticism
from Greek times to our own will observe that it has taken two
principal forms—the analytic and the impressionistic. The analyst's purpose has been to lay down rules and establish universal standards of judgment; the impressionist's, to set up no god
but his own taste, and to write a history of the voyage of his soul
among masterpieces. The value of his criticism has thus depended
upon the value of his soul—always an uncertain factor; and
though writing of this school, when practised by men of quality, has yielded great treasures, the liberty, the artist's privilege
necessary to impressionistic criticism has been shamefully abused
and is nowadays too often made an excuse for arrogant and disorderly variations on the pronoun "I." There is, in modern criticism, a real danger of anarchy if its erratic movements cannot
by some means be related and stabilized. With every development of dramatic technique and every departure from classical
structure, the need increases of a new discussion which, observing the changes of definition since Dryden and the vast accumulation of material since Lessing, shall establish for the stage not

125

indeed a formal rule but an aesthetic discipline, elastic, reasoned, and acceptable to it in modern circumstances.

It is my purpose, then, to discover the principle from which such a discipline might arise. This principle I call the principle of illusion.

Before attempting a more precise and technical definition of illusion, I will strive to give a general impression of it and to show that the idea is a necessary foundation of criticism.

There has been in recent years a tendency among serious critics to revolt against what they call the literary criticism of plays. Drama, they say, is a composite art, and to criticize it as though it were the work of the dramatist alone is unreasonable and unjust. With this statement of their case we may all agree, but they have gone much further. Wishing to depose the dramatist from an exaggerated pre-eminence, they have attempted to establish another monarch in his place; and they differ in their choice of a successor. Mr. Gordon Craig's emphasis is all on the designer of scenery and costume; Mr. Ashley Dukes, though a dramatist himself, writes unblushingly of the director as the artist-in-chief; and they have powerful supporters, for the appearance in Europe of stage artists of genius—men of the quality of Stanislavsky, Reinhardt, and Craig himself—has drawn eager and worshipping eyes to the director's share in the theatrical collaboration. This kind of enthusiasm, though we may not share it, is useful if we examine its psychological origins. What is the genuine need underlying this modern critical revolt against the dramatist? What is the genuine need which prompted the Americans to invent—as I am now inventing—a new critical term? I call mine "illusion" and struggle to define it; the Americans call theirs "theatre." Unfortunately the true meaning of the American word "theatre" has been blunted by common usage. When they say now that a play is "good theatre" or "bad theatre," they mean that it has punch or is tediously lacking in it—in brief that it is, or is not, vigorously theatrical; and they are able to declare that, though a piece has no genuine critical value, it is, for all that, good theatre. But what lay at the root of this American word was, I am sure, a desire to find a critical term which should express the unity of a stage representation, the same spiritual unity which made the productionists revolt against the dramatist's pre-eminence.

This unity, this essence of the drama, which I call illusion, is not the same with the Aristotelian unities of action, time and place, though in plays that accept the Aristotelian form they are included in it. It is, perhaps, best thought of as being to the drama what the soul is to the mind, and those who deny, or say that they cannot perceive, a distinction between soul and mind and will not therefore concede the real existence of the soul, will certainly refuse to recognize the real existence of illusion.

I will not press the comparison, which is intended to be illustrative and no more. What I am certain of is that every playgoer has been made aware now and then of the existence in the theatre of a supreme unity, a mysterious power, a transcendent and urgent illusion, which, so to speak, floats above the stage action and above the spectator, not merely delighting and instructing him as Dryden says, or purging his Aristotelian emotions, but endowing him with a vision, a sense of translation and ecstasy, alien to his common knowledge of himself. The hope of this illusion is the excitement, and the experience of it the highest reward, of playgoing. Strangely enough we become conscious of its approach, as though there were a sound of wings in the air—before the play begins. The curtain is still down, the houselights are still up, but we are in a theatre and, if experience has not embittered us, are dreaming that this evening or another evening the beat of wings will grow louder in our silences, the supreme illusion will stoop down and gather us, the hosts will speak. Again and again we are disappointed. The curtain rises and the play is found to be an ugly bag of tricks; instead of the authentic currency of experience we are given a trickle of counterfeit coin, rubbed for generations between the fingers of plagiarists. But now and then a persistent playgoer's hope, or a part of it, is fulfilled. The order of his experience is always the same—a shock, and after the shock an inward stillness, and from that stillness an influence emerging, which transmutes him. Transmutes *him*—not his opinions. This great impact is neither a persuasion of the intellect nor a beguiling of the senses. It does not spring from the talent of the dramatist alone, or of the actor alone, or of the musician alone, or from an aggregate of their talents. It is not the work of any one artist-in-chief whose name is written on an earthly programme. It is the enveloping movement of the whole drama upon the soul of man. We surrender and are changed. "The outward sense is gone, the inward essence feels," until, betrayed by some flaw in the work of art or failure in ourselves, we begin to perceive again, not the drama, but its parts.

> When the ear begins to hear, and eye begins to see
> When the pulse begins to throb—the brain to think again—
> The soul to feel the flesh, and the flesh to feel the chain—

—then illusion is broken. We return to our little prisons and through the bars are the critical spectators of a play.

I do not wish to suggest that a play which fails to produce illusion of this intensity ought to be condemned, for I have just written of that rare extreme which creates ecstasy in the audience—a veritable rebirth, a carrying out of the senses which seem to bound our humanity. What I wish to establish is that, though the intensity of our experience of it may greatly vary, there is something, some power, some influence, some underlying unity, latent in the drama which has never yet been given its due place in criticism. You may think of it in what terms you will—as a synthesis of the arts of the theatre, as a hypostasis proceeding from their perfect unity, or you may say that it has no concrete existence but is at best a philosophical idea, a critical fiction. Well, beauty itself has no concrete existence and is, perhaps, a critical fiction, but it is one of the necessities of thought. And I suggest that as a wise man bases his criticism of life, not upon judgement of its parts, but upon apprehension of its unity, so judgement of the drama is to be founded on its illusion and not on its form or on the emotion it creates.

That is a general impression of what I mean by illusion. Let me now consider it more closely and indicate one of its distinguishing qualities.

It is a common error to praise a play because, as the lady in the stall behind me never tires of saying, it is "exactly like life." This is an error for two reasons: first, that if a play were exactly like life it would be a bad play; second, that no play has ever been or ever can be exactly like life, and the lady is a liar. What she means, of course, is that the play does not outrage the naturalistic convention which she accepts. She will look at a photograph of her own son, whom she ought to know, and exclaim that it is exactly like him—whereas what she means is that the photograph represents him to her in an accepted convention of black and white. If she had lived in ancient Egypt and had been given by the gods the same son and the same photograph but different pictorial conventions, it is very possible that she would not have recognized her offspring, and would have greatly preferred something more rectilinear. But fascinating though the subject of varying convention may be, I must not now pursue it. The lady's first error is more relevant to my general argument.

Aristotle said at the opening of the *Poetics* that "Epic and tragic composition, also comedy, the writing of dithyrambs and most branches of flute- and harp-playing are all, if looked at as a whole, imitations." Against this my own statement that "if a play were exactly like life it would be a bad play" may look a little small. The lady in the stall behind me would, if she were familiar with the *Poetics*, quote Aristotle with gusto. But Aristotle is one of those men of genius whose sentences, if taken out of their context, can be made to mean anything. To read a little farther into the *Poetics*—to observe indeed that Aristotle includes dithyrambs and flute- and harp-playing in his group of imitations—is to realize that he was by no means a photographic naturalist of the same aesthetic school with the lady in the stalls. It is true that art is rooted in imitation, and that, when it is cut off from that root and becomes decoration only or didacticism only, it dries up and withers. It is rooted in imitation—but in imitation of what? Do not let us say of ordinary life, for the phrase, though Aristotle himself uses it, has no precise meaning. Mr. Baldwin is said to be a representative Englishman; his life is presumably the ordinary life of an English ex-Prime Minister; but I do not see him as you see him, nor do we see him as Shelley would have seen him. How, then, is art to imitate him? It cannot. It can imitate my view of him or yours or Shelley's, but in each of these imitations there will be more of Shelley or you or me than of the hypothetical ordinariness of Mr. Baldwin. All that art can do in the way of imitation of a given subject is, first, to negative a spectator's own preconceptions of that subject so that he lies open to imaginative acceptance of a different view, the artist's view, of it, and secondly, to impregnate him with this fresh, this alien understanding. Illusion is the impregnating force—in masterpieces permanently fruitful, in lesser works of art existent but without endurance, and from machine-made plays, however well made, absent. How often we say of a play that it was "a good story" or "an admirable entertainment"; that it was "cleverly constructed," or that its "characters were natural and alive"; and, having thus praised it, add with a vague sense of disappointment, "but there was nothing in it." What is the critical equivalent of that evasive phrase? The formalists have no answer; the impressionists have none. Does not the phrase mean that the play had no impregnating power? Though it had a thousand other virtues it was without illusion.

The lady of whom I have spoken believes that, in the photograph of her son, she has seen her own impression of him. Evidently she has done nothing of the kind. She has been persuaded to forget her view of him and to accept the camera's as her own. When she goes to a play which seems to her exactly like life, she has been persuaded to abandon her own view of life and to accept the dramatist's. It is true that, when the dramatist is of her own imaginative and intellectual kin, the exchange is not revolutionary, but, when he is a man of genius and has power to persuade her to take his view of *A Doll's House* or to see with his eyes the lamp thrown at wife and mother by Strindberg's Father, the results are prodigious. The lamp of Strindberg's still hurtles through the domestic air, and by Nora a million feminine squirrels were converted into tigresses whose cubs still embarrass us.

And why? Not because the lady in the stalls had ever before thought of herself as resembling the lady of Strindberg's lamp; not because, if she was a squirrel, she had ever perceived until Ibsen pointed it out to her, the limitations of her comfortable cage; not because these great plays were like life as she had formerly understood it; but because her own preconceptions were stilled and afterwards impregnated. What stirred her, what influenced her, was not delusion, which is of herself, but illusion—that divine essence above the battle—which is of the drama. Wordsworth of all men helps to make this point clear. He is expressing his dislike of chatter:

> I am not One who much or oft delight
> To season my fireside with personal talk
> Of Friends who live within an easy walk.

He is not attracted by—

> . . . ladies bright
> Sons, mothers, maidens withering on the stalk. . . .

Better than these, he says, does—

> . . . silence long,
> Long, barren silence, square with my desire;
> To sit without emotion, hope or aim,
> In the loved presence of my cottage fire,
> And listen to the flapping of the flame,
> Or kettle whispering its faint undersong.

The remarkable word in this passage is "barren." The later stanzas show that he means not barren absolutely, but a silence barren of trivial and personal thoughts which might be a bar to a more profound impregnation.

> Dreams, books are each a world, and books we know
> Are a substantial world, both pure and good.
> Round these, with tendrils strong as flesh and blood,
> Our pastime and our happiness will grow.
> There find I personal themes, a plenteous store,
> Matter wherein right voluble I am. . . .

What he is speaking of here is the impregnating power of artistic illusion working upon a mind naturally silent, naturally meditative. In the theatre there is no natural meditation, no flapping flame and, unhappily, no kettle. Dramatic art has, therefore a double function—first to still the preoccupied mind, to empty it of triviality, to make it receptive and meditative; then to impregnate it. Illusion is the impregnating power. It is that spiritual force in dramatic art which impregnates the silences of the spectator, enabling him to imagine, to perceive, even to become, what he could not of himself become or perceive or imagine.

Inquiry, now, into the nature and origin of this impregnating force will expose the root of the theory. Illusion, as I conceive it, is form in suspense. The phrase is obscure and must be explained.

Analytical critics have all supposed that form is valuable in itself. They have based their judgements on a study of form, first establishing by general argument what they consider a perfect form for tragedy or comedy, then asking us to match particular plays with it. It is not surprising that they so often weary themselves in crying "This is not a play" when they encounter dramatic expression that does not correspond with their ideal form. Their confusion, and it is a confusion that has run through the ages, springs from their failure to perceive one plain truth —that in a play, form is not and cannot be valuable *in itself*, only the suspense of form has value. In a play, form is not and cannot be valuable in itself, because until the play is over form does not exist.

Form is *in itself* valuable only in those works of art into which the time-factor does not enter, and which, therefore, come to us whole. Painting, sculpture and architecture come to us whole; they are directly formal arts. An epic poem does not come to us whole, but a short lyric or a particular line therein may almost be said to do this, so slight, by comparison with an epic, is the time-factor involved. A play's performance occupies two or three hours. Until the end its form is latent in it. It follows that during the performance we are not influenced by the form itself, the completed thing, but by our anticipations of completion. We are, so to speak, waiting for the suspended rhyme or harmony, and this formal suspense has the greater power if we know beforehand, as the Greeks did, what the formal release is to be.

This suspense of form, by which is meant the incompleteness of a known completion, is to be clearly distinguished from common suspense—suspense of plot—the ignorance of what will happen, and I would insist upon this distinction with all possible emphasis, for suspense of plot is a structural accident, and suspense of form is, as I understand it, essential to the dramatic art itself. The desire to know what will happen, when it exists at all, is a quality of the audience's delusion; it springs from their temporary belief that they are witnessing, not art, but life; it is the product of deluded curiosity, and is often strongest in the weakest minds. It is obviously stronger in a housemaid watching a play by Mr. Edgar Wallace than in a cultivated spectator of the Aeschylean *Prometheus,* and it would become progressively less strong even in the housemaid as by repeated visits to the theatre the designs of Mr. Wallace were made more familiar to her. I do not wish to speak contemptuously of suspense of plot, for it often contributes to the pleasure of playgoing and reading; it has this value—that it keeps our eyes on stage or book. It may draw attention to a work of art and has been used by great artists for that purpose, but it is not essential to the art itself. Suspense of form, on the contrary, is one of those things without which drama is not.

It may be objected that without form there can be no suspense of form, and that to this extent a formal critic is justified. My argument is that he is wrong in insisting that particular dramatic forms are valuable in themselves. What rhyme is begun matters less than that the rhyme be completed; what harmony is used matters less than that it be resolved; what form is chosen, though it is true that some forms are more beautiful than others, matters less than that while the drama moves *a* form is being fulfilled.

Dramatic illusion, then, is the suspense of dramatic form, and is to be thought of as men think of divinity—an essence in which they may or may not partake, a power which may or may not visit them.

The task of applying this theory of illusion to particular plays must be left to the twentieth-century Lessing, who writes the book to which this paper is a foreword. Having defined the idea, I must be content to give a few indications of its practical value, and of the effect that its acceptance might produce on criticism.

Its value rests in its universality. Not long ago Mr. Granville Barker, speaking on "The Coming of Ibsen," quoted the damning judgement of many critics of the 'eighties on plays now acknowledged to be masterpieces. They were very disturbing to a man who, within little more than an hour after each performance, writes his opinion on nearly two hundred plays a year. It is alarming to think that Mr. Granville Barker, whose youth is perpetual, will rise up in 1980 and make hay with a file of *The Times* newspaper fifty years old. Even the closest study of the theory of illusion will not make any man infallible, but I do believe that it will protect critics from many of the errors into which our predecessors so easily fell. The adverse judgements of Ibsen, which now seem to us unreasonable, prove upon examination to have been inspired by the old prejudice about form. Ibsen, intent upon introducing new subjects to the stage, was creating new shapes to contain them, and the rigid formalists, clinging to prescribed form, condemned him. For the same reason Strindberg has been denied the recognition due to him, though the time will certainly come when it will be perceived that, in such works as *To Damascus* and *The Dream Play,* he prepared the way for what is best in the modernist movements. He was an Expressionist long before Expressionism, as a cult, was heard of, and did with genius what hundreds of charlatans are now attempting to do without it. Ibsen has partly broken through the formalists; Strindberg has not; and both are considered freaks because they do not bow down to that spirit which still presides powerfully over the English theatre—the spirit of Sardou. The reason is that English playgoers and critics are still bound, consciously or subconsciously, to the idea that suspense means suspense of plot, and that form in drama, as in the plastic arts, is a static thing and valuable in itself. A critic who understands the theory of illusion would never fall into the error of saying that Ibsen, because he did not strive for suspense of plot, was ignorant of the theatre, or that Strindberg, because he created new forms and rhythms, was not writing a play. Instead of making these rash errors the critic would say to himself, "Here is something with which I am unfamiliar. Here is a man struggling for a new form. I cannot judge his work as I would judge sculpture or architecture in which there is no time element. While the play is in progress I must yield myself to this moving, developing, organic thing, the suspense of form, and must realize that only when the complete form is known will the suspense of it have full effect on me."

If the critics of the 'eighties had said that to themselves when they took up their pens, Mr. Granville Barker would have been robbed of his powder and shot. The theory of illusion is universal, because it enables criticism to keep its balance amid the shock of new forms.

It is universal, too, because it establishes a standard of judgement which may, with intelligence, be applied to plays of all kinds—to tragedy, to comedy, and even to farce. The illusion of tragedy is the highest of all; the illusion of farce is, I admit, a cripple who has lost a leg. It is barren; it impregnates no silences. But a farce, if it be good of its own kind, has a unity, an "essence above the battle," and it certainly has suspense of form. Indeed, there is hardly to be found a more illuminating distinction between suspense of form and suspense of plot, or between illusion and delusion, than may be perceived in a good farce. Who cares in a farce what will happen? Who believes that anything is happening? We are not deluded by the fantastic narrative nor made curious by it. Our pleasure, if we are pleased, arises from the farce's skill in binding us by its own peculiar symmetry, and from its power to create an illusion, which is never delusion, of a world good-humouredly insane.

The theory of illusion has a third and very important claim to universality—namely, that it may be applied, as no other critical theory can, to plays that do not depend on a conflict of individual character, and thus supplies a link between very ancient and very modern drama. Nearly all criticism has presumed that such a conflict is an essential part of the drama. I am persuaded that it is not, and that if critics remain wedded to this idea of individual struggle and bound to the forms appropriate to it, they will blunder in their judgement of the drama of the future as critics in the past blundered in their judgement of Ibsen and Strindberg. This was deeply impressed upon me when I went to Delphi to see in the ancient theatre performances of Aeschylus—the *Prometheus* and *The Suppliants*. What I wrote then returns to me with increasing force whenever I contemplate the problem of illusion:

It has often been pointed out as remarkable by commentators on *The Suppliants* that Aeschylus, having decided to use the actor and having latent in him that prodigious power to thrust forward the history of the drama of which his extant pieces are evidence, should here have employed the actor so little. Only in the sharp dialogue between the Argive King and Herald, it has been said, is there contest of individuals and a complete, though momentary, emancipation of the dramatic from the narrative or ritualistic form. The reason commonly given for this, and indeed the only reason deducible from an unacted text, is that Aeschylus was as yet half-blind to his own discovery; that he held the actor in his hands as a child holds a strange toy, knowing not how to use him. This explanation, this misunderstanding of Aeschylus, lies, I believe, at the root of the charges of obscurity and primitiveness that have been brought against the play. In performance at Delphi it is neither primitive nor obscure. When once the chorus is felt as a living presence with collective individuality and character, the play appears, not as a primitive struggling towards a new drama, but as a fully developed product of an older tradition. In departures from this tradition Aeschylus was certainly experimenting, but the impression given by the performance is that the experiments were being made as much in reluctance as in eagerness. Whenever the actor shows his head above the choral unity we feel instantly that, though the tension (or suspense of plot) is increased, an extraordinary composure, a deep and passionate perfection of design, is being dissipated. What was this composed perfection that our drama is without and that Aeschylus, for all the promise of a different form, was reluctant to sacrifice? May it not have consisted in this—that the collective formalism of fifty Danaïds may more serenely express the universal truths of the spirit than the particularized portrait of one woman? Is it not possible that the pre-Aeschylean drama held already a key that gave it freedom from the bonds of naturalism (and of individual character)—a key for which modern dramatists from Strindberg to Lenormand have been desperately seeking? The Chorus, we know, had other and less aesthetically conscious origins, but by the time of Aeschylus it had probably become a highly conscious aesthetic instrument used not merely ritualistically and lyrically, but as a synthesis of humanity that our particularized and personal stage has lost.[1]

A synthesis, I would add, towards which our stage is now moving. Perhaps the most significant evidence of this movement—this link between modernism and the pre-Aeschylean theatre—has been in London, Mr. O'Casey's attempt in *The Silver Tassie*

[1] *The Times*, May 12, 1930.

to rediscover the Chorus, and to reintroduce the compression of verse into drama with a contemporary setting. This play was rejected by the Abbey Theatre and Mr. W. B. Yeats; it was condemned by many critics in the same tones of misunderstanding and intolerance with which Ibsen was condemned; fifty years hence Mr. Granville Barker will have them all on his list. And it is not surprising that, in an age which still bases its judgement on Aristotelian forms or on Dryden's definition of a play, criticism should be at fault, for neither Aristotle nor Dryden leaves room for the pre-Aeschylean and Twentieth-century synthesis. Our criticism is rooted in Dryden's idea of a "just and lively representation of human nature . . . for the delight and instruction of mankind"—an idea that denies Strindberg and the pre-Aeschylean chorus, and will, unless it is revised, deny much more in the days to come. The theory of illusion, if received as a basis of criticism, would make unnecessary these fatal denials. While maintaining, in the idea of form in suspense, much that is good in the old critical disciplines, and so preserving criticism from the impressionistic anarchy that threatens it, it would, in the complementary idea of illusion as an impregnating force, restore to criticism a spiritual liberty and boldness that it has lost.

The Plays of Chekhov

ROBERT W. CORRIGAN

In our times no playwright is more respected and less understood than Anton Chekhov. For most theatre people he is like Faulkner's Miss Emily—"a tradition, a duty, and a care; a sort of hereditary obligation." His plays are thought to be moody, complex, soulful, vague, and impossible to do successfully on the American stage. For the most part, readers and audiences have agreed with that critic who, on seeing the famous Cornell-Anderson-Gordon production of *Three Sisters* in 1942, remarked that she "could not see much sense in three adults spending four acts in *not* going to Moscow when all the time they had the price of a railroad ticket." But since then conditions have changed, and today Chekhov's plays seem to have a startling and refreshing contemporaneity; they reflect as few plays do the spirit of our time. What accounts for this belated popularity? Why, a hundred years after he was born, do we think Chekhov has something significant to say to us today?

Part of the answer lies in the fact that all of his plays reflect the mood of spiritual discouragement which permeates the anxieties of the mid-twentieth century. In an age dominated by the fear of nuclear war, the tension of cold war diplomacy, and the insecurity of a defense economy, people wonder what, if anything, can be done to resolve the apparently insoluble prob-

139

lems of life. All of his life Chekhov, too, despaired of the fact
that he was unable to answer life's important questions. "Life,"
he said, "is an insoluble problem." At the end of the first act of
The Sea Gull, Dorn—one of the many doctors in Chekhov's
plays—is trying to comfort the distraught and unhappy Masha,
but all he can find to say is, "But what can I do, my child?
Tell me, what can I do? What?" This question, "What can I do?"
runs like a leitmotiv through all of Chekhov's works. This is
the clue to Chekhov's great modernity.

Chekhov more than any dramatist of the late nineteenth and
early twentieth centuries was very conscious of the existential
loneliness of the human condition. In fact, the central theme of
all his plays is estrangement. He was conscious of man's helplessness before the overpowering forces of circumstance; he was
aware of man's littleness, his insignificance in a gigantic and impersonal universe; he knew that no matter how closely men
huddled together they could never really communicate. In
short, he was aware of the fact that the very conditions of life
doom man to failure and that there was nothing anyone could
do about it. He knew the utter impossibility of finding an answer to the question "What can I do?"

In their ontological solitude, Chekhov's characters are like
those helpless travelers described by Kafka in his *Notebooks:*

> We are in the situation of travellers in a train that has met with an
> accident in a tunnel, and this at a place where the light of the be-
> ginning can no longer be seen, and the light of the end is so very
> small a glimmer that the gaze must continually search for it and is
> always losing it again, and, furthermore, both the beginning and the
> end are not even certainties. Round about us, however, in the con-
> fusion of our senses, or in the supersensitiveness of our senses, we
> have nothing but monstrosities and a kaleidoscopic play of things
> that is either delightful or exhausting according to the mood and
> injury of each individual. What shall I do? or: Why should I do it?
> are not questions to be asked in such places.

The train of Chekhov's characters' lives has been wrecked too;
there is no continuity upon which they can depend; everything

seems ludicrous and absurd, painful and hopeless. Ivanov cannot extricate himself from the morass of his lassitude; nobody succeeds in finding love in *The Sea Gull;* no one achieves his goal in *Uncle Vanya;* the sisters do not go to Moscow (and it would not have solved their problems if they had); and the cherry orchard is not saved. In short, there is nothing one can do in such a situation, and we notice that increasingly, as Chekhov matures, nothing is even attempted. Ivanov's and Treplev's suicides are at least solutions, albeit negative ones, to their problems. Uncle Vanya is incapable of even such a negative solution. In *Three Sisters* the nearest attempt is Irina's and Tusenbach's decision to get married and at least try to make a new life. But even this attempt fails, for despite man's best efforts, a meaningless and mocking fate will destroy him even before he begins. (And we must remember that the couple's approaching marriage was not anticipated joyfully, for Irina did not love Tusenbach.) Finally, in *The Cherry Orchard* nothing is attempted. The sending of Gaev to the auction is little more than an afterthought, a pitiful reminder that nothing can be done, for the cherry orchard—the symbol of their lives—is doomed, no matter who owns it, from the beginning.

But this is not the whole story. If it were, Chekhov's plays would be little more than unrelieved pictures of gloom, and this we know they are not. They are not, because Chekhov, in spite of his realization that man was alone and doomed to failure in all of his attempts to find meaningful relationships and meaningful action, never abdicated his sense of responsibility for human life. Even though Chekhov knew there were no solutions, all his life he sought to find an answer, and his plays are a record of that quest. Thomas Mann, in his perceptive essay on Chekhov, was conscious of this when he wrote:

One has to face the fact that man is a failure. His conscience, which belongs to the spirit, will probably never be brought into harmony with his nature, his reality, his social condition, and there will always be "sleeplessness" for those who for some unfathomable reason feel responsible for human fate and life. If anyone ever suffered from

this, it was Chekhov the artist. All his work was honorable sleeplessness, a search for the right, redeeming word in answer to the question: "What are we to do?" The word was difficult, if not impossible,
to find.

This, I believe, was the central and creative tension in all of
Chekhov's life and work. His own life was filled with the kind
of experience that made him ever aware of the inevitability of
failure and the absurdity of a man's attempts to triumph over his
fate. All of his early years—and he did not have many years to
live—were spent in an erosive struggle against poverty, and only
shortly before he died did he achieve any kind of personal and
financial independence. Finally, after years of hard work, he
succeeded only to discover—before he could enjoy the fruits of
his labor—that he was dying as a young man of tuberculosis. All
of his life was a constant and quiet search for love, and he finally
seemed to have found it in his marriage with the great actress Olga Knipper. But their happiness was at best sporadic—
their careers kept them apart much of the time—and was never
free of the engulfing shadow of his approaching death, a death
which came less than three years after they were married. The
same characteristic was true of his relationship with Stanislavsky
and Danchenko at the Moscow Art Theatre. Without the encour-
agement and support of these two men, Chekhov very likely
would never have succeeded as a playwright; in fact, it is
doubtful that he would have written his last three plays. But
his relationship with Stanislavsky was never a happy one and
was a constant source of frustration to him, for Stanislavsky
never understood what Chekhov was trying to do in the theatre
and "ruined" his plays in production. Finally, his approaching
death itself, which Chekhov as a physician was the first to di-
agnose, and the reality of which, because he was a physician, he
could not escape in the mists of illusion, made the playwright
ever aware of the loneliness and absurdity of his own existential
nature. Death, and therefore, as we shall see, life also, was not
an abstraction for Chekhov. He, like all men, was born to die;

but unlike most of us, Chekhov lived his life with the full awareness of his unique, dying self.

Yes, Chekhov had good reason to know that life is loneliness,
failure, and absurdity, but as I said earlier, that is not the whole
story and this second aspect of his life is the source of strength
for the other half of that creative tension which informs his
plays. Chekhov countered the reality of his death with an
equally powerful weapon—his own life. He met his dying life
with honesty, with reserve, with integrity, and simplicity; and
above all, as an artist, a doctor, and a man he had great sympathy for others and an abiding respect for the dignity of human life. Chekhov's career both as a dramatist and a physician
took its nourishment from a single source; his great capacity to
observe and cherish life; not life as an abstraction or as an ideal,
but as a doomed phenomenon of which he was a part. His tol-
erance, sympathy, wisdom, and his hard-headed vision made it
possible for him to achieve, as few writers do, an unflinching but
generous perspective on life; a perspective which is a victory
over our absurdities, but a victory won at the cost of humility,
and won in a spirit of charity and enlightenment. Maxim Gorky,
Chekhov's younger colleague, caught some of this when he
wrote of Chekhov:

> I think that in Anton Chekhov's presence every one involuntarily
> felt in himself a desire to be simpler, more truthful, more one's self.
> . . . All his life Chekhov lived in his own soul; he was always him-
> self, inwardly free, and he never troubled about what some people
> expected and others—coarser people—demanded of Anton Chekhov.
> . . . Beautifully simple himself, he loved everything simple, genuine,
> sincere, and he had a peculiar way of making other people simple.

And thus we find in his plays, as in his life, a regard for his
characters' pathetic destinies, and a nobility in their attempts to
change or overcome that destiny. Goethe once wrote, "It occurs
to me that the hope of persisting, even after fate would seem to
have led us back into the state of nonexistence, is the noblest of
our sentiments." And this is the quality that informs Chekhov's

characters. Vanya is a ridiculous, fumbling, grumbling, ineffec-
tual, self-pitying man, and yet we take him and his plight
seriously (we must or the play would collapse); we do, I
think, because for all his weakness he never loses his sense of
dignity. Tusenbach is a funny little man with his three names,
his ugly appearance, his pampered childishness, and his ridiculous talk about the brick yards. He knows this, and he also
knows that life has no meaning and will not change. But this
does not keep him from making the effort, from asserting the validity of life in the face of death. In his last speech, when he
knows he is going to be shot in the duel with Solyony, when he
is fully aware that just as all his dreams are about to be realized
he will be deprived of them, he is still able to say:

> Really, I feel quite elated. I feel as if I was seeing those fir trees
> and maples and birches for the first time in my life. They all seem
> to be looking at me with a sort of inquisitive look and waiting for
> something. What beautiful trees—and how beautiful, when you think
> of it, life ought to be with trees like these! (*Shouts are heard.*) I must
> go, it's time. . . . Look at that dead tree, it's all dried up, but it's still
> swaying in the wind along with the others. And in the same way, it
> seems to me that, if I die, I shall still have a share in life somehow
> or other. Goodbye, my dear. . . . (*Kisses* IRINA's *hands.*)

We could continue this catalogue: the three sisters themselves,
Nina, Lyubov, Gaev, in fact, just about every character Chekhov
ever created. But the point is this: the creative tension of Chekhov's work springs from his recognition that in all men there
is a great disparity between the facts of their animal existence
and the aspiring ideals by which they attempt to live. But he
accepted both and he saw the life of a man as the meaningful
and at the same time pathetic, ludicrous, and tragic attempt to
bridge this gap. In Chekhov's plays this conflict is seen in his
characters who embody both a terrible earnestness of purpose
and an awkward and ridiculous acting out of that purpose. In
his own life this conflict is reflected in the very act of writing
itself. For Chekhov, as Thomas Mann has pointed out:

Work, pursued relentlessly to the end with the awareness that one has no answers to the final questions, while one's conscience pricks one for throwing dust in the eye of the reader, remains a strange obligation in spite of all. It comes to this: One 'entertains a forlorn world by telling stories without ever being able to offer it the trace of a saving truth.' To poor Katya's question (in "A Tedious Tale"): 'What am I to do?' one can but answer: 'upon my honor and conscience, I don't know.' Nevertheless, one goes on working, telling stories, giving form to truth, hoping darkly, sometimes almost confidently, that truth and serene form will avail to set free the human spirit and prepare mankind for a better, lovelier, worthier life.

One of the reasons that Chekhov's plays seem so difficult to audiences and critics alike is the fact that they are so different. Until recently, with the advent of the plays of Beckett, Ionesco, Adamov, Albee, and Pinter on our stages (Chekhov, I believe, is the legitimate father of the so-called "absurdist" movement in the theatre), we went to the theatre expecting to see a story about someone doing something; "character in action" is the way the critics put it. This story also usually involved some kind of "message" or "statement" about an aspect of human experience: life can be good if we are honest with ourselves (*Pillars of Society*); life is always doomed because our irrational drives are at variance with our conscious aims (*Ghosts* and a host of other plays); one's marriage is doomed if as a husband you act and react like a soldier (*Othello*). In short, one of the things that we expect of a dramatic action is that it express some kind of completion to the statement: "Life is ———!"

Shortly before he died, Chekhov's wife asked him what he thought the meaning of life was. He replied: "You ask me what life is? It is like asking what a carrot is. A carrot is a carrot, and nothing more is known." Herein lies the basic secret, both in meaning and form, of Chekhov's drama. He did not believe that "life is something"; all of his plays are expressions of the proposition that "life is." This is what he meant in his oft-quoted and usually misinterpreted remark about what the nature of the theatre should be:

A play ought to be written in which the people should come and go, dine, talk of the weather, or play cards, not because the author wants it but because that is what happens in real life. Life on the stage should be as it really is and the people, too, should be as they are and not stilted.

Such an idea of the theatre has tremendous implications for the drama, and we are just now becoming aware of them. First of all, it abolishes the traditional linear plot because Chekhov was not interested in presenting an action in any Aristotelian sense, but rather he was dramatizing a condition. Whenever one asks what the central action of a Chekhov play is, he comes a cropper. Is it Treplev's suicide? Vanya's attempted murder? The three sisters' attempt to go to Moscow? The sale of the cherry orchard? The answer in each case must be "no," for these are only small parts of the plays and not everything that hapens in the plays is directly related to these events; "action" for Chekhov was an artificial concept. He was concerned with showing life as it is, and in life there is no central action, there are only people and the only thing that is basic to each individual is the ontological solitude of his being. As one of my students put it recently: "Chekhov's plays do not tell stories. What do stories have to do with life? To be about life, a story must either be myth, invention, or chronicle; it must have a protagonist or center. But then it becomes a personal narrative or history, either real or imaginary. Chekhov, on the other hand, is not interested in describing a personal history: he has no Oedipus, no Lear, no Macbeth. In showing us life as it is, he has no use for seeing particular men in particular world systems. Chekhov's subject matter is life itself, not 'the life of a great man named Othello,' or 'the life of a school teacher named Medvedenko.'" As a result, Chekhov sought to create in his plays a situation which would reveal the private drama that each man has inside himself and which is enacted every day in the random, apparently meaningless, and undramatic events of our common routine.

But because Chekhov is more concerned with the inner lives of his characters and is not interested in presenting an action, his plays seem lifeless, timeless, static. Such plays of "wrecked travelers" are bound to be the antithesis of an Aristotelian action. Like the characters in the novels of Kafka, Proust, and Joyce, the people in Chekhov's plays talk and plan a great deal, but they do nothing. In fact, part of each play's meaning derives from this disparity between language and action. And we notice that as he develops as a playwright, Chekhov increasingly seems to doubt the possibility of meaningful action (even negative) at all. Ivanov, Uncle George, and Treplev are able to commit suicide, but Uncle Vanya fails in his attempt at murder; in *Three Sisters* and *The Cherry Orchard* nothing happens, and in the latter play not even a gun is fired and no one dies. All of the traditional ingredients of dramatic action—love, murder, suicide, revenge—are present in the Chekhovian drama, but they are used differently, used to serve different ends. They are not ends in themselves or plot devices to further the action, but are used as indirect means of focusing our attention on the inner lives of the characters themselves.

Or again, we notice the quality of timelessness in the plays. This is a strange effect, for all of the plays are structured within a variation of an arrival-departure pattern and there is a great specificity of time in each of the plays; we are conscious of dates, ages, the passage of years, the time of day, the seasons. We know that the cherry orchard is to be sold on August 22; Irina, Masha, and Olga are respectively 20, 22, and 28 at the beginning of *Three Sisters*; they are 24, 26 and 32 at the end; the carnival party will be coming at nine; and the daily routine of the Serebryakov estate with "tea at eight, dinner at one, and supper in the evening" has been upset by the Professor's arrival. And yet, in spite of this frame of a time pattern, we have no real sense of time passing. Chekhov for all his apparent attention to temporal concerns has been interested only in revealing more and more fully the continually shifting and changing state of consciousness within each of the characters. And when the characters, if they do, come back momentarily to temporal reality they shout painfully as Vanya does:

But, my God! Why are my thoughts so entangled? Why am I so old? Why won't she understand me? I despise all that rhetoric of hers, that indolent morality, that absurd talk about the destruction of the world. . . . [*A pause.*] Oh, how I have been deceived!

Or they sob with Irina:

Where. . . . Where has it all gone? Where is it? Oh, God, I've forgotten. . . . I've forgotten everything. . . . Everything's so confused. . . . I don't remember what the Italian for 'window' is, or for 'ceiling'. . . . Every day I'm forgetting more and more, and life's slipping by, and it will never, never return. . . .

"Where has it all gone?" And in between these moments of painful discovery, they have not been concerned with time. Most of Chekhov's characters are like the three sisters, ageless and no age at all. Only those characters whose inner life Chekhov was not interested in revealing are conscious of time and change. The Natashas, Lopahins, and Yashas for the most part live only in the world of events and appointments to be kept; they make things happen, they are interested in time. Natasha asks what time it is; Lopahin is constantly looking at his watch. But most of the characters in Chekhov's world have no sense of time; as Kulygin points out to the three sisters, their clock "is seven minutes fast."

Further, Chekhov made it quite clear that what his characters do want in time is really nothing at all, only an illusion: Astrov's planting of forests, Nina's achievement on the stage, Serebryakov's articles, Irina's desire for work and dreams of true love, Vershinin's happiness in two or three hundred years, the trip to Moscow, finally the cherry orchard itself. If the orchard means so much to Lyubov, why does she do so little to save it? The fact is that Lyubov loves the orchard and at the same time does not care about it at all. It is her life, but her life is meaningless. The orchard is at once the great cause, and nothing at all. All of Chekhov's characters finally arrive at that point where their most deep-felt needs are nothing, that existential nothingness which confronts Kafka's wrecked travelers. They want to be free of time; in fact, they wish to be free of life itself.

Finally, what it all boils down to is this: for Chekhov to show "life as it is" each of his characters must be defined by his solitude and estrangement from life and not by his participation in life. Each man's existence is ultimately solitary, and his unique self can be known only, if it ever can, after all of his social contexts have been stripped away. And yet, although this may be true, no man can exist in the vacuum of self, albeit Chekhov's characters try to. Each of them attempts to build and then operate in his own little world, with no sense of social responsibility, totally unaware of the sufferings of others. Each character has his own thoughts and problems with which he is usually morbidly consumed. As a result, the people in Chekhov's plays never seem to hear or notice one another. Each has room only for himself and each acts in a social vacuum. And yet it is not always easy to keep the walls of these private worlds from breaking down. We notice that Chekhov generally sets his characters in restricted areas. The interiors are always closely confined rooms, the exteriors are usually attached to the house or are nearby. For this reason, if none other, Chekhov's characters are always in contact with each other and it is sometimes difficult to maintain a complete self-centeredness. As a result, each of his characters must have one or more protective escapes to which he can resort if too much is demanded of him. The plays are filled with escapes from social reality; for some it is drinking; for others like Sonya it is blind religious belief; for Vanya it is sleep; for Astrov it is beauty; for Gaev it is billiards and gum drops; for Andrey it is his violin, his books, his gambling; and for many it is work. No matter what the nature of the escape may be, they are all means whereby Chekhov's characters can return to their own little private worlds when outside demands become too great.

But Chekhov did not stop here. If he had, his characters would be little more than selfish and unattractive. And although we know that they are so, we also know they are more than that. Chekhov's most profound insight was that in addition to knowing that each man is alone and that he seeks to maintain his solitude, he also knew that for each man solitude is unbearable. Man is aware that finally he is alone in the universe and that he is incapable of being alone. The essential drama of the human condition as it is expressed in Chekhov's plays lies in this tension between the uncertainty of each man's relationship to others and the uncertainty of his relationship to himself.

As I indicated earlier, Chekhov's plays are different from most plays that we are accustomed to seeing or reading; and I suggested as a reason that he was attempting to say something different and thus required new dramatic forms and techniques. Therefore, I must now say something about certain dominant aspects of Chekhov's dramaturgy. From the very beginning we are faced with a difficult problem: it is impossible to use any of the usual procedures of dramatic criticism—narrating the plot line, describing the characters, thematic analysis—because the texture and density of a Chekhovian play defies such methods. To analyze these plays properly one would have to begin with the opening speech and then, making cross-relationships, work through the entire play until the final curtain in much the same manner one would give a critical reading of a poem. Such a procedure would not be to our purposes here; rather, I shall illustrate some of the major devices used by Chekhov to achieve his dramatic effects.

However, before I do this I must discuss in greater detail the more general problem of form in a Chekhovian play. Earlier, I said that these plays are not imitations of an action in any Aristotelian sense. Chekhov was dramatizing a condition, and therefore he needed a dramatic form which, as Ionesco put it, "progressed not through a predetermined subject and plot, but through an increasingly intense and revealing series of emotional

states." Such a drama must from the beginning then dispense
with the traditional linear plot. Such a plot is sequential; it
starts at a certain moment in time and then moves through a
series of events to a conclusion. Everything that occurs in this
kind of play—each speech, every action, any symbols—is a part
of the play's forward movement and is causally related to the
sequence of events. It is this sequential nature of dramatic action, of which plot is the first form, that Aristotle was referring
to when he said that tragedy is an imitation of an action "which
has a beginning, a middle, and an end."

But as we said, Chekhov was not interested in "imitations of
actions," he wanted to show "life as it is." Life as it is lacks the
direction, the external causality, the cathartic effect of completed events. Like so many painters, composers, poets, novel-
ists, and now, fifty years later, playwrights, Chekhov was aware
that the crises which are so neatly resolved by the linear form
of drama are not so neatly resolved in life. To be alive is to be
in a continual state of crisis; in life as one crisis is resolved another is always beginning. He wanted his plays to express the
paradox, the contradiction, and the incompleteness of experience; he wanted to suggest the raggedness, the confusion, the
complexity of motivation, the "discontinuous continuity," and
the basic ambiguity of all human behavior. Chekhov believed
that the drama as he knew it could never express the "is-ness"
of experience because it was under the destructive tyranny of
a sequential and chronological structure. So in its place he invented a form which might be called, to use the terminology
of the new criticism of poetry, a contextual or concentric action.
(It is hardly fitting to use the word plot here, for, because of
its usual connotations, it can only be misleading.) The structure of a Chekhovian play is epiphanic; its purpose is to reveal
—literally, "to show forth"—the inner lives of his characters. In
such a drama the plot has been twisted into a situation that is
to reveal the psychic lives of the characters. There are many
dramatic situations in a plot; here a single situation has been

stretched to take the place of the plot. This inflation of the situation into the source of the dramatic action, so that it replaces the plot, is the vital secret of Chekhovian dramaturgy. To capture "the aimless, unclimactic multiplicity" of his characters' lives Chekhov has created a form based on what Marvin Rosenberg has called "the tensions of context, rather than direction, of vertical depth, rather than horizontal movement." Chekhov takes a situation and then develops it concentrically, like a series of inscribed but tangential circles. For example, in *The Cherry Orchard*, the situation at the beginning of the play is simply that Lyubov has arrived home because the cherry orchard is to be sold; at the end of the play the orchard has been sold and everyone leaves. Nothing happens really, the situation is single and static; in the four acts the situation has taken one—and only one—forward step; but Chekhov has revealed a great deal about the way "life is" for twelve people as they are related to that situation.

This is a new kind of drama and the devices which Chekhov used to create it and achieve meaning through it will appear by traditional standards to be untheatrical—or, to use the language of his present-day followers, "antitheatrical." And yet, as was pointed out earlier, Chekhov does use the techniques of the earlier realistic drama; only he uses them for different reasons and in different ways. It is quite proper, therefore, that his plays have been called "dramas of indirection."

Before examining the techniques of indirection, however, I should like to make one more point. In discussing the use of time in the plays we noticed that there was a great specificity about time. This is but one example of the great specificity which informs Chekhov's drama, and this fact does much to account for the enduring quality of his art. The greatest danger that faces an artist when he is dealing with man's inner life is that in his presentation of that life he will of necessity become too private, too personal, too subjective—since such a life is the ultimate in subjectivity; but such subjectivity tends to cancel out all communication. If, as Chekhov maintains, all men are solitary and ultimately unknowable, how can the equally solitary reader or member of an audience enter into the private worlds that are being presented on the stage? How, and why, should they have relevance for us? Who really cares—except perhaps our psychiatrist—about the *psyche* of another, and even if we might care, how can we ever comprehend it? I believe Chekhov does much to overcome this problem—and it is a lesson that Beckett and Ionesco would do well to learn—by enclosing his subjective "actions" in an objective frame of specific external details. He was trying to capture the private inner lives of each of his characters, but he did so by means of those everyday events, objects, and expressions that as human beings, in all places and in all times, each of us shares. Chekhov was the great observer, and his plays are filled with the details of his observation. As a man Chekhov cared deeply for all of his fellow human beings; as an artist he always maintained complete objectivity. It is the fusion of these two characteristics that makes his work great, and more important, makes them work as plays.

Keeping in mind, then, that all of Chekhov's plays are framed in great specificity of detail, what are some of the techniques of indirection which he employed to reveal the inner lives of his characters? The most obvious was his refusal to use the big scene, the stereotyped dramatic situation. There are no "obligatory" scenes or great dénouements in a Chekhov play. Traditionally, such scenes were used to reveal through action the truth about a play's central characters. But for Chekhov, the truth is not dramatic in this way nor is it necessarily full of consequence; more likely, it is quite commonplace. We are accustomed to the "big" scenes and have come to expect them; when Chekhov refuses to give them to us we feel cheated. But Chekhov was not trying to fulfill our conditioned expectations and responses, he was showing "life as it is." We are moved by Othello's "Soft you; a word or two before you go" as his universe crashes down upon him, but in life our universes, if they do cave in, do not usually do so quite so dramatically; rather such times are hushed and of no great consequence to most people. So *The Sea Gull* ends with Dorn taking Trigorin aside and quietly telling him: "The fact is, Konstantin Gavrilovitch has shot himself. . . ."

But the very muted and underplayed quality of the scene is precisely what gives it its effect. It may not be as theatrically exciting as Hedda Gabler's suicide, for instance, but it is much truer to life and in the long run its impact upon us is probably more lasting and horrible. Chekhov had a great distrust of the artificiality of the conventional big curtain scene of the well-made play, and his work shows that he gradually discarded it altogether. In his early plays (*Platonov, Ivanov,* and *The Wood Demon* are for the most part structured according to the conventions of the well-made play) he uses the big curtain. For example, in Ivanov, Act I ends with Anna's decision to follow her husband to the Lyebedev's, Act II ends with her discovery of Ivanov and Sasha in each other's arms, Act III with Ivanov's brutal revelation to his wife that she is soon to die, and Act IV with Ivanov's suicide. But Chekhov gradually came to see that such scenes were phony and while he was working on *The Wood Demon* he wrote:

The demand is made that the hero and the heroine should be dramatically effective. But in life people do not shoot themselves, or hang themselves, or fall in love, or deliver themselves of clever sayings every minute. They spend most of their time eating, drinking, running after women or men, or talking nonsense. It is therefore necessary that this should be shown on the stage.

The Sea Gull was the first play to manifest this change of attitude. The suicide is still there, but, as we have shown, it was used in a very different way. The only "dramatic" event in *Uncle Vanya* is Vanya's botched attempt to shoot Serebryakov near the end of the third act. In *Three Sisters* Tusenbach is shot by Solyony in a duel, but his death is off stage and the shot is muffled. Finally, in *The Cherry Orchard* none of the traditional dramatic events take place and even the sad departure of Lyubov and Gaev is undercut by the final appearance of the bumbling Firs. But more important than the gradual elimination of such theatrically effective scenes is the fact that when Chekhov uses them they are no longer ends in themselves but rather they serve as pointers to the more powerful, albeit less theatrical, drama that is taking place within the characters who are on the stage. By underplaying the big, exciting, dramatic events we are better able to see the drama and the complexity of the seemingly trivial, the inconsequential, and the simple that is the very tissue of the human situation. Chekhov had learned well the wisdom of *Hamlet*: "By indirections find directions out."

Chekhov's use of obligatory scenes, then, was ironic, and this irony leads us to another aspect of his dramaturgy. Throughout his life Chekhov constantly made the statement that "the truth about life is ironical" and since he was showing "life as it is" almost all of his dramatic devices were ironic. The irony is best seen in the disparity between what his characters say and what they do. Thus we find in all of his plays characters making brilliantly incisive remarks about themselves and other people, and yet they are said in such a way and are put in such an incongruous and ludicrous context that we do not stop to take them seriously when we hear them. The force of these statements is driven home cumulatively; we are suddenly aware as the play ends that in their actions the characters have done just the opposite to what in their dialogue they have expounded they should do. These flashes of self-revelation have been more than static, isolated, and disconnected statements of opinion; despite all their apparent ludicrousness, they have become ironically true. Thus, Yelena says to Sonya in the second act of *Uncle Vanya*, "You must not look at people that way. It isn't right. You must trust and believe in people, *(pause)* or life becomes impossible." Even at this point in the play we know that this is precisely what Yelena does not do. We tend to laugh at the incongruity of the situation; but as we leave the theatre our stomachs begin to squirm as the truth of her statement begins to sink in. Looking at Yelena, one can see in dramatic terms just how impossible life can really become. But Chekhov has achieved his effect indirectly.

We find something similar in the third act of *The Cherry Orchard,* when Trofimov is telling Lyubov, "You mustn't deceive yourself; for once in your life you must face the truth!" To be sure, Trofimov has spoken the truth about Madame Ranevsky, but it tells us very little about the Russian equivalent to our perpetual graduate student. After all, it is easy for almost anyone to make that observation about Lyubov (Lopahin has been telling her the same thing from the beginning of the first act); what is more important in the scene is how Trofimov reacts when Lyubov rebuffs him: "This is awful! I can't stand it! I'm going. (*He goes off, but at once returns.*) All is over between us!" By exaggerating (one of Chekhov's chief ironic techniques) his reaction, Chekhov points up the melodramatic quality of his exit and in so doing shows Trofimov as a comic butt. He underscores this by having Trofimov run out of the room and fall down the stairs in the midst of a chorus of laughter.

Or, to take a final example of this kind of ironic disparity between speech and action, let us look briefly at Treplev in *The Sea Gull.* Treplev is a typical adolescent writer—today we find his counterpart taking courses in creative writing and going to "writing workshops" in the summer. Treplev has lofty ideals, but he is a bad writer. (Chekhov makes this clear by contrasting him to Trigorin, who, although not great, is a good craftsman.) We learn of Treplev's ideals when he attacks the theatre:

But in my opinion our theatre's in a rut. It's nothing but clichés and shopworn conventions. When the curtain opens on those three-walled "living rooms," and I see those famous and talented actors, those high priests of that sacred art, parade about in their costumes in front of the footlights showing the way people eat, drink, make love, and walk about; when I hear them try to squeeze a moral out of commonplace phrases and meaningless events—some cliché that everyone knows and is suitable for home consumption; when they give me a thousand variations of the same old thing over and over again. . . . I have to leave! . . . we need new forms, and if we can't have them, then it's better to have nothing at all!

Now all this may be true, but the fact that he says it does not make him a playwright. That Treplev is a bad writer is made very clear when his own play is produced:

Men, lions, eagles, and partridges, horned deer, geese, spiders, and the silent fish of the deep, starfish and creatures which cannot be seen by the eye—all living things, all living things, all living things, having completed their cycle of sorrow, are now extinct. . . . I am alone. Once in a hundred years I open my lips to speak, and then my voice echoes mournfully in the void, unheard by all. . . . You, too, pale spirits do not hear me.

This is drivel (it seems to foreshadow the plays of the bad expressionists) and the disparity between what Treplev says about the theatre and what he writes for it is part of Chekhov's point. I think, as much as anything, it is Treplev's recognition of this fact that drives him to suicide. (But already I am aware that such analysis as this has falsified the significance of his death, for it tends to reduce the many interlocking meanings of the play to a single action.) We notice just before Nina's final appearance that the young writer is struggling over a description of a moonlight evening:

And the description of the moonlight's no good either. Trigorin's worked out his own techniques, so it comes easily for him. . . . He'd just mention the neck of a broken bottle glittering in a mill stream and the black shadow of a mill wheel—and he's got a moonlight night. But for me it's the shimmering light, the silent twinkling of the stars, and the distant sounds of a piano, dying away in the still, fragrant air. . . . It's terrible.

We know from a letter written by Chekhov to his brother Alexander in 1886 that the playwright approves of the "Trigorin method," for in that letter he uses word for word the example of the moonlit night that appears in Konstantin's speech. And, finally, as Nina leaves him she not only confesses that she still loves Trigorin, she also goes out the door reciting the lines of Treplev's ill-fated play. The final truth about Konstantin Treplev is very sad and pathetic, but it has been revealed to us indirectly by the ironic devices of Chekhov's method.

I have already indicated that Chekhov often achieves his irony by the use of an undercutting speech. Such a device does much to give the plays their comic quality (we shall discuss the nature of Chekhov's comedy presently), but it also is a means whereby Chekhov can reveal some truth about the inner lives of his characters. For instance, in the first act of *Uncle Vanya*, Vanya has been arguing with his mother and he is finally shut up. An awkward pause follows, and to relieve the tension of this pause Yelena remarks, "It's a fine day, not too hot," and Vanya self-pityingly replies, "It is a fine day to hang oneself!" This line is immediately followed by Marina's coming in to look for the chickens. She says, "Here chick, chick, chick." In her world, in which she is doing her job, this is a perfectly logical line; but coming as it does immediately after Vanya's ironic self-dramatizing, it is not only immensely funny, but it acts as a commentary on Vanya's line. The result is a kind of grotesque humor which makes us laugh with a lump in our throats. It is funny until we realize the total implication of our laughter.

We find much the same thing in the opening act of *The Cherry Orchard*. Lyubov has just arrived and she is gushing about her "dear, beautiful nursery" and Gaev is talking about efficiency, and exactly at this point Charlotta, in a conversation with Pischik, announces that "My dog eats nuts, too." In short, all this talk is just so much gabble. Or to take a final example: in the opening scene of *Three Sisters* Olga and Irina are talking about how wonderful it would be to go back to Moscow. Tusenbach, Chebutykin, and Solyony are carrying on their own conversation in the adjoining room; we catch only snatches of their talk, but notice how Chekhov uses it:

OLGA. I wanted so much to go home again. Go home to Moscow!

CHEBUTYKIN, *sarcastically to* SOLYONY. A small chance of that!

TUSENBACH, *also to* SOLYONY. Of course, it's nonsense.

A few lines later the dialogue goes as follows:

IRINA. Go back to Moscow! Sell the house, leave everything here, and go back to Moscow.

OLGA. Yes, to go back to Moscow! As soon as possible.

CHEBUTYKIN *and* TUSENBACH *laugh.*

No more need be said; from the beginning of the play the sisters' talk of returning to Moscow is an idle dream, but it has been shown to us by the ironical device of the undercutting speech.

I should like to point out one more ironic device. It is a commonplace that Chekhov's characters are addicted to making speeches. Gaev makes a speech to the book case; Trofimov is constantly carrying on about the "brave new world" that is approaching; Vershinin and Tusenbach, when they have nothing better to do, philosophize; Vanya is continually making speeches; and so on. But, beginning with Stanislavsky, many interpreters of Chekhov have missed the point of this speechifying. T. S. Eliot was very perceptive on this point when he wrote in his essay "Rhetoric and Poetic Drama":

Speechmaking in a play can serve useful dramatic ends. Genuine rhetoric is a device of great effect when it occurs in situations where a character in a play *sees himself* in a dramatic light. In plays of realism we often find parts which are never allowed to be consciously dramatic, for fear, perhaps, of their appearing less real. But in actual life, in many of those situations in actual life which we enjoy consciously and keenly, we are at times aware of ourselves in this way, and these moments are of very great usefulness to dramatic verse. They are valuable because they give us a new clue to the character, for we discover the angle from which he views himself.

"We discover the angle from which he views himself"—not the

way we see him, or the other characters see him, or the playwright sees him. Thus by contrasting the way the characters see
themselves with what they do and with the way the other characters view them, Chekhov, again by indirection, is able to reveal the way life really is.

A few words should probably be said about Chekhov's use of
symbols. It has often been noted that the modern drama, beginning with Ibsen, has been increasingly dependent upon non-
verbal symbolism and the imagery of inanimate objects—Cocteau's "poetry of the theatre"—to achieve emotional depth within
theatrical conventions which are, for the most part, committed
only to external reality. Ibsen, beginning with *A Doll's House*
and *Ghosts,* and most explicitly in *The Wild Duck,* used symbols to give a metaphoric meaning that a predominantly naturalistic theatre denied him. Chekhov also used this kind of symbolism, but in a fashion quite different from his contemporaries
(or, indeed, those that followed him). Unlike Ibsen's "ghosts,"
Chekhov's symbols are never abstractions, nor are they simply
analogous to the play's action; they are always concrete, they
are a part of the life of the people in his plays, in a word,
they are organic to the texture and meaning of the play. Nor,
like the "wild duck," are they bizarre superimpositions on the
action. (I believe the wild-duck symbolism works, but the Ekdal
attic stretches conventions of naturalistic verisimilitude almost
to the breaking point. What is more crucial, one has the feeling
that the wild-duck metaphor existed prior to the writing of the
play, as a kind of symbolic framework, and that Ibsen then
created an action to fit the frame.) There are big, almost all-
inclusive symbols—the sea gull, Astrov's forests, Moscow, the
cherry orchard—in a Chekhov play, and these symbols do give
meaning and depth to large segments of the plays of which they
are a part. But these extending symbols are effective because
they grow out of the action and are not imposed upon it, and,
more important, because they rest upon the less noticeable but
more significant symbolic underpinning of the whole play. For

example, Moscow is the symbol of the three sisters' dream of happiness. This happiness we know is an illusion and their belief in this illusion shows how out of touch with reality they are. And yet the play is filled with less obvious symbols that make it clear that everyone in the play—with the exception of Natasha—has to some degree lost touch with reality. These lesser symbols support the overarching Moscow symbol and, what is more, give it its organic quality. To point out but one instance: As the play opens Irina is celebrating her birthday (more exactly the anniversary of her baptism) and old Dr. Chebutykin, who perhaps more than all the others has lost touch with reality, with great ceremony brings Irina her present—a silver samovar. Everyone gasps, and with protestations of "you shouldn't have done it" and "it costs too much money" the incident is dropped as quickly as possible. The point is that in Russia a silver samovar is the traditional gift of a husband to his wife on their silver wedding anniversary. Nothing could have more effectively nor more completely shown just how out of touch with reality the doctor had become; nor, we might add, have revealed the lifetime of pain and disappointment that was the result of Irina's mother's decision to marry Brigadier General Prozorov rather than young Dr. Chebutykin.

In *Uncle Vanya* we notice how Chekhov uses a symbol to achieve another effect. Several of the plays have references to the watchman's rattle or stick. In nineteenth-century Russia the watchman would go about the estate clacking his sticks—much as our present-day nightwatchmen make the rounds with clock and key; the purpose was both to frighten any prowlers that might be about and to let the members of the household know that they were being protected. But Chekhov did not include this effect for verisimilitude alone; he also used it as a thematic symbol.[1] Such is the use of the watchman at the end

---

[1] Chekhov did not believe in verisimilitude for its own sake. He was constantly quarreling with Stanislavsky over just this point. The famous director was always trying to introduce realistic touches—the croaking of

of the second act of *Uncle Vanya:* Yelena and Sonya have just
had an honest talk with each other and because of it they are
capable of feeling. The windows are open, it has been raining,
and everything is clean and refreshed. Yelena thinks she can
play the piano again; as Sonya goes to get permission, the
watchman's rattle is heard; Yelena has to shut the window—the
source of refreshment—and Serebryakov says "no." Their whole
life of feeling has been so protected by the "watchmen" of their
lives that they have no feelings left.

There are countless examples such as these in the plays.
All of Chekhov's symbols have this same kind of organic quality; they deepen and enhance the play's meaning, but more
importantly they too serve as a means of pointing, indirectly, to
that inner drama which is at the heart of each of the plays.

There is one more aspect of Chekhov's art which I should like
to discuss; the tendency on the part of his characters to aestheti-
cize life. All of the people in Chekhov's plays are shown to be
either consciously or unconsciously aware of their own inadequacies as people. They realize that in one way or another
they have failed as human beings, and they therefore attempt
to make their lives like the more perfect world of art. This desire to identify with art manifests itself in various ways. The most
obvious is the tendency on the part of several of the characters
to identify with great artists of the past or with great heroes from
literature. Serebryakov as he suffers from the pains of old age
and a life of retirement (not to mention the probable realization that his life and work as a scholar may have been as meaningless as Vanya says it was), identifies with Turgenev, when
he says at the opening of the second act of *Uncle Vanya,* "They

---

frogs, the barking of dogs, crying children—that served no organic function
in the play. When Stanislavsky defended his actions by saying that such
effects did occur in real life, Chekhov replied: "Quite true, but the stage
demands a certain amount of convention. You have no fourth wall, for
instance. Besides, the stage is art; the stage reflects the quintessence of life.
Nothing superfluous should be introduced on the stage."

say Turgenev got heart trouble from gout. I'm afraid I'm getting it too." In *Three Sisters,* Solyony is constantly insulting and antagonizing people because he feels inferior to them. In a quiet moment with Tusenbach, whom he later kills, he confesses: "When I'm alone with someone I'm all right, I'm just like everybody else. When I'm in a group of people, I get depressed and shy, and. . . . I talk all sorts of nonsense." This shy captain wears the mask of Lermontov: he is always quoting the Russian Byron; he has been in several duels; and he will brook no rivals in love. Vanya, unable to stand the final disillusionment of his life's work, shouts "My life's ruined. I'm gifted, I'm intelligent, I'm courageous. . . . If I'd had had a normal life, I might have become a Schopenhauer, a Dostoyevsky." Finally, in *The Sea Gull,* Treplev, out of the despair of his mother's rejection, identifies himself with Hamlet.

This aestheticizing tendency is also seen in the way Chekhov's characters are more conscious of *how* they say things than what they say. In the third act of *The Cherry Orchard,* Epihodov says to Varya: "I wish you'd express yourself more delicately." He does not care what is said so long as it is said beautifully. Or, in *Three Sisters,* Vershinin has just made one of his typical speeches about how beautiful life will be in two or three hundred years, and Irina, oblivious to the meaning of what he has said, says with a sigh, "Really, someone should have written all that down."

The desire for beautiful expression is directly related to the many quotations and literary allusions which we find in the plays. There are quotations from Shakespeare, Pushkin, Krylov, Lermontov, and Gogol to name but a few, and allusions to Ostrovsky, Balzac, Batushkov, and Turgenev. Chekhov's characters are always quoting and talking—in short, finding comfort in words. They are attempting to give a meaning to their otherwise empty and meaningless lives through words by giving their words artistic form.

Finally, and most profoundly, the aestheticizing of life is

carried to its furthest verge by those characters who seek to make their own lives into works of art. Consider Astrov's remarks about Yelena in the second act of *Uncle Vanya*:

In a human being, everything ought to be beautiful: face and dress, soul and thoughts. She is very beautiful, there's no denying it, but, after all, all she does is eat, sleep, go for walks, fascinate us by her beauty and—nothing more. She has no duties, other people work for her.

Later, he says to Sonya:

I am old, tired, unimportant; my feelings are dead. I could never care for any one again. I don't love anyone, and I don't think I shall ever love anyone. The only thing that appeals to me is beauty. I just can't remain indifferent to it. If, for example, Yelena wanted to, she could turn my head in a day.

Finally, he forces the affair with Yelena; his outburst is not one of physical passion but a reaction to her beauty which culminates in his asking her to keep a tryst in a beautiful forest arbor. We are reminded of Hedda Gabler's request that Lövborg shoot himself beautifully—through the head. Thus the man who has failed, who is incapable of loving anyone, attempts to substitute an erotic picture of idyllic love for a mature and demanding relationship. It is a relationship that is symbolized by the "Autumn Roses" Vanya brings to Yelena; such roses—like all the love affairs in Chekhov's plays—are very beautiful, but they discolor and disintegrate the moment they are touched.

This tendency is most fully developed in Trofimov in *The Cherry Orchard*. Like Astrov, he has become a walking vegetable, an emotional turnip. He loves life and the beauties of nature, but he hates anything animal or physical. Thus his whole relationship with Anya is vegetative. He wants to look at her, but even the slightest trace of physical desire is repulsive. "We are above love," he says. He cannot accept the responsibility of human-animal existence and must escape into the ideal world of art which is bloodless but extremely beautiful. This, then, is but another of the dramatic processes of indirection, as opposed to the tendency toward statement which is so prevalent in the modern theatre, which Chekhov employs to reveal the absorbing drama of "life as it is."

Finally, something must be said about Chekhov and comedy. Critics are continually telling us that Chekhov is funny, and further we know that both *The Sea Gull* and *The Cherry Orchard* were called comedies by their author, and that he conceived none of his plays (despite Stanislavsky's interpretations) as tragedies. But Chekhov's plays are so unlike most of the comedies we know, that we are not sure we should trust even the author's assurances that they are. Perhaps a better way of understanding what is meant when Chekhov is referred to as a comic writer, is to recall that he was writing a drama that was to show "life as it is." Another way of describing "life as it is" is expressed in Santayana's statement that "Everything in Nature is lyrical in its ideal essence, tragic in its fate, and comic in its existence." This provides a very important insight into the form of Chekhovian drama, and it also accounts for the complex overtones that are present in the plays, for Chekhov's characters respond to all three of Santayana's levels with an especial intensity. They are comedians by necessity, smitten with a tragic sense of life, lyrically in love with the ideal in a world poorly equipped to satisfy such aspirations.

The essential quality of the "is-ness" of life is, as was said earlier, its absurdity, its futility. Some would argue that this is tragic, perhaps the most tragic condition of all, but as Dorothy Sayers has wisely pointed out, "the whole tragedy of futility is that it never succeeds in achieving tragedy. In its blackest moments it is inevitably doomed to the comic gesture." Thus, when man comes to see his existence as absurd, that it is governed by the irrational, the inexplicable, and the nonsensical, he moves into the realm of the comic. For comedy presupposes such a world, a world being made and turned upside down. As Gautier put it, "Comedy is the logic of the absurd," and thus it can admit the disorderly and the improbable into the realm of art.

Chekhov was aware that the fragmentary, schizoid life that each of us lives is an existential comedy. His plays suggest that man lives in the midst of so many irreconcilable forces—both within and without—that the only way that life can be given form in art is in comedy. But it is a special kind of comedy, a grotesque kind of comedy, which makes us, as I said earlier, laugh with a lump in our throats. It does so because for all of its awareness of the absurdity of experience, it is also extremely conscious of the suffering, struggle, and failure of experience. Christopher Fry wrote in his essay "On Comedy":

I know that when I set about writing a comedy the idea presents itself to me first of all as tragedy. The characters press on to the theme with all their divisions and perplexities heavy about them; they are already entered for the race to doom, and good and evil are an infernal tangle skinning the fingers that try to unravel them. If the characters were not qualified for tragedy there would be no comedy, and to some extent I have to cross the one before I can light the other. In a century less flayed and quivering we might reach it more directly; but not now unless every word we write is going to mock us.

Chekhov, I think, would have seen the applicability of Fry's remarks to [his own plays,] for they too contain such a vision of life, a vision that may be summed up by the closing prayer of Joyce's *Finnegans Wake:*

> Loud, heap miseries upon us yet entwine
> Our arts with laughters low. In the name
> Of the former and of the latter and of
> Their holocaust, All men.

And yet, somehow, I am not content to stop here. Traditionally, we think of tragedy as a form which celebrates man's capacity to suffer and aspire even though he is doomed to destruction by the inexorable workings of fate. Comedy, on the other hand, celebrates man's capacity to endure. It is *terribly* conscious of the resilience of the human spirit. Fry, in the essay just quoted, distinguished the two forms in this way:

The difference between tragedy and comedy is the difference between experience and intuition. In the experience we strive against every condition of our animal life: against death, against the frustration of ambition, against the instability of human love. In the intuition we trust the arduous eccentricities we are born to, and see the oddness of a creature who has never got acclimatized to being created.

Perhaps this explains the mysterious quality of affirmation that we sense in Chekhov's plays. There have been many playwrights in the modern theatre who were conscious of the doomed nature of human experience, but I know of none who accepted this fact and still had such trust in the enduring qualities of those "arduous eccentricities we are born to," as did Anton Chekhov.

Melodrama

JAMES L. ROSENBERG

I would like to defend a dirty word. Like a lot of dirty words, it is dirty, I feel, only through association—and mistaken association, at that.

The word is "melodrama."

It qualifies, I should say, as just about the dirtiest word in the lexicon of the modern critic of the drama—second only, perhaps, to "sentimental." In fact, it seems to have become a sort of universally applicable term of abuse; like "communism," roughly speaking, it seems to mean "bad."

Thus, when M. Ionesco wants to take a crack at M. Sartre, he calls him a writer of "political melodramas" (a masterpiece of ploymanship, combining two dirty words into a sort of portmanteau term of insult). One of the recurring and almost unceasing critical debates on the American dramatic scene has to do with the question of whether Arthur Miller and Tennessee Williams write melodramas or tragedies—with the clear assumption that to convict them of the former is to discredit them artistically. Mr. Kitto, in trying to come to prickly grips with that thorniest of dramatists, Euripides, finds himself forced—with every evidence of dismay—to conclude that a number of Euripides' plays can be described only as "melodramas"—and so much the worse for Euripides. (As Kitto says, of the *Iphigenia in Aulis,* "Now this is not a bad story, but it is not really tragic, and Euripides knows it." Not a bad story, but not really tragic—does this not sum up our critical attitudes, if they may be dignified by such a term, toward melodrama?)

What does the latest handbook of dramatic terms have to tell us? "Melodrama" is "a play wherein characters clearly virtuous or vicious are pitted against each other in sensational situations filled with suspense, until justice triumphs. The situations, not the characters, are exciting. . . . Melodrama is sometimes said to be tragedy with character left out." Another book tells us that "melodrama . . . has always been regarded as the lowliest form of drama, fit only for the critic's scorn and laughter." And still another defines the opprobrious word as "A play which is sensational, implausible in characterization, dialogue, and situation, abounds in thrilling struggles between heroic and villainous figures, and ends happily in the romantic triumph of virtue."

In short, this form is so ludicrously bad one wonders how and why it has survived from Euripides to the present day. It is, as the King of Siam would say, a puzzlement. But Siamese puzzlement can, if pursued, become the beginnings of wisdom—or at least a gleam of insight.

For instance, do you feel, as I do, a faint uneasiness over the awareness that such plays as *Medea* and *Electra* and *Richard III* and *The Revenger's Tragedy* and *The White Devil* and *Cyrano de Bergerac* have all been pretty universally—and, I think, quite accurately—described as "melodramas"? Are these *really* "fit only for the critic's scorn and laughter"? Are they "tragedy with character left out"? Does any one of them "end happily in the romantic triumph of virtue"?

To make matters infinitely worse, some of the very same critics who speak so disparagingly of melodrama as a form are among those who label some of the foregoing plays as melodramatic.

It is all very well for Emerson to say that a foolish consistency is the hobgoblin of little minds, or for a Walt Whitman to bellow "Do I contradict myself? Very well, then, I contradict myself!" and go striding away to sweat perfume. Emerson was a Transcendentalist and Whitman a poet, which means, I suppose, that they are exempt from the laws of logic and lucidity. But a critic is not—or should not be. He works with terms—terms that should be rational and meaningful, not only to him but to his readers; and, if they are not, he is in the lunatic position of the mathematician who works with numbers which have no value. Criticism becomes—as, I suspect, modern drama criticism has become, to a great degree—a sort of Alice in Wonderland conversation around the Mad Hatter's tea table. Humpty Dumpty could make words mean whatever he wanted them to, because he was insane and in a lunatic world, but the critic who does so falsifies and betrays the very essence of his being and reason for his existence. Yet I submit that no one can read very far in the realms of more or less contemporary dramatic criticism without becoming aware of the fact that our critical terminology has serious bugs in it. "Back to the old drawing board!" cries the cheerful little Peter Arno scientist as the experimental plane goes down in flames—and maybe it's not a bad idea for us.

Just how clear and workable are even our most hallowed and cherished generic terms? How many of us have been guilty —how often?—of prattling away glibly about "tragedy," invoking the ghost of Aristotle and handing down the tables of the law from the Sinai of the lecture platform, the desk, or the armchair? And yet how many of us, I wonder, have *really* looked at what Aristotle said (or reputedly said) and laid it alongside the general body of so-called "Greek tragedy"? If and when we do this, does it not strike us that not just some Greek tragedies, but most, do not conform to the standards for Greek tragedy? (I would be willing to argue that only one does—and how valuable is a critical term which refers to exactly one out of the millions of plays that have been written since the first actor crawled painfully out of the primeval ooze—never, some would say, to advance much further?) *Oedipus at Colonus* and the *Oresteia* end happily; it is not even clear who the tragic protagonist is in *Antigone* and *Philoctetes;* the heroine of *Medea* is a villain; the unities are cheerfully broken in a half dozen others one could mention.

And, as for "comedy"—! I have a standing offer of a pound of my flesh, which I will quite blithely bestow upon anybody who can give me a definition of comedy which will cogently and adequately embrace twenty or so "comedies" from Aristophanes to Ionesco (a disconcerting journey in itself, come to think of it).

And what one is to do with plays like *The Misanthrope* or *The Wild Duck* or *The Cherry Orchard,* I frankly don't know. Only the truly pedantic mind could put them into one of the pigeonholes labeled "tragedy" or "comedy" and feel satisfied with his choice. Maybe only the truly pedantic mind would *want* to.

I would like to submit that the first order of business today for those seriously interested in the drama as an art form rather than a branch of hucksterism is to start cleaning out our vocabularies and honing our definitions to a sharper edge. For working with critical terminology is like looking into a microscope: if the focus isn't razor sharp, you're wasting your time.

I'm afraid I have neither the time nor the ability to undertake the rehabilitation of such sweeping terms as "tragedy" and "comedy." But "melodrama" is a somewhat simpler and more glaring problem, and it is to this that I address myself, hopeful, if not of regaining lost ground, at least of raising questions in the minds of others who can perhaps set to work to do so.

What I have said so far should suggest, I hope, that we are in trouble when it comes to the word "melodrama." The word, as it is popularly defined, does not fit some of the most famous plays in the *genre*—just as in the case of "tragedy" and "comedy"—and its use as a generalized term of abuse certainly does not seem to conform to our experience in either the theatre or the library.

Why and how has this state of affairs come about?

Let's look a little more closely at the term. What seem to be the general objections to or misgivings about "melodrama," as they reveal themselves in nearly all the definitions we have considered? Are they not really two, mainly: (1) melodrama is inferior to tragedy—the other form of "serious" drama; and (2) melodrama "falsifies" life. (Notice the adjectives applied to it: "sensational," "thrilling," "romantic," "implausible." "Implausible," above all, is, I suspect, a key word.)

Well, suppose we start by trying to lay these two ghosts. "Melodrama is inferior to tragedy"—or, as one book put it, "Melodrama is . . . tragedy with character left out." An interesting observation, that, implying that Medea and Richard III and Vindice and Cyrano are somehow not very interesting as "characters"! But for the moment I am even more concerned with the supposition underlying this whole line of thinking, which is that melodrama is trying to be tragedy and not quite making it. And if you assume, as most critics seem to, that tragedy is *per se* the pinnacle of dramatic art, then any comparison with it becomes, by definition, an invidious one. But why must generic classification necessarily degenerate into a game of hierarchies? Is it not enough to perceive that there are various modes of perception—the tragic, the comic, the melodramatic, the farcical, the pastoral, the epic (I am beginning to sound, and feel, like Polonius!)—can we not perceive these various modes without lusting hotly after hierarchical arrangement? Tragedy is certainly "different from" melodrama; this fact does not necessarily make it "better than." Can we not be satisfied with saying that tragedy and comedy and melodrama and farce are different modes of perception, each with its own validity, none necessarily better or worse than the others? (Just in passing, I would like to insist, too, on these *genres* as modes of perception, not techniques of writing. Melodrama, like tragedy, is a way of seeing, not a trick of writing. You write a melodrama—a *good* melodrama—because you see the world that way, not because you think: "Today I think I'll write a melodrama.")

I would like, further, to italicize that adjective, *good*—for is it not noteworthy that nearly all discussions of "melodrama" are actually discussions about *bad* melodramas of the heroine-tied-to-the-railroad-tracks variety—but discussions *as though bad melodramas were the norm?* It's as though critics were to base all their considerations of tragedy on Jonson's *Sejanus* or Addison's *Cato,* or, let us say, their considerations of comedy on *Getting Gertie's Garter*—always with the unspoken assumption that these are outstanding and typical examples of the form. It is perfectly easy to dismiss melodrama as trash if you confine your examination of it to Kotzebue and Boucicault and their inferiors. But just how fair is this assumption? And is it really asking too much of the critic that he be, if not perceptive, at least fair? And that he have the intellectual rigor to question and examine the received terminology instead of, well, just receiving it? But how treacherously easy it is to just repeat the critical commonplaces of yesteryear without testing them for a heartbeat, and how painful and difficult it is to actually think through a set of terms.

But let us press on with this painful and difficult—but, I hope, ultimately rewarding—business. What of the somewhat more serious objection that melodrama falsifies life? This objection is based, of course, on another curious and revelatory presupposition: that it is the business of drama, and art generally, to deal "honestly" with life—to present it to us accurately. Here is where naturalism rears its ugly head once more, that odd Zolaesque disease that has spread like acne over the body dramatic for the past hundred years—and whose spread is not yet checked. Ravaged by this spiritual pink-eye, though, we seem to have lost sight of the fact that art, by its very etymology, never has been in any way concerned with this sort of technological verisimilitude. Art, if it involves anything, surely involves selection, arrangement, meaningful distortions and relocations of the data of experience, and the doctrine which would convict an art-form of falsifying or distorting "reality" would lead inevitably to an appreciation of a page of statistics or an accurate newspaper report (if I may be forgiven a contradiction in terms) as the highest art. Does the melodramatist "simplify" his characters and select certain character traits to emphasize? Of course he does. So does Ben Jonson. So does Molière. So does Shaw. So did the *commedia dell'arte*. With few exceptions, what playwright doesn't? Does he "arrange" the elements in his plot with an eye to theatrical effect? Naturally. Doesn't Sophocles? Or Shakespeare? Since when is it opprobrious to try to write a play that will be effective in the theatre? Would it not be even more questionable to try to write a play that would be *in*effective in the theatre? Clearly this line of thinking leads to an appreciation of an instruction manual on how to change a typewriter ribbon as the highest form of art (it's "real" and "true to life"), and—most importantly—it simply banishes imagination. And that, I submit, is what modern popular art has largely become: art without imagination, which is a little like life without love—the only form, I suppose, that a people numbed by fact and desensitized by quantity can adequately respond to.

This situation, if true, is melancholy, but it still does not mean that we, as defenders of the dramatic faith (and imagination), have merely to accede to it. I suggest that there is a positive therapeutic value in attempting to restore "melodrama" to respectability, and above all in trying to see that what are generally considered its weakest points are actually its strongest and most distinctive.

Before we can go very far in an examination of the nature of melodrama, though, it might be well to pause a moment and consider the over-all nature of drama and theatre. "Everything is what it is and not another thing," said Bishop Butler, in the eighteenth century—in one of those breathtakingly bare statements which seem almost childishly simple, like so many of Aristotle's precepts, but which, on closer examination, prove to contain a most profound and subtle truth. (I think particularly of Aristotle's observation that a play should have a beginning, a middle, and an end.) All right. What *is* a dramatic representation, a play as performed in the theatre? What distinguishes it from other forms of art? It employs language? All literature does. It is a narrative form? So is the novel, the short story, sometimes even the poem. It employs physical movement? So does ballet. The possible list of comparisons is almost endless, and mostly, I'm afraid, pretty fruitless.

Ultimately, there are, I believe, only two or three really distinguishing features which define a performed play:

(1) It is an event which occurs both in space (like a picture or a statue) and in time (like a poem or a symphony). Lessing has said about all there is to say about this in his *Laokoon;* the only point I want to make about it for the moment is that the performed drama is distinguished by a kind of *plenitude* which no other art form possesses. Its appeal is rich, varied, and immediate.

(2) The tense of drama is the perpetual present. A play is something which happens—right here and now—with all the illusion of unmediated spontaneity. It is, in the philosophical sense of the word, an accident rather than an essence, and all our experience shows us, I believe, that while we pay lip service to essence, we live by—and are interested in—accidents. See the front page of tonight's newspaper. Who can deny that part of the appeal of the theatre—subconscious, perhaps—is the awareness that at any moment you, as a member of the audience, may see a literal accident: an actor may blow his lines, a piece of scenery may fall. For all the rehearsals and preparations, which are attempts to bring the riotous accidentalism of the universe under man's rational control, the play is happening every time for the first time, and its future is unknown. Why else do we watch the baseball game by television, or the high-wire act at the circus? Isn't it true that somewhere in all of us there lurks the half-hidden hope that the aerialist may make a misstep, the star outfielder may drop a fly ball? And when they do, it's *exciting* (a word I would like now to smuggle into this

discussion). For the real excitement of theatre lies in this accidental immediacy; it is like life in that the future is perpetually unknown, despite all our efforts to shape it. A certain actor in Act Two of a certain play may forget his lines or fall down, but no one knows—least of all, the actor himself!—whether he will or not until the precise second when the words emerge from his mouth. For all the artificial arrangements of script and rehearsal, the living performance is always a universe of perpetual potentiality. A realm, in other words, of excitement.

(3) The material of the theatre is the human form. (I do not overlook the values of light and scenic background; I simply assume that they are merely that—background and context for the human actor. In other words, I assume that if the curtain rose and allowed us to gaze for two hours on a set, we would not consider this a drama.) The material of the painter is paint and canvas; of the sculptor, plaster and stone; of the composer, sound; of the poet, words. But all these—with the exception of sound—are human artifacts, they are impersonal, and can be brought under some fairly consistent sort of human control. But the human being, as material to work with, is—I need scarcely tell any director—a highly volatile and uncontrollable chemical element. Again, we have the element of excitement, of unpredictability, the constant contrast between the infinite variety and malleability of the human organism and the rigid inflexibility of the forms which surround him. (Bergson, in his famous theory of laughter, had hold, I suspect, of an even larger idea.) The human form—flesh and blood—is the very material of the theatre art. It's an interesting thought. Pope said: "The proper study of mankind is man," but he might just as well have amended it to: "The *only possible* study of mankind is man." For is it not true that the one preeminently fascinating subject for us is ourselves—that, indeed, we are properly speaking not even capable of dealing with anything else? Why else do we anthropomorphize our gods and humanize our animals? We may,

to be sure, study the cellular structure of leaves or the motions of the stars, but do we really understand the leafness of leaves and the starness of stars, or do we just read ourselves and our human attitudes into them?

Now, with these elements of the unique nature of theatre in mind, let me shift the focus from the stage to the auditorium and inquire what it is that draws us, as audience, to a theatrical representation. The excitement, the fascination with the human, to be sure—but what does all this add up to? What is this peculiar and potent magic which can draw people to sit jammed together in a large room watching other people in a smaller room move through rituals of imitative action? Is it not, in the final analysis, the same magnetic force that draws people to the cathedral, the football stadium, the beer tavern—in short, any place where life is expressing itself in a more vivid and concentrated form than it does in the ordinary daily round of dull routine?

In other words, what I am working toward here is a fairly simple formula: We go to the theatre (as we do to the church, the athletic arena, the social center) to be made more aware of our aliveness. Whether consciously or not, this, I suspect, is the great drive of all human beings: To express Life. (In this we are like Camus's Caligula, who, bloody, beaten, dying, cries out, in the last line of the play: "I'm still alive!") Is this not the whole rhythm of human existence? Every day, every minute we are dying, and somehow we feel that we want to have made full use of the vital potentiality that was given us at the start instead of just letting it run through our fingers like water, as is the case, for example, with Chekhov's people. Most of us feel much of the time, I suspect, like Chekhov people: We are living at only about 10 per cent of our capacities at best, and the dead hand of routine and boredom lays itself upon the organic vitality of our days, so that we soon find ourselves looking back over a wasteland of missed chances, empty hours, neglected opportunities. But up there on the stage all is different.

There, everything matters; every moment is significant; nothing is wasted; there, life *really* burns with a hard gemlike flame— as it so rarely does on the other side of the footlights.

And—to return deviously and by indirection to my starting point—that everything matters is true above all of the melodramatic stage. There the central actors—Medea, Richard III, Vindice, Cyrano, Dick Dudgeon—are actors in every sense of the word: people who act, who do things, and also people who conceive of themselves consistently in histrionic terms, who stand back, as it were, observing and enjoying their own performances. Their doing so, incidentally, is theatricalism with a vengeance—for here the theatre becomes not merely an analogue of life, but simultaneously a kind of lens through which to see life. But, above all, it is the wonderful, frank, quite self-conscious *vitality* of these melodramatic heroes that delights us and that gives us a vicarious stimulation—for here surely are people living at about 101 per cent of their vital capacity at any given moment, people living every minute of their lives at, in Gerard Manley Hopkins' fine phrase, "the highest pitch of stress."

And if this is the highest and truest function of theatre—indeed, of all art and of religion, as well—to put us in contact with some sort of electrical current of vitality, to recharge our spiritual batteries, to make us—in the fullest sense of the word— more meaningfully alive, then is not melodrama, in which stimulation and vitality and excitement are everything, is it not perhaps the highest, rather than the most contemptible, of dramatic forms?

A heretical notion, to be sure. But all the more reason for examining it. I suppose one of the first heretics was the first man who ate an oyster.

So, having pushed my theory from a tentative defense of melodrama to a flagrant claim for it as the highest form of drama—like a good melodramatist, I believe in nothing if not in excess—let me try now to push it even further.

Earlier, you will recall, I rejected hierarchies. Now, I am constructing one of my own. I suppose it makes a difference whether you feel you are on the defensive or are carrying the fight into the enemy camp. In any case, swollen with *hubris* as I am, indulge me for a minute and let me move on to an aggressive defense—or, at least, a tentative defense—of melodrama as the highest form of dramatic art. Or, let's say, to put it a bit more precisely, the *purest* form. (A good melodramatist should likewise be able to display some fancy footwork from time to time in shifting his terms.)

Let me recall you to the auditorium once more and seat you out there in the fourth row, center section. We have talked about the rewards which theatre offers, the anticipatory excitement you may legitimately feel as the house lights dim and the curtain rises. But what of the other side of the coin? What are some of the drawbacks and problems which peculiarly distinguish theatre? You know some of them as well as I do. There are always those first few moments of foot shuffling, seat banging and program rattling in the auditorium, and there are always those members of the audience who, as soon as the curtain goes up, begin, in the words of a famous critic, "to strum their catarrhs." What is the result of all this? That generally we miss the first few—often vital—moments of exposition. (With the result that the experienced playwright usually gives his exposition, not once, but twice. It makes for clumsy literature, but for sound theatre—and thereby hangs a tale.)

Actually, the theatregoer out front is in one of the most difficult and impractical positions conceivable for a viewer or auditor of the arts. For one thing, he is fixed; he cannot move his position in relation to the performance. For another, he must catch it all on the fly, as it were. If he misses a line or a nuance, he cannot go back and retrieve it; it is lost forever. If he wants to re-examine a passage, he cannot turn back the page and re-read it. I have spoken earlier of the richness of theatre, but that same richness and plenitude can also be a drawback. It can be—and often is—a source of confusion and muddle. Too much is going on in any play at almost any time—too many simultaneous appeals to the ear and to the eye—for the audience to give the play the same kind of intense and almost rapt attention they can give a painting or a poem or a piece of music. Viewing a painting in the stillness and relative solitude of an art gallery is quite a different matter from plunging into the noisy hurly-burly of a theatre. The viewer can move about and view the painting from various angles, as he pleases; his ear is not meanwhile being distracted by music or dialogue; and he can experience the art work at his own pace, in as leisurely a fashion as he desires. *He* sets the rhythm of his perception—the work of art does not impose it upon him. The same thing is true of the man sitting quietly in his library reading a poem or a novel or a play; he can give the work his undivided attention, free of all external distractions. (I am imagining, I confess, a rather idyllic man, completely free of wife, children, dogs, television sets, neighbors, etc., etc. But, after all, this whole thing is pretty much an exercise in pure speculation.) Even the listener in the concert hall, while he suffers some of the limitations imposed upon the theatregoer, is asked to pay attention only with his ears, not his eyes. He may—many concertgoers do, I discover—actually close his eyes while listening, the better to avoid visual distraction and concentrate with the one sense that is being appealed to. But the poor theatregoer cannot close his eyes—nor his ears. All his senses must be brought into simultaneous operation; all are being appealed to—either directly or vicariously—and his attention becomes accordingly diffused.

Hence the frequent charge, especially by literary people, that the theatre is a coarse form. It is, of course—that is its nature—and almost any play will read rather barely and awkwardly, considered in purely literary terms, alongside almost any novel or lyric poem. But of course a play is not just a literary piece, a sort of chamber work designed only to be read; it is designed to be performed, under aesthetically adverse conditions—and thus the rather heavy-handed and awkward "plants" and repetitions in even the best of stage scripts, as compared to the much greater subtlety and complexity of the novel or the poem. But the play has its compensations, as we have already mentioned, in the tremendous immediacy and vividness of its physical impact, which no novel or poem can even approximate.

And, again, I would like to pick up this point—the grossness, the physical immediacy of the stage—and, applying it to melodrama, try to suggest that melodrama presents this better than any other dramatic form, and that this is to be seen, not as a shameful weakness, but as a positive virtue.

The theatre is a physical place. The stage is a place of objects—bodies, planes, solids, lines, colors, lights, etc. It is through these means that it expresses itself. Going to the theatre is not merely an intellectual or an abstractly aesthetic experience; it is above all a sensory experience.

This sensory quality means that the initial impact of a play —again, I would argue, of any work of art—is emotional, rather than intellectual. Or, if you find yourself suspicious of the intellectual-emotional dichotomy, as I do, let's try to sharpen the terminology once more by saying that the initial impact of a dramatic work in the theatre is visceral rather than cerebral. Pure perception precedes rationalization. And—granted that pure perception *without* rationalization amounts to nothing more than a kind of glandular reaction—it is also true that, without a powerful and stimulating initiating sense impression, the rationalizing mind has quite literally nothing to rationalize about. First things first, and "one world at a time, Waldo," as the dying Thoreau said.

And, I would maintain, the peculiar nature of theatre considered as an art form is its ability to present us with these naked moments of pure perception—distorted, heightened, vivified so as to carry outward into the dark neutrality of the auditorium and assault our senses as directly as the odor of a rose or a slap in the face. The intellectualization of the experience—the inevitable second step if the experience is to be meaningful instead of random—comes later. In the auditorium, we don't worry about whether or not Oedipus has an Oedipus complex; we are confronted with a man caught in the meshes of a dilemma. (In fact, is it not fair to say that every really good play that has ever been written can be boiled down to this simple formula: Man in a dilemma? Which is, in itself, the whole myth of human existence.)

"Everything is what it is and not another thing." Theatre is an art form whose materials—flesh and blood—and whose means—public mimetic representation—endow it peculiarly with the power to present us with moments of direct, pure perception. Ergo, that theatrical form which presents them best can be labeled the "best"—i.e., the purest—theatrical form, in that it is the most conformable to the laws of its being. It is not, like the theatre of naturalism, the theatre trying to be the novel, or, like much so-called "poetic" drama, the theatre aspiring to the condition of lyric poetry. It is the Theatre Theatrical, *das Ding an sich.*

And theatre at its most truly theatrical is melodrama.

Now, please note that I am not holding up for approbation a theatre of sheer mindless excitement and Grand Guignol sensation. I cling firmly to my demand for the intellectual nature of theatre—in fact, I'm afraid I must say that I find the distinguishing mark of modern theatre, modern American theatre, particularly, is an extraordinary lack of real intellectual rigor, as compared to the fields of the novel or of lyric poetry. At times, the flabbiness of Broadway's "thinking" is almost beyond belief. But I do say that there is always and inevitably a time lag between perception and conceptualization, that this is true above all of an art of such immediacy as theatre, and that theatre ignores this basic law of its being at its own dire peril.

Is it not noteworthy that, in looking back over the history of the drama for the last seventy-five to a hundred years—the Realists' reign of terror—we see an art form consistently and coyly trying to pretend to be something other than itself? What is the purpose of all these correctly furnished drawing rooms and dining rooms and kitchens, with *real* furniture and *real* rugs and sometimes even, wonderful to relate, *real* water coming out of *real* taps? What is the purpose of all this hugger-mugger except to pretend that theatre is not actually theatre at all, but what we are pleased to call "real life"? In other words, we are in on the deliberate detheatricalization of the theatre, the emasculation of an art form, performed by its own high priests.

The modern trend toward greater "theatricality" is, I think, an inevitable and long-delayed (and, I might add, healthy) reaction to this curious condition, and we find it everywhere we look today—in Brecht, in the absurdists, in Thornton Wilder, in Duerrenmatt and Frisch, in such very new young Americans as Jack Gelber and Edward Albee, in such groups as the Living Theatre and the Actors' Workshop. No art form can defy the very laws of its own being and go on living for very long; in fact, seventy-five years in a moribund state (a marvelous title, come to think of it, for a history of American drama)—this is a long time, even for an Edgar Allan Poe hero. It is high time, in every sense of the word, to pry open the coffin and release the barely living corpse.

You may have noticed that I have smuggled into the discussion a set of definitions and a frame of reference that are somewhat different from those we started with, and that I have now maneuvered melodrama into a corner and rendered it indistinguishable from "Theatre," with a capital "T."

But I announced at the outset that I proposed to redefine "melodrama," and I feel no sense of chicanery in having sneaked up on it in this fashion. Can one equate "melodramatic" with "theatrical"? I think so—and to the greater glory of both words. The whole mainstream of the drama, from Thespis to Arthur Kopit, has been, if you will, melodramatic rather than tragic or comic—and it's about time that we got over our curiously Victorian sense of shame in this matter.

The Greeks, with their chanting and dancing choruses and declaiming masked figures, were not afraid to be "theatrical" and —let's face it—"melodramatic." Nor were the *commedia dell'arte* performers. Nor were Shakespeare and his contemporaries. Nor Molière and his troupe. It is only somewhere along about the eighteenth or nineteenth centuries that the bourgeois sensibility begins to anesthetize the histrionic sensibility, and dramatists and actors begin to feel ashamed of behaving excessively and begin to lose sight of the fact that excess—the "fine excess" of Keats's fine phrase—is not only the nature of their being but the only reason for their existence. A good play should be a fever chart of life, and not a fever chart which has flattened out into a straight line, devoid of monstrous and drastic peaks and valleys, for such a one has—by definition—ceased to be a fever chart. It is simply a report of a normal—and therefore uninteresting—condition.

The function of the drama—of all art—is surely to put us in contact with the abnormal, the unusual, the extraordinary, perhaps to exhort us to aspire toward these peaks of unusualness ourselves, at least to make us more sensitive toward their occasional irruption into the dull and featureless normality of our own daily existence. And to condemn a playwright for writing melodramatically seems to me tantamount to criticizing a painter for using a bit too much color or a composer for writing a shade too melodically. Just as color and sound are the materials of the painter and the composer, so action is the material of the playwright—and to condemn him for using the materials most appropriate to his form is a curious line of criticism, to say the least.

The time, I think, is preeminently ripe for a rallying cry: "Melodramatists of the world, unite! You have nothing to lose but your inhibitions." The theatre, from its Dionysian beginnings, has never been a place of inhibitions—which were, after all, inventions of fairly modern times.

The time is ripe for a truly and greatly melodramatic drama, a drama which will assault us with visions of Man Alive in a Universe of Danger—again, a kind of formula-phrase which suggests the very archetype of Drama. Above all, though, Man Alive—alive and in action, and with Death always just offstage, waiting in the wings.

And this is melodrama. Simply the protoplasmic stuff of which great art has always been made. It is a dirty word only when its means and purposes become directed toward cheap or sentimental ends—as can be done with any art form. But, in the hands of the great melodramatists, like Euripides or Shakespeare, it needs no defense—from me or from anyone. It speaks for itself, powerfully, vividly, conclusively, with the energies of art, and tells us, as all great art does, about ultimate things.

[*Lecture, Carnegie Institute of*
Technology, May, 1962]

PART FIVE

THE CRITICISM OF DRAMA

RONALD S. CRANE

THE VARIETIES OF DRAMATIC CRITICISM

NORTHROP FRYE

SPECIFIC FORMS OF DRAMA

The Varieties of
Dramatic Criticism

R. S. CRANE

There is a sentence in Arthur Mizener's preface to Volume 1 of
the *Carleton Drama Bulletin* which may serve to point the direction of my remarks this evening. It is our ambition, he says,
"to pull together the drama as a thing alive on the stage and
the drama as a thing read, contemplated, and discussed"—in
other words, to conjoin drama in the concrete, as presented to
our eyes, ears, and emotions by producers and actors, with
drama in the abstract, as brought to our minds and through the
concepts and reasonings of dramatic critics. The chief concern
of Mr. Mizener was properly with the kinds of plays that
would best promote union of the living stage and the stage as
formulated art. My concern, on the other hand, will be with the
second element in the combination: namely, with the conditions under which, in such a program, the reading and study of
dramatic criticism may help to advance rather than to hinder
the realization of its double aim.

For it is surely better to remain innocent of dramatic criticism altogether than to read even a great deal of it in the expectation that it will automatically make us more competent

189

judges of the plays we see. The effect, indeed, may be just the
reverse of that. There is always a temptation, when we come
upon an especially clear-cut and persuasively argued statement
of doctrine about the drama, to attach ourselves to it in a kind
of exclusive faith, and so close our minds for the time being at
least, to those characteristics and values in plays for which
our favorite theory makes no provision, in the manner so abundantly illustrated in the history of Shakespearean criticism from
Thomas Rymer and Voltaire to William Archer and Wilson
Knight. And the results are little better when as an alternative
to such discipleship, we try to eke out a critical education in
the drama by picking and choosing among pieces of the various theories we meet in our reading: we are able, in that case,
to say more things about any play, but at the cost of not knowing very clearly why we say them.

What is lacking in both of these uses of dramatic criticism is
a properly critical view of that criticism itself. It is the business
of critics of the drama to make propositions about plays or
about the art of which plays are products, and it is our business, as students of the drama, to utilize these propositions to
the end of improving our capacity for contemplating and discussing the plays we happen to read or see. But we cannot do
this intelligently or fruitfully if we are content to concentrate,
in our reading, merely upon what is explicitly said about this
or that topic. For the propositions of critics, or at least of those
most likely to repay our study, are never either fully intelligible or completely verifiable in themselves as independent
judgments or statements of doctrine. They are not propositions
simply but reasoned propositions, and as reasoned propositions
they derive their meaning and validity not only from their relations to the objective dramatic things they refer to, but, more
immediately, from their place in a network of other propositions,
not all of them expressed, which serve both to fix their terms
and to provide a warrant for their assertion. If we are really to
profit, therefore, from our study of critical writings about the

drama, we must form the habit of reading them with a view not merely to what they say about a certain subject but to why they say this, whatever it may be, rather than something else. We must consider, that is, not only the doctrines and judgments of critics but the basic reasons, or as Dryden puts it in his essay on tragedy, the "grounds of criticism," upon which these rest.

Why is it, for instance, that although no important critics in the Seventeenth Century ever thought of making a sharp separation between poetry and drama, such a separation is to be met with on all sides in the criticism of our time? Or why is it that Aristotle can make plot "the first principle and as it were the soul" of tragedy, with character second, whereas, for William Archer, the "noblest part" of drama—that which makes it live—is not action but character? The history of dramatic criticism is full of such conflicts of doctrine, which can never be satisfactorily resolved without taking into account something more fundamental to the positions of the various critics than appears on the surface of their statements or than can be discovered by a direct appeal to facts or to changing fashions in taste.

That something may be called the necessity of the critic's principles. It is the more or less impersonal compulsion, with respect to what a critic is able to say, or will find it appropriate and relevant to say, on any question, which comes from the fact that he has chosen, however undeliberately, to set up his problems in terms of one rather than any other of the many distinct aspects or relationships in which drama may be viewed, and to solve them by one rather than any other of the several possible methods of critical inquiry. For what has been said by Étienne Gilson of philosophers is no less true of dramatic critics: they "are free to lay down their own sets of principles, but once this is done, they can no longer think as they wish—they think as they can." We ought therefore to examine into the nature and variety of the compulsions by which dramatic critics are led to say the kinds of things they do and not to say the kinds of things which other critics say who are ostensibly discussing the same subjects, but under the compulsion of different principles. Only by doing this, I believe, can we make of the dramatic criticism of the past and present something more than a collection of arbitrary dogmas or statements of personal opinion and put ourselves in a position to utilize it sensibly toward the improvement of our powers of judgment. It is all a matter of grasping the basic reasons of what we read; and I have thought that I could best illustrate concretely what that means by taking as the subject of this lecture the major varieties of dramatic criticism which have been developed, between the Greeks and ourselves, as a result of the choice by different critics of different sets of compulsive first principles.

I

It will make a very great difference, in the first place, if you are a critic of the drama, whether you assume, on the one hand, that the drama can be adequately discussed in terms of principles peculiar to the drama itself, as a distinctive form of art, or hold, on the other hand, that the truth about the drama must be deduced from the truth about something else, to which the drama is related as a part or a means. Of these two fundamentally different ways of considering the drama, the great early representative of the first was Aristotle, of the second Plato; and the two modes of discussion have persisted as more or less distinct traditions, though often borrowing elements from one another, throughout the subsequent history of dramatic criticism.

The criticism in the "Platonic" tradition, in spite of the great variety of forms which it has taken and the many conflicting views of the drama to which it has given currency, can be identified by one common characteristic. It is essentially a criticism that looks upon the drama as an activity or function in the context of other human activities or functions, and hence is governed by principles that signify or point to some larger good than that of the drama itself which the drama ought to serve if it is to become what it can be or even to be tolerated in society. The larger good may be so conceived that the activities of dramatists in bringing actors on the stage who mimic many characters, good and bad, and excite the passions of audiences are bound to seem a perpetual threat to its realization. This is of course the line taken by Plato himself: with pretty completely negative results in *The Republic,* where the final good, in the light of which drama is condemned, is that of the ideally just state ruled by philosopher-kings; more moderately in *The Laws,* where the drama is allowed a place in the second-best state depicted in that work, but under heavy censorship. The extreme negativism of *The Republic* has its modern counterpart in the Puritan attacks on the stage, such as Sidney undertook to answer in his *Apology for Poetry,* while the somewhat more tolerant position of *The Laws* has descended to us both in the numerous efforts of moralists, like Jeremy Collier and Rousseau, to expose the ethical imperfections and dangers of the existing stage and to direct it to more innocent ends, and in the attempts of politicians, like the present rulers of Russia, to assimilate the drama, in its themes and techniques, to the governing apparatus of the regime.

But there is nothing in the "Platonic" approach as such that prevents its being turned to more positive uses in the criticism of the drama. All that you need for this purpose is a conviction that the drama as it is, collectively, is imperfect, and a set of ideas, embodying some conception of the good of society or of human conduct or knowledge or of art in relation to these, by means of which you can argue to what the drama at its best ought to be. This is so natural a pattern of argument, indeed, that one is embarrassed to know which illustrations of it to select out of the many that come to mind. Here is Bernard Shaw, writing of that high conception of the uses of the theater which had guided him as a weekly critic of plays for the *Saturday Review.* "Only the ablest critics," he says, "believe that the theater is really important: in my time none of them would claim for it, as I claimed for it, that it is as important as the Church was in the

Middle Ages and much more than the Church was in London in the years under review." Hence the Church, he goes on, "is giving way to that older and greater Church to which I belong: the Church where the oftener you laugh the better, because laughter only can destroy evil without malice, and affirm good fellowship without mawkishness." And this would be a very good thing "if the theatre took itself seriously as a factory of thought, a prompter of conscience, an elucidator of social conduct, an armory against despair and dullness, and a temple of the Ascent of Man. I took it seriously in that way, and preached about it instead of merely chronicling its news and alternately petting and snubbing it as a licentious but privileged form of public entertainment." And here is T. S. Eliot, concluding a lecture on how he has attempted in his own plays to bring poetry back into the drama with an eloquent suggestion of an ideal end to be served by poetic drama beyond anything he has been able to achieve: "I should not like to close . . . without attempting to set before myself and, if I can, before you, though only in dim outline, the ideal towards which it seems to me that poetic drama should strive. It is an attainable ideal: and that is why it interests me, for it provides an incentive towards further experiment and exploration, beyond any goal which there is prospect of attaining. It is a function of all art to give us some perception of an order in life, by imposing order upon it. . . . To go as far in this direction as it is possible to go, without losing that contact with the ordinary everyday world with which the drama must come to terms, seems to me the proper aim of dramatic poetry. For it is ultimately the function of art, in imposing a credible order upon ordinary reality, and thereby eliciting some perception of an order *in* reality, to bring us to a condition of serenity, stillness, and reconciliation; and then leave us, as Virgil left Dante, to proceed toward a region where that guide can avail us no further." And here is Christopher Fry, arguing to the superiority of "the theater of poetry" over "the theater of prose" from a distinction between two orders of perception: a lower order in which human existence is taken for granted and a higher order in which human existence is an incredible and fantastic surprise. The first is the sphere of the ordinary prose drama, and of that we have perhaps had enough. But the language "in which man explores his own amazement" is poetry, and a shift to the poetic theater could "help us to see ourselves and the world freshly, as though we had just rounded the corner into life. . . . This change of viewpoint would be no escapism or fantasy. Nothing could be so wildly, perilously, incomprehensibly fantastic as reality itself, and we may as well dare to look at it, and like it."

I will mention one more contemporary example of this approach. It is Francis Fergusson's *The Idea of a Theater,* the very title of which betrays its intellectual origins. The main intention of the book is to exhibit the drama as it is, in its best forms, today, in the light of "the perennial idea" of a drama devoted to the "imitation" of human life and action in the most comprehensive sense. A theater "formed at the center of the culture of its time, and at the center of the life and awareness of the community," "focusing all the available insights—historical, ethical, religious—upon 'two boards and a passion.'" Mr. Fergusson's "idea of a theater" is thus a kind of Platonic paradigm, which has, however, come close to realization in two dramatists of the past, Sophocles and Shakespeare, and is embodied most usefully for us, outside the drama, in *The Divine Comedy,* which is "the very pattern of the imitation of action—mirroring the greatest height and depth of human experience, as Eliot says— in the most comprehensive scene-of-human-life to be found in our tradition." Needless to say, we have no such theater now, nor has one existed since Shakespeare: the whole modern age has been one of limited realizations and "partial perspectives," and it is hard to see how it can be otherwise in the future. "But we need the 'Idea of a Theater,'" Mr. Fergusson says, "both to understand the masterpieces of drama at its best, and to get our bearings in our own time."

II

By contrast with the approach represented in these writers, we can identify the dramatic criticism in the "Aristotelian" tradition, not only by its relative indifference to the exalted views and eloquent language of the "Platonic" critics, but, more significantly, by its insistence on finding principles that are dictated in some sense by the peculiar nature of the drama as an art or craft. It is essentially a criticism of forms and techniques, and it seeks to establish criteria for these by considering not so much the social or moral functions of drama as the necessities and possibilities determined for the dramatic artist by such things as the character of his medium, the nature of his subjects, the psychology of his audiences, or the standards set by earlier practitioners of his art. In the long history of this criticism from Aristotle to the present day, we can distinguish two principal phases, which differ rather clearly from one another according to which of two aspects of the drama is taken as the central object of attention. The distinction is suggested by Aristotle himself in Chapter 3 of the *Poetics,* where, after summarizing the three respects in which poetic "imitations" may differ—namely, in their means, in their objects, and in their manner—he goes on to remark that "as an imitator Sophocles will be on one side (i.e., with respect to the quality of the objects imitated) akin to Homer, both portraying good men; and on another (i.e., with respect to the manner of imitating) to Aristophanes, since both present their personages as acting and doing. This in fact, according to some, is the reason for plays being called dramas, because in a play the personages act the story." It is possible, in other words, to discuss the art of drama either from the point of view of the particular poetic forms, such as tragedy and comedy, which it embodies dramatically or from the point of view of its general character as dramatic representation and the requirements and opportunities which this defines for the playwright regardless of his more specific formal aims. The history of dramatic criticism in this tradition is in large part, as

I shall try to show, a history of the eventual triumph, which has never become quite complete, of the second of these two varieties of consideration over the first.

There can be no question as to which was primary for Aristotle himself. We cannot read the *Poetics,* it is true, without becoming convinced of his strong interest in the theater and his great respect for the drama as a mode of literary art. Out of the twenty-six chapters of the treatise as it has come down to us, seventeen are devoted to tragedy and only two to epic, and the treatise ends with an argument for the superiority of the dramatic method of representation characteristic of tragedy over the narrative method characteristic of epic. The culminating stage, moreover, in the history of poetry outlined in Chapters 4 and 5, is the emergence of drama, in its two extreme forms of tragedy and comedy, out of the epic; and here and elsewhere the great praise of Homer is that he knew how to give a "dramatic" quality to his imitations of both serious and comic actions by keeping himself out of sight as far as possible and letting his characters act and speak his story. It is little wonder that the *Poetics* has always been hailed as the great classic of dramatic criticism in our tradition.

And yet, in a very significant sense, it is this only incidentally. The nature of dramatic representation is a principle in the argument, but a secondary one. Inferences can indeed be drawn from it, as when Aristotle distinguishes between the shorter actions proper to plays and the longer actions possible in epic, or as when he discusses the difficulty of making the marvelous seem credible on the stage. But when we look at the context of these remarks, we see that they belong to an inquiry in which tragedy and comedy are being considered primarily, not as kinds of drama but as forms of imitative poetry, the notion of drama, in the sense of dramatic manner, being a differentia merely, though an important one, rather than the controlling genus of the discussion.

Nor could it well be otherwise, given the special subject matter and aims of poetic science as Aristotle conceived them. For the task of poetic science, in the view he took of it, is to inquire into the art, in the sense of the habits of correct artistic reasoning, which poets must possess (along, of course, with poetic genius) if they are to make poems that have a maximum of excellence in their respective kinds. The science must start, therefore, by distinguishing the various species of poetry that now exist, since these obviously present to the poet quite different problems of artistic construction. It must attempt, moreover, to formulate the peculiar nature of each kind in its concrete wholeness, as it appears in completed individual poems, since without a clear intuition of the whole to be constructed in any given case the poet would be unable to reason to what he ought to do in any of its parts, if the poem is to be beautiful. The kinds of poems Aristotle proposes to deal with are those—including tragedy, epic, and comedy—which happen, as he says, to be "imitations," that is to say, artistic productions using speech as their medium which achieve their effects by bringing before us interesting or moving semblances of human actions, characters, and passions. Hence it is primarily as "imitations" that they must be considered; and the wholeness of any of them will involve the combination of four things: the moral quality of the action imitated (as serious or ludicrous, for example), the specific character of the means used (as merely verse or verse with music), the manner of the imitation (as dramatic, narrative, or mixed), and the peculiar emotional "working or power" to which everything is directed in a good poem. The first principles of poetics, accordingly, will be definitions of poetic forms or species in which all four of these variables are specified in proper correlation, with the object of imitation primary, as in the definition of tragedy in Chapter 6. Nothing short of this will serve the practical needs of poetics in Aristotle's meaning of the term, inasmuch as the wholes which any poet seeks to construct can be brought into successful existence only if he has acquired the total art of using a certain means and a certain manner of imitating to body forth a certain object in such a way as to yield a certain definite emotional effect. Hence it is that the generic art of drama is subordinated in Aristotle, as merely one kind of poetic manner, to the specific arts of making tragedies or comedies. For no dramatist ever writes drama merely, but always tragedy or comedy or something else of a similarly formal sort, with respect to which mastery of dramatic manner is only one condition of artistic excellence in subordination to the more distinctively poetic mastery required by the peculiar natures of the objects to be represented and of the emotional effects to be achieved.

Poetry and the forms of poetry are thus the primary considerations in Aristotle's dealings with the drama. The same thing, however, can be said of a good many later critics, and if we are to grasp what is special in the approach to dramatic criticism exemplified in the *Poetics*, we must take note of two further points, the first of which has to do with Aristotle's conception of poetry and the second with his conception of poetic forms.

Now in the most distinctive sense, for Aristotle, poetry is the art of constructing wholes of which the matter is language, used either simply or as embellished with meter and music, and the organizing form the pattern of some kind of human action or passion such as can be made credible and emotionally effective for us in the words and rhythms of the completed work. The poet must therefore be one skilled in language and meter, and also, if he writes plays, in the techniques of the dramatic manner; but these are only necessary conditions: he becomes a poet, essentially, by reason of his ability to imitate, that is, to construct wholes in which everything that he does with his words and rhythms, and with his techniques of representation, is made to contribute to the beauty and peculiar "power" of the represented action. Hence poetry, for Aristotle, is not what it has commonly been for later critics. It is not the art or faculty of writing verse as distinct from the art or faculty of writing prose, nor is it a certain quality of language or thought or sensibility which ought to be present, but is not always, in writings conventionally called poems. Poetry is a character, rather, that belongs to all imitations in words—and to these as wholes—by virtue simply of the fact that they are imitations. And this means that the great modern problem, which I shall touch upon later, of the relations between "drama" and "poetry" does not exist for him. The drama, in the sense of the forms of tragedy and comedy (or whatever other forms employ a dramatic manner), *is* poetry, and the makers of such works *are poets,* by definition; the only question we can sensibly ask is how good, in its kind, and irrespective of the verbal medium that happens to be used, any given dramatic work is.

The view which Aristotle took of the nature of poetic, and hence of dramatic, forms is clearly discernible in his analysis of tragedy, and here again he stands in sharp contrast with the majority of later critics who have concerned themselves with this question. The analysis begins, as we all know, with the definition of a class of poetic works, called "tragedy," the essential nature of which, as induced from an inspection of existing plays, is the imitation in embellished language of a serious action (that is, an action in which good men are confronted with issues of life-and-death import) which is complete and of a certain extent; the imitation being effected dramatically rather than narratively, and so conducted that its peculiar "power" is the bringing about, through incidents arousing pity and fear for the protagonist, of a catharsis or resolution of these and the other painful emotions excited by the plot. And this definition is followed by an elaborate deduction of its consequences for the ways in which the constituent parts of such a work—especially its plot in the two aspects of plot and tragic plot, its rendering of character, its thought, and its diction—ought to be conceived and handled if the work is to embody the tragic form with a maximum of poetic beauty and emotional power. Now what I should especially like to emphasize here is the character of the critical reasoning underlying this whole procedure. We can imagine Aristotle saying to himself something like this: "There does now actually exist in our theaters, as a result of the successive efforts of many earlier poets, trying to improve on what their predecessors had discovered, a class of productions called tragedies, which appear, when I examine them analytically, to be imitations of complete and extended serious actions, in embellished language, that gain their effects through dialogue and acting; and I observe further that the most powerful and most prized of these are so constructed as to excite and resolve emotions which I would identify roughly as pity and fear. I will concentrate, therefore, on this form and try to make evident the artistic reasoning which the best achievement of it must presuppose, and in doing this I will not consider whether or not tragedy is now fully developed in all its possible species, but simply what, if future poets should want to write works of the special existing kind I have isolated, are the essential causes of success and failure, artistically speaking, in such an effort." Tragedy, in short—and the same thing holds true of comedy—is for Aristotle merely a particular species of literary art that exists and has the characteristics he assigns to it solely because poets have happened to write dramatic works possessing these characteristics. It does, indeed, have a natural basis, both in the instinctive delight which all men take in imitation and in the capacity of men to respond emotionally in certain ways to the crimes and sufferings of other men. But it is not in itself a natural form, or the embodiment of a natural form, in any sense that requires us, in judging of particular tragedies, to refer for our criteria to some Platonic "idea" of tragedy or to some doctrine as to what is and is not essentially "tragic" in life.

III

I said that there is a sharp contrast between Aristotle's conception of the forms of drama and the conceptions of these forms to be found in most of the later criticism of the drama which

has given a primary place to distinctions of dramatic form.
The decisive cause of the change was undoubtedly the disap-
pearance of Aristotle's inductive method of definition. Had this
been revived in the Renaissance along with the doctrines about
tragedy and comedy it was used to state, the consequence might
well have the recognition and analysis, in a scientific undog-
matic spirit, of many possible forms of serious drama besides the
one species of tragedy Aristotle talks about, and the development, similarly, of a poetics of comedy and the intermediate
forms of drama more nearly adequate to modern achievements
in these forms than anything we now have. But the method was
not revived, with the result that the criticism of dramatic forms
which has been built upon the *Poetics* since the Sixteenth Century, while it has retained the traditional names of "tragedy"
and "comedy," and added others like "tragicomedy," has tended
to treat the nature of the realities signified by these names in
a quite un-Aristotelian way.

It is the difference between a criticism that would have
asked about Arthur Miller's *Death of a Salesman*, for instance,
What, precisely, is the form, old or new, being aimed at in this
play, and how fully are its possibilities realized? and a criticism that asks of Miller's drama, Is it or is it not a tragedy in
the true sense of that word? The modern method, in short, has
not been one that proceeds typically by induction from what
dramatists have done, on the assumption that the forms of drama
are determined merely by differences in the artistic principles
that happen to govern the making of existing plays; it is a
method, rather, in which the nature of any dramatic form is deduced from principles more general than drama or even art
itself, on the assumption that the common name of any such
form must necessarily correspond to some more or less fixed and
unitary idea or essence which can be defined dialectically in
relation to other literary ideas or essences and, as so defined,
be made to yield rules to direct poets in constructing plays
and criteria to guide critics in analyzing and judging them. The

result has been to confer a kind of ideal and invariant character upon the entities designated by such words as "tragedy" and "comedy." They are still forms, but forms in the sense of quasi-Platonic patterns or models rather than in that of particular animating principles of concrete artistic wholeness; and they can be defined, therefore, in abstraction from the works in which they are embodied, in much the way in which we define the concepts of mathematics; as when we are told, for example, without any indication of what works the critic has in mind, that "tragedy shares with comedy its concern with man's limitations, but differs from it, in one respect at least, in presenting these limitations as both disastrous and part of the ultimate configuration of life itself; tragedy, at its best and as distinct from mere pathos or melodrama, rests upon and implies a universal import in the structure of man's situation in the world."

As the nature of the method might lead one to expect, the history of this later mode of discussing the forms of drama has been marked, since its emergence in the Renaissance, by a tendency toward ever more general and comprehensive definitions of these forms and toward definitions increasingly remote from the actual conditions of artistic production. For many if not most of the critics of the Neoclassical period, the governing assumption continued to be that which Horace had stated when he advised poets to let each peculiar species of writing fill with decorum its proper place. It was primarily a question, that is, of what actions, what characters, what sentiments, what forms of language, what moral and emotional effects are proper to, or appropriately go with, the idea of comedy as distinct from that of farce or tragedy, the idea of tragedy as distinct from that of epic, and so on; I refer you for example to Dryden's dramatic essays or, if you prefer more extreme specimens, to the comments of Rymer and Voltaire on Shakespeare. The ideas of comedy, tragedy, tragicomedy, farce, and the like, in this criticism, were still, for the most part, rather limited ideas, of which the reference was bounded by the sphere of art;

when these critics talked about comedy and the comic or tragedy and the tragic, they had in view forms and qualities which owed their existence to the contrivances of poets rather than to the nature of things or of the human mind, however often they might appeal to moral or psychological principles in support of their conclusions as to what comic and tragic poets ought to do.

The definitions of these Neoclassical critics were more general than anything Aristotle had thought worth attempting, but the definitions developed in the Nineteenth Century, under the influence of idealist philosophy, were more general still. The discussion of dramatic forms, it was now widely assumed, must start from something fundamental in the nature of human existence and thought that can be taken as the basic tragic or comic "fact" or the basic tragic or comic "view of life"; it must then proceed to draw out deductively the consequences of this hypothesis for what dramatic poets have done or should do. Thus for August Wilhelm Schlegel the basis of tragedy is "that longing for the infinite which is inherent in our being" and which is "baffled by the limits of our finite existence. . . . This is the tragic tone of mind; and when the thought of the possible issues out of the mind as a living reality, when this tone pervades and animates a visible representation of the most striking instances of violent revolutions in a man's fortunes, either prostrating his mental energies or calling forth the most heroic endurance—then the result is *Tragic Poetry*. We thus see how this kind of poetry has its foundation in our nature. . . ." For Hegel the "essentially tragic fact" is something still more abstract: it is "the self-division and intestinal warfare of the ethical substance, not so much the war of good with evil as the war of good with good" —for example, the conflicting claims of the family and the state in *Antigone*, of love and honor in Corneille's *Le Cid*—and the end of the conflict is the denial of both of the exclusive claims. For Andrew Bradley, whose paraphrase of Hegel's definition I quote, this is true as far as it goes, but the definition needs to be generalized still further if it is to give us "the common essence of all tragedies"; and he proposes a more inclusive formula, according to which *"any* spiritual conflict involving spiritual waste is tragic" provided the conflicting values are sufficiently great.

We are still largely under the influence of this characteristic Nineteenth Century desire for maximum generality in the definitions of literary forms. Idealist metaphysics, however, is much less to our taste nowadays than analytical psychology and cultural anthropology; and the latest phase in the long series of modern attempts to give to the traditional distinctions among dramatic forms a fixed and natural basis in some kind of dialectic of universal essences has been dominated by concepts deriving from the speculations of anthropologists like Sir James Frazer and Jane Harrison and of psychologists like Sigmund Freud and C. G. Jung. The common ambition of the critics who have taken this line has been to renew our understanding of the existing forms of artistic drama by exploring the broad analogies between them and the more general forms of primitive religious ritual and myth, or of the unconscious operations of the psyche, from which they must be supposed to have emerged; as, for example, in the writings of Gilbert Murray and F. M. Cornford on Greek tragedy and comedy, in Maud Bodkin's Jungian discussion of the universal "tragic pattern" in her *Archetypal Patterns in Poetry,* and in parts of Francis Fergusson's *The Idea of a Theater.* I shall not dwell here on the results of these efforts except to say that the criticism of dramatic forms seems now to have moved a long way from its original starting-point in Aristotle's inductive definitions of tragedy and comedy as highly particularized forms of developed art.

IV

There remains the second major variety of dramatic criticism in the "Aristotelian" line: the variety that results when critics take as the special object of their concern not the species of drama but the drama as such, and talk primarily of those principles which constitute tragedies, comedies, tragicomedies, farces, and the like, as plays simply rather than as kinds of poetry in dramatic form. The possibility of such a criticism, as I have said before, is clearly indicated in the *Poetics* itself, where it remains, however, a subordinate mode of consideration. Its chief representative in antiquity was Horace in the *Ars Poetica*, but the full development of its potentialities has come only in modern times. We can see it taking form, first of all, perhaps in Castelvetro, with his radical substitution of the character of the theatrical audience for the nature of tragedy or comedy as the first principle of dramatic criticism, and then, more clearly still, in such works of the mid-Seventeenth Century as the Abbé d'Aubignac's *La Pratique du Théatre* (translated under the significant title of *The Whole Art of the Stage*), Corneille's *Discours,* and Dryden's *Essay of Dramatic Poesy.* It was the characteristic approach, in the Eighteenth Century, of writers like Johnson, Diderot, and Lessing; but the great flourishing period of the method has been in the century and a half since 1800, when it has become probably the most widely accepted frame of reference for writers on the dramatic arts—the controlling concept of works as diverse in other respects as August Wilhelm Schlegel's *Lectures on Dramatic Art and Literature,* Gustav Freytag's *Technique of the Drama,* Francisque Sarcey's *Theory of the Theater,* Ferdinand Brunetière's "Law of the Drama," Brander Matthews' *Study of the Drama* and *Principles of Play Making,* William Archer's *Play-Making* and *The Old Drama and the New,* and George Pierce Baker's *Dramatic Technique,* to mention merely a few of the more familiar titles.

The most obvious feature of most of these writings, as well as of the earlier ones I have mentioned, is their preoccupation, in a thoroughly practical spirit, with questions of dramatic manner in Aristotle's sense, as determined by the common requirements of literary composition for the stage irrespective of the particular forms which that composition takes. How should plays, of whatever kind, be written if they are to be actable in theaters to the satisfaction of spectators?—that is the simple form to which the dramatic theorists in this tradition tended to reduce their problems, as a consequence of their decision to theorize to practical ends about the drama as such. The collective result has been a large body of more or less useful advice to playwrights concerning a great variety of technical topics, ranging from the question of how to get ideas for plays and what stories can and cannot be put on the stage, through questions of general dramatic construction (for example, the shaping of the theatrical act on through its stages of exposition, rising action, climax, falling action, dénouement; the functions of the successive acts; the unities of place and time), to more particular questions of probability, foreshadowing, suspense and surprise, the better and worse ways of beginning and ending plays, the structure and connection of scenes, the delineation of character, the writing of dialogue, the use of choric devices, the relative advantages of blank verse and rhyme or of verse and prose, and so on.

If we ask how such advice can be validated, the answer is that it can be validated, in the first place, by arguments from example: the critic can point to earlier or contemporary plays in which the procedure he is recommending has achieved brilliant or at least successful results; and of arguments of this kind there are innumerable instances in the critical works we are considering. If the rules of dramaturgy, however, are to be put on a really firm foundation, something more general and basic is obviously needed than a mere appeal to precedent; and it is clear that such ultimate reasons cannot be found where Aristotle found them—namely, in principles of specific form; they must be looked for in common character of all play-writing as an art which issues in public performances in theaters. For the great majority of these modern critics, therefore, the first principle of dramatic criticism has been that principle which received its classic statement in Dr. Johnson's famous line: "The drama's laws the drama's patrons give." It is a principle that permits of a wide range of interpretations, from the merest box-office expediency to the idealism expressed by Dryden when he identified the proper audience for the dramatic poet with those spectators whose taste has been formed on Virgil. But in one formulation or another it has been the starting-point from which most of the generalizing critics of the drama have reasoned, from Horace in antiquity and Castelvetro in the Sixteenth Century to the present day.

"It is an indisputable fact," Francisque Sarcey wrote in 1876, "that a dramatic work, whatever it may be, is designed to be listened to by a number of persons united and forming an audience. . . . No audience, no play. The audience is the necessary and inevitable condition to which dramatic art must accommodate its means. I emphasize this point because it is the point of departure, because from this simple fact we can derive all the laws of the theater without a single exception." And here, closer to our time, is William Archer: "The art of theatrical story-telling," he says, "is necessarily relative to the audience to whom the story is to be told. One must assume an audience of a certain status and characteristics before one can rationally discuss the best methods of appealing to its intelligence and sympathies. . . . The painter may paint, the sculptor model, the lyric poet sing, simply to please himself, but the drama has no meaning except in relation to an audience. It is a portrayal of life by means of a mechanism so devised as to bring it home to a considerable number of people assembled in a given place." All of which means that the whole art of the drama, for the critics who thus take the satisfaction of the audience as a first principle rather than merely as a necessary condition of dramatic production, inevitably assumes the character of a kind of rhetoric (the dramatic poet's occupation, said Schlegel, "coincides with that of the orator"), all the special problems involved in the making of plays being assimilated to the central problem of how "as promptly as possible to win the attention of the audience" and how "to hold that interest steady or, better, to increase it till the final curtain falls." And the task of the dramatic theorist is to discover and sort out the commonplace devices available to playwrights for exciting and sustaining interest in any kind of play, producing conviction or illusion, and eliciting emotional responses. In this context distinctions among the specific forms of drama may still be recognized, but only as subordinate principles qualifying the applicability of particular general rules; and questions of better and worse in drama tend to become questions primarily either of the playwright's genius or seriousness of purpose or of the quality of the audience he is attempting to please—for example, as more or less intelligent or "adult."

Not all the critics in this tradition, however, have been content to view drama merely as a manner or technique or "mechanism," with rules determined by the character of theatrical audiences. It is natural for theorists in any special field to want to give to their ruling concepts as much territory to rule over as they can; and once the concept of "drama" had been taken as the controlling theme of dramatic criticism, it was doubtless to be expected that its original scope of meaning would sooner or later be considerably enlarged. This at any rate is what happened in the Nineteenth Century, and under the influence of the same philosophical spirit in criticism to which we owe those extreme generalizations of the concepts of "tragedy" and "comedy" I have already spoken of. It was at this time that drama began to be discussed, not as a technique merely, but as a comprehensive form of art, co-ordinate with the two other great literary arts of lyric poetry and epic (the latter including the modern novel), but distinct from these in its essential nature. It became necessary, therefore, to define that essential nature; and so it was that the question, "What is dramatic?" came to be a burning question for a long line of theorists through the Nineteenth Century and into the Twentieth. It was answered, of course, in a good many different ways, but nearly always in terms that involved, in the first place, a comparison of drama with lyric poetry and with the epic or novel and, in the second place, an insistence on finding the essence of drama, not merely in its character as a mode of representation, but in some attribute common to all the human experiences or actions which drama may represent, that is to say, in the least common denominator of all properly dramatic plots. The method and the kind of results it could yield are well illustrated in what became perhaps the most famous and influential of all these attempts, Brunetière's essay on "the law of the drama." Will any argument, however ingenious," he asks, "alter the fact that all poetry is either lyric, epic, or dramatic? Certainly not." And does it not follow, if such-and-such tragedies, comedies, farces are admittedly dramatic, that "all these works, so different, must nevertheless have not merely a few points of contact or vague resemblance, but an essential characteristic in common? What is this characteristic?" Brunetière's answer is simply that the essence of drama is "the spectacle of a *will* striving towards a goal, and conscious of the means which it employs." This is what separates drama from lyric poetry and from the epic or novel (which is indeed the contrary of drama inasmuch as it represents men not as willing particular ends but as being acted upon by external conditions); and Brunetière goes on to show how this principle may be used to distinguish the various essential species of the drama and to illuminate the history of the drama in relation to the spiritual conditions of the different ages in which it has either flourished or declined.

The predictable result of all these attempts to declare the independence of the drama as a complete art form in its own right has been to raise the question, which was not a question at all for Aristotle or the "Neo-Aristotelian" critics of the early modern period, of how the concept of "drama," as thus enlarged, is related to the concept of "poetry." I want to touch on this matter briefly by way of conclusion because the very fact that we ask the question at all illustrates rather vividly, I think, the main thesis I have been trying to expound in this lecture, of the necessary relativity of the problems and doctrines of dramatic criticism to the nature of the principles upon which that criticism, at any given time or in any given critic, happens to be based. For I suggest that we should never have thought of using the term "poetic drama," as we nearly all do, in a specialized and exclusive sense, or of writing, as T. S. Eliot has done, about "Poetry and Drama," or of distinguishing, as Christopher Fry has done, between "the theatre of poetry" and "the theatre of prose," had it not been for two major developments in critical theory during the past hundred and fifty years. One of these is the change of fashions in the principles of dramatic criticism itself which I have just been speaking of. The other is a parallel change in the criticism of poetry, which has brought it about that, for most critics since at least the end of the Eighteenth Century, the term "poetry" no longer signifies the art of imitating human actions in appropriate speech but stands for something much more general than that—a certain quality of expression, commonly identified with verse rather than with prose, a certain way of feeling or conceiving things, a certain power of unifying experience imaginatively. . . .

Thus both of our terms have been radically redefined and, as a consequence, made to refer to two entities that need have no intimate relation with one another. Drama, that is to say, may or may not be also poetry, as the terms "poetry" and "drama" are now conceived; and a new problem is thereby generated for critics, of making up their minds as to whether the two ought or ought not to be united in one composite whole. The orthodox answer, down almost to our own time, has been an affirmative one. A dramatic work, wrote Schlegel, may be regarded from a double point of view—how far it is *poetical*, and how far it is *theatrical*. "The two," he adds, "are by no means inseparable," but his own position is that there can be no good drama in which a "poetical" element is not present, in the sense not of metrical language necessarily but of a certain "spirit and de-

sign" in a play which may exist in as high a degree when the
medium is prose as when it is verse; and he identifies this "higher
excellence" with the mirroring in the play of "thoughts and
feelings which in their character are necessary and eternally
true, and soar above this earthly life." There were few critics,
during the next hundred years, who would have quarreled with
this, however differently they might define the essence of "poetry." But then at last came William Archer. Dramatic criticism
has not yet completely recovered from the shock that was administered, in the early twenties of the present century, by his
famous book on *The Old Drama and the New.* For what Archer
did, in effect, was to take the current notion that drama at its
best is a combination of two distinct things, drama and poetry,
and to oppose to this a conception of "pure" or "unmixed" drama,
that can come to exist only when the essence of drama, which,
for Archer, is the faithful "imitation" of life as we know it, is
freed from the "poetical" or "lyrical" elements, including verse,
which had been imposed upon it by its religious origins; the
thesis of his book is that the history of English drama has been
a progress, culminating in the realistic prose plays of Pinero,
Galsworthy, and Granville-Barker, from a "mixed and heteroge-
neous art" to "a pure and logical art form." Archer saw the whole
matter, in short, in the framework of terms already adopted by
Schlegel and many others; he merely insisted on separating
sharply what they had kept joined together. And the same
thing has been true of most of those who have pleaded the
cause of "poetic drama" since his book appeared. He has been
answered many times, but nearly always, I think, by critics who
have been content to accept, without question, the principles
he used in stating his case for "the theatre of prose"—the antithesis of "poetry" and "drama" and the opposition of "pure" and
"mixed" forms—and who, accordingly, have had no way of re-
futing him except by turning his scale of values upside down
(so that the "drama" in Shakespeare, for instance, is said to be
less important than the "poetry," and *Macbeth* is praised as a

"poem" of the order of *The Waste Land*), or else by arguing that since each element in the combination of "drama" and "poetry" is incomplete by itself, the best drama must be such a union of the two elements as that envisaged in the theories, among many others, of T. S. Eliot and Christopher Fry.

I dwell on this as one final instance of that compulsive influence of principles in dramatic criticism which critics can never escape, however unaware they may be of what is happening to them, and which we, as readers of such criticism, would do well to take constantly into account, lest, by not grasping clearly why different critics are impelled to say the things they do, we fail to profit as much as we might from what the many varied critical approaches to the drama, ancient and modern, have to tell us about the nature and possibilities of that art.

Specific Forms of Drama

NORTHROP FRYE

We have now to see whether this expansion of perspective, which enables us to consider the relation of the *lexis* or verbal pattern to music and spectacle, gives us any new light on the traditional classifications within the genres. The division of dramas into tragedies and comedies, for instance, is a conception based entirely on verbal drama, and does not include or account for types of drama, such as the opera or masque, in which music and scenery have a more organic place. Yet verbal drama, whether tragic or comic, has clearly developed a long way from the primitive idea of drama, which is to present a powerful sensational focus for a community. The scriptural plays of the Middle Ages are primitive in this sense: they present to the audience a myth already familiar to and significant for that audience, and they are designed to remind the audience of their communal possession of this myth.

The scriptural play is a form of a spectacular dramatic genre which we may provisionally call a "myth-play." It is a somewhat negative and receptive form, and takes on the mood of the myth it represents. The crucifixion play in the Towneley cycle is tragic because the Crucifixion is; but it is not a tragedy in the sense that *Othello* is a tragedy. It does not, that is, make a tragic *point;* it simply presents the story because it is familiar and significant. It would be nonsense to apply such tragic conceptions as hybris to the figure of Christ in that play, and while pity and terror are raised, they remain attached to the subject, and there is no catharsis of them. The characteristic mood and resolution of the myth-play are pensive, and pensiveness, in this context, implies a continuing imaginative subjection to the story. The myth-play emphasizes dramatically the symbol of spiritual and corporeal communion. The scriptural plays themselves were associated with the festival of Corpus Christi, and Calderon's religious plays are explicitly *autos sacramentales* or Eucharist plays. The appeal of the myth-play is a curious mixture of the popular and the esoteric; it is popular for its immediate audience, but those outside its circle have to make a conscious effort to appreciate it. In a controversial atmosphere it disappears, as it cannot deal with controversial issues unless it selects its audience. In view of the ambiguities attaching to the word myth, we shall speak of this genre as the *auto*.

When there is no clear-cut distinction between gods and heroes in a society's mythology, or between the ideals of the nobility and the priesthood, the *auto* may present a legend which is secular and sacred at once. An example is the No drama of Japan, which with its unification of chivalric and otherworldly symbols and its dreamy un-tragic, un-comic mood so strongly attracted Yeats. It is interesting to see how Yeats, both in his theory of the *anima mundi* and in his desire to get his plays as physically close to the audience as possible, reverts to the archaic idea of corporeal communion. In Greek drama, too, there is no sharp boundary line between the divine and the heroic protagonist. But in Christian societies we can see glimpses of a secular *auto*, a romantic drama presenting the exploits of a hero, which is closely related to tragedy, the end of a hero's exploit being eventually his death, but which in itself is neither tragic nor comic, being primarily spectacular.

Tamburlaine is such a play: there the relation between the hero's hybris and his death is more casual than causal. This genre has had varying luck: more in Spain, for instance, than in France, where the establishing of tragedy was part of an intellectual revolution. The two attempts in France to move tragedy back towards heroic romance, *Le Cid* and *Hernani*, each precipitated a big row. In Germany, on the other hand, it is clear that the actual genre of many plays by Goethe and Schiller is the heroic romance, however much affected they have been by the prestige of tragedy. In Wagner, who expands the heroic form all the way back to a sacramental drama of gods, the symbol of communion again occupies a conspicuous place, negatively in *Tristan*, positively in *Parsifal*. In proportion as it moves closer to tragedy and further from the sacred *auto*, drama tends to make less use of music. If we look at the earliest extant play of Aeschylus, *The Suppliants*, we can see that close behind it is a predominantly musical structure of which the modern counterpart would normally be the oratorio—it is perhaps possible to describe Wagner's operas as fermented oratorios.

In Renaissance England the audience was too bourgeois for a chivalric drama to get firmly established, and the Elizabethan secular *auto* eventually became the history-play. With the history-play we move from spectacle to a more purely verbal drama, and the symbols of communion become much attenuated, although they are still there. The central theme of Elizabethan history is the unifying of the nation and the binding of the audience into the myth as the inheritors of that unity, set over against the disasters of civil war and weak leadership. One may even recognize a secular Eucharist symbol in the red and white rose, just as one may recognize in the plays that end by pointing to Elizabeth, like Peele's *Arraignment of Paris*, a secular counterpart of a mystery play of the Virgin. But the emphasis and characteristic resolution of the history play are in terms of continuity and the closing up both of tragic catastrophe and (as in the case of Falstaff) of the comic festival. One may compare Shaw's "chronicle play" of *Saint Joan*, where the end of the play is a tragedy, followed by an epilogue in which the rejection of Joan is, like the rejection of Falstaff, historical, suggesting continuity rather than a rounded finish.

The history merges so gradually into tragedy that we often cannot be sure when communion has turned into catharsis. *Richard II* and *Richard III* are tragedies insofar as they resolve on those defeated kings; they are histories insofar as they resolve on Bolingbroke and Richmond, and the most one can say is that they lean toward history. *Hamlet* and *Macbeth* lean toward tragedy, but Fortinbras and Malcolm, the continuing characters, indicate the historical element in the tragic resolution. There seems to be a far less direct connection between history and comedy: the comic scenes in the histories are, so to speak, subversive. *Henry V* ends in triumph and marriage, but an action that kills Falstaff, hangs Bardolph and debases Pistol is not related to comedy in the way that *Richard II* is related to tragedy.

We are here concerned only with tragedy as a species of drama. Tragic drama derives from the *auto* its central heroic figure, but the association of heroism with downfall is due to the simultaneous presence of irony. The nearer the tragedy is to *auto*, the more closely associated the hero is with divinity; the nearer to irony, the more human the hero is, and the more the catastrophe appears to be social rather than a cosmological event. Elizabethan tragedy shows a historical development from Marlowe, who presents his heroes more or less as demigods moving in a kind of social ether, to Webster, whose tragedies are almost clinical analyses of a sick society. Greek tragedy never broke completely from the *auto*, and so never developed a social form, though there are tendencies to it in Euripides. But whatever the proportions of heroism and irony, tragedy shows itself to be primarily a vision of the supremacy of the event or *mythos*. The response to tragedy is "this must be," or, perhaps more accurately, "this does happen": the event is primary, the explanation of it secondary and variable.

As tragedy moves over towards irony, the sense of inevitable event begins to fade out, and the sources of catastrophe come into view. In irony catastrophe is either arbitrary and meaningless, the impact of an unconscious (or, in the pathetic fallacy, malignant) world on conscious man, or the result of more or less definable social and psychological forces. Tragedy's "this must be" becomes irony's "this at least is," a concentration on foreground facts and a rejection of mythical superstructures. Thus the ironic drama is a vision of what in theology is called the fallen world, of simple humanity, man as natural man and in conflict with both human and non-human nature. In nineteenth-century drama the tragic vision is often identical with the ironic one, hence nineteenth-century tragedies tend to be either *Schicksal* dramas dealing with the arbitrary ironies of fate, or (clearly the more rewarding form) studies of the frustrating and smothering of human activity by the combined pressure of a reactionary society without and disorganized soul within. Such irony is difficult to sustain in the theatre because it tends toward a stasis of action. In those parts of Chekhov, notably the last act of *Three Sisters,* where the characters one by one withdraw from each other into their subjective prison-cells, we are coming about as close to pure irony as the stage can get.

The ironic play passes through a dead center of complete realism, a pure mime representing human life without comment and without imposing any sort of dramatic form beyond what is required for simple exhibition. This idolatrous form of mimesis is rare, but the thin line of its tradition can be traced from Classical mime-writers like Herodas to their *tranche-de-vie* descendants in recent times. The mime is somewhat commoner as an individual performance, and, outside the theatre, the Browning monodrama is a logical development of the isolating and soliloquizing tendencies of ironic conflict. In the theatre we usually find that the spectacle of "all too human" life is either oppressive or ridiculous, and that it tends to pass directly from one to the other. Irony, then, as it moves away from tragedy, begins to merge into comedy.

Ironic comedy presents us of course with "the way of the world," but as soon as we find sympathetic or even neutral characters in a comedy, we move into the more familiar comic area where we have a group of humors outwitted by the opposing group. Just as tragedy is a vision of the supremacy of *mythos* or thing done, and just as irony is a vision of *ethos*, or character individualized against environment, so comedy is a vision of *dianoia*, a significance which is ultimately social significance, the establishing of a desirable society. As an imitation of life, drama is, in terms of *mythos*, conflict; in terms of *ethos*, a representative image; in terms of *dianoia*, the final harmonic chord revealing the tonality under the narrative movement, it is community. The further comedy moves from irony, the more it becomes what we here call ideal comedy, the vision not of the way of the world, but of what you will, life as you like it. Shakespeare's main interest is in getting away from the son-father conflict of ironic comedy towards a vision of a serene community, a vision most prominent in *The Tempest*. Here the action is polarized around a younger and an older man working in harmony together, a lover and a benevolent teacher.

The next step brings us to the extreme limit of social comedy, the symposium, the structure of which is, as we should expect, clearest in Plato, whose Socrates is both teacher and lover, and whose vision moves toward an integration of society in a form like that of the symposium itself, the dialectic festivity which, as is explained in the opening of the *Laws*, is the controlling force that holds society together. It is easy to see that Plato's dialogue form is dramatic and has affinities with comedy and mime; and while there is much in Plato's thought that contradicts the spirit of comedy as we have outlined it, it is significant that he contradicts it directly, tries to kidnap it, so to speak. It seems almost a rule that the more he does this, the further he moves into pure exposition or dictatorial monologue and away from drama. The most dramatic of his dialogues, such as *Euthydemus,* are regularly the most indecisive in philosophic "position."

In our own day Bernard Shaw has tried hard to keep the symposium in the theatre. His early manifesto, *The Quintessence of Ibsenism,* states that a play should be an intelligent discussion of a serious problem, and in his preface to *Getting Married* he remarks approvingly on the fact that it observes the unities of time and place. For comedy of Shaw's type tends to a symposium form which occupies the same amount of time in its action that the audience consumes in watching it. However, Shaw discovered in practice that what emerges from the theatrical symposium is not a dialectic that compels to a course of action or thought, but one that emancipates from formulated principles of conduct. The shape of such a comedy is very clear in the bright little sketch *In Good King Charles's Golden Days,* where even the most highly developed human types, the saintly Fox and the philosophical Newton, are shown to be comic humors by the mere presence of other types of people. Yet the central symposium figure of the haranguing lover bulks formidably in *Man and Superman,* and even the renunciation of love for mathematics at the end of *Back to Methuselah* is consistent with the symposium spirit.

The view of poetry which sees it as intermediate between history and philosophy, its images combining the temporal events of the one with the timeless ideas of the other, seems to be still involved in this exposition of dramatic forms. We can now see a mimetic or verbal drama stretching from the history-play to the philosophy-play (the act-play and the scene-play), with the mime, the pure image, halfway between. These three are specialized forms, cardinal points of drama rather than generic areas. But the whole mimetic area is only a part, a semicircle, let us say, of all drama. In the misty and unexplored region of the other semicircle of spectacular drama we have identified a quadrant that we have called the *auto,* and we have now to chart the fourth quadrant that lies between the *auto* and comedy, and establish the fourth cardinal point where it meets the *auto* again. When we think of the clutter of forms that belong here, we are strongly tempted to call our fourth area "miscellaneous" and let it go; but it is precisely here that new generic criticism is needed.

The further comedy moves from irony, and the more it rejoices in the free movement of its happy society, the more readily it takes to music and dancing. As music and scenery increase in importance, the ideal comedy crosses the boundary line of spectacular drama and becomes the masque. In Shakespeare's ideal comedies, especially *A Midsummer Night's Dream* and *The Tempest,* the close affinity with the masque is not hard to see. The masque—or at least the kind of masque that is nearest to comedy, and which we shall here call the ideal masque—is still in the area of *dianoia:* it is usually a compliment to the audience, or an important member of it, and leads up to an idealization of the society represented by that audience. Its plots and characters are fairly stock, as they exist only in relation to the significance of the occasion.

It thus differs from comedy in its more intimate attitude to the audience: there is more insistence on the connection between the audience and the community on the stage. The members of a masque are ordinarily disguised members of the audience, and there is a final gesture of surrender when the actors unmask and join the audience in a dance. The ideal masque is in fact a myth-play like the *auto,* to which it is related much as comedy is to tragedy. It is designed to emphasize, not the ideals to be achieved by discipline or faith, but ideals which are desired or considered to be already possessed. Its settings are seldom remote from magic and fairyland, from Arcadias and visions of earthly Paradise. It uses gods freely, like the *auto,* but possessively, and without imaginative subjection. In Western drama, from the Renaissance to the end of the eighteenth century, masque and ideal comedy make great use of Classical mythology, which the audience is not obliged to accept as "true."

The rather limited masque throws some light on the structure and characteristics of its two far more important and versatile neighbors. For the masque is flanked on one side by the musically organized drama which we call opera, and on the other by a scenically organized drama, which has now settled in the movie. Puppet-plays and the vast Chinese romances where, as in the movie, the audience enters and leaves unpredictably, are examples of pre-camera scenic masques. Both opera and movie are, like the masque, proverbial for lavish display, and part of the reason for it in the movie is that many movies are actually bourgeois myth-plays, as half a dozen critics suddenly and almost simultaneously discovered a few years ago. The predominance of the private life of the actor in the imaginations of many movie-goers may perhaps have some analogy with the consciously assumed disguise of the masque.

Opera and movie possess, unlike the masque, the power of producing spectacular imitations of mimetic drama. The opera can only do this by simplifying its musical organization, otherwise its dramatic structure will be blurred by the distortion of acting which the highly repetitive structure of music makes necessary. The movie similarly must simplify its spectacle. In proportion as it follows its natural bent for scenic organization, the movie reveals its affinities with other forms of scenic masque: with the puppet-play in Chaplin and others, with the commedia dell'arte in recent Italian films, with the ballet and pantomime in musical comedies. When the movie succeeds in imitating a mimetic drama, the distinction between the two forms is not worth making, but the generic difference shows itself in other ways. Mimetic drama works towards an end which illuminates, by being logically connected with, the beginning: hence the parabola shape of the typical five-act mimetic structure, and hence the teleological quality in drama expressed by the term discovery. Spectacular drama, on the other hand, is by nature processional, and tends to episodic and piecemeal discovery, as we can see in all forms of pure spectacle, from the circus parade to the revue. In the *auto* too, on the other side of spectacular drama, the same processional structure appears in the long continued stories of Shakespearean history and scriptural pageant. In the rotating performance and casual attendance of the movie, and the sequence of arias forcibly linked to dramatic structure by recitative in the opera, one can see the strong native tendency to linear movement in spectacular forms. In Shakespeare's first experimental romance, *Pericles,* the movement toward processional structure, a sequence of scenes "dispersedly in various countries," is very clear.

The essential feature of the ideal masque is the exaltation of the audience, who form the goal of its procession. In the *auto,* drama is at its most objective; the audience's part is to accept the story without judgement. In tragedy there is judgement, but the source of the tragic discovery is on the other side of the stage; and whatever it is, it is stronger than the audience. In the ironic play, audience and drama confront each other directly; in the comedy the source of the discovery has moved across to the audience itself. The ideal masque places the audience in a position of superiority to discovery. The verbal action of *Figaro* is comic and that of *Don Giovanni* tragic; but in both cases the audience is exalted by the music above the reach of tragedy and comedy, and though as profoundly moved as ever, is not emotionally involved with the discovery of plot or characters. It looks at the downfall of Don Juan as spectacular entertainment, much as the gods are supposed to look at the downfall of Ajax or Darius. The same sense of viewing the dramatic mimesis through a haze of spectacular exhilaration is also of central importance in the movie, as it is even more obviously in the puppet-play from which the movie is chiefly descended. We move from ironic to ideal comedy through the symposium, and we note that at the conclusion of Plato's *Symposium* the prophecy is made that the same poet should be able to write both tragedy and comedy, though the ones who have done so most successfully are those who, like Shakespeare and Mozart, have had a strong interest in spectacular forms.

For our next step we must return to the masque proper. The further comedy moves from irony, the less social power is allowed to the humors. In the masque, where the ideal society is still more in the ascendant, the humors become degraded into the uncouth figures of the Jonsonian antimasque, who are said to be descended from a dramatic form far older than the rest of the masque. Farce, being a non-mimetic form of comedy, has a natural place in the masque, though in the ideal masque its natural place is that of a rigorously controlled interlude. In *The Tempest,* a comedy so profound that it seems to draw the whole masque into itself, Stephano and Trinculo are comic humors and Caliban an antimasque figure, and the group shows the transition very clearly. The main theme of the masque involves gods, fairies, and personifications of virtues; the figures of the antimasque thus tend to become demonic, and dramatic characterization begins to split into an antithesis of virtue and vice, god and devil, fairy and monster. The tension between them partly accounts for the importance of the theme of magic in the masque. At the comic end this magic is held by the benevolent side, as in *The Tempest;* but as we move further away from comedy, the conflict becomes increasingly serious, and the antimasque figures less ridiculous and more sinister, possessed in their turn of powers of enchantment. This is the stage represented by *Comus,* which is very close to the open conflict of good and evil in the morality play. With the morality play we pass into another area of masque which we shall here call the archetypal masque, the prevailing form of most twentieth-century highbrow drama, at least in continental Europe, as well as of many experimental operas and unpopular movies.

The ideal masque tends to individualize its audience by pointing to the central member of it: even the movie audience, sitting in the dark in small units (usually of two), is a relatively individualized one. A growing sense of loneliness is noticeable as we move away from comedy. The archetypal masque, like all forms of spectacular drama, tends to detach its settings from time and space, but instead of the Arcadias of the ideal masque, we find ourselves frequently in a sinister limbo, like the threshold of death in *Everyman,* the sealed underworld crypts of Maeterlinck, or the nightmares of the future in expressionist plays. As we get nearer the rationale of the form, we see that the *auto* symbol of communion in one body is reappearing, but in a psychological and subjective form, and without gods. The action of the archetypal masque takes place in a world of human types, which at its most concentrated becomes the interior of the human mind. This is explicit even in the old moralities, like *Mankynd* and *The Castell of Perseveraunce,* and at least implicit in a good deal of Maeterlinck, Pirandello, Andreyev, and Strindberg.

Naturally, with such a setting, characterization has to break down into elements and fragments of personality. This is why I call the form the archetypal masque, the word archetype being in this context used in Jung's sense of an aspect of the personality capable of dramatic projection. Jung's persona and anima and counsellor and shadow throw a great deal of light on the characterization of modern allegorical, psychic, and expressionist dramas, with their circus barkers and wraithlike females and inscrutable sages and obsessed demons. The abstract entities of the morality play and the stock types of the commedia dell'arte (this latter representing one of the primitive roots of the genre) are similar constructions.

A sense of confusion and fear accompanies the sense of loneliness: Maeterlinck's early plays are almost dedicated to fear, and the constant undermining of the distinction between illusion and reality, as mental projections become physical bodies and vice versa, splits the action up into a kaleidoscopic chaos of reflecting mirrors. The mob scenes of German expressionist plays and the mechanical fantasies of the Čapeks show the same disintegration at work in a social context. From the generic point of view, one of the most interesting archetypal plays is Andreyev's powerful *The Black Maskers,* in which its author saw reflected not only the destruction of an individual's *nobile castello*, which is its explicit theme, but the whole social collapse of modern Russia. This play distinguishes two groups of dissociative elements of personality, one group connected with self-accusation and the other with the death-wish, and it exhibits the human soul as a castle possessed by a legion of demons. It is evident that the further the archetypal masque gets from the ideal masque, the more clearly it reveals itself as the emancipated antimasque, a revel of satyrs who have got out of control. The progress of sophisticated drama appears to be towards an *anagnorisis* or recognition of the most primitive of all dramatic forms.

At the far end of the archetypal masque, where it joins the *auto*, we reach the point indicated by Nietzsche as the point of the birth of tragedy, where the revel of satyrs impinges on the appearance of a commanding god, and Dionysos is brought into line with Apollo. We may call this fourth cardinal point of drama the epiphany, the dramatic apocalypse or separation of the divine and the demonic, a point directly opposite the mime, which presents the simply human mixture. This point is the dramatic form of the point of epiphany, most familiar as the point at which the Book of Job, after describing a complete circuit from tragedy through symposium, finally ends. Here the two monsters Behemoth and Leviathan replace the more frequent demonic animals.

The Classical critics, from Aristotle to Horace, were puzzled to understand why a disorganized ribald farce like the satyr-play should be the source of tragedy, though they were clear that it was. In medieval drama, where the progression through sacred and heroic *auto* to tragedy is so much less foreshortened, the development is plainer. The most clearly epiphanic form of scriptural drama is the Harrowing of Hell play, which depicts the triumph of a divine redeemer over demonic resistance. The devils of that play are the Christian forms of figures very like the Greek satyrs, and dramatic groups generically very close to the satyrs are never far from any scriptural play that deals directly with Christ, whether tamed and awed as in the *Secunda Pastorum,* or triumphantly villainous, as in the crucifixion and Herod plays. And just as Greek tragedy retained and developed the satyr-play, so Elizabethan tragedy retains a satyric counterpoint in its clown scenes and the farcical under-plots of *Faustus* and many later tragedies. The same element provides those superb episodes of the porter in *Macbeth,* the grave-diggers in *Hamlet,* and the serpent-bearer in *Antony and Cleopatra,* which so baffled Classically-minded critics who had forgotten about the satyr-play. Perhaps we could make more dramatic sense out of *Titus Andronicus* if we could see it as an unharrowed hell, a satyr-play of obscene and gibbering demons.

The two nodes of the scriptural play are Christmas and Easter: the latter presents the triumphant god, the former the quiet virgin mother who gathers to herself the processional masque of the kings and shepherds. This figure is at the opposite end of the masque from the watching queen or peeress of an ideal masque, with the virtuous but paralyzed Lady of *Comus* halfway between. A female figure symbolizing some kind of reconciling unity and order appears dimly at the end of the great panoramic masques of *Faust* and *Peer Gynt,* the "eternal feminine" of the former having some of its traditional links. Modern examples of the same epiphanic form range from Claudel's Annunciation play to Yeats's *Countess Cathleen,* where the heroine is really a female and Irish Jesus, sacrificing herself for her people and then cheating the devils by the purity of her nature, very much as in the pre-Anselm theory of the atonement. As Yeats remarks in a note, the story represents one of the supreme parables of the world.

PART ONE

THE PLAYWRIGHT

THORNTON WILDER

SOME THOUGHTS ON PLAYWRITING

FRIEDRICH DUERRENMATT

PROBLEMS OF THE THEATRE

EUGÈNE IONESCO

EXPERIENCE OF THE THEATRE

Some Thoughts on Playwriting

THORNTON WILDER

Four fundamental conditions of the drama separate it from the other arts. Each of these conditions has its advantages and disadvantages, each requires a particular aptitude from the dramatist, and from each there are a number of instructive consequences to be derived. These conditions are:

1. The theatre is an art which reposes upon the work of many collaborators;

2. It is addressed to the group-mind;

3. It is based upon a pretense and its very nature calls out a multiplication of pretenses;

4. Its action takes place in a perpetual present time.

I. THE THEATRE IS AN ART WHICH REPOSES UPON THE WORK OF MANY COLLABORATORS

We have been accustomed to think that a work of art is by definition the product of one governing selecting will.

A landscape by Cézanne consists of thousands of brushstrokes each commanded by one mind. *Paradise Lost* and *Pride and Prejudice,* even in cheap frayed copies, bear the immediate and exclusive message of one intelligence.

It is true that in musical performance we meet with intervening executants, but the element of intervention is slight compared to that which takes place in drama. Illustrations:

1. One of the finest productions of *The Merchant of Venice*
in our time showed Sir Henry Irving as Shylock, a noble,
wronged and indignant being, of such stature that the Merchants
of Venice dwindled before him into irresponsible schoolboys.
He was confronted in court by a gracious, even queenly, Portia,
Miss Ellen Terry. At the Odéon in Paris, however, Gémier
played Shylock as a vengeful and hysterical buffoon, confronted in court by a Portia who was a *gamine* from the Paris
streets with a lawyer's quill three feet long over her ear; at the
close of the trial scene Shylock was driven screaming about
the auditorium, behind the spectators' back and onto the stage
again, in a wild Elizabethan revel. Yet for all their divergences
both were admirable productions of the play.

2. If there were ever a play in which fidelity to the author's
requirements were essential in the representation of the principal role, it would seem to be Ibsen's *Hedda Gabler,* for the
play is primarily an exposition of her character. Ibsen's directions read: "Enter from the left Hedda Gabler. She is a
woman of twenty-nine. Her face and figure show great refinement and distinction. Her complexion is pale and opaque. Her
steel-gray eyes express an unruffled calm. Her hair is an attractive medium brown, but is not particularly abundant; and she
is dressed in a flowing loose-fitting morning gown." I once saw
Eleonora Duse in this role. She was a woman of sixty and made
no effort to conceal it. Her complexion was pale and transparent. Her hair was white, and she was dressed in a gown that
suggested some medieval empress in mourning. And the performance was very fine.

One may well ask: why write for the theatre at all? Why
not work in the novel where such deviations from one's intentions cannot take place?

There are two answers:

1. The theatre presents certain vitalities of its own so inviting and stimulating that the writer is willing to receive them in compensation for this inevitable variation from an exact image.

2. The dramatist through working in the theatre gradually learns not merely to take account of the presence of the collaborators, but to derive advantage from them; and he learns, above all, to organize the play in such a way that its strength lies not in appearances beyond his control, but in the succession of events and in the unfolding of an idea, in narration.

The gathered audience sits in a darkened room, one end of which is lighted. The nature of the transaction at which it is gazing is a succession of events illustrating a general idea—the stirring of the idea; the gradual feeding out of information; the shock and countershock of circumstances; the flow of action; the interruption of action; the moments of allusion to earlier events; the preparation of surprise, dread, or delight—all that is the author's and his alone.

For reasons to be discussed later—the expectancy of the group-mind, the problem of time on the stage, the absence of the narrator, the element of pretense—the theatre carries the art of narration to a higher power than the novel or the epic poem. The theatre is unfolding action and in the disposition of events the authors may exercise a governance so complete that the distortions effected by the physical appearance of actors, by the fancies of scene painters and the misunderstandings of directors, fall into relative insignificance. It is just because the theatre is an art of many collaborators, with the constant danger of grave misinterpretation, that the dramatist learns to turn his attention to the laws of narration, its logic and its deep necessity of presenting a unifying idea stronger than its mere collection of happenings. The dramatist must be by instinct a storyteller.

There is something mysterious about the endowment of the storyteller. Some very great writers possessed very little of it, and some others, lightly esteemed, possessed it in so large a measure that their books survive down the ages, to the confusion of severer critics. Alexandre Dumas had it to an extraordinary degree, while Melville, for all his splendid quality, had it barely sufficiently to raise his work from the realm of nonfiction. It springs, not, as some have said, from an aversion to general ideas, but from an instinctive coupling of idea and illustration; the idea, for a born storyteller, can only be expressed imbedded in its circumstantial illustration. The myth, the parable, the fable are the fountainhead of all fiction and in them is seen most clearly the didactic, moralizing employment of a story. Modern taste shrinks from emphasizing the central idea that hides behind the fiction, but it exists there nevertheless, supplying the unity to fantasizing, and offering a justification to what otherwise we would repudiate as mere arbitrary contrivance, pretentious lying, or individualistic emotional association spinning. For all their magnificient intellectual endowment, George Meredith and George Eliot were not born storytellers; they chose fiction as the vehicle for their reflections, and the passing of time is revealing their error in that choice. Jane Austen was pure storyteller and her works are outlasting those of apparently more formidable rivals. The theatre is more exacting than the novel in regard to this faculty, and its presence constitutes a force which compensates the dramatist for the deviations which are introduced into his work by the presence of his collaborators.

The chief of these collaborators are the actors.

The actor's gift is a combination of three separate faculties or endowments. Their presence to a high degree in any one person is extremely rare, although the ambition to possess them is common. Those who rise to the height of the profession represent a selection and a struggle for survival in one of the most difficult and cruel of the artistic activities. The three endowments that compose the gift are observation, imagination, and physical co-ordination.

1. An observant and analyzing eye for all modes of behavior about it, for dress and manner, and for the signs of thought and emotion in one's self and in others.

2. The strength of imagination and memory whereby the actor may, at the indication in the author's text, explore his store of observations and represent the details of appearance and the intensity of the emotions—joy, fear, surprise, grief, love, and hatred, and through imagination extend them to intenser degrees and to differing characterizations.

3. A physical co-ordination whereby the force of these inner realizations may be communicated to voice, face and body.

An actor must *know* the appearances and the mental states; he must *apply* his knowledge to the role; and he must physically *express* his knowledge. Moreover, his concentration must be so great that he can effect this representation under conditions of peculiar difficulty—in abrupt transition from the non-imaginative conditions behind the stage; and in the presence of fellow-actors who may be momentarily destroying the reality of the action.

A dramatist prepares the characterization of his personages in such a way that it will take advantage of the actor's gift.

Characterization in a novel is presented by the author's dogmatic assertion that the personage was such, and by an analysis of the personage with generally an account of his or her past. Since, in the drama, this is replaced by the actual presence of the personage before us and since there is no occasion for the intervening all-knowing author to instruct us as to his or her inner nature, a far greater share is given in a play to (1) highly characteristic utterances and (2) concrete occasions in which the character defines itself under action and (3) conscious preparation of the text whereby the actor may build upon the suggestions in the role according to his own abilities.

Characterization in a play is like a blank check which the dramatist accords to the actor for him to fill in—not entirely blank, for a number of indications of individuality are already there, but to a far less definite and absolute degree than in the novel.

The dramatist's principal interest being the movement of the story, he is willing to resign the more detailed aspects of characterization to the actor and is often rewarded beyond his expectation.

The sleepwalking scene from *Macbeth* is a highly compressed selection of words whereby despair and remorse rise to the surface of indirect confession. It is to be assumed that had Shakespeare lived to see what the genius of Sarah Siddons could pour into the scene from that combination of observation, self-knowledge, imagination, and representational skill, even he might have exclaimed, "I never knew I wrote so well!"

II. THE THEATRE IS AN ART ADDRESSED TO A GROUP-MIND

Painting, sculpture, and the literature of the book are certainly solitary experiences; and it is likely that most people would agree that the audience seated shoulder to shoulder in a concert hall is not an essential element in musical enjoyment.

But a play presupposes a crowd. The reasons for this go deeper than (1) the economic necessity for the support of the play and (2) the fact that the temperament of actors is proverbially dependent on group attention.

It rests on the fact that (1) the pretense, the fiction on the stage would fall to pieces and absurdity without the support accorded to it by a crowd, and (2) the excitement induced by pretending a fragment of life is such that it partakes of ritual and festival, and requires a throng.

Similarly the fiction that royal personages are of a mysteriously different nature from other people requires audiences, levees, and processions for its maintenance. Since the beginnings of society, satirists have occupied themselves with the descriptions of kings and queens in their intimacy and delighted in showing how the prerogatives of royalty become absurd when the crowd is not present to extend to them the enhancement of an imaginative awe.

The theatre partakes of the nature of festival. Life imitated is life raised to a higher power. In the case of comedy, the vitality of these pretended surprises, deceptions, and the *contretemps* becomes so lively that before a spectator, solitary or regarding himself as solitary, the structure of so much event would inevitably expose the artificiality of the attempt and ring hollow and unjustified; and in the case of tragedy, the accumulation of woe and apprehension would soon fall short of conviction. All actors know the disturbing sensation of playing before a handful of spectators at a dress rehearsal or performance where only their interest in pure craftsmanship can barely sustain them. During the last rehearsals the phrase is often heard: "This play is hungry for an audience."

Since the theatre is directed to a group-mind, a number of consequences follow:

1. A group-mind presupposes, if not a lowering of standards, a broadening of the fields of interest. The other arts may presuppose an audience of connoisseurs trained in leisure and capable of being interested in certain rarefied aspects of life. The dramatist may be prevented from exhibiting, for example, detailed representations of certain moments in history that require specialized knowledge in the audience, or psychological states in the personages which are of insufficient general interest to evoke self-identification in the majority. In the Second Part of Goethe's *Faust* there are long passages dealing with the theory of paper money. The exposition of the nature of misanthropy (so much more drastic than Molière's) in Shakespeare's *Timon of Athens* has never been a success. The dramatist accepts this limitation in subject matter and realizes that the group-mind imposes upon him the necessity of treating material understandable by the larger number.

2. It is the presence of the group-mind that brings another requirement to the theatre—forward movement.

Maeterlinck said that there was more drama in the spectacle of an old man seated by a table than in the majority of plays offered to the public. He was juggling with the various meanings in the word "drama." In the sense whereby drama means the intensified concentration of life's diversity and significance he may well have been right; if he meant drama as a theatrical representation before an audience he was wrong. Drama on the stage is inseparable from forward movement, from action.

Many attempts have been made to present Plato's dialogues, Gobineau's fine series of dialogues, *La Renaissance,* and the *Imaginary Conversations* of Landor; but without success. Through some ingredient in the group-mind, and through the sheer weight of anticipation involved in the dressing up and the assumption of fictional roles, an action is required, and an action that is more than a mere progress in argumentation and debate.

III. THE THEATRE IS A WORLD OF PRETENSE

It lives by conventions: a convention is an agreed-upon falsehood, a permitted lie.

Illustrations: Consider at the first performance of the *Medea,* the passage where Medea meditates the murder of her children. An anecdote from antiquity tells us that the audience was so moved by this passage that considerable disturbance took place.

The following conventions were involved:

1. Medea was played by a man.

2. He wore a large mask on his face. In the lip of the mask was an acoustical device for projecting the voice. On his feet he wore shoes with soles and heels half a foot high.

3. His costume was so designed that it conveyed to the audience, by convention: woman of royal birth and Oriental origin.

4. The passage was in metric speech. All poetry is an "agreed-upon-falsehood" in regard to speech.

5. The lines were sung in a kind of recitative. All opera involves this "permitted lie" in regard to speech.

Modern taste would say that the passage would convey very much greater pathos if a woman "like Medea" had delivered it—with an uncovered face that exhibited all the emotions she was undergoing. For the Greeks, however, there was no pretense that Medea was on the stage. The mask, the costume, the mode of declamation, were a series of signs which the spectator interpreted and reassembled in his own mind. Medea was being re-created within the imagination of each of the spectators.

The history of the theatre shows us that in its greatest ages the stage employed the greatest number of conventions. The stage is fundamental pretense and it thrives on the acceptance of that fact and in the multiplication of additional pretenses. When it tries to assert that the personages in the action "really are," really inhabit such and such rooms, really suffer such and such emotions, it loses rather than gains credibility. The modern world is inclined to laugh condescendingly at the fact that in the plays of Racine and Corneille the gods and heroes of antiquity were dressed like the courtiers under Louis XIV; that in the Elizabethan age scenery was replaced by placards notifying the audience of the location; and that a whip in the hand and a jogging motion of the body indicated that a man was on horseback in the Chinese theatre; these devices did not spring from naïveté, however, but from the vitality of the public imagination in those days and from an instinctive feeling as to where the essential and where the inessential lay in drama.

The convention has two functions:

1. It provokes the collaborative activity of the spectator's imagination; and

2. It raises the action from the specific to the general.

This second aspect is of even greater importance than the first.

If Juliet is represented as a girl "very like Juliet"—it was not merely a deference to contemporary prejudices that assigned this role to a boy in the Elizabethan age—moving about in a "real" house with marble staircases, rugs, lamps, and furniture, the impression is irresistibly conveyed that these events hap-

pened to this one girl, in one place, at one moment in time.
When the play is staged as Shakespeare intended it, the bare-
ness of the stage releases the events from the particular and
the experience of Juliet partakes of that of all girls in love, in
every time, place and language.

The stage continually strains to tell this generalized truth
and it is the element of pretense that reinforces it. Out of the
lie, the pretense, of the theatre proceeds a truth more compelling than the novel can attain, for the novel by its own laws
is constrained to tell of an action that "once happened"—"once
upon a time."

IV. THE ACTION ON THE STAGE TAKES PLACE IN A PERPETUAL PRESENT TIME

Novels are written in the past tense. The characters in them,
it is true, are represented as living moment by moment their
present time, but the constant running commentary of the novelist ("Tess slowly descended into the valley"; "Anna Karenina
laughed") inevitably conveys to the reader the fact that these
events are long since past and over.

The novel is a past reported in the present. On the stage it
is always now. This confers upon the action an increased vitality which the novelist longs in vain to incorporate into his work.

This condition in the theatre brings with it another important element:

In the theatre we are not aware of the intervening storyteller.
The speeches arise from the characters in an apparently pure
spontaneity.

A play is what takes place.

A novel is what one person tells us took place.

A play visibly represents pure existing. A novel is what
one mind, claiming omniscience, asserts to have existed.

Many dramatists have regretted this absence of the narrator
from the stage, with his point of view, his powers of analyzing
the behavior of the characters, his ability to interfere and sup-

ply further facts about the past, about simultaneous actions not visible on the stage, and above *all* his function of pointing the moral and emphasizing the significance of the action. In some periods of the theatre he has been present as chorus, or prologue and epilogue or as *raisonneur*. But surely this absence constitutes an additional force to the form, as well as an additional tax upon the writer's skill. It is the task of the dramatist so to co-ordinate his play, through the selection of episodes and speeches, that though he is himself not visible, his point of view and his governing intention will impose themselves on the spectator's attention, not as dogmatic assertion or motto, but as self-evident truth and inevitable deduction.

Imaginative narration—the invention of souls and destinies—is to the philosopher an all but indefensible activity.

Its justification lies in the fact that the communication of ideas from one mind to another inevitably reaches the point where exposition passes into illustration, into parable, metaphor, allegory, and myth.

It is no accident that when Plato arrived at the height of his argument and attempted to convey a theory of knowledge and a theory of the structure of man's nature he passed over into story telling, into the myths of the Cave and the Charioteer; and that the great religious teachers have constantly had recourse to the parable as a means of imparting their deepest intuitions.

The theatre offers to imaginative narration its highest possibilities. It has many pitfalls and its very vitality betrays it into service as mere diversion and the enhancement of insignificant matter; but it is well to remember that it was the theatre that rose to the highest place during those epochs that aftertime has chosen to call "great ages" and that the Athens of Pericles and the reigns of Elizabeth, Philip II, and Louis XIV were also the ages that gave to the world the greatest dramas it has known.

Problems of the Theatre

FRIEDRICH DUERRENMATT

Behold the drive for purity in art as art is practised these days.
Behold this writer striving for the purely poetic, another for the
purely lyrical, the purely epic, the purely dramatic. The
painter ardently seeks to create the pure painting, the musician
pure music, and someone even told me, pure radio represents
the synthesis between Dionysos and Logos. Even more remarkable for our time, not otherwise renowned for its purity, is that
each and everyone believes he has found his unique and the
only true purity. Each vestal of the arts has, if you think of it,
her own kind of chastity. Likewise, too numerous to count, are
all the theories of the theatre, of what is pure theatre, pure tragedy, pure comedy. There are so many modern theories of the
drama, what with each playwright keeping three or four at
hand, that for this reason, if no other, I am a bit embarrassed to
come along now with my theories of the problems of the theatre.

Furthermore, I would ask you not to look upon me as the
spokesman of some specific movement in the theatre or of a certain dramatic technique, nor to believe that I knock at your door
as the traveling salesman of one of the philosophies current on
our stages today, whether as existentialist, nihilist, expressionist
or satirist, or any other label put on the compote dished up by
literary criticism. For me, the stage is not a battlefield for the-

ories, philosophies and manifestos, but rather an instrument whose possibilities I seek to know by playing with it. Of course, in my plays there are people and they hold to some belief or philosophy—a lot of blockheads would make for a dull piece—but my plays are not for what people have to say: what is said is there because my plays deal with people, and thinking and believing and philosophizing are all, to some extent at least, a part of human nature. The problems I face as playwright are practical, working problems, problems I face not before, but during the writing. To be quite accurate about it, these problems usually come up after the writing is done, arising out of a certain curiosity to know how I did it. So what I would like to talk about now are these problems, even though I risk disappointing the general longing for something profound and creating the impression that an amateur is talking. I haven't the faintest notion of how else I should go about it, of how not to talk about art like an amateur. Consequently I speak only to those who fall asleep listening to Heidegger.

What I am concerned with are empirical rules, the possibilities of the theatre. But since we live in an age when literary scholarship and criticism flourish, I can not quite resist the temptation of casting a few side glances at some of the theories of the art and practice of the theatre. The artist indeed has no need of scholarship. Scholarship derives laws from what exists already; otherwise it would not be scholarship. But the laws thus established have no value for the artist, even when they are true. The artist can not accept a law he has not discovered for himself. If he can not find such a law, scholarship can not help him with one it has established; and when the artist does find one, then it does not matter that the same law was also discovered by scholarship. But scholarship, thus denied, stands behind the artist like a threatening ogre, ready to leap forth whenever the artist wants to talk about art. And so it is here. To talk about problems of the theatre is to enter into competition with literary scholarship. I undertake this with some misgivings.

Literary scholarship looks on the theatre as an object; for the dramatist it is never something purely objective, something separate from him. He participates in it. It is true that the playwright's activity makes drama into something objective (that is exactly his job), but he destroys the object he has created again and again, forgets it, rejects it, scorns it, overestimates it, all in order to make room for something new. Scholarship sees only the result; the process, which led to this result, is what the playwright can not forget. What he says has to be taken with a grain of salt. What he thinks about his art changes as he creates his art; his thoughts are always subject to his mood and the moment. What alone really counts for him is what he is doing at a given moment; for its sake he can betray what he did just a little while ago. Perhaps a writer should not talk about his art, but once he starts, then it is not altogether a waste of time to listen to him. Literary scholars who have not the faintest notion of the difficulties of writing and of the hidden rocks that force the stream of art into oft unsuspected channels run the danger of merely asserting and stupidly proclaiming laws that do not exist.

Doubtless the unities of time, place and action which Aristotle—so it was supposed for a long time—derived from Greek tragedy constitute the ideal of drama. From a logical and hence also esthetic point of view, this thesis is incontestable, so incontestable indeed, that the question arises if it does not set up the framework once and for all within which each dramatist must work. Aristotle's three unities demand the greatest precision, the greatest economy and the greatest simplicity in the handling of the dramatic material. The unities of time, place and action ought to be a basic dictate put to the dramatist by literary scholarship, and the only reason scholarship does not hold the artist to them is that Aristotle's unities have not been obeyed by anyone for ages. Nor can they be obeyed, for reasons which best illustrate the relationship of the art of writing plays to the theories about that art.

The unities of time, place and action in essence presuppose Greek tragedy. Aristotle's unities do not make Greek tragedy possible; rather, Greek tragedy allows his unities. No matter how abstract an esthetic law may appear to be, the work of art from which it was derived is contained in that law. If I want to set about writing a dramatic action which is to unfold and run its course in the same place inside of two hours, for instance, then this action must have a history behind it, and that history will be the more extensive the fewer the number of stage characters there are at my disposal. This is simply an experience of how the theatre works, an empirical rule. For me a history is the story which took place before the stage action commenced, a story which alone makes the action on the stage possible. Thus the history behind Hamlet is, of course, the murder of his father; the drama lies in the discovery of that murder. As a rule, too, the stage action is much shorter in time than the event depicted; it often starts out right in the middle of the event, or indeed towards the end of it. Before Sophocles' tragedy could begin, Oedipus had to have killed his father and married his mother, activities that take a little time. The stage action must compress an event to the same degree in which it fulfills the demands of Aristotle's unities. And the closer a playwright adheres to the three unities, the more important is the background history of the action.

It is, of course, possible to invent a history and hence a dramatic action that would seem particularly favorable for keeping to Aristotle's unities. But this brings into force the rule that the more invented a story is and the more unknown it is to the audience, the more careful must its exposition, the unfolding of the background be. Greek tragedy was possible only because it did not have to invent its historical background, because it already possessed one. The spectators knew the myths with which each drama dealt; and because these myths were public, ready coin, part of religion, they made the feats of the Greek tragedians possible, feats never to be attained again; they made possible their abbreviations, their straightforwardness, their stichomythy and choruses, and hence also Aristotle's unities. The audience knew what the play was all about; its curiosity was not focused on the story so much as on its treatment. Aristotle's unities presupposed the general appreciation of the subject matter —a genial exception in more recent times is Kleist's *The Broken Jug*—presupposed a religious theatre based on myths. Therefore as soon as the theatre lost its religious, its mythical significance, the unities had to be reinterpreted or discarded. An audience facing an unknown story will pay more attention to the story than to its treatment, and by necessity then such a play has to be richer in detail and circumstances than one with a known action. The feats of one playwright can not be the feats of another. Each art exploits the chances offered by its time, and it is hard to imagine a time without chances. Like every other form of art, drama creates its world; but not every world can be created in the same fashion. This is the natural limitation of every esthetic rule, no matter how self-evident such a rule may be. This does not mean that Aristotle's unities are obsolete; what was once a rule has become an exception, a case that may occur again at any time. The one-act play obeys the unities still, even though under a different condition. Instead of the history, the situation now dominates the plot, and thus unity is once again achieved.

But what is true for Aristotle's theory of drama, namely its dependency upon a certain world and hence its validity relative to that world, is also true of every other theory of drama. Brecht is consistent only when he incorporates into his dramaturgy that *Weltanschauung*, the communist philosophy, to which he—so he seems to think—is committed; but in doing so he often cuts off his own nose. Sometimes his plays say the very opposite of what they claim they say, but this lack of agreement can not always be blamed on the capitalistic audience. Often it is simply a case where Brecht, the poet, gets the better of Brecht, the dramatic theorist, a situation that is wholly legitimate and ominous only were it not to happen again.

Let us speak plainly. My introducing the audience as a factor in the making of a play may have seemed strange to many.
But just as it is impossible to have theatre without spectators,
so it is senseless to consider and treat a play as if it were a
kind of ode, divided into parts and delivered in a vacuum. A
piece written for the theatre becomes living theatre when it is
played, when it can be seen, heard, felt, and thus experienced
immediately. This immediacy is one of the most essential aspects of the theatre, a fact so often overlooked in those sacred
halls where a play by Hofmannsthal counts for more than one
by Nestroy, and a Richard Strauss opera more than one by Offen-
bach. A play is an event, is something that happens. In the theatre everything must be transformed into something immediate,
something visible and sensible; the corollary to this thought,
however, is that not everything can be translated into something
immediate and corporeal. Kafka, for example, really does not
belong on the stage. The bread offered there gives no nourishment; it lies undigested in the iron stomachs of the theatre-going
public and the regular subscribers. As luck would have it, many
think of the heaviness they feel not as a stomach ache, but as
the heaviness of soul which Kafka's true works emanate, so that
by error all is set aright.

The immediacy sought by every play, the spectacle into
which it would be transformed, presupposes an audience, a theatre, a stage. Hence we would also do well to examine the theatres for which we have to write today. We all know these
money-losing enterprises. They can, like so many other institutions today, be justified only on an idealistic basis: in reality,
not at all. The architecture of our theatres, their seating arrangements and their stages, came down from the court theatre or, to
be more precise, never got beyond it. For this reason alone, our
so-called contemporary theatre is not really contemporary. In
contrast to the primitive Shakespearean stage, in contrast to this
"scaffold" where, as Goethe put it, "little was shown, everything
signified," the court theatre made every effort to satisfy a crav-

ing for naturalness, even though this resulted in much greater unnaturalness. No longer was the audience satisfied to imagine the royal chamber behind the "green curtain"; every attempt was made to show the chamber. Characteristic of such theatre is its tendency to separate audience and stage, by means both of the curtain as well as having the spectators sit in the dark facing a well-lit stage. This latter innovation was perhaps the most treacherous of all, for it alone made possible the solemn atmosphere in which our theatres suffocate. The stage became a peep show. Better lighting was constantly invented, then a revolving stage, and it is said they have even invented a revolving house! The courts went, but the court theatre stayed on. Now to be sure, our time has discovered its own form of theatre, the movies. But no matter how much we may emphasize the differences, and how important it may be to emphasize them, still it must be pointed out that the movies grew out of theatre, and that they can at last achieve what the court theatre with all its machinery, revolving stages and other effects only dreamed of doing: to simulate reality.

The movies, then, are nothing more nor less than the democratic form of the court theatre. They intensify our sense of intimacy immeasurably, so much so that the movies easily risk becoming the genuinely pornographic art. For the spectator is forced into being a "voyeur," and movie stars enjoy their immense popularity because those who see them come also to feel that they have slept with them; that is how well movie stars are photographed. A larger-than-life picture is an indecency.

Just what then is our present-day theatre? If the movies are the modern form of the old court theatre, what is the theatre? There is no use in pretending that the theatre today is anything much more than a museum in which the art treasures of former golden ages of the drama are put on exhibition. There is no way of changing that. It is only too natural, at a time like ours, a time which, always looking toward the past, seems to possess everything but a living present. In Goethe's time the ancients were rarely performed, Schiller occasionally, but mostly Kotzebue and whoever else they were. It is worthwhile to point out that the movies preempt the theatre of its Kotzebues and Birch-Pfeiffers, and it is hard to imagine what sort of plays would have to be put on today, if there were no movies and if all the scriptwriters wrote for the legitimate stage.

If the contemporary theatre is to a large extent a museum, then this has definite effects on the actors which it employs. They have become civil servants, usually even entitled to their pensions, permitted to act in the theatre when not kept busy making movies. The members of this once despised estate have settled down now as solid citizens—a human gain, an artistic loss. And today actors fit into the order of professional rank somewhere between the physicians and small industrialists, surpassed within the realm of art only by the winners of the Nobel prize, by pianists and conductors. Some actors are visiting professors of sorts, or independent scholars, who take their turn appearing in the museums or arranging exhibitions. The management, of course, takes this into account when it arranges its playbill more or less with an eye to its guest stars; says the management: what play should we put on when this or that authority in this or that field is available to us at such and such a date? Moreover actors are forced to move about in many different acting styles, now in a baroque style, now in a classical one, today acting naturalism, tomorrow Claudel. An actor in Molière's day did not have to do that. The director, too, is more important, more dominant than ever, like the conductor of an orchestra. Historical works demand, and ought to demand, proper interpretation; but directors as yet dare not be as true to the works they put on as some conductors are quite naturally to theirs. The classics often are not interpreted but executed, and the curtain falls upon a mutilated corpse. But then, where is the danger in it all? There is always the saving convention by which all classical things are accepted as perfection, as a kind of gold

standard in our cultural life, with all things looked upon as
gold that shine in Modern Library or Temple classics. The
theatre-going public goes to see the classics, whether they be
performed well or not; applause is assured, indeed is the duty
of the educated man. And thus the public has legitimately been
relieved of the task of thinking and of passing judgments other
than those learned by rote in school.

Yet there is a good side to the many styles the present-day
theatre must master, although it may at first glance appear bad.
Every great age of the theatre was possible because of the discovery of a unique form of theatre, of a particular style, which
determined the way plays were written. This is easily demon-
strable in the English or Spanish theatre, or the Vienna Na-
tional Theatre, the most remarkable phenomenon in the Ger-
man-speaking theatre. This alone can explain the astounding
number of plays written by Lope de Vega. Stylistically a play
was no problem for him. But to the degree that a uniform style
of theatre does not exist today, indeed can no longer exist, to that
extent is writing for the theatre now a problem and thus more
difficult. Therefore our contemporary theatre is two things: on
one hand it is a museum, on the other an experimental field,
each play confronting the author with new challenges, new
questions of style. Yes, style today is no longer a common property, but highly private, even particularized from case to case.
We have no style, only styles, which puts the situation in art
today in a nutshell. For contemporary art is a series of experiments, nothing more nor less, just like all of our modern world.

If there are only styles, then, too, we have only theories of
the art and practice of the theatre, and no longer one dramaturgy.
We now have Brecht's and Eliot's, Claudel's and that of Frisch
or of Hochwaelder: always a new theory of drama for each
dramatic offering. Nevertheless one can conceive of a single
theory of drama, a theory that would cover all particular instances, much in the same way that we have worked out a geometry which embraces all dimensions. Aristotle's theory of
drama would be only one of many possible theories in this dram-

aturgy. It would have to be a new *Poetics,* which would examine the possibilities not of a certain stage, but of the stage, a
dramaturgy of the experiment itself.

What, finally, might we say about the audience without
which, as we have said before, no theatre is possible? The audience has become anonymous, just "the paying public," a matter
far worse than first strikes the eye. The modern author no longer
knows his public, unless he writes for some village stage or Caux,
neither of which is much fun. A playwright has to imagine his
audience; but in truth the audience is he himself—and this is a
danger which can neither be altered now nor circumvented.
All the dubious, well-worn, politically misused notions which
attach themselves to the concepts of "a people" and "society,"
to say nothing of "a community," have perforce also crept into
the theatre. What points is an author to make? How is he to find
his subjects, what solutions should he reach? All these are questions for which we may perhaps find an answer once we have
gained a clearer notion as to what possibilities still exist in the
theatre today.

In undertaking to write a play I must first make clear to
myself just where it is to take place. At first glance that does
not seem like much of a problem. A play takes place in London or Berlin, in the mountains, a hospital or on a battlefield,
wherever the action demands. But it does not work out quite
that way. A play, after all, takes place upon a stage which
in turn must represent London, the mountains or a battlefield.
This distinction need not, but can be made. It depends entirely
on how much the author takes the stage into account, how
strongly he wants to create the illusion without which no theatre can exist, and whether he wants it smeared on thickly with
gobs of paint heaped upon the canvas, or transparent, diapha-
nous and fragile. A playwright can be deadly serious about
the place: Madrid, the Ruetli, the Russian steppe, or he can
think of it as just a stage, the world, his world.

How the stage is to represent a given place is, of course, the task of the scene designer. Since designing scenes is a form of painting, the developments which have taken place in painting in our time have not failed to touch the theatre. But the theatre can really neither abstract man nor language, which is in itself both abstract and concrete, and scenery, no matter how abstract it would pretend to be, must still represent something concrete to make sense, and for both of these reasons, abstraction in scenic design has essentially failed. Nevertheless the "green curtain" behind which the spectators have to imagine the place, the royal chamber, was reinstituted. The fact was recalled that the dramatic place and the stage were not one and the same, no matter how elaborate, how verisimilar the stage setting might be. The fact is the place has to be created by the play. One word: we are in Venice; another, in the Tower of London. The imagination of the audience needs but little support. Scenery is to suggest, point out, intensify, but not describe the place. Once more it has become transparent, immaterialized. And similarly the place of the drama to be shown on the stage can be made immaterial.

Two fairly recent plays which most clearly illustrate the possibility referred to as immaterializing the scenery and the dramatic place are Wilder's *Our Town* and *The Skin of Our Teeth*. The immaterializing of the stage in *Our Town* consists of this: the stage is nearly empty; only a few objects needed for rehearsals stand about—some chairs, tables, ladders and so on; and out of these everyday objects the place is created, the dramatic place, the town, all out of the world, the play, the wakened imagination of the spectators. In his other play Wilder, this great fanatic of the theatre, immaterializes the dramatic place: where the Antrobus family really lives, in what age and what stage of civilization, is never wholly clear; now it is the ice age, now a world war. This sort of experiment may be met quite often in modern drama; thus it is indefinite where in Frisch's play, *Graf Oederland*, the strange Count Wasteland abides; no man knows where to wait for Godot, and in *The Mar-*

riage of Milord Mississippi (*Die Ehe des Herrn Mississippi*) I expressed the indefiniteness of the locale (in order to give the play its spirit of wit, of comedy) by having the right window of a room look out upon a northern landscape with its Gothic cathedral and apple tree, while the left window of the same room opens on a southern scene with an ancient ruin, a touch of the Mediterranean and a cypress. The really decisive point in all this is that, to quote Max Frisch, the playwright is making poetry with the stage, a possibility which has always entertained and occupied me and which is one of the reasons, if not the main one, why I write plays. But then—and I am thinking of the comedies of Aristophanes and the comic plays of Nestroy —in every age poetry has been written not only *for,* but *with* the stage.

Let us turn from these incidental problems to more basic ones. What do the particular problems look like, which I—to cite an author whom I know at least to some, though not the whole extent—have faced? In *The Blind Man* (*Der Blinde*) I wanted to juxtapose the word against the dramatic place, to turn the word against the scene. The blind duke believes he is living in his well-preserved castle whereas he is living in a ruin; he thinks he is humbling himself before Wallenstein, but sinks to his knees before a Negro. The dramatic place is one and the same, but by means of the pretense carried on before the blind man, it plays a dual role: the place seen by the audience and the place in which the blind man fancies himself to be. So also, when in my comedy, *An Angel Comes to Babylon* (*Ein Engel kommt nach Babylon*), I picked for my dramatic locale the city in which the Tower was built, I had essentially to solve two problems. In the first place the stage had to express the fact that there were two places of action in my comedy, heaven and the city of Babylon; heaven, which was the secret point of origin of the action, and Babylon, the locale where that action ran its course.

Well, I suppose heaven could have been simply represented by a dark background to suggest its infinity, but since I wanted to convey in my comedy the idea that heaven was not something infinite, but something incomprehensible and altogether different, I asked for the stage background, the heaven above the city of Babylon, to be occupied entirely by the Great Nebula in Andromeda, just as we might see it through the telescope on Mt. Palomar. What I hoped to achieve thereby was that heaven, the incomprehensible and inscrutable, would take on form, gain, as it were, its own stage presence. In this wise also heaven's rapprochement with the earth was to be brought out, reiterating the coming together of the two that is expressed in the action through the angel's visiting Babylon. Thus, too, a world was constructed in which the result of the action, namely the building of the tower of Babylon, became possible.

In the second place I had to think of how to make the stage represent Babylon, the place in which the action unfolds. I found the idea of Babylon challenging because of its timeliness, its Cyclopean big-city character, its New-York-look with its skyscrapers and slums, and by having the first two acts take place along the banks of the Euphrates I wished to hint at Paris. Babylon, in brief, stands for the metropolis. It is a Babylon of the imagination, having a few typically Babylonian features, but as a modernized parodied version, with its modernities—for instance the convenience of electric street lights. Of course the execution of the scenery, the building of the stage itself, is a job for the scene designer, but the playwright must always decide himself just what kind of stage he wants.

I love a colorful stage setting, a colorful theatre, like the stage of Theo Otto, to mention an admirable example. (I have little use for a theatre that uses black curtains as was the fashion once upon a time, or for the tendency to glory in threadbare poverty which some stage designers seem to aim for.) To be sure the word is important above all else in the theatre; but note: above all else. For after the word there are many other things, which also rightfully belong to the theatre, even a certain wantonness. Thus when someone asked me quite thoughtfully with respect to my play *Mississippi,* where one of the characters enters through a grandfather-clock, whether or not I thought a four-dimensional theatre possible, I could only remark that I had not thought of Einstein when I did it. It is just that in my daily life it should give me great pleasure if I could enter into a company and astonish those present by coming into the room through a grandfather-clock or by floating in through a window. No one should deny us playwrights the opportunity to satisfy such desires now and then at least on the stage, where such whims can be fulfilled. The old argument of which came first, the chicken or the egg, can be transformed in art into the question of whether the egg or the chicken, the world as potential or as rich harvest, is to be presented. Artists might very well be divided then into those favoring the egg and those favoring the chicken. The argument is a lively one. Alfred Polgar once said to me, it was odd that while in the contemporary Anglo-Saxon drama everything came out in the dialogue, there was always much too much happening on the stage in my plays and that he, Polgar, would sometimes like to see a simple Duerrenmatt play. Behind this truth, however, lies my refusal to say that the egg came before the chicken, and my personal prejudice of preferring the chicken to the egg. It happens to be my passion, not always a happy one perhaps, to want to put on the stage the richness, the manifold diversity of the world. As a result my theatre is open to many interpretations and appears to confuse some. Misunderstandings creep in, as when someone looks around desperately in the chicken coop of my plays, hoping to find the egg of Columbus which I stubbornly refuse to lay.

But a play is bound not only to a place, but also to a time. Just as the stage represents a place, so it also represents a time, the time *during* which the action takes place as well as the time *in* which it occurs. If Aristotle had really demanded the unity of time, place and action, he would have limited the duration of a tragedy to the time it took for the action to be carried out (a feat which the Greek tragedians nearly achieved), for which reasons, of course, everything would have to be concentrated upon that action. Time would pass "naturally," everything coming one after the other without breaks. But this does not always have to be the case. In general the actions on the stage follow one another but, to cite an example, in Nestroy's magical farce, *Death on the Wedding Day* (*Der Tod am Hochzeitstag*), there are two acts taking place simultaneously and the illusion of simultaneity is skillfully achieved by having the action of the second act form the background noise for the first, and the action of the first act the background noise for the second. Other examples of how time is used as a theatrical device could be easily recalled. Time can be shortened, stretched, intensified, arrested, repeated; the dramatist can, like Joshua, call to his heaven's orbits, "Theatre-Sun, stand thou still upon Gideon! And thou, Theatre-Moon, in the valley of Ajalon!"

It may be noted further that the unities ascribed to Aristotle were not wholly kept in Greek tragedy either. The action is interrupted by the choruses, and by this means time is spaced. When the chorus interrupts the action, it achieves as regards time—to elucidate the obvious like an amateur—the very same thing the curtain does today. The curtain cuts up and spreads out the time of an action. I have nothing against such an honorable device. The good thing about a curtain is that it so clearly defines an act, that it clears the table, so to speak. Moreover it is psychologically often extremely necessary to give the exhausted and frightened audience a rest. But a new way of binding language and time has evolved in our day.

If I cite Wilder's *Our Town* once again, I do so because I assume that this fine play is widely known. You may recall that in it different characters turn toward the audience and talk of the worries and needs of their small town. In this way Wilder is able to dispense with the curtain. The curtain has been replaced by the direct address to the audience. The epic element of description has been added to the drama. For this reason, of course, this form of theatre has been called the epic theatre.

Yet when looked at quite closely, Shakespeare's plays or Schiller's *Goetz von Berlichingen* are in a certain sense also epic theatre. Only in a different, less obvious manner. Since Shakespeare's histories often extend over a considerable period of time, this time span is divided into different actions, different episodes, each of which is treated dramatically. *Henry IV, Part I,* consists of nineteen such episodes, while by the end of the fourth act of *Goetz* there already are no less than forty-one tableaux. I stopped counting after that. If one looks at the way the over-all action has been built up, then, with respect to time, it is quite close to the epic, like a movie that is run too slowly, so that the individual frames can be seen. The condensation of everything into a certain time has been given up in favor of an episodic form of drama.

Thus when an author in some of our modern plays turns toward the audience, he attempts to give the play a greater continuity than is otherwise possible in an episodic form. The void between the acts is to be filled; the time gap is to be bridged, not by a pause, but by words, by a description of what has gone on in the meanwhile, or by having some new character introduce himself. In other words, the expositions are handled in an epic manner, not the actions to which these expositions lead. This represents an advance of the word in the theatre, the attempt of the word to reconquer territory lost a long time ago. Let us emphasize that it is but an attempt; for all too often the direct address to the audience is used to explain the play, an undertaking that makes no sense whatever. If the audience is moved by the play, it will not need prodding by explanations; if the audience is not moved, all the prodding in the world will not be of help.

In contrast to the epic, which can describe human beings as they are, the drama unavoidably limits and therefore stylizes them. This limitation is inherent in the art form itself. The human being of the drama is, after all, a talking individual, and speech is his limitation. The action only serves to force this human being on the stage to talk in a certain way. The action is the crucible in which the human being is molten into words, must become words. This of course, means that I, as the playwright, have to get the people in my drama into situations which force them to speak. If I merely show two people sitting together and drinking coffee while they talk about the weather, politics or the latest fashions, then I provide neither a dramatic situation nor dramatic dialogue, no matter how clever their talk. Some other ingredient must be added to their conversation, something to add pique, drama, double meaning. If the audience knows that there is some poison in one of the coffee cups, or perhaps even in both, so that the conversation is really one between two poisoners, then this little coffee-for-two idyl becomes through this artistic device a dramatic situation, out of which and on the basis of which dramatic dialogue can develop. Without the addition of some special tension or special condition, dramatic dialogue can not develop.

Just as dialogue must develop out of a situation, so it must also lead into some situation, that is to say, of course, a new situation. Dramatic dialogue effects some action, some suffering, some new situation, out of which in turn new dialogue can again develop, and so on and so forth.

However, a human being does more than just talk. The fact that a man also thinks, or at least should think, that he feels, yes, more than anything feels, and that he does not always wish to show others what he is thinking or feeling, has led to the use of another artistic device, the monologue. It is true, of course, that a person standing on a stage and carrying on a conversation with himself out loud is not exactly natural; and the same thing can be said, only more so, of an operatic aria. But the monologue (like the aria) proves that an artistic trick, which really ought not be played, can achieve an unexpected effect, to which, and rightly so, the public succumbs time and again; so much so that Hamlet's monologue, "To be or not to be," or Faust's, are among the most beloved and most famous passages in the theatre.

But not everything that sounds like a monologue is monologue. The purpose of dialogue is not only to lead a human being to a point where he must act or suffer, but at times it also leads into a major speech, to the explanation of some point of view. Many people have lost the appreciation of rhetoric since, as Hilpert maintains, some actor who was not sure of his lines discovered naturalism. That loss is rather sad. A speech can win its way across the footlights more effectively than any other artistic device. But many of our critics no longer know what to make of a speech. An author, who today dares a speech, will suffer the same fate as the peasant Dicaeopolis; he will have to lay his head upon the executioner's block. Except that instead of the Acharnians of Aristophanes, it will be the majority of critics who descend on the author—the most normal thing in the world. Nobody is more anxious to bash out someone's brains than those who haven't any.

Moreover, the drama has always embodied some narrative elements; epic drama did not introduce this. So, for instance, the background of an action has always had to be related, or an event announced in the form of a messenger's report. But narration on the stage is not without its dangers, for it does not live in the same manner, is not tangible the way an action taking place on the stage is. Attempts have been made to overcome this, as by dramatizing the messenger, by letting him appear at a crucial moment, or by making him a blockhead from whom a report can only be extracted with great difficulties. Yet certain elements of rhetoric must still be present if narration is to succeed on the stage. Stage narratives can not exist without some exaggeration. Observe, for instance, how Shakespeare elaborates on Plutarch's description of Cleopatra's barge. This exaggeration is not just a characteristic of the baroque style, but a means of launching Cleopatra's barge upon the stage, of making it visible there. But while the speech of the theatre can not exist without exaggeration, it is important to know when to exaggerate and above all, how.

Furthermore, just as the stage characters can suffer a certain fate, so also their language. The angel that came to Babylon, for example, grows more and more enthusiastic about the earth's beauty from act to act, and hence his language must parallel this rising enthusiasm until it grows into a veritable hymn. In the same comedy the beggar Akki relates his life in a series of *makamat*, passages of a rich and stately prose interspersed with rhymes, refined in grammar, rhetoric, poetic idiom and tradition, that come from the Arabic and flourished a thousand years ago. In this way I try to convey the Arabic character of this personage, his joy in inventing stories and in duelling and playing with words, without at the same time wandering off into another form, the chanson. The *makamat* or anecdotes of Akki are nothing less than the most extreme possibilities offered by his language, and therefore they intensify his being. Through the *makamat* Akki has become all language and this is just what an author must always strive for, so that there are moments in his plays in which the characters he has created with the written word become living language and nothing less.

A danger lurks here, too, of course. Language can lead a writer astray. The joy of being able all of a sudden to write, of possessing language, as it came over me, for instance, while I was writing *The Blind Man*, can make an author talk too much, can make him escape from his subject into language. To keep close to the subject is itself a great art, achieved only by masterful control of the impetus to talk. Dialogue, like playing on words, can also lead an author into byways, take him unawares away from his subject. Yet ideas flash into his mind again and again, ideas which he ought not resist, even if they disrupt his carefully laid plans. For in addition to being on guard against some of these tempting flashes of ideas, a writer must also have the courage to follow some of them.

These elements and problems of place, time, and action, which are all, of course interwoven and are but hinted at here, belong to the basic material, to the artistic devices and tools of the craft of the drama. But let me make it clear here and now, that I make war upon the notion of "the craft of the drama." The very idea that anyone who makes a sufficiently diligent and steadfast endeavor to achieve something in that art will succeed in the end or even that this craft can be learned is a notion we thought discarded long ago. Yet it is still frequently met with in critical writings about the art of play-writing. This art is supposed to be a sound-and-solid, respectable and well-mannered affair. Thus, too, the relationship between a playwright and his art is considered by some to be like a marriage in which everything is quite legal when blessed with the sacraments of esthetics. For these reasons, perhaps, critics often refer to the theatre, much more than to any other form of art, as a craft which, depending on the particular case, has been more or less mastered. If we investigate closely what the critics really mean by "the craft of the drama," then it becomes obvious that it is little else but the sum of their prejudices. There is no craft of the theatre; there is only the mastery of the material through language and the stage or, to be more exact, it is an overpowering of the material, for any creative writing is a kind of warfare with its victories, defeats and indecisive battles. Perfect plays do not exist except as a fiction of esthetics in which, as in the movies, perfect heroes may alone be found. Never yet has a playwright left this battle without his wounds; each one has his Achilles' heel, and the playwright's antagonist, his material, never fights fairly. It is cunning stuff, often not to be drawn out of its lair, and it employs highly secret and low-down tricks. This forces the playwright to fight back with every permissible and even non-permissible means, no matter what the wise exhortations, rules and adages of the masters of this craft and their most honored trade may say. Best foot forward won't get an author anywhere in the drama, not even his foot in the doorway. The difficulties in writing for the drama lie where no one suspects them; sometimes it is no more than the problem of how to have two people say hello, or the difficulty in writing an opening sentence. What is sometimes considered to be the craft of the drama can be easily learned inside half an hour. But how difficult it is to divide a given material into five acts and how few subjects there are which can be divided that way, how nearly impossible it is to write today in iambic pentameter, those things are hardly ever suspected by the hack writers who can slap a play together any time and without trouble, who can always divide any subject into five acts, and who have always written and still write with facility in iambic pentameter. They really pick their material and their language in the way some critics think this is done. They are not so much amateurs when they talk about art as when they tailor art to their talk. No matter what the material is like, they always fashion the same bathrobe to be sure the audience will not catch cold and that it will sleep comfortably. There is nothing more idiotic than the opinion that only a genius does not have to obey those rules prescribed for writers of talent. In that case I should like to be counted among the geniuses. What I want to emphasize strongly is that the art of writing a play does not necessarily start out with the planning of a certain child, or however else a eunuch thinks love is made; but it starts out with love making of which a eunuch is incapable. Though really the difficulties, pains and also fortunes of writing do not lie within the realm of things we mean to talk about or even can talk about. We can only talk about the craft of the drama, a craft that exists only when one *talks* of drama, but not when one writes plays.

The craft of the drama is an optical illusion. To talk about plays, about art, is a much more utopian undertaking than is ever appreciated by those who talk the most.

Employing this—really non-existent—craft, let us try and give shape to a certain material. Usually there is a central point of reference, the hero. In theories of the drama a difference is made between a tragic hero, the hero of tragedy, and a comic hero, the hero of comedy. The qualities a tragic hero must possess are well known. He must be capable of rousing our sympathy. His guilt and his innocence, his virtues and his vices must be mixed in the most pleasant and yet exact manner, and administered in doses according to well-defined rules. If, for example, I make my tragic hero an evil man, then I must endow him with a portion of intellect equal to his malevolence. As a result of this rule, the most sympathetic stage character in German literature has turned out to be the devil. The role of the hero in the play has not changed. The only thing that has changed is the social position of the character who awakens our sympathy.

In ancient tragedy and in Shakespeare the hero belongs to the highest class in society, to the nobility. The spectators watch a suffering, acting, raving hero who occupies a social position far higher than their own. This continues still to impress audiences today.

Then when Lessing and Schiller introduced the bourgeois drama, the audience saw itself as the suffering hero on the stage. But the evolution of the hero continued. Buechner's Woyzeck is a primitive proletarian who represents far less socially than the average spectator. But it is precisely in this extreme form of human existence, in this last, most miserable form, that the audience is to see the human being also, indeed itself.

And finally we might mention Pirandello, who was the first, as far as I know, to render the hero, the character on the stage, immaterial and transparent just as Wilder did the dramatic place. The audience watching this sort of presentation attends, as it were, its own dissection, its own psychoanalysis, and the stage becomes man's internal milieu, the inner space of the world.

Of course, the theatre has never dealt only with kings and generals; in comedy the hero has always been the peasant, the beggar, the ordinary citizen—but this was always in comedy. Nowhere in Shakespeare do we find a comic king; in his day a ruler could appear as a bloody monster but never as a fool. In Shakespeare the courtiers, the artisans, the working people are comic. Hence, in the evolution of the tragic hero we see a trend towards comedy. Analogously the fool becomes more and more of a tragic figure. This fact is by no means without significance. The hero of a play not only propels an action on, he not only suffers a certain fate, but he also represents a world. Therefore we have to ask ourselves how we should present our own questionable world and with what sort of heroes. We have to ask ourselves how the mirrors which catch and reflect this world should be ground and set.

Can our present-day world, to ask a concrete question, be represented by Schiller's dramatic art? Some writers claim it can be, since Schiller still holds audiences in his grip. To be sure, in art everything is possible when the art is right. But the question is if an art valid for its time could possibly be so even for our day. Art can never be repeated. If it were repeatable, it would be foolish not just to write according to the rules of Schiller.

Schiller wrote as he did because the world in which he lived could still be mirrored in the world his writing created, a world he could build as a historian. But just barely. For was not Napoleon perhaps the last hero in the old sense? The world today as it appears to us could hardly be encompassed in the form of the historical drama as Schiller wrote it, for the reason alone that we no longer have any tragic heroes, but only vast tragedies staged by world butchers and produced by slaughtering machines. Hitler and Stalin can not be made into Wallensteins. Their power is so enormous that they themselves are no more than incidental, corporeal and easily replaceable expressions of this power; and the misfortune associated with the former and to a considerable extent also with the latter is too vast, too complex, too horrible, too mechanical and usually simply too devoid of all sense. Wallenstein's power can still be envisioned; power as we know it today can only be seen in its smallest part for, like an iceberg, the largest part is submerged in anonymity and abstraction. Schiller's drama presupposes a world that the eye can take in, that takes for granted genuine actions of state, just as Greek tragedy did. For only what the eye can take in can be made visible in art. The state today, however, can not be envisioned for it is anonymous and bureaucratic; and not only in Moscow and Washington, but also in Berne. Actions of state today have become *post-hoc* satyric dramas which follow the tragedies executed in secret earlier. True representatives of our world are missing; the tragic heroes are nameless. Any small-time crook, petty government official or policeman better represents our world than a senator or president. Today art can only embrace the victims, if it can reach men at all; it can no longer come close to the mighty. Creon's secretaries close Antigone's case. The state has lost its physical reality, and just as physics can now only cope with the world in mathematical formulas, so the state can only be expressed in statistics. Power today becomes visible, material only when it explodes as in the atom bomb, in this marvelous mushroom which rises and spreads immaculate as the sun and in which mass murder and beauty have become one. The atom bomb can not be reproduced artistically since it is mass-produced. In its face all of man's art that would recreate it must fail, since it is itself a creation of man. Two mirrors which reflect one another remain empty.

But the task of art, insofar as art can have a task at all, and hence also the task of drama today, is to create something concrete, something that has form. This can be accomplished best by comedy. Tragedy, the strictest genre in art, presupposes a formed world. Comedy—in so far as it is not just satire of a particular society as in Molière—supposes an unformed world, a world being made and turned upside down, a world about to fold like ours. Tragedy overcomes distance; it can make myths originating in times immemorial seem like the present to the Athenians. But comedy creates distance; the attempt of the Athenians to gain a foothold in Sicily is translated by comedy into the birds undertaking to create their own empire before which the gods and men will have to capitulate. How comedy works can be seen in the most primitive kind of joke, in the dirty story, which, though it is of very dubious value, I bring up only because it is the best illustration of what I mean by creating distance. The subject of the dirty story is the purely sexual, which because it is purely sexual, is formless and without objective distance. To be given form the purely sexual is transmuted, as I have already mentioned, into the dirty joke. Therefore this type of joke is a kind of original comedy, a transposition of the sexual onto the plane of the comical. In this way it is possible, today in a society dominated by John Doe, to talk in an accepted way about the purely sexual. In the dirty story it becomes clear that the comical exists in forming what is formless, in creating order out of chaos.

The means by which comedy creates distance is the conceit. Tragedy is without conceit. Hence there are few tragedies whose subjects were invented. By this I do not mean to imply that the ancient tragedians lacked inventive ideas of the sort that are written today, but the marvel of their art was that they had no need of these inventions, of conceits. That makes all the difference. Aristophanes, on the other hand, lives by conceits. The stuff of his plays is not myths but inventions, which take place not in the past but the present. They drop into their world like bomb shells which, by throwing up huge craters of dirt, change the present into the comic and thus scatter the dirt for everyone to see. This, of course, does not mean that drama today can only be comical. Tragedy and comedy are but formal concepts, dramatic attitudes, figments of the esthetic imagination which can embrace one and the same thing. Only the conditions under which each is created are different, and these conditions have their basis only in small part in art.

Tragedy presupposes guilt, despair, moderation, lucidity, vision, a sense of responsibility. In the Punch-and-Judy show of our century, in this back-sliding of the white race, there are no more guilty and also, no responsible men. It is always, "We couldn't help it" and "We didn't really want that to happen." And indeed, things happen without anyone in particular being responsible for them. Everything is dragged along and everyone gets caught somewhere in the sweep of events. We are all collectively guilty, collectively bogged down in the sins of our fathers and of our forefathers. We are the offspring of children. That is our misfortune, but not our guilt: guilt can exist only as a personal achievement, as a religious deed. Comedy alone is suitable for us. Our world has led to the grotesque as well as to the atom bomb, and so it is a world like that of Hieronymus Bosch whose apocalyptic paintings are also grotesque. But the grotesque is only a way of expressing in a tangible manner, of making us perceive physically the paradoxical, the form of the unformed, the face of a world without face; and just as in our thinking today we seem to be unable to do without the concept of the paradox, so also in art, and in our world which at times seems still to exist only because the atom bomb exists: out of fear of the bomb.

But the tragic is still possible even if pure tragedy is not. We can achieve the tragic out of comedy. We can bring it forth as a frightening moment, as an abyss that opens suddenly; indeed many of Shakespeare's tragedies are already really comedies out of which the tragic arises.

After all this the conclusion might easily be drawn that comedy is the expression of despair, but this conclusion is not inevitable. To be sure, whoever realizes the senselessness, the hopelessness of this world might well despair, but this despair is not a result of this world. Rather it is an answer given by an individual to this world; another answer would be not to despair, would be an individual's decision to endure this world in which we live like Gulliver among the giants. He also achieves distance, he also steps back a pace or two who takes measure of his opponent, who prepares himself to fight his opponent or to escape him. It is still possible to show man as a courageous being.

In truth this is a principal concern of mine. The blind man, Romulus, Uebelohe, Akki, are all men of courage. The lost world order is restored within them; the universal escapes my grasp. I refuse to find the universal in a doctrine. The universal for me is chaos. The world (hence the stage which represents this world) is for me something monstrous, a riddle of misfortunes which must be accepted but before which one must not capitulate. The world is far bigger than any man, and perforce threatens him constantly. If one could but stand outside the world, it would no longer be threatening. But I have neither the right nor the ability to be an outsider to this world. To find solace in poetry can also be all too cheap; it is more honest to retain one's human point of view. Brecht's thesis, that the world is an accident, which he developed in his *Street Scene* where he shows how this accident happened, may yield—as it in fact did—some magnificent theatre; but he did it by concealing most of the evidence! Brecht's thinking is inexorable, because inexorably there are many things he will not think about.

And lastly it is through the conceit, through comedy that the anonymous audience becomes possible as an audience, becomes a reality to be counted on, and also, one to be taken into account. The conceit easily transforms the crowd of theatre-goers into a mass which can be attacked, deceived, outsmarted into listening to things it would otherwise not so readily listen to. Comedy is a mousetrap in which the public is easily caught and in which it will get caught over and over again. Tragedy, on the other hand, predicated a true community, a kind of community whose existence in our day is but an embarrassing fiction. Nothing is more ludicrous, for instance, than to sit and watch the mystery plays of the Anthroposophists when one is not a participant.

Granting all this there is still one more question to be asked: is it permissible to go from a generality to a particular form of art, to do what I just did when I went from my assertion that the world was formless to the particular possibility for writing comedies today. I doubt that this is permissible. Art is something personal, and something personal should never be explained with generalities. The value of a work of art does not depend on whether more or less good reasons for its existence can be found. Hence I have also tried to avoid certain problems, as for example the argument which is quite lively today, whether or not plays ought to be written in verse or in prose. My own answer lies simply in writing prose, without any intentions of thereby deciding the issue. A man has to choose to go one way, after all, and why should one way always be worse than another? As far as my concepts of comedy are concerned, I believe that here, too, personal reasons are more important than more general ones that are always open to argument. What logic in matters of art could not be refuted! One talks best about art when one talks of one's own art. The art one chooses is an expression of freedom without which no art can exist, and at the same time also of necessity without which art can not exist either. The artist always represents his world and himself. If at one time philosophy taught men to arrive at the particular from the general, then unlike Schiller who started out believing in general conclusions, I can not construct a play as he did when I doubt that the particular can ever be reached from the general. But my doubt is mine and only mine, and not the doubt and problems of a Catholic for whom drama holds possibilities non-Catholics do not share. This is so even if, on the other hand, a Catholic who takes his religion seriously is denied those possibilities which other men possess. The danger inherent in this thesis lies in the fact that there are always those artists who for the sake of finding some generalities to believe in accept conversion, taking a step which is the more to be wondered at for the sad fact that it really will not help them. The difficulties experienced by a Protestant in writing a drama are just the same difficulties he has with his faith. Thus it is my way to mistrust what is ordinarily called the building of the drama, and to arrive at my plays from the unique, the sudden idea or conceit, rather than from some general concept or plan. Speaking for myself, I need to write off into the blue, as I like to put it so that I might give critics a catchword to hang onto. They use it often enough, too, without really understanding what I mean by it.

But these matters are my own concerns and hence it is not necessary to invoke the whole world and to make out as if what are my concerns are the concerns of art in general (lest I be like the drunk who goes back to Noah, the Flood, original sin and the beginning of the world to explain what is, after all, only his own weakness). As in everything and everywhere, and not just in the field of art, the rule is: No excuses, please!

Nevertheless the fact remains (always keeping in mind, of course, the reservations just made) that we now stand in a different relationship to what we have called our material. Our unformed, amorphous present is characterized by being surrounded by figures and forms that reduce our time into a mere result, even less, into a mere transitional state, and which give excessive weight to the past as something finished and to the future as something possible. This applies equally well to politics. Related to art it means that the artist is surrounded by all sorts of opinions about art and by demands on him which are based not upon his capacities, but upon the historical past and present forms. He is surrounded therefore by materials which are no longer materials, that is possibilities, but by materials which have already taken on shape, that is some definitive form. Caesar is no longer pure subject matter for us; he has become the Caesar whom scholarship made the object of its researches. And so it happened that scholars, having thrown themselves with increasing energy not only upon nature but also upon the intellectual life and upon art, establishing in the process in-

tellectual history, literary scholarship, philosophy and goodness knows what else, have created a body of factual information which can not be ignored (for one can not be conscious of
these facts and at the same time pretend to be so naive that one
need pay no attention to the results of scholarship). In this way,
however, scholars have deprived the artist of materials by doing what was really the artist's task. The mastery of Richard
Feller's *History of Berne* precludes the possibility of an historical drama about the city of Berne; the history of Berne was thus
given shape before some literary artist could do it. True, it is
a scholastic form (and not a mythical one which would leave
the way open for a tragedian), a form that severely limits the
field for the artist, leaving to art only psychology which, of
course, has also become a science. To rewrite such a history in
a creative literary manner would now be a tautology, a repetition by means which are not suitable or fitting, a mere illustration of scholarly insights; in short, it would be the very thing
science often claims literature to be. It was still possible for
Shakespeare to base his Caesar upon Plutarch, for the Roman
was not a historian in our sense of the word but a storyteller,
the author of biographical sketches. Had Shakespeare read
Mommsen he could not have written his Caesar because he
would of necessity have lost the supremacy over his materials.
And this holds true now in all things, even the myths of the
Greeks which, since we no longer live them but only study,
evaluate, investigate them, recognizing them to be mere myths
and as such destroying them, have become mummies; and these,
bound tightly round with philosophy and theology, are all too
often substituted for the living thing.

Therefore the artist must reduce the subjects he finds and runs
into everywhere if he wants to turn them once more into real
materials, hoping always that he will succeed. He parodies his
materials, contrasts them consciously with what they have actually been turned into. By this means, by this act of parody,
the artist regains his freedom and hence his material; and thus
material is no longer found but invented. For every parody pre-

supposes a conceit and an invention. In laughter man's freedom becomes manifest, in crying his necessity. Our task today is to demonstrate freedom. The tyrants of this planet are not moved by the works of the poets. They yawn at a poet's threnodies. For them heroic epics are silly fairy tales and religious poetry puts them to sleep. Tyrants fear only one thing: a poet's mockery. For this reason then parody has crept into all literary genres, into the novel, the drama, into lyrical poetry. Much of painting, even of music, has been conquered by parody, and the grotesque has followed, often well camouflaged, on the heels of parody: all of a sudden the grotesque is there.

But our time, up to every imaginable trick there is, can handle all that and nothing can intimidate it: the public has been educated to see in art something solemn, hallowed and even pathetic. The comic is considered inferior, dubious, unseemly; it is accepted only when it makes people feel as bestially happy as a bunch of pigs. But the very moment people recognize the comic to be dangerous, an art that exposes, demands, moralizes, it is dropped like a hot potato, for art may be everything it wants to be so long as it remains *gemütlich*.

We writers are often accused of art that is nihilistic. Today, of course, there exists a nihilistic art, but not every art that seems nihilistic is so. True nihilistic art does not appear to be nihilistic at all; usually it is considered to be especially humane and supremely worthy of being read by our more mature young people. A man must be a pretty bungling sort of nihilist to be recognized as such by the world at large. People call nihilistic what is merely uncomfortable. Then also people say, the artist is supposed to create, not to talk; to give shape to things, not to preach. To be sure. But it becomes more and more difficult to create "purely" or however people imagine the creative mind should work. Mankind today is like a reckless driver racing ever faster, ever more heedlessly along the highway. And he does not like it when the frightened passengers cry out, "Watch out" and "There's a warning sign! Slow down" or "Don't kill that child!" What is more, the driver hates it even worse when he is asked, "Who is paying for the car?" or "Who's providing the gas and oil for this mad journey?", to say nothing of what happens when he is asked for his driver's license. What unpleasant facts might then come to light! Maybe the car was stolen from some relatives, the gas and oil squeezed from the passengers, and really not gas and oil but the blood and sweat of us all; and most likely he wouldn't even have a driver's license and it would turn out that this was his first time driving. Of course, it would be embarrassing if such personal questions were to be asked. The driver would much prefer the passengers to praise the beauty of the countryside through which they are traveling, the silver of the river and the brilliant reflection of the ice-capped mountains in the far distance, would even prefer to have amusing stories whispered into his ear. Today's author, however, can no longer confine himself with good conscience to whispering pleasant stories and praising the beautiful landscape. Unfortunately, too, he can not get out of this mad race in order to sit by the wayside, writing the pure poetry demanded of him by all the non-poets. Fear, worry, and above all anger open his mouth wide.

How very nice it would be if we could end now on this emphatic note. It would be a conclusion that could be considered at least partially safe and not wholly impossible. But in all honesty we must ask ourselves at this point if any of this makes sense today, if it were not better if we practiced silence. I have tried to show that the theatre today is, in the best sense of the word to be sure, in part a museum, and in part a field of experimentation. I have also tried to show here and there what these experiments are. Is the theatre capable of fulfilling this, its latter destiny? Not only has the writing of plays become more difficult today but also the rehearsing and performing of these plays is harder. The very lack of time results at best in only a decent attempt, a first probing, a slight advance in what might be the right direction. A play that is to be more than a merely conventional piece, that is really to be an experiment, can no longer be solved at the writing desk. Giraudoux's fortune was that he had Jouvet. Unhappily this happens only once or twice. The repertory theatre of Germany can afford less and less to experiment. A new play must be gotten rid of as quickly as possible. The museum's treasures weigh too heavily in the scales. The theatre, our whole culture, lives on the interest of the well invested intellect, to which nothing can happen any more and for which not even royalties have to be paid. Assured of having a Goethe, Schiller or Sophocles at hand, the theatres are willing now and then to put on a modern piece—but preferably only for a premiére performance. Heroically this duty is discharged, and sighs of relief are breathed all around when Shakespeare is performed next time. What can we say or do? Clear the stages completely! Make room for the classics! The world of the museum is growing and bursts with its treasures. The cultures of the cave dwellers have not yet been investigated to the nth degree. Let the custodians of the future concern themselves with our art when it is our turn. It does not make much difference then if something new is added, something new is written. The demands made of the artist by esthetics increase from day to day. What is wanted is the perfection which is read into the classics. And let the artist even be suspected of having taken one step backwards, of having made a mistake, just watch how quickly he is dropped. Thus a climate is created in which literature can be studied but not made. How can the artist exist in a world of educated and literate people? This question oppresses me, and I know no answer. Perhaps the writer can best exist by writing detective stories, by creating art where it is least suspected. Literature must become so light that it will weigh nothing upon the scale of today's literary criticism: only in this way will it regain its true worth.

[*Translated by Gerhard Nellhaus*]

Experience of the Theatre

EUGENE IONESCO

When I am asked the question: "Why do you write plays?" I always feel very awkward and have no idea what to answer. Sometimes it seems to me that I started writing for the theatre because I hated it. I used to enjoy reading literature and essays and I used to go to the movies. Occasionally I would listen to music and visit the art galleries; but I almost never went to the theatre.

When I did go, it was quite by accident, to keep someone company or because I had been unable to turn down an invitation, because I *had* to go.

It gave me no pleasure or feeling of participation. The acting embarrassed me: I was embarrassed for the actors. The situations seemed to me quite arbitrary. I felt there was something phony about it all.

A theatrical performance had no magic for me. Everything seemed rather ridiculous, rather painful. For example, it was beyond me how anyone could dream of being an actor. It seemed to me that actors were doing something unacceptable and reprehensible. They gave up their own personalities, repudiated themselves, changed their own skins. How *could* they consent to being someone else and take on a character different from their own? For me it was a kind of vulgar trick, transparent, inconceivable.

Besides, an actor did not even become someone else, he just pretended, which was, I thought, far worse. I found this very distressing and in a way dishonest. "What a good actor," the audience used to say. In my view, he was a bad actor, and acting was a Bad Thing.

For me, going to a public performance meant going to see apparently serious people making a public exhibition of themselves. And yet I am not one of those completely matter-of-fact types. I am not opposed to make-believe. On the contrary, I have always considered imaginative truth to be more profound, more loaded with significance, than everyday reality. Realism, socialist or not, never looks beyond reality. It narrows it down, diminishes it, falsifies it, and leaves out of account the obsessive truths that are most fundamental to us: love, death and wonder. It presents man in a perspective that is narrow and alien; truth lies in our dreams, in our imagination: every moment of our lives confirms this statement. Fiction precludes science. Everything we dream about, and by that I mean everything we desire, is true (the myth of Icarus came before aviation, and if Ader or Blériot started flying, it is because all men have dreamed of flight). There is nothing truer than myth; history, in its attempts to "realize" myth, distorts it, stops halfway: when history claims to have "succeeded," this is nothing but humbug and mystification. Everything we dream is "realizable." Reality does not have to be: it is simply what it is. It is the dreamer, the thinker or the scientist who is the revolutionary; it is he who tries to change the world.

The fictional element in the novel did not worry me at all and I accepted it in the cinema. I can believe as naturally in the potential reality of fiction as in my own dreams. Film acting did not fill me with the same indefinable malaise, the same embarrassment as acting in the theatre.

Why could I not accept the truth of the theatrical reality? Why did it seem false to me? And why did the false seem to want to pass as true and take the place of truth? Was it the fault of the actors? Of the text? Or my own fault? I think I realize now that what worried me in the theatre was the presence of characters in flesh and blood on the stage. Their physical presence destroyed the imaginative illusion. It was as though there were two planes of reality, the concrete, physical, impoverished, empty and limited reality of these ordinary human beings living, moving and speaking on the stage, and the reality of imagination, face to face, overlapping, irreconcilable: two antagonistic worlds failing to come together and unite.

Yes, that was it: every gesture, every attitude, every speech spoken on the stage destroyed for me a world that these same gestures, attitudes and speeches were specifically designed to evoke; destroyed it even before it could be created. It seemed to me an absolute abortion, a fatal mistake, sheer fatuity. If you stop up your ears to shut out the dance music an orchestra is playing but go on watching the dancers, you can see how ridiculous they look, how fantastic their movements are; in the same way, if someone were present for the first time at the celebration of some religious rite, the whole ceremony would seem to him incomprehensible and absurd.

It was in a spirit you might call unsanctified that I paid my rare visits to the theatre, and that was why I did not like it, did not respond to it, did not believe in it.

In a novel you are *told* a story; it does not matter whether it is invented or not, nothing stops you believing it. In a film you are *shown* a fictional story; it is a novel in pictures, an illustrated novel. So a film too tells a story; of course, the fact that it is visual in no way changes this and you can still believe it. Music is a combination of notes, a story in notes, adventures in sound. A painting is an organization or a disorganization of forms, colors and planes, and the question of belief or disbelief does not arise; it is there, as evidence: all that is required is that the various elements satisfy the exacting ideals of comparison and pictorial expression. The novel, music and painting are pure structural form, containing no elements that are extraneous; that is why they can stand alone, they are admissible. Even the cinema can be accepted, because it is a succession of pictures, which means that it too is pure, whereas the theatre seemed to me essentially impure: the fictional element was mixed with others that were foreign; it was imperfectly fictional, yes, raw material that had not yet undergone the transformation or mutation that is indispensable. In short, everything about the theatre exasperated me. When I saw actors, for example, identifying themselves completely with their parts and weeping real tears on the stage, I found it unbearable, positively indecent.

When on the other hand I saw an actor who was too much in control of his part, out of character, dominating it, detached from it, which was what Diderot and Jouvet and Piscator and, after him, Brecht all wanted, I was just as dissatisfied. This too seemed to me an unacceptable mixture of true and false, for I felt a need for the essential transformation or transposition of a reality that only imagination and artistic creation can make more meaningful, more dense, more "true," that the didactic doctrines of realism merely overload, impoverish and reduce to the level of a second-rate ideology, I did not like stage actors, stars, who for me represented an anarchical principle, breaking up and destroying to their own advantage the organized unity of the stage, attracting all attention to themselves to the detriment of any coherent integration of the elements of drama. But the dehumanization of the actor, as practiced by Piscator or Brecht, a disciple of Piscator, who turned the actor into a simple pawn in the chess game of drama, a lifeless tool, denied passion, participation or personal invention, this time to the advantage of the production, which now, in its turn, attracted all attention to itself—this priority given to organized unity exasperated me just as much and made me feel, quite literally, that something was being smothered: to squash the actor's initiative, to kill the actor, is to kill both life and drama.

Later, that is to say quite recently, I realized that Jean Vilar had managed to strike the necessary balance in his productions

—respecting the need for cohesion on the stage without de-humanizing the actor and thus restoring to drama its unity and to the actor his freedom—half way between the style of the *Odéon* (and so an advance on the rantings of a Sarah Bernhardt or a Mounet-Sully) and that of the Brechtian or Piscatoresque discipline. This is not, however, with Vilar an expression of theories about the theatre or hard and fast dogmatism, but a question of tact and instinctive sense of theatre.

But I still could not quite see how to get rid of that positive feeling of malaise produced by my awareness of the "impurity" of acted drama. I was by no means an agreeable theatregoer, but on the contrary, sulky, grumbling, always discontented. Was this due to some deficiency in myself alone? Or was it some-think lacking in the theatre?

I was dissatisfied even by the plays I had managed to read. Not all of them! For I was not blind to the merits of Sophocles, Aeschylus or Shakespeare, nor a little later to some of the plays of Kleist or Büchner. Why? Because, I thought, all these plays make extraordinary reading on account of their literary qualities, which may well not be specifically theatrical. In any case, after Shakespeare and Kleist, I do not think I have enjoyed reading a play. Strindberg seemed to be clumsy and inadequate. I was even bored by Molière. I was not interested in those stories of misers, hypocrites and cuckolds. I disliked his unmetaphysical mind. Shakespeare raised questions about the whole condition and destiny of man. In the long run Molière's little problems seemed to me of relatively minor importance, sometimes a little sad of course, dramatic even, but never tragic; for they could be resolved. The unendurable admits of no solution, and only the unendurable is profoundly tragic, profoundly comic and essentially theatrical.

On the other hand, the gestures of Shakespeare's plays seemed to be diminished in performance. No Shakespearean production ever captivated me as much as my reading of *Hamlet, Othello* and *Julius Caesar,* etc. As I went so rarely to the theatre, perhaps I have never seen the best productions of Shakespeare's drama. In any case, in performance I had the impression that the unendurable had been made endurable. It was anguish tamed.

So I am really not a passionate theatregoer, still less a man of the theatre. I really hated the theatre. It bored me. And yet . . . when I was a child, I can still remember how my mother could not drag me away from the Punch and Judy show in the Luxembourg Gardens. I would go there day after day and could stay there, spellbound, all day long. But I did not laugh. That Punch and Judy show kept me there open-mouthed, watching those puppets talking, moving and cudgeling each other. It was the very image of the world that appeared to me, strange and improbable but truer than true, in the profoundly simplified form of caricature, as though to stress the grotesque and brutal nature of the truth. And from then until I was fifteen any form of play would thrill me and make me feel that the world is very strange, a feeling so deeply rooted that it has never left me. Every live show awoke in me this feeling for the strangeness of the world, and it impressed me nowhere more than at the theatre. And yet, when I was thirteen, I wrote a play, my first piece of writing, which had nothing strange about it. It was a patriotic play: extreme youth is an excuse for anything.

When did I stop liking the theatre? From the moment when, as I begin to grow more clearsighted and acquire a critical mind, I became conscious of stage tricks, of obvious theatrical contrivance, that is to say from the moment I stopped being naïve. Where are the *monstres sacrés* of the theatre who could give us back our lost naïveté? And what possible magic could justify the theatre's claim to bind us in its spell? There is no magic now, nothing is sacred: there is no valid reason for this to be restored to us.

Besides, there is nothing more difficult than writing for the theatre. Novels and poems last well. Their appeal is not blunted even by the centuries. We still find interest in a number of minor works from the nineteenth, eighteenth and seventeenth centuries.

And how many even older works do we not still find interesting? All painting and music resist the passage of time. The moving simplicity of the least significant sculptured heads on countless cathedrals still remains fresh and alive, intact; and we shall go on responding to the architectural rhythms of great monuments of the most distant civilizations, which speak to us directly through them in a language that is clear and revealing. But what of the theatre?

Today the theatre is blamed by some for not belonging to its own times. In my view it belongs only too well. This is what makes it so weak and ephemeral. I mean that the theatre *does* belong to its own times, but not quite enough. Every period needs something "out of period" and incommunicable to be introduced into what is "period" and communicable. Everything is a circumscribed moment in history, of course. But all history is contained in each moment of history: any moment in history is valid when it transcends history; in the particular lies the universal.

The themes chosen by many authors merely spring from a certain ideological fashion, which is something *less* than the period it belongs to. Or else these themes are the expression of some particular political attitude, and the plays that illustrate them will die with the ideology that has inspired them, for ideologies go out of fashion. Any Christian tomb, any Greek or Etruscan stele moves us and tells us more about the destiny of man than any number of laboriously committed plays, which are made to serve a discipline, a system of thought and language different from what is properly their own.

It is true that all authors have tried to make propaganda. The great ones are those who failed, who have gained access, consciously or not, to a deeper and more universal reality. Nothing is more precarious than a play. It may maintain its position for a very short time, but it soon falls apart, revealing nothing but contrivance.

In all sincerity, Corneille bores me. Perhaps we like him (without believing in him) only from habit. We cannot help it. He has been forced on us at school. I find Schiller unbearable. For a long time now, Marivaux's plays have seemed to me futile little comedies. Musset's are thin and Vigny's unactable. Victor Hugo's bloody dramas send us into fits of laughter; whereas it is difficult to laugh, whatever people say, at most of Labiche's funny plays. Dumas fils, with his *Dame aux Camélias,* is ridiculously sentimental. As for the others! Oscar Wilde? Facile. Ibsen? Boorish. Strindberg? Clumsy. A recent dramatist, Giraudoux, not long dead, does not always get across the footlights now; like Cocteau's, his drama seems to us superficial and contrived. It has lost its sparkle: with Cocteau the theatrical tricks are too obvious; with Giraudoux the tricks and contrivances of language, distinguished though they may be, still remain tricks.

Pirandello himself has been left behind the times, for his theatre was built on theories about personality or the multiformity of truth, which now seem clear as daylight since psychoanalysis and psychology plumbed the depths. In testing the validity of Pirandello's theories, modern psychology, inevitably going further than Pirandello in its exploration of the human psyche, certainly confirms Pirandello's findings, but at the same time shows him to be limited and inadequate: for what has been said by Pirandello is now said more thoroughly and scientifically. So the value of his theatre does not rest on his contribution to psychology but on the quality of his drama, which must inevitably lie elsewhere: what interests us in this author is no longer the discovery of the antagonistic elements in human personality, but what he has made of them dramatically. The strictly theatrical interest of his work lies outside science, beyond the limits of his own ideology. All that is left of Pirandello is his dramatic technique, the mechanics of his theatre: which again proves that drama founded on ideology or philosophy, exclusively inspired by them, is built on sand and crumbles away. It is his dramatic idiom, his purely theatrical instinct that keeps Pirandello alive for us today.

In the same way, it is not Racine's psychological insight into the passions that sustains his theatre, but what Racine has made of it as a poet and man of the theatre.

If we were to go through the centuries and count the dramatists who can still move an audience, we should find about twenty ... or at the most thirty. But the paintings, poems and novels that still mean something to us can be counted in their thousands. The naïveté essential to a work of art is lacking in the theatre. I do not say a dramatist of great simplicity will not appear; but at the moment I see no sign of him on the horizon. I mean a simplicity that is lucid, springing from the inmost depths of our being, revealing them, revealing them to ourselves, restoring our own simplicity, our secret souls. At the moment there is no naïveté, in audience or writer.

What faults are there then to be found in dramatists and their plays? Their tricks, I was saying, that is to say their too obvious contrivances. The theatre may appear to be a secondary, a minor form of literature. It always seems rather coarse-grained. There is no doubt it is an art that deals in effects. It cannot do without them, and this is the reproach leveled against it. And these effects have to be broad. One has the impression that the texture has been roughened. The textual refinement of literature is ironed out. Drama of literary subtlety soon wears thin. Half-tones are deepened or banished by light that is too brilliant. No shading, no nuance is possible. Problem plays, *pièces à thèse*, are rough-hewn pieces of approximation. Drama is not the idiom for ideas. When it tries to become a vehicle for ideologies, all it can do is vulgarize them. It dangerously oversimplifies. It makes them too elementary and depreciates them. It is "naïve," but in the bad sense. All ideological drama runs the risk of being parochial. What would, not the *utility,* but the proper *function* of the theatre be, if it was restricted to the task of duplicating philosophy or theology or politics or pedagogy? Psychological drama is not psychological enough. One might as well read a psychological treatise. Ideological drama is not philosophical enough. Instead of going to see a dramatic illustration of this or that political creed I would rather read my usual daily paper or listen to the speeches of my party candidates.

Dissatisfied with the gross naïveté and rudimentary character of the theatre, philosophers, literary men, ideologists and poets of refinement, all intelligent people try to make their drama intelligent. They write with intelligence, with taste and talent. They put their thoughts into it. They express their conception of life and the world, and believe that writing a play should be like presenting a thesis in which problems find their solution on the stage. They sometimes construct their work in the form of a syllogism, with the two premises in the first two acts and the conclusion in the third.

There is no denying the construction is sometimes first-rate. And yet this does not answer the demands we make of drama, because it fails to lift the theatre out of an intermediate zone that lies somewhere between where discursive reasoning can be only one ingredient—and the higher realms of thought.

Should one give up the theatre if one refuses to reduce it to a parochial level or subordinate it to manifestations of the human spirit that impose different forms and modes of expression? Can it, like painting or music, find its own autonomous existence?

Drama is one of the oldest of the arts. And I can't help thinking we cannot do without it. We cannot resist the desire to people a stage with live characters that are at the same time real and invented. We cannot deny our need to make them speak and live before our eyes. To bring phantoms to life and give them flesh and blood is a prodigious adventure, so unique that I myself was absolutely amazed, during the rehearsals of my first play, when I suddenly saw, moving on the stage of the *Noctambules,* characters who owed their life to me. It was a terrifying experience. What right had I to do a thing like that? Was it allowed? And how could Nicolas Bataille, one of my actors, turn into Mr. Martin? . . . It was almost diabolical. And so it was only when I had written something for the theatre, quite by chance and with the intention of holding it up to ridicule, that I began to love it, to rediscover it in myself, to understand it, to be fascinated by it: and then I knew what I had to do.

I told myself that the too intelligent playwrights were not intelligent enough that is was no use for thinkers to look to the theatre for the idiom of a philosophical treatise; that when they tried to bring too much subtlety and refinement into the theatre it was not only too much but not enough; that if the theatre was merely a deplorable enlargement of refined subtleties, which I found so embarrassing, it merely meant that the enlargement was not sufficient. The overlarge was not large enough, the unsubtle was too subtle.

So if the essence of the theatre lay in magnifying its effects, they had to be magnified still further, underlined and stressed to the maximum. To push drama out of that intermediate zone where it is neither theatre nor literature is to restore it to its own domain, to its natural frontiers. It was not for me to conceal the devices of the theatre, but rather make them still more evident, deliberately obvious, go all-out for caricature and the grotesque, way beyond the pale irony of witty drawing-room comedies. No drawing-room comedies, but farce, the extreme exaggeration of parody. Humor, yes, but using the methods of burlesque. Comic effects that are firm, broad and outrageous. No dramatic comedies either. But back to the unendurable. Everything raised to paroxysm, where the source of tragedy lies. A theatre of violence: violently comic, violently dramatic.

Avoid psychology or rather give it a metaphysical dimension. Drama lies in extreme exaggeration of the feelings, an exaggeration that dislocates flat everyday reality. Dislocation, disarticulation of language too.

Moreover, if the actors embarrassed me by not seeming natural enough, perhaps it was because they also were, or tried to be, *too* natural: by trying not to be, perhaps they will still appear natural, but in a different way. They must not be afraid of not being natural.

We need to be virtually bludgeoned into detachment from our daily lives, our habits and mental laziness, which conceal from us the strangeness of the world. Without a fresh virginity of mind, without a new and healthy awareness of existential reality, there can be no theatre and no art either; the real must be in a way dislocated, before it can be reintegrated.

To achieve this effect, a trick can sometimes be used: playing against the text. A serious, solemn, formal production or interpretation can be grafted onto a text that is absurd, wild and comic. On the other hand, to avoid the ridiculous sentimentality of the tear jerker, a dramatic text can be treated as buffoonery and the tragic feeling of a play can be underlined by farce. Light makes shadows darker, shadows intensify light. For my part, I have never understood the difference people make between the comic and the tragic. As the "comic" is an intuitive perception of the absurd, it seems to me more hopeless than the "tragic." The "comic" offers no escape. I say "hopeless," but in reality it lies outside the boundaries of hope or despair.

Tragedy may appear to some in one sense comforting, for in trying to express the helplessness of a beaten man, one broken by fate for example, tragedy thus admits the reality of fate and destiny, of sometimes incomprehensible but objective laws that govern the universe. And man's helplessness, the futility of our efforts, can also, in a sense, appear comic.

I have called my comedies "anti-plays" or "comic dramas," and my dramas "pseudo-dramas" or "tragic farces": for it seems to me that the comic is tragic, and that the tragedy of man is pure derision. The contemporary critical mind takes nothing too seriously or too lightly. In *Victims of Duty* I tried to sink comedy in tragedy: in *The Chains,* tragedy in comedy or, if you like, to confront comedy and tragedy in order to link them in a new dramatic synthesis. But it is not a true synthesis, for these two elements do not coalesce, they coexist: one constantly repels the other, they show each other up, criticize and deny one another and, thanks to their opposition, thus succeed dynamically in maintaining a balance and creating tension. The two plays that best satisfy this condition are, I believe: *Victims of Duty* and *The New Tenant.*

Similarly, one can confront the prosaic and the poetic, the strange and the ordinary. That is what I wanted to do in *Jack, or the Submission,* which I called "a *naturalistic* comedy" too, because after starting off in a naturalistic tone I tried to go beyond naturalism.

In the same way *Amédée, or How to Get Rid of It,* where the scene is laid in the flat of a *petit bourgeois* couple, is a realistic play into which fantastic elements have been introduced, a contrast intended at one and the same time to banish and recall the "realism."

In my first play, *The Bald Soprano,* which started off as an attempt to parody the theatre, and hence a certain kind of human behavior, it was by plunging into banality, by draining the sense from the hollowest clichés of everyday language that I tried to render the strangeness that seems to pervade our whole existence. The tragic and the farcical, the prosaic and the poetic, the realistic and the fantastic, the strange and the ordinary, perhaps these are the contradictory principles (there is no theatre without conflict) that may serve as a basis for a new dramatic structure. In this way perhaps the unnatural can by its very violence appear natural, and the too natural will avoid the naturalistic.

May I add that "primitive" drama is not elementary drama; to refuse to "round off the corners" is a way of providing a clear outline, a more powerful shape; drama that relies on simple effects is not necessarily drama simplified.

If one believes that "theatre" merely means the drama of the word, it is difficult to grant it can have an autonomous language of its own: it can then only be the servant of other forms of thought expressed in words, of philosophy and morals. Whereas, if one looks on the word as only *one* member of the shock troops the theatre can marshal, everything is changed. First of all, there is a proper way for the theatre to use words, which is as dialogue, words in action, words in conflict. If they are used by some authors merely for discussion, this is a major error. There are other means of making words more theatrical: by working them up to such a pitch that they reveal the true temper of drama, which lies in frenzy; the whole tone should be as strained as possible, the language should almost break up or explode in its fruitless effort to contain so many meanings.

But the theatre is more than words: drama is a story that is lived and relived with each performance, and we can watch it live. The theatre appeals as much to the eye as to the ear. It is not a series of pictures, like the cinema, but architecture, a moving structure of scenic images.

Nothing is barred in the theatre: characters may be brought to life, but the unseen presence of our inner fears can also be materialized. So the author is not only allowed, but recommended to make actors of his props, to bring objects to life, to animate the scenery and give symbols concrete form.

Just as the words are complemented by gesture, acting and pantomime, which can take their place when words are no longer adequate, so they can be amplified by the scenic elements of the stage as well. The use of props is yet another question. (Artaud had something so say about that.)

When people say that the theatre should be purely social, do they not really mean that the theatre should be political, slanted, of course, in this or that direction? It is one thing to be social; to be "socialist" or "marxist" or "facist" is another—this is the expression of a kind of stock-taking that does not go far enough: the more I see of Brecht's plays , the more I have the impression that time, *and* his own time, escape him; Brechtian man is shorn of one dimension, the writer's sense of period is actually falsified by his ideology, which narrows his field of vision; this is a fault common to ideologists and people stunted by fanaticism.

Then one may be a social being in spite of oneself, since we are all of us caught in a kind of historical complex and belong to one special moment in history—which is, however, far from absorbing us entirely but rather expresses and contains only the least essential part of us.

I have spoken mainly about a certain technique, about a theatrical idiom, an idiom which is all its own. Social themes or subjects may very well form the subject and themes of drama, if they remain within this idiom. It is perhaps only through subjectivity that we become objective. The individual is linked to the generality of men, and society is obviously an objective fact: and yet I see this social element, and by that I mean rather the expression of history, of the period we belong to, even if it only appears in our natural idiom (and all idiom too is historical, limited to its own time, that is undeniable), I see this expression of history as being naturally inherent in a work of art, whatever one's conscious intentions, but vital and spontaneous rather than deliberate or ideological.

Besides contemporaneity does not conflict with timelessness and universality: on the contrary, it is subservient.

There are some states of mind, some intuitions that lie positively outside time, outside history. When, one day of grace, I awake some morning, not only from my night's sleep but also from the mental sleep of habit, and suddenly become aware of my existence and of a universal presence, when all seems strange and yet familiar, when I am possessed by the wonder of living, this is a feeling or intuition that can come to any man at any time. You can find this spirit of awareness expressed in practically the same terms by poets, mystics and philosophers, who experience it exactly as I do, and as all men have surely experienced it unless they are spiritually dead or blinded by their preoccupation with politics; you can find exactly the same spirit clearly expressed both in antiquity and the Middle Ages as well as in any of the so-called "historical" centuries. At this timeless moment in time philosopher and shoemaker, "master" and "slave," priest and layman are reconciled and indistinguishable.

The historical and the non-historical are joined and welded together in poetry and painting too. The identical picture of a woman dressing her hair is found in certain Persian miniatures, in Greek and Etruscan steles and in Egyptian wall paintings; a Renoir or a Manet or painters from the seventeenth and eighteenth centuries did not need to know the paintings of other periods to find and catch the same attitude, imbued with the same unfailing sensual grace and inspiring the same emotion. As with my first example, we are here dealing with permanent emotions. The pictorial style in which the image is rendered differs (though often very little) according to period. But this "difference," which is of secondary importance, upholds and illumines a permanent value. All the evidence is there to show how contemporaneity or "historicity," to use a word in vogue, meets and merges with timelessness, universality and superhistoricity, how each lends support to the other.

Let us choose a great example in our own field: in the theatre, when the fallen Richard II is a prisoner in his cell, abandoned and alone, it is not Richard II I see there, but all the fallen kings of this world; and not only all fallen kings, but also our beliefs and values, our unsanctified, corrupt and worn-out truths, the crumbling of civilizations, the march of destiny. When Richard II dies, it is really the death of all I hold most dear that I am watching; it is *I* who die with Richard II. Richard II makes me sharply conscious of the eternal truth that we forget in all these stories, the truth we fail to think about, though it is simple and absolutely commonplace: I die, he dies, you die. So it is not history after all that Shakespeare is writing, although he makes use of history; it is not History that he shows me, but *my* story and *our* story —*my* truth, which, independent of my "times" and in the spectrum of a time that transcends Time, repeats a universal and inexorable truth. In fact, it is the nature of a dramatic masterpiece to provide a superior pattern of instruction: it reflects my own image, it is a mirror; it is soul-searching; it is history gazing beyond history toward the deepest truth. One may find the reasons given by this or that author for wars and civil strife and struggles for power true or false, one may or may not agree with these interpretations. But one cannot deny that all those kings have faded from the scene, that they are dead; and an awareness of this reality, of this lasting evidence of the ephemeral nature of man, contrasted with his longing for eternal life, is obviously accompanied by the most profound emotion, by the most acute consciousness of tragedy, passionately felt. Art is the realm of passion, not of pedagogy; in this tragedy of tragedies we are concerned with the revelation of the most painful reality; I learn or reconsider something that has passed from my mind, I learn it in the only way possible with poetry, by an emotional participation that is not distorted by mystification and has burst through the paper dams of ideology and of a narrowly critical or "scientific" spirit. I only risk being taken in when I see a play, not with evidence to *offer*, but with a thesis to *prove*, an ideological, committed play, a play that is bogus and not true profoundly and poetically, as only poetry and tragedy can be true. All men die a lonely death, all values fall into contempt: that is what Shakespeare tells me. "Richard's cell is indeed the cell of all our solitudes." Perhaps Shakespeare *wanted* to tell the story of Richard II; if that was all he had told us, *the story of someone else,* he would not move me. But Richard II's prison is a truth that has not been swept away with history: its invisible walls still stand, whereas countless philosophies and ideologies have vanished for ever. And this truth still holds, because it is couched in the idiom of living evidence and not of demonstrative and rational judgment; Richard's prison is there before me, more vivid than any demonstration. Drama *is* this eternal and living presence: there is no doubt that it can reproduce the essential structure of tragic truth and theatrical reality. The evidence it offers has nothing to do with the uncertain truths of abstract thought or with the so-called ideological theatre: we are now concerned with the essence of the theatre, with theatrical archetypes, with theatrical idiom. An idiom that has been lost in our own times, when allegory and academic illustration seem to have been substituted for the living image of truth, which must be rediscovered. Every idiom develops, but development and renewal do not mean self-surrender and a change in kind; they mean a constant rediscovery of self, at each historical moment of time. One develops with the framework of one's own personality. The idiom of the theatre can never be anything but the idiom of the theatre.

As the idioms of painting and music have developed, they have always adjusted to the cultural style of their day, but without ever losing their pictorial or musical nature. And the development of painting, for example, has never been anything but a rediscovery of painting, its idiom and its essence. The direction taken by modern painting shows us this clearly. Since Klee, Kandinsky, Mondrian, Braque and Picasso, painting has done nothing but try to shake of all that is not painting: literature, story-telling, history and photography. Painters are trying to rediscover the basic fundamentals of painting, pure form, color for its own sake. Nor is it in this case a question of estheticism or what is nowadays rather improperly called formalism, but of the expression of reality in pictorial terms, *in an idiom as revealing as the language of words and sounds.* Even if this first appeared to us as a disintegration of the pictorial idiom, fundamentally it was the ascetic pursuit of purity, the rejection of a parasitic idiom. Similarly, it is only when we have pulled apart the conventional characters in our plays, only when we have broken down a false theatrical idiom, that we can follow the example of painting and try to put it together again—its essential purity restored.

Theatre can be nothing but theatre, although some contemporary specialists in "theatrology" consider it not true that a thing can be identified with itself—which seems to me the most bewildering and unlikely form of paradox.

For these "specialists" the theatre, being something different from the theatre, is ideology, allegory, politics, lectures, essays or literature. This is as much an aberration as it would be to claim that music was archaeology, that painting was physics or mathematics; and tennis anything you like but tennis.

Even if you admit that my views are not untrue, you may well tell me they are by no means new. If you went on to say these truths were elementary, I should be delighted, for there is nothing more difficult that the rediscovery of elementary truths, fundamental premises, or certitudes. Even philosophers go chiefly in search of sound premises. Elementary truth is precisely what one loses sight of, what one forgets. And that is why we breed confusion, why we fail in mutual understanding.

Besides, what I have just said is not a preconceived theory of dramatic art. It has not come *before,* but *after* my own personal experience of the theatre. Thinking about my own plays, good or bad, has provoked these few ideas. The reflections came afterward. I have no ideas *before* I write a play. I have them when I have *finished* it, or while I am *not* writing any at all. I believe that artistic creation is spontaneous. It is for me. Once again, all this is chiefly valid for me; but if I could believe I had discovered instinctively in myself the basic framework and permanent character of the objective reality of drama, or thrown even a little light on what the essence of the theatre is, I should be very proud. All ideologies are derived from knowledge that is second-hand, indirect, devious and false; nothing borrowed from others is true for the artist. For an author nicknamed "avant-garde," I shall earn the reproach of having invented nothing. I believe that as one invents, one discovers, and that invention *is* discovery or rediscovery; and it is not my fault if I am taken for an avant-garde author. It is the critics who say so. It is of no importance. This definition is as good as the next. It means nothing at all. It is just a label.

Surrealism is not new either. All it did was discover and bring to light, in the process of reinventing, a certain way of knowing, or certain tendencies in human nature that centuries of rationalism frowned upon and suppressed. What, in short, does surrealism try to release? Love and dreams. How can we have forgotten that man is quickened by love? How not have noticed that we dream? Like all revolutions, the surrealist revolution was a reversion, a restitution, an expression of vital and indispensable spiritual needs. If finally it became too rigid, if one can now talk of academic surrealism, it is because every idiom wears out in the end; a lively tradition hardens into traditionalism, it becomes set in its forms and is "imitated"; in turn it too must be rediscovered: besides, as is well known, surrealism is itself a rejuvenation of romanticism; its origin, or one of its sources, is in the German romantics' power to dream. An extension of the frontiers of known reality depends upon a rediscovery of method and a rejuvenation of idiom. A genuine avant-garde movement can only be of value if it is more than a fashion. It can only spring from intuitive discovery, followed by a reassessment of neglected models from the past, which require constant rediscovery and rejuvenation. I believe that in recent times we have forgotten what theatre is. And I am not excepting myself; I believe that, step by step, I have discovered it once more for myself, and what I have just described is simply my own experience of the theatre.

Obviously, a large number of problems have not been touched on. It remains to be seen, for example, how it comes about that a playwright like Feydeau, although the technique and mechanics of his theatre are beyond reproach, is not nearly so great as other playwrights whose technique may or may not be so perfect. In one sense, it is because everyone is a philosopher: by that I mean that everyone discovers some part of reality, the part that he can discover for himself. When I say "philosopher," I do not mean the specialist in philosophy, who merely exploits other people's vision of the world. Insofar as an artist has a personal apprehension of reality, he is a true philosopher. And his greatness is a result of the breadth, the depth and acuity of his authentically philosophical insight, of his living philosophy. The quality of a work of art directly depends on how "alive" philosophy is, on the fact that it springs from life and not from abstract thought. A philosophical system withers away as soon as a new philosophy or a new system goes a step further. Works of art, however, which are live philosophies, do not invalidate one another. That is why they can co-exist. The great works of art and the great poets seem to find confirmation, completion and corroboration in one another; Aeschylus is not cancelled out by Calderon, or Shakespeare by Chekhov, or Kleist by a Japanese Nō play. One scientific theory can cancel out another, but the truths found in works of art complement one another. Art seems the best justification for belief in the possibility of a metaphysical liberalism.

[*Translated by Donald Watson*]

PART TWO

THE ACTOR

MORRIS CARNOVSKY

DESIGN FOR ACTING

PETER SHAFFER

THE CANNIBAL THEATRE

FREDERIK SCHYBERG

WHAT IS AN ACTOR?

Design for Acting:
The Quest of Technique

MORRIS CARNOVSKY

I'm glad that the name and purpose of these conferences define my function here along lines that happen to be congenial to myself. The Factor of Acting in the Working Theatre—the subject is organic in my life to an overwhelming degree. I think I've gone beyond the point where it would be possible for anyone to ask me, as a woman put it to me bluntly years ago, "What's uppermost in you, the actor or the man?" The answer, I hope, is now, "Both." For I've learned that if you endeavor to express your life without some form to receive it, you're apt to produce a chaotic mess—and on the other hand, if you play-act at life, well, there you'll certainly come a cropper.

Though what's implied in the question above is one of the fundamental challenges of the creative life. Form and content. The style—and the man himself. Stanislavsky chose his title "My Life in Art" and meant it quite literally, for he literally immolated himself in the search for the methods and materials of his craft. I don't know whether in the sum of things he emerged as a great actor, but as a searcher, he was a very great man.

For myself, I say I only hope that I've somewhat narrowed

the gap between what I am and what I do. If that sounds deliberately modest let it stand. I don't aim to practice modesty for its own sake; that would be inartistic. The modesty I feel is a "technical" thing, and stems from a healthy respect for the lifelong difficulties of the task every true craftsman sets himself. It is a *key*, to objectivity, if you will, a kind of objectivity which it is necessary to assume, by an act of will, before you can say: What am I up against? What is my relation to my medium? What does it want of me? How do we effect the bridge? By what means do we arrive at a common conclusion? In what sign shall I conquer? And also: How shall I know my enemies?—my difficulties and my limitations?

A moment ago I referred to modesty as a *technical* matter. The word "technique" has to be explained especially in regard to my own craft, since for many it still retains the atmosphere of a bright and glossy competence, something machine-made, inevitable in the way it functions—"you put it in here and it comes out there"—particularly adapted to sparkling dialogue and sophisticated effects, "timing," creased trousers and secure *décolletage*, smart deaths and entrances. Measured sobs and gusts of professional laughter to account for the anguish of loss and the joy of living. An actor of my acquaintance has made a tidy career for himself out of something called "footwork"—this, he solemnly assured me, was the underlying secret of all good acting. Malvolio might have said it: " 'Tis but footwork—all is but footwork." My friend neglected to tell me what happened when he was sitting down! However—

In the Twenties, when I first came to New York and to the service of the theatre, the stage was the stamping ground of many an attitude and fixed persuasion such as the above. It was a field day for every sort of exhibitionism, dominated by "stars" who were expected to be the exhibitionists par excellence. It was a competition not so much of living or cultural values as of showmanship. The lily of truth was often unrecognizable for the gilding that weighed it down. Among these stars there were some, of course, that burned with a purer light; it was as if they didn't know how to conceal the thing they *were*. David Warfield, with one shoe on the rich soil of the Ghetto, the other getting a shine up in the Lambs' Club. Otis Skinner, using every trick in the bag to convey the juiciest romanticism I have ever seen. Mrs. Fiske, Mistress of the Theatrical Inn, barely disguising a warm heart beneath her devastating and witty rhythms. "Whizzing exhalations" like Emily Stevens and Jeanne Eagels burning in their comets' flight with an alcoholic blue flame, giving themselves to the fires with obstinate grandeur—what else was there to do?

If the student of acting took these as his models, he was more likely to absorb their foibles and eccentricities than the magnificence of their *Idea*. To talk and walk brightly with crisp "stylish" diction in the hectic manner of the day, this was what they'd learned in "School"—that is, by observation, by Stock, and the threat of losing their job. They were often pathetically self-conscious about this "technique" of theirs. A very good actor I knew and admired had a singular trick of elongating vowel sounds in the most unlikely places—monosyllables like "if," "as," "but," particularly "but." "Bu-u-ut," he would say, "Bu-u-ut screw your courage to the sticking point a-a-and we'll not fail. Or "I—i-if you be-e-e." Etc. I asked him about it once and he answered promptly and with pride, "Why, that's my sostenuto *but!*"

Now, you must not think because I describe these interesting phenomena as quirks that I dismiss them entirely as unworthy of the craft of acting. Or that I regard a pleasant, fastidious, and crisp manner of speech and presence as a sign of decadence. In our last decade poor Marlon Brando has precipitated upon his head the reputation and credit for having restored the Yahoo to his rightful place in society, but we need not admire him the less for that. All innovators must take their chances. And there is generally a deeper reason for odd behavior stemming from something that is striving to be said.

For myself, I learned as much as I could, largely by imitation, from the "technique" of these older actors. I even think I now understand what they were driving at. For example, my friend of the "footwork." I now believe that he had discovered for himself a useful and comfortable arcanum in the area of physical rhythm, a very important thing for actors. He had found through experience that it was blissfully reassuring to be in the right place at the right time! His dukes and his butlers were never caught flatfooted, as they say in boxing. Out of the balance between his words and his movements he had perfected a kind of personal dance. This pleased him and gave him ultimate confidence. . . . And what of him of the sostenuto "but"? He was a lover of words—*all* words, even those that are customarily neglected. He rescued them from oblivion and gave them dignity. But (bu-u-ut) more importantly, he made them *act!* There was a warning note in that "but" of his, a promise in his "and," a threat in his "if." I find that most interesting, because it betokened an *inner* life and energy that was the mark of this man's talent, his brush-stroke, as it were.

The actors of the Twenties often seemed to be all dressed up with no place to go. Except into the Thirties—which is what they did, eventually. They went pitching down the funnel of the years, practicing all the techniques they knew, believing in their own effectiveness and their own sincerities. And reaching out, too, for a better language of craft, more expanse to their horizons, greater satisfaction for their spirits. They had no leadership. It was each man for himself. The murmurs that reached them from foreign shores, murmurs of vibrant new names—Craig, Appia, Jessner, Reinhardt, Stanislavsky, Copeau—these seemed to promise a new kind of showmanship, but there was no one around—with the exception of a few scene designers who began to sit up and take notice—to interpret the swelling theme of a new *Theatre* to them. The theatre understood, possibly for the first time, as a profound organic experience shared by *all* its elements, audience, designers, lighting experts, producers, directors—and, of course, actors.

I say there was no one around to utter a warning or to say: "Be of good cheer! At last you are about to receive a vessel for your talents. Not a knighthood nor an empty citation, nor a cigar banded with your name. No champagne banquets with speeches to inflate your vanity and encourage you in your worst professional habits. No fan clubs milling about the stage door and shouting your name in the worn, ironic streets. Not these things, but a place—a place where your actors' nature will be understood and used, through work, through discipline, through struggle, through proper organization, to the end that you will inherit the only thing worth having—namely, your Self."

In the clarion tones of this annunciation, I realize that I am anticipating history in the shape of such possible headlines as "American Theatre Finds Its Way Out!" or "Actors Break Their Chains As Dead Hand Shrivels" (or at least "When The Saints Come Marching In"). But history, as we know, is never that easy, even in its best conclusions. Because the struggle continues. "That's for sure," as we say in our pungent idiom. The American Theatre hasn't found its way out, nor has the dead hand entirely relaxed its grip. But there have been tremendous advances. An interchange of movements, bloods, languages, nationalities; an intermingling of ideas. The depression jolted us back on our heels; when our eyes cleared, their expression was simpler, more modest, more compassionate. The war made us reach out our hands to our friends in all places.

I was part of this transformation as far as it applied to theatre, since I lived through it. It was in a very real sense a revolution. Like all such changes, it cast its shadow before as well as after. There was this leaderless, troubled floundering as through swamps in the dark; the dawn when it came was yet uncertain and it is still working its strength up toward the full light of day. As far as acting technique was concerned, there was much honest striving in the Twenties. I came in contact with some of the best of it in six years of the Theatre Guild. In the Guild, the *spécialité de la maison* was the good play. Its directors gambled on the intelligent, fretting public, suffering the indigestion of so

much questionable food in the theatre; they gambled and won.
They found themselves with the responsibility of serving up
their good plays—Shaw, O'Neill, Behrman, Molnar—with the as-
sistance of actors who were not only competent and worldly, but
intelligent. The demand created a supply. And eventually the
Guild (pushed to it, no doubt, by economic as well as artistic necessity) took the truly noble step of supporting their
program of plays with a hand-picked "permanent" acting company. The idea was abandoned as unworkable after a few rather
glorious years. Many successes, happy, well-fed actors, radiant
box-offices. The Bible records that "Jeshurun waxed fat and he
kicked." Hollywood slithered around the corner and stepped up
the volume of her siren-song: Oh come, all ye unfaithful; and
some of the actors disappeared, not without a sheepish back-
ward glance. But I'm not sure that that was the reason for the
failure of the company-idea. The Guild had become, by repetition and success, a show-shop on a higher plane. They no
longer *needed* an acting company, preferring the freedom and
variety of the open market.

However, this particular emphasis need not detain us. Speaking for myself, I had every obvious reason to be satisfied during
this period. I played a succession of good parts, my colleagues
were some of the finest actors of the day—Dudley Digges,
Henry Travers, the Lunts, Edward G. Robinson, many others.
We all came together most amiably to perform the play, but
few among us had any real connection with their fellows, either
socially or in the matter of a common understanding of what they
had to say or of how they said it. If we had absorbed any basic
life-values, you could not read our minds' construction in our
faces, or in our behavior at rehearsals or on the stage. It was curious, but none of these good craftsmen seemed able or willing
to discuss their craft. They were undoubtedly passionate about
their work, but the passion produced no babies, as it were. The
Guild survivors would probably interrupt at this point to exclaim: Oh yeah? What about your beloved Group Theatre? But

that birth was not exactly organic. It's true that many of the expenses of the *accouchement* were borne by Guild funds, and for this we must be eternally grateful—I say it without irony. Nevertheless, the Group was regarded for years (and probably still is) as a kind of biological sport, a hag-whelp, a Caliban spawned by some obscure Sycorax, worshipping strangely at the altars of Setebos Sergeitch Stanislavsky!

But the "Drang" toward the Group Idea was far from inorganic. It was rooted in the poignant needs of real people who were ready to strike hands and say, in the British phrase, "Come on, mates, let's have a bash at it!" Separation and loneliness, they felt, were not good for the soul, even though the body was well-fed. "What *is* this thing we love, the theatre?" they seemed to say. "And if you love a thing, you *do* something about it, *for* it. We know that this medium to which we have committed our lives is a collective one. The unit of it is the living actor. Because he is unashamedly alive, he turns his eyes outward to behold his brother-actor, lost in the same human predicament. When their eyes meet, the scene begins. When their ideas collide, they move forward in the service of the play, and possibly to a commonly shared point of view about life and art. What else is it to be what Hamlet calls 'the abstract and brief chronicles of the time'?"

To be or not to be—a moment of choice. Our elders would have judged that we were expressing ourselves rather flamboyantly. "Youth, youth." And not all the young actors felt as I have described, precious few, in fact. Despite the gathering clouds of the Depression, many actors were comfortably entrenched, and any change seemed ominous, irrational. Why look a gift-horse in the teeth? they would complain irritably. And as for learning, it's experientia that docets the stultos, not blind experiment! One of these younger actors, a dear, good fellow, very witty and explosive, called me all kinds of a damn fool when I told him I was thinking of leaving the Guild and joining the Group; then later, when we got talking about calmer subjects, he confided to me that (dammit!) acting presented him with one curious problem—in the middle of a scene, he would lift his hand in an impulsive gesture to about here (shoulder high), and then for the life of him he didn't know how to get it down! I wasn't able to help him at the time. A simple case of hypertension.

Certainly in those days I wasn't very articulate about my own notions of craft—I hadn't earned the right to be. It was a case of no foundation all along the line. I was acquainted with my friend's tensions, since I recognized them full well in myself. Tension of the body, mirrored by inner tension, leading inevitably to forced, mechanical, exhibitionistic action (Get that laugh! Nail down that effect!), with here and there a saving grace of truthful feeling that would disentangle itself and float upward like a wisp of smoke into the flies. When it didn't happen, squeeze as I might, I was unhappy. I was considered a good actor, too, and *that* made me ashamed. I was fed up with fumbling. I was undoubtedly learning many valuable lessons along the way, but I didn't know them by name. I see now that the effort to depict the character led me too far from its proper roots in my own individuality. I had misplaced my Self, which was far worse than a hand left dangling in the air. I yearned for my own return and I didn't know how to get it back. I think it could be said of me then, as now, that I was *seeking my Image*. Call it a wholeness, integrity; *my* life in Art, if you will.

I was not alone, as I discovered more and more when the Group Theatre got under way. My fellow-workers all aspired to earn the name of Actor. The smell of grease-paint was but one element in the confused aroma that drifted our way from the gardens of this brave new world. We set sail into the Thirties on the good ship Nonconformity. The isle as we approached it was full of noises, and we aimed at making sense of it all. We were eager to get down to First Causes, even if it meant making fools of ourselves—which history records we often did.

We were at once exploring for the lost Adam and the gold of Peru. If the memory of our endeavors vibrates somewhat with a fuzzy romanticism, I'm not too concerned. Shakespeare may have had his fellow-actors in mind when he put it down: We are such stuff as dreams are made on. (I seem to be quoting *Tempest* quite a lot.) We *were* romantic, from necessity—and necessity for whatever reason is very real. We needed, as I said, a Place for our exercises; we needed peace, in which to learn the grammar of struggle.

Please bear in mind, in spite of appearances, that I am still getting around to Actors' Technique—that property of any art which (as Michael Chekhov quotes it) "is sometimes apt to dampen, as it were, the spark of inspiration in a *mediocre* artist; but the same techniques in the hands of a master can fan that spark into an unquenchable flame." . . . Consummation devoutly to be wished. And that's how we wanted it—devoutly, passionately. Not everyone in the same way; some of us were monks by temperament, some were sybarites, others opportunists, a crank or two—for it takes all kinds to make a Group. At our best, though, there was a glow about us; we had been chosen, and in a sense had chosen each other. We respected our three directors who had taken us for better or worse, and were far ahead of us in their separate intuitions about the difficulties of this childlike safari in an inimical world.

The glow came, I think, from the sharing of the common task. The age around us was a discombobulated one; our relationship to it was not clear to us. We experienced a kind of sanity in the very act of concentrating on the problems of acting. It forced us to look inside ourselves. We scrutinized ourselves minutely, ourselves through each other; we anatomized ourselves; we taught ourselves to become intensely aware; we stalked our own weaknesses remorselessly. We built on our momentary successes and discoveries with the satisfaction of Egyptians piling up a pyramid stone by stone. We were each other's guinea-pigs, and from observation and criticism of our experiments we learned to describe the actor's equipment in terms that became a new Esperanto. The poet Francis Thompson has an image somewhere of Science. "Science, old noser, that with anatomizing scalpel tents its three-inch of thy skin and brags 'All's bare.'" Our tendency to probe and break things down became a nuisance and good friends warned us of the fate of Humpty-Dumpty. But we have spent the rest of our lives putting ourselves together again. The proof of this particular synthesis lies in the eating, if I may mix puddings and rainbows, in the practical kitchen of the Theatre.

If our sight had remained so fanatically focused only on the dark and private world of our actors' organism, we might really have emerged as "old nosers," with new "footworks" and "sostenuto buts." But—aside from the fact that we were mindful of our bodies and took normal delight in them, the more so as we sensed the organic interflow of mind and body, the sovereignty of will and Imagination to arouse and control them—aside from this fact, the new-found concentration on our functions as actors, forced us also to turn our eyes outward upon the nature of the *objective* world. Our citizenship in this world was acquiring a gravity and an interconnection and even a responsibility that we hadn't dreamed of in that other time before we'd crossed the Jordan. The world of music and plastic movement, the world of painting and photography, of current history and politics, of the many cultures that made our American culture, the consequences of the Depression and the grim incredible prevalence of the shivering breadline and the apple-seller. That new awareness of ours expanded in all directions; according to temperament and capacity, each person drank of the world around him, even though sometimes it ran like a bitter liquor through his veins. Sympathy or repulsion—they were bred of objective circumstances, a look at the world. "Watchman, what of the night!" When we returned to our exercises we had something to say about it.

Plus ça change; but *plus* not altogether *la même chose*. The interpenetration of the two longings I have described—intense consciousness of Self combined with an insatiable thirst to understand our contemporaries and their times—produced a "new" type of actor. Shall we label him actor-philosopher, or actor-citizen? Or, socially-conscious actor? One hesitates to encase this fly in amber; better to call him—just—actor. "Abstract and brief chronicle of the time"—that word "abstract," though Shakespeare didn't altogether intend it so, permits me to say this: as one of these creatures, I am not willing to see the wild flutter of its wings nailed down upon a ticketed board. The important point lies in the fact that the amalgamation I speak of provided an enormous quickening of the imagination, and when that happens, laws and labels are apt to fly out of the window. The creative impulse—like Ariel—is essentially wild and homeless, chafing against limitations. Somewhere in the heart of this impatient shimmering movement is a spirit, heedless of normal lets and hindrances. It craves to release itself, in a burst of music. All the more, therefore, unless it is to be allowed to attain freedom beyond all recognition, does it need the bondage imposed upon it by some master-force and will. The name of Setebos will have to yield to Prospero—Prospero Sergeitch.

Stanislavsky. . . . Adam in the Garden of Eden apparently had no difficulty at all about the names he chose for all created things. He was divinely inspired! Even in translation from Edenese, they come across magnificently: tiger, lamb, elephant, hyena, cat—most satisfactory. But if you want to know what really was happening, and how the struggle for concrete forms takes place without supernatural prompting—then consider *My Life in Art* by Stanislavsky.

On rereading this book recently, I was struck again and again by the quantity of things that we already take for granted these days about ourselves as actors. "But of course," we say, "how obvious!" It is the case again of Columbus' egg—very clear, once it's been demonstrated. The touching quality in Stanislavsky's book is the first one he confesses in himself, his obstinacy.

To the very last page, for all his majesty of presence and over-whelming knowledge and sophistication, he remains a child, with the concentrated purposefulness of a child learning to walk. "Strange," he seems always to be muttering to himself, "Strange, very strange. I fall. But—let's try again." Like a good Captain, he shares every hardship of his men; he bivouacs on the bare cold ground. He loves them for every glimmer of progress they show; he growls at their laziness, their complacency, their vanities. He presides over his province with farsighted roving eyes, with the look of a skeptical lion. "Know your enemies," he seems to rumble in his throat, "False pathos, cheap tricks, artificiality, disrespect, timidity, tension, fashionableness. And again, laziness!" . . . "*I don't believe you!*"—his actors flinched and quailed before that dreaded battle cry of his, roared out of the depths of the auditorium. And yet, on opening nights, when Stanislavsky, being often ill was obliged to stay home from the theatre, they would call him on the telephone to be reassured and steadied by the sound of his voice.

Toward the end of the book (it is 1914—Stanislavsky is almost 60 and the sea gull on the curtain of the Moscow Art Theatre has come to rest permanently in the imagination of the world), there is a moving section called simply "The Voice." It might also have been called "Let's Face It!" Stanislavsky has faced this matter of the voice thousands of times in his life, and yet, here he faces it again with a kind of wistful and defiant finality. Nowhere does the beacon of art that draws him on burn more purely than in this chapter. It is there for you to read, but I would like to quote only this:

As for me, some people praised me, others (and there were more of them) criticized me. In this book, both before and now, I judge myself not by press reviews and public opinions, but by my own feelings and thoughts. I would not exchange my failure for any success in the world, for it taught me a great deal. . . . Music helped me to solve many problems that had been racking my brain and it convinced me that an actor should know how to speak. . . . Isn't it strange that I had to live almost sixty years *before I felt with all my being* this simple and well-known truth, a truth that most actors do not know?

The target, the summary of his beliefs and teachings, is stated in his last chapter. This is no *"Ave atque vale,"* for Prospero is just buckling down to work and continued quest, and there are many years before him. He quotes the painter Dégas as saying: "If you have a hundred thousand francs' worth of skill, spend another five sous to buy more." Then he goes on to speak of "The torch of living tradition and the conscious road to the gates of the unconscious, the true foundation of theatrical art."

This is a torch which can be passed only from hand to hand, and not from the stage; through instruction, through the revelation of mysteries, on the one hand, and through exercises and stubborn and inspired effort to grasp these mysteries, on the other.

        *   *   *

The main difference between the art of the actor and all other arts is that other artists may create whenever they are inspired. The stage artist, however, must be the master of his own inspiration and must know how to call it forth at the time announced on the theatre's posters. This is the chief secret of our art. Without this, the most perfect technique, the greatest gifts, are powerless. . . . The inability to find a conscious path to unconscious creativeness led actors to disastrous prejudices which deny inner, spiritual technique. They became stagnant and mistook theatrical self-consciousness for true inspiration.

        *   *   *

What will my rôle be in this future task? (i.e., the sphere of the actor's inner and outer technique.) In my last years of life, I would like to be what I am in reality, what I must be on the strength of the laws of nature according to which I have lived and worked in art.

        *   *   *

Fundamentally, the processes of stage creation remain the same for the younger generation as they were for the older. It is precisely in this sphere that young actors distort and maim their nature. We can help them, we can warn them in time.

The result of my life-long search is my so-called "system," the method of acting that I have discovered and that allows the actor to create images, reveal the life of the human spirit, and naturally incarnate it in a beautiful artistic form on the stage.

Stanislavsky did not dread change. He welcomed it. It was with joy that he saw younger actors and directors, in his lifetime, absorb what he had taught and give it forth in new forms. Michael Chekhov, Vakhtangov, many others. Though he referred to it as "my system," he was never "Sir Oracle" about it. He gloried in the fact that the voices to which he listened were but promptings from the greatest technicians of the past, and confirmed by the most stirring practice of his own youthful observation—Salvini, Rossi, Chaliapin, Yermolova, Duse. The "system" was for those that needed it. To Harold Clurman he once said: "One only asks, is it truthful, is it beautiful. And if I see such beautiful acting anywhere, shall I say, Just a moment there! It's true, you act marvellously, I am deeply moved, nevertheless, I must reject it because you've never been to my School!" He may have talked of "mysteries," but he was much more concerned with the "revelation" that might make them clear as day. For the actor there is only one "mystery" and it lies in the interrelationship of the refractory body with the wayward soul. The particular solution may determine *anyone's* life in art. The key that Stanislavsky placed in the hands of the actor was—the actor's own consciousness.

What does this include? Everything. Everything that comes within the grasp of his five senses and is subject to his will. The use of his body, his voice, his inner gifts, sense of rhythm, response to imagery, his sympathies, even his moral point of view. Always, his *conscious recognition* of these things. As he grows in their service, he will grow to love himself, but not with self-love, only as a vessel of craft. If it's Shakespeare he's playing, or Aeschylus, or Molière, or Shaw, he will love their words because they have been chosen and arranged with deep craft, almost with guile—a camouflage to deceive mortality. The wonder and simplicity of *"Tu l'as voulu, Dandin!"* Or. . . . "She never told her love, but let concealment like a worm i' the bud feed on her damask cheek. She pined in thought, and with a green and yellow melancholy she sat like patience on a monument, smiling at grief." Or the sheer rippling delight of exclaiming: "Cry to it, Nuncle, as the cockney did to the eels when she put 'em i' the paste alive! She knapped 'em o' the coxcombs with a stick and cried, 'Down, wantons, down!' It was her brother who in pure kindness to his horse, buttered his hay." . . . Or the despair of ever coming within a mile of "Light thickens; and the crow Makes wing to th' rooky wood: Good things of day begin to droop and drowse; Whiles night's black agents to their preys do rouse. . . ."

Such are the splendors and the miseries of the actor's world. But one thing is certain, mere thinking won't make it come to pass. It's not a general matter of "work to be done," but of concrete tasks, consciously undertaken and mastered by repetition. They are the irreducible minimum of our business. Specific things done, moment to moment. Grasp this, and at once there's a clearing of the decks—all reliance on so-called actors' instinct, inspiration, divine fire, and such-like dangerous fantasies must go. Not that these things don't matter in their place; there will be a time for such a word, to misquote Macbeth. But for the actor they are the consequence, not the shapers of action. One must not be in a hurry to dismiss divine fire when it happens. But it *is* a matter of *when* it occurs. Perhaps this *"Gott-sach,"* as the Germans call it, has to do with our ingrained memories. We are the sum of what we have experienced, yes, but more deeply, we are what we remember in our bones. The poet Rilke says:

For the sake of a few lines one must see many cities, men and things. One must know the animals, one must feel how the birds fly and know the gesture with which the small flowers open in the morning. One must be able to think back to roads . . . meetings . . . partings . . . days of childhood . . . parents . . . nights of travel . . . many nights of love . . . screams of women in labor . . . the dying . . . the dead . . . And still it is not enough to have memories. One must be able to forget them when they are many, and one must have the great patience to wait until they come again. For it is not yet the memories themselves. Not until they have turned to blood within us, to glance, to gesture, nameless and no longer to be distinguished from ourselves—not until then can it happen that in a most rare hour the first word of a verse arises in their midst and goes forth from them.

Here, at the threshold of the unconscious, as Stanislavsky called it, is the continental divide of our discussion. It is time we climbed down to the flatlands. Since I have hinted at some of the rapt possibilities, I expect you to ask: But how?—just how do you go about achieving them? Even now, I have an impulse to shirk the answer—to say merely: go to the ant, thou sluggard!—in this case, the mighty ant Konstantin Sergeitch. For it is all there, in his books and in the evidence of his practical collected works.

Not always were his followers capable of seizing upon the full meaning of his work, or enlarging upon it. The exception was Eugene Vakhtangov, the brilliant young director, or better still, the partnership of Vakhtangov-Michael Chekhov, since it was the latter who has left us (in a single smallish volume —*To the Actor*) the conclusions that followed from their flint-and-steel collaboration. I knew Chekhov. He was an immensely complicated man, an Ariel, a great teacher. Simplicity is a very complicated thing, and Michael Chekhov set out to simplify the vast implications of his Master's artistic struggles. The basic discoveries having already been made, he took them into his body, so to speak, filtered them through his own powerful individuality and imagination, and gave them an even more elementary character. It is interesting to set some of their terminology side by side. Where Stanislavsky spoke of "Relaxation of Muscles," Chekhov did not hesitate to call it "Feeling of Ease."

Where Stanislavsky broke off his brilliant observations on Action and Objective, Chekhov combined them with Character in his marvelous intuition of the Psychological Gesture. Most of all, he understood the harmony of "Body and Psychology," as he put it. "Listen to your bodies," he would say, "and they will interpret the movement of your *inner* impulses." Great intellect though he was, he scorned its usefulness for the actor, preferring to obey what one might call the "muscularity" of the Imagination.

But to return to your question of "How?" . . . Perhaps it will be useful to imagine, to visualize exactly what is happening, in a play we are looking at. Not so much *in,* as *behind* it, *through* it. As an audience, let us say we are fortunate; we are witnessing a realistic play of stature performed by a company of highly trained craftsmen, sensitive and experienced men and women. We are familiar with their work; we like them even before the curtain rises, but this only sharpens our sense of responsibility. It is they who have taught us what to expect of them; it is for us to be alert and fully attentive. In this way we will be able to give the play back to them; by seeing the point, we will confirm them in their power to make us *see* the point. We want them to be what they have always been—the beautiful, expressive voices, the subtle, sinewy bodies, their lightness and resiliency of spirit, their moody transformations, their seeming worship of the ultimate good in life. We want all of these things all over again, yet offered to us somehow in a new light, as these fine technicians know how to turn them.

The curtain rises. Within the music of the playwright's words we begin to perceive an issue that embodies a basic struggle. The decision lies in the hands of a group of characters who battle it out to the final curtain, and even beyond, in the aroused responses of the spectators. That much could be the summary of almost any play in the doing. But we are here for a special pleasure—to observe our actors, to tent them to the quick. The first five or ten minutes seem to pass in a kind of sparring, easy yet tentative, as if they hadn't quite made up their minds. And then, here it comes, as so often before, stealing upon us before we are aware, the realization that those people are in the highest degree in *connection* with each other. And this they are without strain, by no overt means. Not offhand; if these actors *wanted* to be offhand, they would *be* offhand. But as if they were saying with simple deliberation: I am here—you are here—we are here—and we are in this together. We sense again the peculiar and reassuring pleasure there is in watching our actors *look*, simply look; their eyes are full of vision, when they look, they *see*. They see not only what they want to see by an act of special concentration which explores the significance of the moment, they also prepare for future looks, future significances. Already this is life, but it is above life. It is the same with their listening. They not only listen, they hear. And so with their other senses, of which perhaps touching is the most obvious. But one sense cannot be divided from the others. These actors come alive all in one piece; they can touch with their eyes, taste and smell with their ears. And what's more, they talk. That is to say, they truly communicate by means of words and silences.

The dialogue begins to prepare for a small event—one of the actors has a speech to which the others all listen. You know in advance that he loves this speech, for there's a glow of anticipation in him as it comes near, the mouth of his imagination begins to water—he launches into it, tearing at it with little nips, the speech feeds him with imagery and his eyes light up as he *sees* ever more and more. He enjoys the responses of his fellows—they give him strength and a strange freedom as he goes plunging along to the end. In the chorus of yesses that follows, enters one bearing a gift. He is elderly, self-deprecating, though his heart is full of love. But these qualities are not yet fully established in him; we sense him alternately feeding at

some center within himself and reaching out to find some object or person with which or whom he can establish outer
connection. Before long he has it; eye meets eye, an intangible
circle is defined, he snuggles into his character as into a warm
coat; life in the form of the ensuing action radiates from him
without effort, with infectious reality. . . . There is another,
who has been brooding to one side of the stage. We know him
as the Bear. He seems apart from the others, objective, critical.
But his inner attitude, not yet revealed, scorns any obvious
indications, bodily or facial; it simply radiates out of some energy he has known how to store up in himself. The speech of
the previous young actor has apparently stayed with him; now,
strolling lazily toward the group, he harks back to it with challenge and contempt. He cuts through the scene like a hot
ploughshare; challenge and contempt become welded into a private grief—his face becomes ironed out into a moving simplicity,
strangely classical. He remains connected with some image
within himself, tears stand in his eyes, he disdains them with an
angry lift of his head, you can see they have come unbidden
and we divine in this moment that actor and man have found an
intense union. They, too, are connected. . . . A woman has wandered in during this last outburst; she is the one we call Greensleeves. We know about her. Life has dealt her many a hard
blow, but she has found in herself the strength to resist bitter-
ness. Now her lovely face is molded into an expression past suffering, compassionate and pure. *There* is one of her characteristic gestures, head on the side, a quizzical fleeting smile, the
partly open hand raised and let fall. She hears the man's words,
her face becomes grave; she wants to stay out of it, she turns
away and describes little circles with her finger on the table;
then she hears a strange tone in the man's voice, she turns to
see the tears glistening—a flash of sullen resistance crosses her
face, "What have I to do with you?," followed by a sigh. She is
connected with him through understanding—her face is a mask

of compassion. She folds her arms and waits, filled with some special grace for which there is no name but her own, and which is yet not static, but suspended, in conflict. Two powers seem to fill the stage with dramatic potential—the power of masculine integrity and the power of love.

In the performance of these four or five little "pictures" that I have pilfered from various places and strung together at random, I want to point out that there is nothing *calculated*—not the man's tears, nor the woman's sigh, nor the old man's radiations, nor the young man's abandonment. These actors do what they have to do—it is a second nature by now—out of obedience to certain fundamental stimulations which make everything else come to pass. They are too wise to fall into the error of copying themselves. Nevertheless, night after night they are capable of conveying the content of the play without superficial indication or studied effectiveness, simply by safeguarding the truth. One notices that (1) They accept themselves; they open themselves, too; they know how to leave themselves free to receive all impressions. (2) They accept and relate to each other. (3) They adapt to the circumstances of the play with intelligence and sensitiveness. (4) They give and take through their senses; also through action and reaction. (5) They have rhythm in speech and action. (6) They are constantly in contact with something, whether it be an inanimate object, their partners, a thought, an image, or a memory. (7) As a result of all these, their emotions simply occur, easily, abundantly.

There are larger vistas beyond—the completion of the Main Action, the grades and climaxes, the whole composition of the play. But I deliberately set these aside in order to examine the intimate condition of the actor at work. One is rightly suspicious of readers' digests as substitutes for a man's life-long labor. But I think we can agree that the unit of what happens when that curtain goes up is the Moment. The Moment is the responsibility of the actor at work. And if I had to reduce the

great gold vein of Stanislavsky's mine to a single practical nug-
get, I would say—that for the actor there is no moment on
the stage that cannot be examined and accounted for in terms
of three basic elements—the Self, the Object, and the Action.

The actor, like all craftsmen, brings himSelf to the work. He
also finds himSelf *in* the work, and he brings back this perpetually renewed Self time after time, *to* the work. Technically,
this is what I understand by Stanislavsky's Relaxation, Chekhov's Feeling of Ease. You may take it as relaxation and leave
it at that if you prefer. But for me, it is a more central and intimate way of feeling at home on the stage. More than that, it is
a source of power, and inexhaustible. The Self is all we have
—it is well to realize it, to accept it, and most importantly, to
use it. Does this seem obvious?—then why is our stage still
afflicted with tensions of all kinds, tensions of the body and the
mind, contortions of the spirit? When the curtain rose on those
little "pictures" of ours it was the first thing we sensed—these
actors were not self-conscious, they were Self-possessed. We will
return, in the end, to Self.

Michael Chekhov prefaces one of his chapters with this remark by Leonardo da Vinci: "The soul desires to dwell with
the body because without the members of the body it can neither
act nor feel." In much the same way, the Self needs the objective world—otherwise it has no meaning, it is like a motor idling, it is not connected. May we not think of our waking
day (and according to the Freudians much more importantly
our sleeping time!) as an uninterrupted succession of pictures, ideas, thoughts, fantasies, actualities. We are constantly seeing, even when our eyes are closed. The actor's Self utilizes
this fact significantly; collaborating with the Author's lines, and
between the lines as well, he weaves a continuous tissue of these
objects, these "lies like truth," amusing fictions, coruscating images, grim deeds and memories. He is on intimate terms with
them, unbidden as they frequently are when they come. In

return they "give" him something, as we say—a focus of concentration, a storehouse of reassurance. As long as they are alive, he is alive. That actor of ours, brooding off there on the side, was drinking deep of this flow of objects; the woman Greensleeves, drawn in almost against her will, the victim of memories and faiths of which she herself has become the sacrifice—then, when they could contain themselves no more, they overflowed in action.

Which is the third of our three ingredients. Action, considered thus, may be thought of as an expression of the *energy* which is set up between the Self and the Object. As such it has an "oscillating" character—back and forth, back and forth. Is this to consider it too curiously? And are we discarding Stanislavsky's orthodox dictum of desire: I want, therefore I act? Well— have we actors not found in practice that often and often even the word, desire, killeth? But isn't desiring the electrical continuum of looking and seeing? "And the eyes of them both were opened and they knew that they were naked." (Genesis 3,7) The Bible comes to the support of Prospero Alexeitch. And once we have set that energy *going,* will it be so difficult to know what we *want?* Again, I must warn you, as I warn myself, that these things must not be taken mechanically, lest we fall again into the error of the "old noser." They are neither a formula nor a recipe. They are the shorthand, as it were, of a long experience. Symbols. All symbols have to be earned, and paid for with the usual legal tender—blood, sweat, and tears.

I hope that you will let me share with you a private experience which properly falls outside the limits of this discussion. And yet, not so, since it stemmed organically from what I was thinking about all these subjects. It is not accidental, that from time to time, as you noticed, I have been referring in one way or another to Shakespeare's *Tempest.* It happens to be one of the plays we will do this summer at Stratford. I stand in awe, as all of us do, before the work of this man, the more as I have had to struggle with the fact of playing him. I think that as men change and progress, their understanding of him will progress and change. Each age will evaluate him in its own terms, for "others abide our question, thou art free." Now, as for *Tempest*, I had long ago caught its "message" of ultimate reconciliation of man with man, in the form of an allegory that seemed to measure the relative goodness and spirituality of created things in a series of contrasts. Wisdom and brute stupidity. Disembodied beauty and earthbound carnality. Unworldliness and malevolence. Innocence and bitter knowledge. True, these things are there, and we may arrange them in a gorgeous banquet of moralities, if we wish (enclosing a card from W.S.). But I don't think so. Not now. It was not only for these things that Prospero broke his staff. The inner event had to do with Shakespeare's resignation from the kingdom of poesy. This has been remarked before, as we know. But I can only say that for myself I had never felt the special poignancy, the *technical* poignancy, if you will, of this resignation, as I did while I was struggling to put down the ideas of this very technical paper. Beauty is truth—but truth is also beauty. The truth of the lifelong struggle, for the right word, the right cadence, the right pause ("That's my dainty Ariel"), the right storm ("My brave spirit"), the right tranquillity ("Delicate Ariel, I'll set thee free for this"), the right object, the right action, the right sense of Self (sound of staff, breaking).

These are the thoughts I wanted to share with you (I feel they are the "right" thoughts), principally to point out that they came to me as intimation arising out of this whole consideration of actors' technique. It's how a craftsman's mind works—that is how we actors find our correct objectives. It is a matter of many levels, not one.

Postscript on Self. . . . There's a homely American story. It tells of an Indian and a white trapper who went out hunting together. They blundered into some very wild country, farther and farther away from familiar surroundings and the ancestral teepee. Night was falling and the coyotes beginning to howl. The white man stopped and said: "Look here, Eagle Feather, you know what I think? I think we're lost!" To which the noble savage replied: "Me not lost. Teepee lost."

The Cannibal Theatre

PETER SHAFFER

I shall always remember my first encounter with actors, probably because it so disappointed and depressed me. It occurred in a B.B.C. studio at the rehearsal of my first play, a piece for radio. That day was certainly the most exciting of my life up till then: the acceptance of the play (after many rejections of plays and ideas for plays); the invitation to attend rehearsal; a Sunday journey to London into the peeling, cracked, almost defeated shabbiness (1947 shabbiness) of Marylebone. I remember a long corridor, red lights on and off, and then the vast studio itself and the control room into which I was ushered in a flurry of half-rising figures, whispered greetings, and uncompleted handshakes. The actors were grouped around the microphone, out in the middle of the floor. I listened, and suddenly a huge wave of joy bashed over my head: the sound, the first irrecapturable sound of my words being spoken by professionals! My words! For five minutes they made no sense; the surf of pleasure pounded inside me. Then, when this hurricane of self-approbation was over, I began to listen critically. They weren't very good lines, but at least I had selected them from all possible combinations, and that thought gave me an encouraging sense of my own existence. More, it gave me a curious sense of proprietorship in the actors, a vain, childlike, rather thrilling emotion. It was soon to be dispelled.

At the lunch interval I was introduced to this cast I mentally owned. Nervously I went with them to a pub nearby, all exposure and anxious amiability. They asked me what I'd like to drink; I said beer. That was our whole conversation. Thereafter nobody said anything to me at all. For the rest of the hour the actors talked shop among themselves, workaday shop with all the unromantic trivia of the true professional. Finally they returned to work, briskly performed my play, and walked off together, forgetting even to say good night. Suddenly it was all over. I found myself in the subway, feeling injured and disappointed. It was my first taste of that deep sense of rejection which nonacting playwrights feel around actors. They went their way, I went mine; they together, I alone.

This is always how it is, at least on the surface. Actors, no matter how solipsistically mad they are, live in a fraternity, an indissoluble Order. They take vows to join it, largely unspoken; they feel safe with other members of it, even though they often resent them: behind their most irresponsible displays is the awareness of a Calling. Though here, of course, as elsewhere, few are chosen.

My first reaction was one of annoyance, concealing envy. It must be so good to belong, to be sustained by the professional warmth, the intimacy, the pattern of dressing-room life, and the inalienable duty to play, whatever happens. I have never lost this envy, although when I tell an actor so he rarely believes it. For his part, the actor is made nervous by authors; as often as he can he retreats behind a screen of simple-mindedness ("I'm just the actor") which is only partly sincere. If you say to an actor, "How do you remember all those lines?" he will spit in your eye; but that same actor will say to an author, or wonderingly imply, turning on him the half-mocking, half-impressed blue eye of theatrical innocence, "However do you think of it all? I wish I were clever like that!" Now, behind all this banter, and behind even the deep yearnings to belong, or to be "clever like that," is a deep, grave antagonism which cannot be eradicated. Between actors and playwrights exists, at best, a violent, desperate, irrefragable relation which makes reconciliation in a conventional sense impossible between them, and even undesirable. It is perhaps the most profoundly loving, because the most urgently needful, of all relations—that between hungry beings and their prey.

Over the years my simple view of actors, as a jolly company of people to be wistfully envied, changed and deepened as I came to see their exclusiveness and their ultimate indifference to writers as something infinitely more profound than mere trade unionism. What I had first observed as a fraternity was also in fact a primitive tribe, with which I was intimately and terribly connected—over which, indeed, for a short spell, and with the inevitable penalty, I had to rule.

The rehearsal of a serious play is an elaborate and quietly awful ceremony of fertilization; a ritual, despite its frequent appearance of disorganization and its very real air of friendliness, of sacrifice and rebirth. At the beginning, the playwright is accepted as God-King; he is felt to contain some truth without which the players cannot live. He is treated with deference, consulted, danced before. He speaks, or his interpreter speaks for him, and is eagerly obeyed.

For a spell the tribe, still weak and undernourished, moves at his nod; he sits enthroned in the secrets they require, assured, assuring, needed. Then, gradually the actors gain strength—his strength: they learn his words, his secrets; they cut off his hair. They take away everything he has, at first tentatively, and then boldly, with increasing assurance. They catch his quick sentences and acquire his speed; they subdue his big speeches and take away his gravity; they tear out his jokes and leave him humorless or imperceptive. They must invade him entirely and search for their nourishment in his darkness; they need his potency, and do not rest—cannot rest—until they have it. *For the actor dies between roles, and comes to work seeking his spring.* It is not an accident that we speak of the theatrical "season." Under that trivial word you may see primal planting, the earth wetted with lifeblood, the shoots emerging, thickening, talling, harvested, and eaten: a corn of text, and words becoming flesh.

It is an awesome thing for a playwright to watch good modern actors who have played his parts for a year on the stage become suddenly obliged, say for a new production somewhere else, to take up the actual scripts again and do a reading of the play. They stumble and slur, they look resentfully at the lines, they are surprised and at times quite thrown by minute alterations between the original typescript and what they have been saying for months. They are made uneasy by the printed page, by the return of flesh to word. (Re-productions of plays with the same cast in another city can never be easy; they represent a reversal of the order of nature. How does one resurrect the dismembered body of an author, or turn back the process of ingestion, except by vomiting?) Actors will tell you, and tell you rightly, that they can do nothing until they have thrown away the text—until, that is, *they have thrown away you,* until there does not survive a single punctuation mark to remind them of your vanished power, or a word remaining undissolved in their blood streams.

And when this happens, you feel your death. You are the least needed person in the theater; you are totally superfluous. The actors go on stage and forget you; they even forget they had to memorize your words. They must do this. The parts, all parts of the parts, the very private parts, are theirs now. You may have brought John into the world, but like a mother who learns about her children from everyone else, you must accept the fact that John has become Mr. A., the actor, and that with a dazzling arrogance which you cannot but acknowledge, he can truly say: "I (John) don't feel it like that," "I would never do that," and even, when your rewrites are disputed, "I would never say that." When the actor comes to say this last, the sacrifice is really complete, there is nothing left of the author at all.

Of course, the playwright doesn't merely accept this role; he needs and demands it. He also seeks rebirth, and the only way for him to achieve it is to be liberated from his old play, to have the obsessional demon who first beat it from the cover of his unrest haled out of his body in the fullness of performance. The actor is the playwright's exorcist.

But the actor, too, needs freeing. He also lives in isolation and needs to be released, through the harness of a text, from intensity of feeling unyoked to purpose. Thus each of these incomplete beings is living in the other and released by the other, as in an inevitable love affair. Unease must remain, for the writer, quite simply, writes; and this hard process of setting down is never really acknowledged by the actor, who to be true to himself must believe that the words are born in his living throat without any intermediary process. Paper, for the actor, is a commodity which does not exist; for the author, it is the focus of his reverence. Still, each is united to the other with a true force, without which none of this ritual, this loosing of carnivores, would be tolerable.

I have noted that actors are a fraternity and take vows. In England, certainly, they are regarded with extreme suspicion. Something deep in the conforming heart is disturbed by the thought of the actor's nonattachment to homes and steady visits to offices. And something is also puzzled and offended by a certain indifference in him to social reality, political iniquity, world danger—a seeming frivolity he shares with priests. Our attitude toward actors is always uneasy; though we are hardly aware of it, and actors themselves do not understand it, we treat them with the same half-scornful, half-flattering wariness which we would show to priests of some incomprehensible but rather awesome cult. Which is certainly the right way to regard them.

What is their article of faith? It is simple and immense. Every man contains in himself the history of man. No man is an island; he isn't even a continent: he is, viewed rightly, the world. Therefore, no pattern of behavior should be incomprehensible to us, and no feeling in another inaccessible to us. We fail in our sympathy over and over again, because of our preconceptions and our unexercised imaginations, and because our hearts shrink in the effort to present to the world an image of ourselves.

The actor is not concerned with this at all; in his dual nature he can succeed where we fail, and in a real sense succeed (as in all art) *for us*. He has therefore an almost divine function in society, for to survive as a true speaker for us he must find in himself what most of us deny is there—the experience of the race. He must refuse in himself the pressured right we claim to prejudice; he must take on all lonelinesses and fears, relish confidence where he himself has none, enjoy many kinds of jokes, though he himself has but one sense of humor. Ideally, no hunger is too acute, no perversion too obscure for him to live it out imaginatively, and to do this he must set aside, as a barrier, all personal condemnation. The moral purpose of actors, which is the exorcism not only of playwrights but of society, can be accomplished only by slaying the mortal enemy of truth, preconception.

And in the same degree the playwright does likewise. This is where we meet, on moral ground. We both sense what charge is laid upon us, what dark journeys have to be made in the way of business, descents into Nibelheim to gratify Wotan. The encyclopedic imagination which is necessary to the actor is needed as urgently by the playwright; he must list from within himself an inventory of authentic emotions enough to furnish all the mansions of the blessed and unblessed. Many actors fail— I don't mean technical failure—because of their inability to meet these demands in full or because they don't even realize unconsciously that the demands are being made, which means that they are bad actors. The strictures of good actors on bad actors are harsher than in any other profession, for this reason: to a dedicated player, a bad piece of acting is a betrayal, and a bad actor is a whisky priest. And most playwrights fail for the same reason. Both are moral agents.

One last thought: the playwright has an added duty, specifically to the actor. He has an obligation to write good parts. Without them, despite what theatrical fans say, the actor can do very little. What good is it to own the Tarnhelm, if all you are asked to do is turn yourself into a frog? There is no excuse under heaven for creating people whose sole reason for living is to hear a pistol shot, to say the carriage is without, to announce Lady Bore's arrival, to hold a spear or a Martini. These parts are betrayals. I would be truly ashamed if an actor told me a part of mine wasn't, in the real sense, big enough—even though, as often as not, the actor will prove to be foolish enough to have counted the lines and not the heartbeats of the part.

So, on this frail bridge of obligation, the baker can meet the starving boy: he offers him homemade bread; the boy snatches it and waves him impatiently away. The baker goes, dismissed, knowing that in a little while the boy will be hungry again and will wander the streets hollow-eyed, seeking his shop, praying there will be something in it worth eating.

And that is the prayer of the playwright too: to be full again.

What Is an Actor?

FREDERIK SCHYBERG

In a famous speech about actors in 1928, Max Reinhardt called the art of theatre "the oldest, most powerful, most immediate of the arts, combining the many in one." The statement may appear exaggerated, but it is only a weak echo of statements which great minds in the past have been inspired to make. Voltaire called the theatre "the noblest and most useful thing invented by the human mind," and Victor Hugo designated the drama, in his well-known manifesto, the preface to *Cromwell,* as "complete poetry," the "ocean" into which all the other streams of poetry flow. But I do not intend to speak of the theatre in general, only of the art of acting; partly because it seems to me that problems in the art of acting have had a profound effect upon the current as well as the eternal state of the art of theatre (does not the contemporary drama and film owe much to actors?), and partly because this distinctive art form has virtually never been the subject for scholarly analysis. It is the least known, least explored area of theatre esthetics.

The drama as art form, as literary genre, has been a subject of research and recognition for three hundred years, but uncertainty and insufficient knowledge of the subject, coupled with scorn on the part of scholars, has caused the art of acting to be regarded as a pariah. In the middle of the nineteenth century a prominent theatre critic, pupil of Hegel, and university man in Berlin, Heinrich Theodor Rötscher, wrote a book entitled *Die Kunst der dramatischen Darstellung* (1841), in which he made an attempt to distinguish methodically between the literary and performing arts. His work is idealistic, but Prussianistically pedantic and naïve—and scarcely readable today. No stimulating scholarly insights emanated from the work, and it inspired no sequels. The German dramatist Otto Ludwig in his *Shakespeare-Studien,* which was published in 1871, conceived a new fresh view of the works of the great dramatist by considering them in terms of the technical aspects of acting, and he found that certain important plays—even those of Shakespeare—seemed to be written only "to furnish a foundation for the art of acting," a fruitful and at that time completely new point of view which he rightfully recommended as the fundamental theoretical view for "the second part of a work on the art of dramatic composition." But this second part has yet to be written, and, in academic circles, his point of view has not been acknowledged.

Professors of esthetics and humanities have found it difficult from the start to assign an appropriate place in their systems to the art of acting, and as often as not they have ignored or belittled it. Obviously it was not an independent art; it was only a reproducing, a second-hand, and therefore second-rate art. At the turn of the century the Danish actor Karl Mantzius, author of the comprehensive *The History of Theatrical Art* (1897–1916), a work which enjoys an international reputation because it is—despite its great limitations—the only exhaustive work of its kind to date in any language, took a stand against the university professors of the time who had placed the art of acting, in their esthetic writings, rather low in the ranks of the liberal arts. Professor Claudius Wilkens at the University of Copenhagen included it only with hesitation among the other art forms in his esthetics, but without reservation he also included—to Mantzius' justified chagrin—gardening. And Professor Carl Lange, in his otherwise excellent study of the physiology of pleasure (1899), placed acting among the lowest of the liberal arts, under equilibristic performances, that is, among circus attractions, inasmuch—as he expressed it—as the art of acting was the least independent of the arts. It functions only as the servant and intermediary agent of dramatic poetry.

Even if the art of acting has risen somewhat in academic prestige during this century and generally is no longer ranked with acrobatics and the care of the garden, it cannot yet be said to possess the hallmark of a liberal art. On the other hand, in Germany, America, and just recently in Sweden, the history of the theatre has become an academic discipline as a subdivision of the history of culture. The dead theatre at Pompeii and Herculaneum, buried under the streams of lava and rains of ashes of the past, has been found worthy of excavation and exposure—but what of the living theatre? Right up to our own time scholars carefully have steered clear of the art and esthetics of acting. Even though the art constitutes the primary energizer of the artistic complex of the theatre, the study of acting has been entrusted entirely to outsiders or to actors themselves. Even in Germany, the most hospitable milieu anywhere for theatrical frenzy, theatrical romance, and the adoration of actors throughout the last century, the situation is the same. Except for a pair of isolated contributions by theatre critics, it has been left up to actors themselves to express expert opinions about their art. Just after World War I, in 1919, two capable, experienced theatre people, actors Ferdinand Gregori from Berlin and Adolph Winds from Dresden, wrote a pair of creditable books, filled with useful statements and valuable hints, but with pessimistic conclusions. Gregori regretted that the nature and uniqueness of the art of acting had remained a secret right up to our time, which is particularly regrettable for the profession of acting, since, he said, it "is still not completely accepted among the 'honorable' occupations, and, moreover, is only reluctantly accepted as art." Winds finishes the preface to his book by expressing a hope that he might see this art form placed on a par with the other art forms! It sounds strange and anachronistic today, but that is how it is—or so it is expressed by both of these eminent theatre people in any case. The admittance (*Aufnahme*) of the art of acting into the academic art forms on a line with and granted equality of rights with literature, painting, music, and architecture, which Lessing fought for two hundred years ago with the publication of his little book *Beiträge zur Historie und Aufnahme des Theaters* (1751), really cannot be said to have taken place yet; perhaps it has in the mind of the public, but not in the world of scholars.

As an art form, acting awaits its investigation, its delimitation, its definition and its classification, and its professors. The source materials are rich and enticing in a historical sense, but even more in a sociological, esthetic, and psychological sense. The task will be: to decide, as Holberg formulated the question in Just Justesen's preface to the first volume of his comedies (1723), to what extent it is "indecent for the children of fine men to permit themselves to be used in theatrical exercises"; (Holberg answered this intricate, amusingly formulated question with a no, but actually it stands open to this very day—and is an object for the most divergent opinion. Many people attend the theatre, but a considerable number still find it anything but proper.); to determine the actor's social and sociological position and significance in the life of his community; to determine the rightful place of the genuine actor, the scenic artist, in the esthetic system as well as in the manifold, exciting ensemble of conflicting, contributing factors and elements in the theatrical performance; and to investigate and illuminate the complex psychological picture of the actor, who, while on the stage, *acts* and *is* at the same time! What is especially attractive to me in this investigation is, among other things, the possibility of gaining access, through the study of the actor, to the mechanical process of artistic creation itself. The art of acting is the only art form in which the creative moment, the great psychological puzzle of all art forms, the secret of talent, is to a certain degree, under conscious control of the artist, and therefore can be observed, because the actor must create at a certain hour of the day, and therefore must have worked out the means to master the necessary process. Because of his profession, the actor must create consciously. He cannot, like other artists, wait for the well-known inspiration, nor—if he wishes to assert his authority as an artist—can he satisfy himself with perfunctory office-work, inasmuch as his art demands warmth, life, concentration, and radiance at a given hour. That which lies concealed in subconscious darkness in other art forms, in this art form alone comes to the surface at the bidding of the artist and can be measured and recorded. This is indeed a subject, a series of subjects, to examine and investigate.

What material do we have then to work with? The mixing, by university people, of better judgment and naïveté in connection with the theatre, their lack of confidence in the art form, and often their total lack of knowledge of the theatre world's always ambiguous and strange complexity of talents and passions, with subsequent disdain as a result, has—together with the biased insistence upon the artistic primateship of the *literary work* made by the esthetic theoreticians—led to the rejection of acting as an art form. The academicians have left us nothing to study. By way of recompense for this rejection, actors have developed a defiant over-estimation of themselves, which is understandable and excusable. They have been forced to take the matter into their own hands and win their victories and recognition on their own ground: the theatre. Scholars have looked with distrust upon actors, but there is no doubt that the distrust is mutual. Actors have no cause to display confidence either. They are on their guard against what is said or written about them. No one shall teach *them* anything. "No one really understands their art!" This certainly is their viewpoint generally. But hence it follows that the critical-theoretical literature on the art of acting that is known to exist has never been adequately paid attention to, and up to now this material has been as good as unexploited. Except for the two great literary figures Diderot and Lessing, the writers who have dedicated themselves to writing principally about the art of acting have, without exception, been allotted the fate of working without being noticed by scholars and being scorned or ignored by the actors! Their names cannot be found in handbooks of literary history, and neither are they listed in histories (such as Mantzius' book) on the art of acting. Inasmuch as Mantzius was himself an actor, he shared his profession's disdain for "literary people." I shall not tire the reader with an enumeration of the names of these writers—from Aristotle to Rötscher—of which Mantzius seems totally ignorant—but I shall return to them in another context. I only wish to mention that the first real theoretician on the art of acting, the Frenchman Rémond de Sainte-Albine, predecessor of Lessing and Diderot, who wrote his first book, *The Actor,* in 1747, has never been made the subject for an esthetic-dramaturgical examination, even though two hundred years before Stanislavski, he established a number of themes later developed by the great Russian and answered a number of crucial theoretical questions related to the art form in a wise and knowing way. Albine deserves better treatment, and he will surely get it! From him, and from a number of writers of comparable quality and with a comparable love of the art, one can derive a significant source of raw materials for the developing of an esthetic system for the art of acting. Actors themselves will probably be the most surprised of all about this.

Without hesitation, the acting profession allots itself the position of leadership within the walls of the theatre. "It is to the actor and to no one else that the theatre belongs," said Reinhardt, originally an actor himself, in his earlier cited *Rede über den Schauspieler.* And Stanislavski, in his memoirs *My Life in Art,* says, "The only king and ruler of the stage is the talented actor." As a useful corrective agent for these arbitrary and typical expressions by this century's two most brilliant men of the theatre, let me cite several lines from a letter written to the Danish actress Betty Hennings in 1891, by Victor Rydberg: "It sometimes happens that the theatrical artist is a more finely sensitive writer and a more astute psychologist than the author which he or she has to interpret." It really happens—and more often than we might think. At this point let us use these three statements to form a point of departure, since they contain a truth and an important viewpoint.

At one time or another we have all fallen victim to the thrilling, bewildering, eloquent, and compelling effect which great acting exerts. On what is this effect dependent? With what means is it created? We are all grateful to the great actors—but for what? I do not know. But perhaps I can suggest the contours of this complicated problem. From my own observations and from the materials assembled by the despised literary people, I will follow several threads, prescribe several outlines, attempt, in a short abstract, to give something which later I hope to have the opportunity to elaborate into a more satisfactory whole, and delineate several problems and principles which up to now have not been esthetically defined in an adequate manner. This is only the beginning of something—but something that must be embarked upon. I do not intend going through the great names in the art of acting. The intention is to probe into theatre psychology rather than theatre history. Several actors will be mentioned as typical and used as examples: Garrick, Talma, Johanne Luise Heiberg, Sarah Bernhardt, Joseph Kainz, Johannes Poulsen, and Gösta Ekman—but this selection must not be interpreted as an appraisal, it is only an illustration. Examples can be chosen from among the great actors of the present, whether from the stage or from motion pictures. The whole world is our theatre.

The following can be divided into three isolated sections: one historical, one about the actor's technique, and one containing psychological viewpoints. The latter two sections can be divided, like Bernard Shaw's drama, into a pleasant and an unpleasant part. The last of the sections, "The Actor as Phenome-

non," is a very unfriendly section, but I hope that it will answer
Holberg's question about the extent to which it is indecent for
the children of fine people to participate in theatrical exercises
—without suggesting that the answer should be used as professional advice. To begin with, we shall approach our subject,
the art of acting, by considering its origin.

*   *   *

All human knowledge begins and ends with a question mark.
We go through existence, each one aspiring to formulate an answer. But the conditions of human existence are such that even
our answers become questions. This holds true for the great
subjects as well as the small ones. It holds true also for science
and art, the two fields in which man has come closest to giving
something resembling an answer to his disquietude, his longing,
and what the American dramaturgist Brander Matthews once
called "man's insatiable curiosity about himself." The subject
we shall now discuss, dealing with man's curiosity regarding himself, begins with the seemingly simple question: What is an actor?

There is no need to introduce the name of one or another well-
known actor, Leslie Howard or Edward Persson, Rita Hay-
worth or Tora Teje, Viveca Lindfors or Louis Jouvet. The names
are impressive, but the answer is much simpler. The problem
goes deeper. In the depths of their hearts, all people are actors.
We all play-act. "All the world's a stage / And all the men and
women merely players." Two-thirds of our lives are spent performing, rather than *being*. The occupation which society has
assigned to each and every one of us, forces us, particularly if
we are not happy with it, to play it as a role for the rest of our
lives. The different vocational types are to a large measure performed character parts. We are all acquainted with people who
have played the part of minister, doctor, teacher, business execu-
tive, lawyer, professor, theatre director, yes, even actor, all their
lives, without ever being it. The compulsion to perform is a con-

dition which the struggle for existence has imposed upon human beings. More often than we generally admit existence forces us to appear to be something we are not. And we all go about with a craving to perform a role. This craving would be most distressing if we did not possess simultaneously, deep in our being, the ability to perform. The desire to play-act is a primitive impulse in human nature.

For a moment let us leave the present, seek the very distant past, and probe more deeply into the subject. We go to children and savages, two aspects of the same subject. In the play of children we witness an early phase in the history of the development of the theatre. Children imitate the reality of their elders; driven by a spontaneous mimetic instinct, they act out the parts of adults. But they do not restrict themselves to imitating reality; they also create reality. A chair, a table, a cupboard is transformed into a train, a house, a mountain. A pillow or a doll becomes a small, living child, and is handled like a small, living child. In the play of children we see two of the secrets of acting revealed, the secrets called concentration and imagination. In terms of the strength of enchantment, no theatrical illusion can match the illusion by which talented children enter in and abandon themselves to their festive game at the same time knowing and taking delight in the fact that it *is* a game. They are simultaneously authors and performers. In them we see the primitive joy of performing. They are primitive actors. But they do not perform for others, or in any case, seldom successfully. Generally when children play, they are their own both faithful and exacting audience.

In this way they resemble primitive people, but with the latter the situation is more involved. We now stand at the very origin of the art of acting, the oldest of all art forms. Where and when it comes into existence and takes form, we do not know. On the whole we know very little for certain about these prehistoric phenomena and processes. But by observing the primitive people still living on earth, we can see how it came about.

It begins, as it does in the case of children, with mimicry and the joy of watching it succeed. This develops into organized narrative. Scenes of glory from the life and history of the tribe are represented in mimetic form in primitive dances. But the dance evolves from imitation and narrative until one day it becomes a sorcery of higher powers, man's attempt to come into contact with his demons, his gods, to impress the good and to placate or banish the evil.

Primitive peoples take their game just as seriously as children do—no, more seriously. It is not only a game; it has a practical purpose. It becomes an integral part of the struggle for life. One day it takes on the character of ecstasy, the dimensions of the cult of the worship of gods. .

Having arisen from play, the game becomes bewitchery and rapture. The prayer for ecstasy is granted. Led by the medicine-man or shaman, the tribe achieves union with its gods in the torch-lit dark of night. The people are possessed by the god— the ecstatic dancers sense that they are filled to the very brim with the power that they have invoked and beseeched. They feared their demons, but the demons answered their prayers, and their fear is transformed into courage.

In this primitive arena we find both a foundation for, and an explanation of, the origin of the art of theatre assembled in a synthesis. The theatre in its original form. The exhilarating mimicry and the ecstasy in fear. Man becomes one with his gods. And man receives the courage to take up the struggle with the powers that he conjured up. The game becomes religion. And one day the religion becomes art.

Out of the Thracian worship of Dionysus, out of the primitive Dionysiac cultist actions, which ended in wild orgies involving the devouring of the raw meat of goats and bulls (and even human beings), the Greek theatre, after several centuries of refinements, arose. Religion becomes art. The art of theatre, in another sense, became the art which is occasionally a man-eating art. From the Corybantian dancers' demonic illusion of *being* the ghastly characters which they portrayed arose the finer and better intended illusion of the art of theatre, which on occasion can produce an air of demonism. And while the spectator and performer had originally been one—*one* performing, dancing, and conjuring crowd—it is now divided into two parts: those who "play" and those who observe. The primitive synthesis of dramatist and actor united in the same person still survives for a short time. Then comes the dramatic moment when they separate. The signal is sounded for the beginning of the present-day theatre, and for the problem of this theatre, which is the separating of something which was originally assembled, the subdividing of something which was one from the beginning! The drama, as an art form, is born! We stand on the threshold of culture, of civilization—and consequently close to the question which concerns us. *What* is an actor? *Who* becomes an actor?

From religion and ecstasy we proceed down to a purely psychological plane in order to find out what it is that causes us so-called civilized people to play-act. We have the desire present in us as a mimetic instinct, as a joy of and a zest for playing. But civilization has set up barriers for so many of our other instincts and desires. What about this one? Surely we are not savages or children—or are we?

At the bottom of the mystery of the art of acting lies something which is at the bottom of most of the mysteries of human behavior: egoism. Or let us use the more pleasant expression: self-assertion. He who play-acts asserts himself abruptly by talking and doing, by creating. He provokes laughter or admiration. He *is* somebody, and he rises above the others, both above those whom he imitates, and above those who are degraded into spectators: see what *I* can do? Man is vain, and he strives to be admired; man is lonely, and he seeks contact. Art is one of the means to these ends. In acting, man finds an outlet and an opportunity to reveal himself in play and in art, an opportunity of a more organic nature than any of the other art forms provide, because acting is created with the human body itself as the medium and the raw material. In its primitive phase, the art of acting is man giving vent in play to his inner vision, and in this way satisfying a deep need. The child plays a beautiful game, and the peacock spreads his gaudy tail feathers! At the bottom of the primitive acting temperament, we find three elements: loneliness, egoism, and eroticism.

We all feel, as previously stated, the instinct to act. We encounter it every day in ourselves and in others. Every day we act in front of our superiors and our inferiors, and even before complete strangers on the street or in the streetcar. Even when we pick up a telephone receiver, we act for the operator. She is supposed to notice that we are a somebody. We must convince ourselves that we are a somebody. If we are not, we can at least *play the part*. In this modern life, where all primitive expressions of vitality are overlaid with a veneer of education, of convention, which curtails the opportunities to find a spontaneous outlet for the feelings which stir within us, the need to act becomes doubly strong. Man must express himself, or else suffocate. I am acquainted with fine, respectable people, who, when they cannot find an outlet for their feelings in any other way, go to the office or go home to their wives and make a scene. No matter how irrational or without cause the scene might be, it still reduces tensions and leaves a feeling of pleasure. This digression is introduced only to illustrate the universal human instinct to act, man's natural need of self-assertion, to obtain a share of existence when he cannot experience it by at least transforming it into theatre. This spiritual need is also a physical need, which is an important fact to notice if one wishes to understand the acting mentality, and of course this is our goal. In actors, the physical need to perform can be so strong that the actor who is unemployed for a time literally can become ill because of it.

Ordinary people do not generally behave in this fashion. This is the distance which separates the stage from the auditorium.

Certain fortunate individuals, whose vocational life gives full, free passage to a diversified active reality, rarely find their way to the theatre other than to obtain several hours of diversion. And they are likely to regard the theatre as folly. And then there are certain narrow individuals, completely satisfied with their listless commonplace existence, who will never have any need to perform and will not understand this need in others. There is no reason to talk about these categories any further. But the rest of us love and understand the theatre, the oldest of the art forms, originating as a spontaneous expression of a human need: man's primitive instinct to reveal himself, privately and collectively, individually and communally; man's instinct to communicate and be understood, to seek contact, to provoke admiration and delight. We understand the theatre. We share its play and its desire and its suffering. In our temperament we have part of these people, whose lives pursue their courses by being other than what they are. At times we too wish fervently to be other than what we are, or show ourselves as we think we really are—disguise ourselves in order to conceal qualities we are ashamed of, or to develop qualities we admire and are jealous of in others. We too would like to be free behind a mask, to feel ourselves free and feel superior. This is a partial explanation of the power of the theatre to attract and entrance, and an explanation of the problem which one could advance as a contrast to the question "What is an actor?": What is a *spectator?*

We have settled the question of what an actor is. It is clear that he is a person who reveals and liberates himself by acting. But how does this fortunate egoist ever get anyone to want to see him perform? This is the key problem involving art and its appreciation. We human beings seek answers to our questions. If we cannot find and formulate these answers ourselves, others must give them to us. Here we have the social purpose of the theatre. The theatre as liberation, as release and diversion, something which the ancient Greeks understood very well when they opened their theatres to the Dionysian dancers and transformed a primitive, instinctive ecstasy into a game and an art, the objective of which was to bring about a purification, a *catharsis*, of the spectators' senses.

The theatre is release and relaxation. We experience this, not through personal participation, but through inner feeling by means of imagination and empathy. "*Wir sehen handeln, wenn wir nicht selbst bedeutend handeln können,*" said A. W. Schlegel in his definition of the theatre. Seated in the theatre, we are simultaneously participators and spectators in the game, the game which is reality freed from reality's element of danger, and yet which still has a profound effect upon the entire range and register of our emotional life. We rejoice over the free play of the forces involved, and at the same time are raised above it, not imprisoned or hampered by its problems.

In the theatre, we experience the things which existence cheats us out of or spares us from; our potentialities, our longings, our desires and illusions are realized in the play. We achieve understanding; we acquire self-reliance and a feeling of superiority by watching our own problems interpreted and brought to life by others.

Someone might say that this applies to all art. What then is characteristic about the art of acting? It is its powerful, intensive, living immediacy—more pronounced than in any other art. All art is expression and interpretation. But all other art is man's attempt to cling to and preserve, to explain and to hold on to the fleeting instant, a part of man's dream of eternity. On the other hand, the art of acting, which is itself so transitory, is the raising of the instant to a higher power, the complete instant, the complete moment, the moment with everything, not only what it contains, but what it can contain. The *complete expression*, which Lessing therefore quite rightly demanded from the complete actor, if he was to satisfy an audience to the fullest extent. Not one or another accidental human utterance, but the full, meaningful expression, the expression as symbol and idea, the selected expression "*so wie es nicht besser und nicht vollständiger ausgedruckt werden kann.*"

With this we have set boundaries to our subject and approached a definition of what an actor is. *He is the one who can render this expression.* He is not just anyone, nor is he like one of us who confines the joy of playing or the instinct to imitate to our private lives. He is neither child nor savage, although he shares traits with both of them. He is neither you nor I with our roles in everyday life. But he is both you and I with all our commonplace roles. We are dilettantes. He is an artist. He is one who can perform. He is the one who appears on the day when the performance is no longer a game, but an art, when the play—paradoxically enough—becomes a profession for the person who, by virtue of special talents, is capable of expressing the very thing which the rest of us seek to express, and who has the strongest need of all to express himself. He is a professional; therefore we have a right to make demands upon him.

He is the one who magnetically draws everyone's attention to himself when he acts. He radiates something which we cannot clearly define. He can ignite his talent and his radiance at an appointed hour. He is the medicine man, the shaman, the spiritual conjurer who causes our emotions to dance. He can unite us with our gods, arouse our sense of joy, calm our anguish, and instill courage in us. He can accomplish these things only now and then, at propitious moments. But his play, his profession, his trade has many sides and many facets. He can also confine himself just to trifling with us and diverting us. The mysterious thing called talent, an attribute which cannot be defined, is the common qualification for all who perform and—be it duly noted —wish to win audience approval for their performance. We can observe a common ability and common requisites within a whole category of people who otherwise are not ordinarily called actors. The clown in the circus ring, even the tightrope walker and the magician, the ballad singer, the revue performer, the nightclub singer, the lecturer, etc., etc.—all have this common ability: a mixture of the joy of playing and the power to charm; egoism and magnetism; something simultaneously primitive and highly complicated, but subject to control by the will of the person who practices the craft of acting; the power to concentrate, which Per Lindberg once designated as the ability to enhance and distill, to fortify and heighten the sense of being alive, and in this way release this sense in others through tears and laughter.

In our observations, we have not yet come to the level of the art theatre, the higher form of theatre. We have reached only the budding talent itself, the primal ability present in the professional player, the professional actor. For that matter, the leap from the clown to the "fine" actor is not great (it is often a leap in taste, not in ability). The clown can satisfy our need for expression, our questioning, our joy, our anguish, just as intensely as the great actor. The same "purification" can be present in a clown act as in a high tragedy (it all depends on the character, standards, and composition of the audience). In reference to the purification and release through art, Johannes V. Jensen, in one of his earlier fables, "Knokkelmanden" ("Death, the King of Terrors"), has written a number of unforgettable lines, using a cheap variety show as a point of departure. I am eager to cite these lines because they touch upon one of the fundamental problems in the art of the theatre. While on a trip, the writer found himself in a small German factory town and in the evening made his way to a third-class music hall. There he saw a duet between an ugly and grotesque clown who played a lute and a pale and confused girl, Kate, who sang a song—thin, lucid tones to a broken and bleating accompaniment. It had a wonderfully intense effect. Kate's delicate dreamy song and the bleating accompaniment—so musically shaky and so awful. "Everyone in the audience was quiet. And when that strange duet on the stage had finished, there were silent lamentations! I saw the spectators sigh in such a way that their troubles were lifted, and I saw in their eyes that a twinge of pain had passed healingly through their senses."

In this perceptive account of an act in a variety show, the writer has described the very process which took place in the theatre of Dionysus in Athens during a performance of one of the tragedies of Sophocles or Euripides—and he has told us something about why, and for what purpose, the theatre exists; about that mysterious and magical artistic process which the art of acting involves; and about the significance of the controversial concept of catharsis: there were silent lamentations. A twinge of pain had passed *healingly* through their senses.

*   *   *

The inclination to play-act is very ancient, just as is the need to see theatre. To perform and to witness, to give and to receive, to be admired and to admire. But a crucial psychological and cultural phenomenon occurs when the art of acting changes from a game to an occupation, when actors become professionals, deserters from orthodox social behavior, people who perform for money, people who—as they say—live on imagination! In Greece the first professional actors were called *hypokrites,* a word which early came to signify dissemblers, but generally they were highly respected people in this art-loving land. It was otherwise in Rome, the military state; puritanical Rome, where art found no great favor during the early centuries, where clowns were looked upon as despicable—an occupation for foreigners and slaves.

The dubious reputation with which the acting profession as profession has been cursed, and with which, as a matter of fact, it is still cursed even today in the eyes of many, stems from the *infamy* which was thrust upon the profession by Roman law. The actor was placed in the same category with slaves and prostitutes. Free-born citizens were not permitted ·to be seen on the streets in their company. Free-born people who became actors lost their citizenship rights. They were denied freedom of speech. They could not testify in court. In certain instances free-born citizens could kill actors without having to answer for their actions in court.

Right from the beginning, the great statesmen and legislators of the day regarded plays and actors with apprehension.

Plato had warned against theatrical performances, in the work of his old age, *Laws and the State*. Through these performances, he said, the spectators learn to surrender themselves to imaginary passions. How shall they succeed in controlling real passions in a manner befitting Greeks? It was in answer to Plato's attack and condemnation from a social viewpoint that Aristotle summarized the argument *for* the theatre a few years later in his *Poetics* and, as a defense, formulated his doctrine of the "catharsis" in order to demonstate that the theatre performed a useful service and could not be dispensed with.

But Aristotle, who found much to admire in the art of drama, did not hold actors in high esteem. "Dramatic ability is a natural gift, and can hardly be taught," he wrote in his *Rhetoric*. "Ye are to judge of players, indeed, by their voice, but of orators by the gravity of their sentence," said Demosthenes. Nowadays one is tempted sometimes to twist this thesis around in order to be able to accept its meaning, but the statement is typical of the attitude toward the art of acting which was held by the ancients (and furthermore, also tells us something of the nature of the art). Cicero, who was in agreement with Plato that theatrical performances sooner irritated audience sentiments than acted as diversion for them, thus ministering to passions more than manners (a viewpoint later adopted by the Christian moralists), admired, as a unique exception, his friend Roscius, the foremost name in acting in classical antiquity. He said of him: "He is such a good actor, that no one else seems worthy to set foot upon the stage"—but Cicero added—"and is such a noble person, that he seems too good for it." Here in a nutshell we have the view of the acting profession held by classical antiquity. But even in ancient times the public's worship of actors assumed the same proportions in terms of enthusiasm and devotion that we know today; adoration was lavished upon the great virtuosos of theatre in the same way that the film stars of our time are pampered. People loved the theatre then as they do now and divided their enthusiasm equally between the great, eloquent declaimers; the comic and tragic *histrionem;* and the popular actors who specialized in low comedy, the *mimes*, who were the counterparts of contemporary popular comedians and revue artists. The art of acting is always Janus-faced—the sides corresponding to the perennial symbols of the theatre: the masks of comedy and tragedy. There are also two different ways of judging the art—a fact worth noting. Its distinctive feature is the combination of the adoration, the deification of certain great actors, together with contempt for the profession in general. This contempt has its origin in the infamy, the aftereffects of which can be traced right up to our time.

Since people—not only individuals, but groups as well—easily become what others believe them to be, the acting profession, over a period of several centuries, became what its members were believed to be: asocial and prostituted. With the exception of certain isolated, brilliant examples, the professional actors of classical antiquity were deeply scarred by the ban under which they lived. When Christianity grew strong actors became a target for violent condemnations made by the fathers of the church. The great church councils denounced the theatre as "the shrine of Venus," the refuge for all sin, the consistory of shamelessness, and, in an effective expression by Tertullian, as "the Church of the Devil." The argumentation, although richly varied in the linguistic styles of the different bishops and princes of the Church—and there were very inspired speakers and writers among the early Christian organizers: Augustine, Justin, Cyprian, Tatian, Tertullian, and John Chrysostom—is not very different from those of Solon and Plato. "The Father of all truth hates dissembling, and each fiction is regarded by Him as adulteration," said Tertullian. And he added a warning to the public that those who could not do without plays ought to wait for the greatest and most harrowing play of all, judgment day, when actors will scream louder than they do in any tragedy.

Fourteen centuries later, Bossuet, called the last of the church fathers, condemned Molière and his actors with a similar expression and analogous argumentation.

The art of acting in ancient times—about which we know virtually nothing concerning its artistic character, manner, and technique, and must satisfy ourselves with guesswork because crucial documents have been lost—died out and, in a manner of speaking, was scorched like weeds by the lightning bolts of the Roman church. Only the thoroughly popular art, the half-realistic, half-stylized comic imitations of reality of the *mimes*, survived in secrecy like a suppressed complex and preserved its character until the Renaissance, when it arose anew in the Italian *commedia dell'arte*.

❖   ❖   ❖

After a period of hibernation which lasted well over a thousand years, acting was revived as an art form during the Renaissance. The process involved in its birth, or rather rebirth, is similar to the one we have already described and similar features are present. The natural joy of playing and the instinct to act find an outlet in theatrical performances which are part of a religious, this time a Christian, cult. During the Middle Ages and the early Renaissance, priests and burghers perform church ceremonies to instruct and amuse the people. The people continually require bread first—and then plays, and the church endures the situation and even derives benefits from it. But soon the popular theatre emancipates itself from the church. The comedians seek out open squares and marketplaces and, with their coarse merriments, sever connections with the solemn ceremonies. At the same time Renaissance scholars rediscover the great dramas of classical antiquity and produce copies of them at aristocratic festivities. The masks of tragedy and comedy reappear as symbols and as realities. First the dilettantes perform—the craft guilds in the cities, the students at the universities, the young noblemen at court—then the professional actors arise, first in Italy and England; jesters and clowns are used regularly as comedians, and able, bombastic declaimers as tragedians. The ban still lies heavily upon them, but they survive defiantly because they are indispensable. Meanwhile a crucial thing has taken place. In the Italian *commedia dell'arte*, which, as previously mentioned, has roots back in the

Roman mimes, the art of acting is liberated, not only from the art of writing, from literature—with which, in this special genre, it has always had only the most unsubstantial connection imaginable—but from the written text altogether. These actors improvise their own words; they write while they act and thus pick up a thread which leads back to the theatre's obscure origin. But in so doing they realize an original theatrical concept in which dramatist and actor are one and the same person. The actor as such asserts his independence and sovereignty. This is actually the starting point for the modern theatre; in any case, it is here that the real art of acting begins, the art of acting as we know it today—acting as an occupation, as a craft, and as an art. Acting has become an independent art form.

At the same time the struggle begins with the literary theatre, with the writers and the scholars who have refused, even till now, to acknowledge that acting was anything but imitative, a subservient and mediatory second-rate art form, the duty of which—and excuse for being—was to subordinate itself to the text, to the drama. The dramatist Robert Greene, a somewhat older contemporary of Shakespeare, has given us evidence of how writers viewed the bold, presumptuous effort towards emancipation made by professional actors in the middle of the sixteenth century. In 1592, in an angry outburst made on behalf of writers and other creative artists, Greene cast his curse upon actors. He talked of apes and "burres" which try to secure themselves, "those Puppets (I meane) that spake from our mouths, those Anticks garnisht in our colours." The enmity between writers and actors, an enmity which can be traced right up to our time despite all apparent mutual respect and interdependence, has found frequent expression more recently in the writings of eminent literary men who could refer to the fact that back in ancient Greece Aristotle had found cause to complain that "in drama the actors now count for more than the poets"—and the complaint is heard repeatedly today. Even Goethe and Diderot, who were in close touch with the practical world of the theatre during important periods in their lives, had harsh experiences with theatre people, and they gave vent to their scorn in a drastic fashion. It was Goethe who, as director of the Weimar Theatre, had a tendency "to play chess" with his actors—that is to say to use them as chess pieces rather than as living individuals in his productions. It was Goethe who scornfully maintained that he wished to undertake "to make an actor out of each well-built grenadier." And Diderot, whose view of actors oscillated remarkably during the course of his life, declared bitterly one day that a great actor in the final analysis was "a most ingenious puppet, and his strings are held by the poet, who at each line indicates the true form he must take!" Writers always have had a great weakness for viewing actors as their marionettes; and consequently actors, by way of recompense, have just as incorrect and as dangerous a conception of writers—as a more or less necessary, but always very troublesome, evil in the contemporary theatre.

In *commedia dell'arte* acting as a profession finds freedom. Alongside the type-comedy, or rather mask-comedy, of *commedia dell'arte*, two kinds of representational art sprouted simultaneously and took form, each clearly bearing the stamp of one of the two genres of the theatre of classical antiquity: the tragic and the comic. A lofty, almost singing, oratorical art intended for the higher drama, tragedy; and a more individualistic, realistically imitative art, rendering types from real life, intended for comedy. But it must be made clear that both genres are still, to an even greater degree than *commedia dell'arte*, in a rather primitive state. Just a mask of make-up conceals the folk jester, the tightrope walker, the marionette manager, the clown.

And so we begin the modern era with Shakespeare and Molière!

This moment is a great one. One of the greatest, not only in theatre history but also in the history of culture, because both names belong among the brilliant, immortal stars in the literary firmament as well. However, we shall deal with them here as theatre men exclusively. Strangely enough, and characteristically enough, they both represent, contemporaneously—a coincidence that seems planned—the remarkable synthesis which is so invaluable to the art of theatre: that of the author and the actor in the same person. Later this synthesis disappeared as a fundamental element in the organization of the theatre to more recent times and reappears only in valuable but rather special circumstances as, for example, in the case of the brilliant Johann Nestroy in Vienna in the middle of the last century, and in our own special case, the unique, many-sided Noel Coward in London, whose representative significance as a theatrical concept far more than as an individual phenomenon should not be underestimated.

* * *

Shakespeare and Molière gave, not in special tracts or dissertations but in the dialogue of their plays, the first definitions of the nature of the modern art of acting. These definitions are in the form of actual guidance for working actors: Shakespeare in Hamlet's famous advice to the players; Molière in his facetious instructions to his troupe in the well-known little play *Impromptu de Versailles,* in which, under his own name and without any costume, Molière himself is the chief performer. In these practical, down-to-earth situations we see both renowned theatre men function personally, in a sense as pioneering guides, as teacher-directors, as we might phrase it today, for a new generation of actors. The key point in their teaching is the reference to *natural acting* as opposed to what Shakespeare in another situation jokingly referred to as doing "it in King Cambyses' vein" (*I Henry IV*, II, iv, 426), and what Molière called *"le brouhaha,"* a famous expression, by which he characterized the exaggerated, bombastic oratorical actions of the dominant French tragic actors. Nature will be the model, say both men—"the modesty of nature." By making clear to us what they revolted against, they draw, indirectly, a very clear picture of the general condition of acting in their time. The advice they offer has a common point of departure, but there is a significant difference in what they stress as essential for a reformation.

Shakespeare's ideal is clearly enough the actor who *feels* his role; Molière's, the actor who *characterizes* it. In this difference lies the seed for a substantial part of the debate about modern theories of acting.

The English and the French schools of acting, two of the most significant within the European theatre, originate with Shakespeare and Molière respectively. From the start the two geniuses set their stamps upon the art of acting of their lands; however, it must be noted that that which they revolt against still continues to exist as a distinctive, contrasting feature of the theatre art of their respective nations. But a freer and finer kind of acting is given a theoretical form by Shakespeare and Molière, who train their actors accordingly. Just behind these giants we still find *commedia dell'arte,* the improvised comedy, the emancipated form of acting, serving as model and taskmaster, at once primitive in its feeling and artistically refined in its form. Behind Shakespeare stands Yorick, poor Yorick, the brilliant clown and improviser Richard Tarleton, whose art was essentially related to, and influenced by, the Italians. Behind Molière stands Scaramuccia, the great Italian comedian Tiberio Fiorelli, from whom Molière took lessons in his youth, and for whom Paris wrote the following epitaph: "He was Molière's teacher, / And nature was his."

Out of the demands made and the definitions given by Shakespeare and Molière there arises a finer, higher art of acting; from a declamatory art, an oratorical art, it becomes an art of representation. But the process of change takes place in different ways and at different speeds in France and England. The first great actor in this new era, and consequently one of the most important names in theatre history, is Molière's pupil and friend Michel Baron, the first French tragedian, who scorned the concept of *déclamation* and ushered in the characterization style of acting even in the tragedies of Corneille and Racine. In England a half-century elapsed before the actor Shakespeare dreamed about appeared; but by way of recompense, he became the greatest actor of the eighteenth century and perhaps one of the greatest of all time—the genius David Garrick.

In the seventeenth century, Shakespeare and Molière throw out the tag-line for the modern art of acting; Baron and Garrick pick up the cue in the eighteenth century.

❋   ❋   ❋

The professional art of acting struggles on toward artistic rank and independence. At the same time—and this event stamps its impression on the modern art of acting right from the beginning —actresses emerge, first in Italy and Spain, next in France, then—in about the middle of the seventeenth century—in England, and last in Germany. But because of this, actors had to fight hard and to some extent in vain for the recognition of their civil rights. In 1641, Louis XIII, instigated by Richelieu, decreed that the infamy over the French and Italian actors was to be lifted on the condition that in the future they would behave and conduct themselves like proper people. But the decree had little effect on public and religious opinion. Theatre people were refused church weddings or Christian burials. Not only Molière himself, but also, a half-century later, Baron's colleague and pupil, the great actress Adrienne Lecouvreur, were buried surreptitiously, and the latter actually in unconsecrated ground. In 1690, Bossuet fulminated against actors, "the hired liars, the exhibited slaves, the lost Christians, within whom all shame is extinguished." As late as 1758, when acting in France had attained its first artistic peak, even Rousseau censured actors on similar grounds: it was humiliating for free men to practice the art of acting for money and thereby offer themselves for sale in public. "The greatest disgrace in the profession of acting—over and above the looseness of its women—is the mendacity in which its practitioners continually, so to speak professionally, live." We have here the most characteristic and ineradicable objection directed against actors by middle-class society: they lend their personality for a price, and thereby surrender it! In France, theatre-happy France, actors were long looked upon in this way, right up to the French revolution—with a special exception, tempered by the nation's erotic temperament, made for actresses. A characteristic French *bon mot* from the end of the eighteenth century reads thusly in all its brevity: "Actors are not people. An actor is less than a man. An actress is more than a woman!"

Scarred deeply by the battle for independence as artists, spiritually hurt by the seemingly fruitless striving to overcome the contempt for actors held by people in prominent circles, the practitioners of the art of acting found their place in society during the last half of the seventeenth and the first half of the eighteenth century. What we have dealt with in these opening remarks then is only the earliest history of acting up to the crucial turning point. Which crucial turning point? The birth of the *modern* art of acting. We place this event about the year 1750, but we trace the threads back to the principles of the art form which were formulated by Shakespeare and Molière—and also to a distinctive characteristic of dramatic art which is deposited in their immortal theatrical creations.

During classical antiquity acting was divided into opposite, clearly defined genres—the tragic and the comic, each one with its fixed register of expression and its widely separated technique. In the earlier European art of acting during the Renaissance, in the art of the amateurs as well as the professionals, a strict distinction was made between the comic and the tragic. The distinction lies deep, not only in the nature and development of the art of acting, but also in the nature and development of the theatre itself. In one way this is still true today to the point where the comic theatre is evaluated by many as a less *fine*, in any case less worthwhile, theatre than the tragic; even now a comic actor is seldom as highly regarded as a tragic

actor. Should there be a fundamental theatrical law in this? A
rule which cannot be broken? Nevertheless we will break it.

In Shakespeare's theatre we meet, for the first time in world
drama, the tragicomic method of character delineation which
makes new, different, and special demands upon the performers
of such roles. There is much to indicate that Shakespeare, who
surely liked to blend the comic and the tragic in his work as an
impressive contrast, did not fully realize the artistic possibilities
of the kind of blending which his brilliant texts afford to the actor during the creation of an individual role. Everything points
to the fact that Shylock and Malvolio, to cite two examples, were
played comically by comedians in Shakespeare's time. But we
know that the adherents of the new art of acting quite rightly
were not content with this. In Molière's theatre the blending of
the two ingredients was even more clearly and completely artistically realized. With Arnolphe in *L'École des maris;* Alceste in
Le Misanthrope; with George Dandin, the unfortunate cuckold;
and not least with the Miser, the cuckold of his money, the tragicomic theatre is born. As an actor, Molière, like many of his later
fellow professionals, was instinctively attracted to tragedy, even
though his natural talent was comic. (That he was an innova-
tor in comic character interpretation, but conventional and hardly
convincing as a tragedian in the eyes of his contemporaries,
is another matter.) His ambitions were first realized in his pupil Baron. But in his plays he supplied material for a different and
richer style of acting, a representation of humanity in the theatre
of deeper truthfulness and greater breadth, than ever before
known.

When the demands made by the roles in Shakespeare and
Molière—together with the demand, the exhortation, that actors
practice natural acting—are realized for the first time, modern
acting is born, and the truly great actor, the *tragicomic actor,*
arises, lives, and suffers before our eyes—the complete actor, something Garrick had in mind when he maintained, using himself

as an example, that a person could not be a good tragic actor if he was not a good comic actor as well. This requirement has been endorsed in our time, although Gösta Ekman, to cite an example, was derided in the early 1930's when, in an interview, he indicated that he considered a sense of humor necessary for the person who wished to succeed in playing Hamlet. The press ridiculed the "comic Hamlet" which it was presumed the great Swedish actor wished to present. Per Lindberg, in an excerpt from his book about Gösta Ekman, quotes him in this way: "I still maintain that an actor must have a sense of humor in order to be able to play tragedy." Ekman has endorsed just what Garrick said and formulated as a categorical requirement. The greatest modern actors are, almost without exception, tragicomedians.

The complete actor is the one who shows us the true face of life in his playing. The comic and tragic masks are only symbols of the Janus-faced theatre. The true face of life is the tragic and comic masks combined in one. The theatre achieves its greatest, its most moving and unforgettable effects, when the tragic and comic elements of existence are united in a whimsical, poignant mixture and whole. It is then that we first experience the true catharsis, and the pain passes healingly through our senses. The actors capable of uniting the two faces into one are the true *histrionem*, the brilliant *hypokrites*, and merit the designation Shakespeare gave his actors in *Hamlet:* the history of the age in brief recapitulation. They give the artistic interpretation and synthesis we seek in the theatre. "They are the abstract and brief chronicles of the Time."

We are reminded of Johannes V. Jensen's fable "Death, the King of Terrors." It dealt only with an act in a variety show, but we return to it in order to note that it also dealt with just a beginning, an outline for an interpretation of what takes place in the theatre. The bleating clown and the thin, pathetic girl in the fable are symbols of the Janus-faced art of theatre, of both masks. Their duet produces, in a primitive way, the double effect characteristic of the theatre. What double effect? Johannes V. Jensen speaks of it in the conclusion of his fable, when he attempts to explain the unforgettable effect which the number had upon him: "It struck me that it was a duet of life and death I heard."

It is this duet which the theatre is supposed to render for us.

[*Translated by Harry G. Carlson*]

PART THREE

THE DIRECTOR

HAROLD CLURMAN

MISTAKEN NOTIONS

STARK YOUNG

THE ART OF DIRECTING

JEAN VILAR

MURDER OF THE DIRECTOR

Mistaken Notions

HAROLD CLURMAN

One of our most popular play reviewers, closing his most recent report of a new production, spoke of its direction as "fast, ingenious, and altogether admirable." The first part of the same review pointed out that the production failed to catch the spirit of the play, or to convey the author's intention. The discrepancy between the first part of the review and its conclusion may pass unnoticed by the ordinary reader; to a theatre man it is sheer nonsense.

The mistake here is not peculiar to a single reviewer. It is general. It is a symptom of the innocence (I refuse to use a harsher word) in regard to direction evinced by most laymen and an alarming number of professionals.

In one sense, the matter is not crucial. There is no need for the theatregoer to examine the separate ingredients that go into the making of a play in order to appreciate it as a whole. What the theatregoer should properly be concerned with is the essential feeling of what he experiences at the play. The fine point he often believes himself constrained to make about production details—such as the play's direction—is usually the imitation and echo of the inane expertness of presumably theatre-wise folk.

In the "old days"—before 1915—hardly any theatregoer and few reviewers mentioned the stage director—except in the case of

David Belasco. In fact few playbills listed the director at all. It was only after the First World War, with our increased interest in foreign examples—the theatre of Max Reinhardt, the theories of Gordon Craig, the repute of the Moscow Art Theatre—that reviewers and, later, playgoers, began to speak with (usually) empty sagacity of the director as if they were alluding to a star with a new sort of sex appeal. It has now come to the point where many hits are ascribed in large measure to the mysterious maneuverings of an invisible magician who the stage director is supposed to be.

My own belief is that while the director is important in the making of the stage play, what and how he does his job in its detail is of little moment to the spectator. What the audience (as well as the critic) have to enjoy and judge is simply the total effect of what they see—which is the play. This does not mean that it is not possible or valuable to understand the director's contribution to the total effect, but the special nature of the director's work (which, to begin with, is collaborative) makes it difficult for any but the most thoroughly trained to measure.

The most common epithets used to evaluate direction emphasize tempo: the direction is "fast," "slow," "lethargic," "well-paced," "rapid-fire," "taut," etc., etc. When you hear these adjectives pronounced as outstanding qualities of a play's direction, you should realize at once that the person who pronounces them knows very little about the matter. (It sounds as silly to a theatre craftsman to hear such opinions as it would be to hear a literary critic sum up a novel by Faulkner as slow and one by Hemingway as fast.) At best, one can say that such judgments confuse staging with direction. Staging has chiefly to do with the physical arrangement of the figures on the stage, and does not affect the heart of the problem except as an attribute of the play's basic direction. Staging is the surface, direction is the core.

Direction of a play involves the creation through actors and all the other elements of the theatre (settings, costumes, lights, music, etc.) of the mood, meaning, and spirit of what we see on the stage. The director's initial material is the dramatist's script. A well-written and well-constructed script on an interesting theme will often prove sufficient in itself to create a satisfying total effect, but it has often been noted that even Shakespeare's plays may seem weak and ineffective when they have not been adequately directed.

The reason for this sharp distinction between the script (what is read) and the play (what is seen on the stage) is that the script is composed of words and a description of action while the play is composed of action itself through the persons of specific men and women, and other real objects. The director employs actors and other concrete materials as the dramatist employs words.

In *I Am a Camera*, the dramatist tells of a girl who lives a rather disordered life in a hectic, almost diseased environment. On the stage, the play's effect is amusing and even charming. This may be due to the delightful personality of the leading player. But it is probable that even the same player might produce a more disturbing or at least more humanly complex impression if the director had chosen to make a different point. The choice of the point to make (hence, the difference of effect) is a primary question of direction.

In *Desire Under the Elms*, the opening scene is, scriptwise, merely expository. The words tell us that two farmers work hard, that they feel crushed by their tyrannical father, and are thinking of abandoning the farm. The director may use this scene to indicate the legendary (or symbolic) intention of the author, the grandiose—non-realistic—key which he thinks the play should strike, the largeness as well as the rude plainness which suits that key. The director's choice may be mistaken—his interpretation is certainly not the only possible one. The point is that a discussion of this scene cannot be couched in terms of tempo, because the tempo is not an abstract feature of the scene, but an organic part of what the director has to say—the effect in feeling and thought he intends to produce.

Criticism of direction is the perception on the part of the audience of what the production has done in relationship to the written material employed. To understand what the director has done, we must ask ourselves what the author must have aimed at in his writing, and what happened to his intention in the passage of the written script to the flesh of the stage. The actors have a great deal to do with the play's immediate physical and emotional impact on us; the director is largely responsible for the intention and significance of the total event.

The Art of Directing

STARK YOUNG

In the course of stage history the director has borne a varied name and a more varied relationship to the theatre. He has sometimes been the owner of the play, sometimes an actor from the company, sometimes the *régisseur,* or director of the entire production in all its parts, sometimes the producer or actor-manager. But whatever the problem of the *régisseur,* or producer, or actor manager may be elsewhere, in our American theatre at present the director is the man with the script in his hand who stands behind the whole performance of the play, who, to varying degrees, prescribes what the interpretation shall be, what the actors shall do, and trains them how to do it. He is the *maestro,* the coach, the general behind the rehearsals.

The director is the artist who takes the drama as it is put into his hands and labors to recreate it in his own technical terms. And this drama, when it is recreated into these terms, becomes theatre and something that is different from what it was before. Directing is an art or it is nothing.

There is no such thing as a play directed exactly as it is written any more than there is a landscape painted as it really is. In any art the material that goes to make up the work suffers a change before it becomes this work, and this change, this something added, derives from the artist working. In Corot's Ville

365

d'Avray the material was the landscape of trees, atmosphere, and light; the medium was the paint. In Houdon's Voltaire the material was a body and the character in that body; the medium the marble. The dramatist's material is men, life, experience; his medium the dramatic form. In the art of the director the drama itself is the material, the actor in the midst of the audience and the designer's decor is his medium. It follows that when a drama emerges from the hands of the director it has undergone a restatement of itself, a translation into the terms of the theatre, and the importance of the thing added will measure the importance of the director.

Most directors are not distinctly one type or another; they belong in the middle ground between two extremes. But at one extreme in directing is the virtuoso. He takes the play into his own hands and does with it what he chooses, twists it, and makes it his own. He may go to the limit in violating its quality, in forcing it to his own ends.

At the other extreme is the director whose aim is to carry out entirely the dramatist's idea. If the play is bombastic he makes his rendering of it bombastic, where it is cold he will be cold, where it is barren he keeps it barren, and so on; he covers nothing, he tries to discover and to restate in theatre terms the play's essential character; to every element in the play he means to give its special quality and intention.

Both these types of directors are artists. If one appears more sharply than the other to be an artist, it is not because of his method, but because what he creates is better or worse. It is a difference in degree, not in kind. We may prefer a performer who tries to play a concerto as closely as he can to what is written rather than one who sweeps it out of itself to his own mood and will. But in the end what finally decides the question as to whether or not either of the performers is an artist is the thing created. With Liszt, Schubert may become not only the material that Liszt interprets but also the material from which he creates something violently his own. The virtuoso director at his peril does what he wills in directing a play. He may be a good artist or a bad, according to the result that he creates, but he is an artist. The result must judge itself. The original drama may almost disappear before such a director has done with it, but, conceivably at least, we may be willing to forget it quite in order to possess the new creation, as we are willing to forget in El Greco the likeness of trees in order to achieve El Greco. In the theatre the trouble, however, with the virtuoso lies in the fact that there will always be few directors who have as much to give us as have the plays that they direct.

Great talents like Gordon Craig may do what they like with a play, and risk the outcome. Gordon Craig might take *Othello*, for example, and change it into what, as a whole, it but slightly could be, or read into it something that it scarcely contains at all, and yet create for us a result magnificent in itself. Or he might lift one element in the play to an importance out of all proportion to the whole of it, and by doing so illumine and dilate forever the region that *Othello* can express. A dozen Gordon Craigs bringing to bear on Shakespeare's tragedy this radiant distortion and dilation in twelve different aspects might increase twelve times *Othello's* radiance and scope. But Gordon Craigs are rare. And we are apt to feel that any one so determined to say what he has to say rather than what the dramatist intended should let the play alone and write another for himself.

The kind of director at the other extreme from the virtuoso would by some persons be rejected entirely as a creative artist— to use a phrase that is often heard but that makes no sense, since an artist is an artist only in so far as he is creative. To reply to that we may best set aside the comparison between the director and the play he uses and El Greco and the trees that go into his painting of a landscape. Shall we say an orchestra leader and his rendering of a Beethoven Symphony, and a director and the play that he presents? In this case what comes to the artist is already established; as was not the case with the landscape, something is already created. The score is ready to his hand. Into it the artist, working in his own terms, strives to create life and thus to express it. But if every instrument in the orchestra rendered exactly the score written for it we should still not have the symphony created. Not in nature, ideas, or art is there any truth that is ready and expressed and the same; it is restated in every man that experiences it and as significantly as the observer is significant. No director can give us a play as it is, however faithful his intention may be and however great his ability to carry out his intention. His ideal may be a fine one; he strives to disappear and to leave the play exposed and expressed, to achieve a style that is an invisible medium, like a laboratory glass that reveals the delicate processes of an experiment. But he remains the artist by whose creation this style and revelation may arrive.

MUSIC AS A BASE

The relation among a play's ideas, remarks, events, and emotions, how they follow one another, how they dispose themselves together and so reveal the whole meaning of the play, is expressed, in so far as concerns their precise meanings and definite points, through words and actions. The exact observation that Hamlet has to make on his own failure in the power to act is expressed when he says:

> Why, what an ass am I! This is most brave
> That I, the son of a dear father murdered,
> Prompted to my revenge by heaven and hell,
> Must, like a whore, unpack my heart with words,
> And fall a-cursing like a very drab,
> A scullion!

When we see Pirandello's hero daub paint on his face and put on the robes of Henry at Canossa, we know exactly what theme and disguise his plan has followed.

But these are more special and particularized elements of a drama. Beneath them lies the main body of the play. In the whole of it there is the emphasis of one part compared with another; the mass is stressed heavily here and lightly there, according to its importance in the whole. One speech leaps out from another, propelled by the inner conflict beneath them. One speech is distant from those near it because it arises from meditation in the speaker or from his continuous habit of thought. One speech is ready in the speaker's heart before the thing it seems to answer has been said, its lips were on the other's lips ere they were born. The pulse or beat of a line or a speech or a scene is here quick, there slow; the emotion or thought exhilarates, it retards. All these are a matter of pure relationships. Beneath the particular situation, the particular thoughts, reactions, deeds, every play can be reduced to this abstract basis. Every play has this abstract pattern of values. On this side it is for the most part closely connected with the art of music. A director can best study the layout of a play as if it were a musical composition.

Music, as every one knows, is of all arts, except architecture perhaps, the most ideal. That is to say, music does not involve imitation or concrete instance or definite concept; its region is pure to itself. Music is the beautiful eternity, the idea, the essence, the general quality. In sum, to take an example, where Hamlet can only say to us,

I have that within which passeth show,

music can put us into the very state itself out of which this poetry or our tears arise. But this, of course, is a commonplace about the art.

In the play the matter of emphasis, themes and characters and events, the speed, the vocal tone, rest all fundamentally and essentially on a base of music. The relation of the stream of points equidistant from one point is a part of the truth of a circle, an abstract thing. The height of a tower is a part of its idea. The quiet of the vowels and the contemplative measure in one of Virgil's pastoral verses is as much its truth as is the precise thing said in words, and to forget this is to forget the nature

of art. To forget this is like saying that a madness to kill is
expressed or conveyed in a remark stating, "I am going to kill
you," rather than in the eye and the onward rush of the murderer. The length, the beat, the duration of a speech in a play
are a part of its idea. The time between two speeches is a
part of their meaning. The tempo at which a cue is taken and
the tone of the voice are as much—and often far more so—the
truth of a speech as the more exact and limiting words that are
said. When Othello says:

> Never, Iago. Like to the Pontic Sea,
> Whose icy current and compulsive course
> Ne'er keeps retiring ebb, but keeps due on
> To the Propontic and the Hellespont;
> Even so my bloody thoughts, with violent pace
> Shall ne'er look back, ne'er ebb to humble love,
> Till that a capable and wide revenge
> Swallow them up—

the main truth of the outburst, the sheer fact that it is an outburst even, is conveyed by a tremendous current in the declamation, by the vocal tone and flood sound rather than by the
special concept in each and every phrase. And unless this outline and rhythm are established, the speech breaks down into
something of forced images and elaborate if not false details.

When Marchbanks, with the poet's insight, says to Prossy of
the arid, hot heart, and bitter, drab profession, that he can see
nothing in Morell but words, pious resolutions, and asks if it is
possible for a woman to love him, and Prossy, after trying to
evade the question, says,

> Yes,

it is obvious that except for her mere acknowledgment of a fact,
the whole moving truth must lie in the time she takes before she
speaks and in the tone of her voice. When Miss Clare Eames
acted the part it was almost wholly her musical sense that made
this particular moment in the play so mordant and touching. The

Hopkins production of *The Deluge*, very interesting in its intention, wore out long before the end, because in this situation, where a group of people, shut in by the flood and faced with death, show reformations and candid fires not usual with them, and later, when safety comes, revert to their daily selves, the more or less dramatic repetition in the scenes depended for its point on a variation in tempo which was not achieved. And, finally, in the case of individual actors it is their time sense, their sense of the exact moment for a cue, a speech, an answer, that does as much as anything else to engage the audience's attention with its constantly fresh vitality and surprise.

VISUAL MUSIC

There is an element, of course, in the performance of a play that speaks entirely to our eyes. When the director begins to consider the expression of this aspect of a play he may wisely study every part of it as a set of pure relationships, a kind of visual music. He can study as he might a symphony what is the essential idea of a play and what groups, motions, positions will most help in expressing through the eye what the other dramatic mediums are expressing through our other faculties or channels of perception. He can define those lines and masses on the stage, and then subordinate what is secondary and omit some of the confusion of empty or extraneous movements. He can study a scene for its last, fundamental idea or characteristic and try to find what line, what visual quality, will most express the essential idea of the scene; and can employ that line as something in itself expressive. And he can seek to establish what is most important of all these, the visual continuity of the scene, its living rhythm in our eyes, from the time it begins till it ends.

THE DIRECTOR'S MEDIUM

Granted a clear or important idea for the play that he will present and the means and ability to carry it through, the director has still a problem like that of any artist, who for the prosperity of a work has to consider what tact and judgment he will use to achieve the right relationship between the work and the public. There is a point beyond which if an artist carries his idea he will lose the sympathy of his public and so defeat his own end, which is to express his idea to them. On the other hand, too much consideration of his public may prevent the artist's going far enough to reach the point at which his idea will get itself expressed. In every art some concession, obviously, is unescapable; music, for instance, has to be loud enough to be audible; the musician must concede that much at least to his public. But in general as an artist you may choose to trim your sails in order to arrive at your wished-for port, or you may choose to miss the temporary destination or success and instead to stretch the bounds of your art, to chart new seas, to sight new forms, new possibilities for expression. You take your choice at your peril and according to your own nature.

But the artist directing in the theatre has to remember that the theatre essentially is an impure medium. It consists not only of what is on the stage but of the audience in front. The director will have to make an imaginative choice and proportionment of parts, so as not to leave out the audience from his creation. However prophetic or illuminating the stage end of his creation may be, if the audience is not rightly involved in it the creation suffers, as might be the case with a pianist who insisted on pouring water into the instrument for the sake of some future aquatic scale, but failed of any sound or anything besides his strong idea or inspiration. The director has to consider what effect he most seeks, what is the truth that he would most express. When this is found he must relate every detail to it, taking his choice as to how far he is creating for a complete present moment and how far for future innovation or extension. A thing admirably right in itself may, when the audience sees it, jump out of the frame and distort the whole picture. An unwelcome detail, however true in itself, may either wreck the truth of a whole scene or send it to a thrilling pitch. To say what has never been allowed said on the stage, what has been more or less banned as crass or outrageous, may swamp the play or may double its expressiveness. The director may take whatever chance he likes, but he has to work in all the elements of his art —the play, the actors, the audience.

RESTATEMENTS OF PLAYS

When a play is new, hot from the author's forge, it may be taken as written for its own time, its idea stated for the dramatist's own generation. The director's business is an interpretation of it in theatrical terms. But when there is a play to be revived, a few years or some centuries from its birth, the director's problem takes on another shift in restatement.

In so far as a play was ever a work of art it was a living thing. Within his dramatic form the dramatist has arrested and found a right body for a section in the stream of life. Life may be said to rise and to fill for a moment such a form. But the very essence of life as distinguished from the dead is this streaming, this ever-changing current of it. The living content, no longer wholly arrested in this form, goes on with its stream and is not to be distinguished from it. The form without the content is empty and dead. In the history of an art the process toward degeneration, and through and past that to a new summit of excellence, a new epoch, consists of two courses: First, there is the survival of the form with less and less of the sustaining life that once brought the form into being; this is the so-called decadence of an art. Second, there is the progress of a new quality of life needing its body and moving toward a form that will contain and express it.

In Euripides's *Bacchae* Dionysos, the god of ever-springing life and enthusiasm and ecstasy, could not be bound; prison-bars, fetters, no obstacle had power to hold him fast. Only the forms of his own passion and of his own thought and his own motion could contain his divine life.

Pirandello, for the modern theatre, has dramatized this idea.

The theme in Pirandello's work is the dualism between Life on the one hand and Form on the other; on the one hand Life pouring in a stream, unknowable, obscure, unceasing; on the other hand forms, ideas, crystallizations, in which we try to embody and express this ceaseless stream of Life. Upon everything lies the burden of its form, which alone separates it from dust, but which also interferes with the unceasing flood of Life in it. In *Henry IV* this man who has taken on Form, a fixed mask in the midst of changing Life, remains in it until the moment when his passion and despair and violent impulse send him back into Life. But only for a moment; the impetuous violence of the Life in him expels him into his masquerade again; in his tragic struggle between Life and Form, Life is defeated, Form remains.

To many a play, when it is revived, comes such a fate as this. The life in the play is defeated, the ironic form remains.

The performance of a play at the director's hands is not a mere matter of the written text. Its truth can arise only from the combination of this text as it stands, plus the audience for whom it is given. In so far as a play is alive the living element in it is an impalpable, on-running, delicately perilous reality on which an illusion of permanence has been imposed by its form. The life in *Macbeth*, for example, seems to be permanently expressed by the play as we read it, and this might seem to hold true even for its performance. But this, in fact, is not the case. In such a performance there might be academic phrases of interest. As history of literature, as drama, as Shakespearean tragedy, it might, if you choose, possess an interest. But such kinds of interest, though studious and engaging, are apart from the play's vitality as art. And this is just the point at which we need most the director's imagination, need the genius in him for re-creating the play in the necessary new terms.

That side of Shakespeare's *Macbeth* that is a living thing, that speaks to the life in us and arouses a response from it, and fecundates and increases the volume of that life, must be restated in every revival—and in a sense, indeed, at every perform-

ance—of the play. The life in this play is not a fact, it is not
a fixed reality, unconfinable, a ceaseless flux, but real. The six-
teenth-century *Macbeth* of Shakespeare derives from an earlier
and more primitive base. It has beneath it such an element of
shock and terror as is to be found nowhere else in drama. This
primitive quality Shakespeare restated in terms of the morality
and the complex style of his own Elizabethan age, and lo, we
have his *Tragedy of Macbeth.* And now, in turn, this primitive
quality and this Elizabethanness must be restated for us. Even
if a director could discover every fact, every piece of business,
exact reading, gesture, tone of the first production of *Macbeth,*
and could reproduce them for us to the last jot, he would not
necessarily convey to us the life in the play. He might give us
only something beautifully curious or antiquarian or historic, exhibitions in facsimile, but not *Macbeth* and its meaning to us. No,
his business as an artist is to discover a rendering for *Macbeth*
—which is his material—through his medium—which is first the
actors and the decor of his theatre—to discover a rendering of
such a kind as will restate for the audience present the significance of the life of the play. There is no right way to produce
Macbeth. It would be a comfort to think so, to have something
to rest upon, just as some right way of living would be a comfort. But with life and with art the same thing holds: the essence
of being alive is a constant, perilous choice and a constant projection of imagination into living forms.

A part of the truth of a Greek play is its distance from us
in time. To be alive it has to be restated for us somewhat as its
original material had to be restated in it. For us a part of a Greek
play's truth is its Greekness, with all that that may mean for
us. In Restoration times a gentleman often carried a little bowl
of gold or silver which he could take from his pocket and rest on
the arm of his chair, and into it from time to time might spit.
Molière's gallants did a smart thing when they took a comb from
their pockets and arranged their curls as they sat in a lady's sa-
lon. But the director who wished to give us the quality of gal-

lant gentlemen in his revival of these social comedies could not show us such details, they would defeat his ends and give us not elegance but only ugliness. These are simple instances, but they illustrate the case. What in these particular instances needs most to be conveyed is the living thing, the permanent idea in them to which we respond—in sum, their elegance. At whatever cost, this must be created or the moment is empty.

The director's revival of a play, then, is a form of creation, and in so far as this is not so the play lies dead on the stage, a mere fact, the empty shell where once there was an engaging life. All compromise, change, or emphasis in a new production of an old play can have but this one end, which is in a way to keep it alive. The extent to which the director preserves closely the play in its original shape, or violates or distorts it, re-creates its essentials in new terms or even forces it so that we hardly recognize it for the same play, may affect the success of his enterprise, but it does not alter the principle involved. There are as many ways of doing *Macbeth* as there are generations of human life; and in its production the perpetual creation of a right body to express its truth is the condition on which alone *Macbeth* is kept not merely a matter of culture but a thing that is alive in our experience.

USE OF THE ACTOR

When the director, as an orchestra leader might, has achieved through the actors under him the desired emphasis throughout the performance, the time values, the tone, and so on, he remains to be considered as any artist in general making use of the means at hand. We may think of him as an artist in the use of his medium.

Of late years there has arisen in the theatre a type of directing that proceeds on the basis of letting the actor alone. Up to the point of collision with the other players the actor can go his own way and almost unmolested in creating his rôle. The principle is to get good actors and let them go ahead. Up to a certain point this policy has worked. But it has been a limited and often fatal method. Provided you get good actors, and in cases where only one or two actors carry the whole burden of the scene and can, perhaps, work it out between the two of them you may succeed. But in general the scheme is almost as hopeless as turning a crew of sailors loose without an officer to run the ship. And moreover, this method leads to a relaxation and laziness in the director himself.

The other extreme in directing actors is an older and more tried policy. In it the one hand controls everything and every one involved in the play, and not only controls the actor but dominates his conception of a role and the entire playing of it. Such a director at such an extreme may even give the actor the tone, the gesture, the movement. He may, when he likes, make the actor an imitation of himself. Up to a certain point this method also has often worked. If we must choose, it is on the whole safer than the opposite extreme. Provided the director himself has ideas that are capable of making the play into something worth while, and has the force or control to work the actors into his will, he may succeed. And the discouraging inferiority of the mass of actors seems to argue for such tyranny. But it obviously throws away no little of the individual resonance of the actor. And it tends to mechanize actors and to make them stale. It gives them stage tricks where real invention is needed; it leads them toward a more or less passive exploitation of themselves.

The necessity of the second method, the one controlling head for the performance, is plain. The whole scale of the play finally depends on that. The good element in the first method, the hands-off-and-let-the-actor-do-it school of directing, consists in the fact that at its best it allows the actor freedom to create and the possibility of succeeding in himself, of happiness in his own soul. It leads him toward becoming a better and better medium in which the director may work. The ideal directing combines the two methods.

But of the actor as medium there is more to say. As the medium in which the director works, the actor may be thought of somewhat as paint is thought of for the painter or marble for the sculptor. In every work of art the artist takes his material from nature or experience and translates it into his medium, creating in it, as he works, something that was not there before. His creation is partly in terms of his material and partly in terms of the medium employed. Our consciousness of the medium is a part of our perception of a work of art and of our pleasure in it. One among the many reasons why Velasquez is a great painter lies in the distinction with which the paint itself is a part of his work: the texture, the brush, the density of the painting medium, and the color as well are a part of the idea that Velasquez's picture presents. In Shakespeare, at his best, along with the dramatic emotion and the thought we have always a sense of words being employed, of sheer phrasing and diction, as a part of our delight. Something of the truth of an Egyptian statue is in the granite of it.

In the director's use of his actors it ought to be true that the more he can use in his scheme of the play the actor's own stuff, the better. The different truths of a great sculpture in wood and a great sculpture in marble will consist partly of the difference between wood and marble. It ought to be the fact that a certain deepening in the truth of an actor's contribution to a play will derive from the actor's getting his results in terms of himself, making up out of his own elements the result that he creates. It will allow a better chance for those explosive accidents that we call inspiration, those moments when the actor is carried beyond his own plan or clear intention. At such moments a certain unexpected contribution to the director's creation may come from the medium itself, which may contribute to his invention, give him an idea. Many an architect has got a design, a motive, a form, from some quality of texture, color, or weight of the stone that he is using. The limitations of marble may invite no little of the sculptor's pattern. This might be called keeping the medium alive. The director brings the actor's own truth to the creation of the larger truth that the director is after.

If, for example, then, you have, as in Lenormand's *Les Ratés*, a scene in which a crude black man is brought suddenly to the discovery of a corpse and cries aloud, it ought to be true that the first thing to do is to let the actor make the cry himself, express his own kind of emotion in his own kind of cry, and then to use all this as far as possible rather than to start by explaining the emotion and giving him a cry to imitate. If an actor, rehearsing for the storm scene in *King Lear,* feels a certain way in the part, the director may use this feeling as far as he can toward the creation of the feeling that he himself wishes to express. He must believe that his actors are souls as well as bodies, and that the creation he seeks is composed of all our human elements. In sum, such a use of the actor medium by the director ought to be the means of keeping his performance alive in all its parts, as a good painter keeps the paint or a good sculptor keeps the marble alive in every inch of his surface.

Murder of the Director

JEAN VILAR

1

The following notes concern only a particular technique of theatrical art, that of transposing a written work from the imaginary realm of reading to the concrete realm of the stage. To look for anything more than "means of interpretation" in these often deliberately cryptic lines would be vain.

When so many theories, *ars poetica* and metaphysics have been made up about this art, it is perhaps necessary that one advance, as a preliminary, a few artisan's considerations.

2

One can never read the play often enough. Actors never read it often enough. They think they understand the play when they follow the plot more or less clearly—a fundamental error.

Sticking my neck out, I would point out that in general, directors underrate the professional intelligence of actors. They are asked to be bodies only, animated pawns on the director's chessboard. The play once read by the director, read a second time *à l'italienne*, the actors are thrust onto the stage. What is the result?

Subjected too early to the demands of physical presence and

action, the actors fall back on their habitual, conventional reactions, and develop their characters conventionally and arbi-
trarily, before their professional intelligence and their sensibilities can grasp the director's intention. Whence, so many hack
performances!

For there are hack performances in the most sensitive actor,
just as a writer will produce hack work when he hurries or is
hurried. How many actors, including some of the best, have
murmured to us for twenty years in the same voice, with the
same bearing and gestures, with the same emotional quality,
in the most diametrically opposed roles!

Hence the necessity for many reading rehearsals: about a
third of the total number. At least. Manuscript in hand, seat
firmly planted on a chair, body in repose. Thus the deepest sensibilities will gradually pitch themselves to the desired note, as
the actor comes to understand, or feel, the new character that is
to become himself.

3

All characters must be *composed*. All good actors are necessarily *composers*. All roles are the result of *composition*.

4

The composition of a character is the work of creation which,
alone, assimilates the actor's craft to the artist's; for composing
a character implies selection, observation, research, inspiration,
and discipline.

5

The actor selects within and around himself.

Around himself, because nature presents to his eyes the most
various and distinct models, for his observation; one might almost say, for his contemplation.

Within himself, because if, on the one hand, the actor cannot sufficiently observe the life teeming around him, neither
can he sufficiently expose his sensibilities to contact with it.

In short, the actor must be able to retain in his visual memory the human types that strike his attention, as also the sympathetic (or sensory) memory of his own wounds and moral suffering. He must know how to use this memory and, better yet, cultivate it.

6

In blocking, the point is to simplify and pare down. Contrary to the usual practice, the idea is not to *exploit* space, but to forget or ignore it.

For a production to have its full power of suggestion, it is not necessary that a so-called scene of action should be "busy" (with acrobatics, fisticuffs, brawling and other "realistic" or "symbolic" activity). One or two gestures, and the text, suffice; provided both are "right".

7

The work of blocking and physical characterization should be fairly quickly completed by good professional actors: say fifteen rehearsals out of forty.

8

An actor's—or a director's—talent does not necessarily lie in the variety and strength of his powers (which are a relatively unimportant gift of Providence), but above all in the refining of his powers, the severity of his selectivity, in his voluntary self-impoverishment.

9

Music-hall theatre: a great actor, a splendid costume, a striking decor, music brimming with genius, strong-colored lighting.

10

No actor worthy of the name imposes himself on the text; he serves it. Humbly. Let the electrician, musician, and designer, accordingly, be even more humble than this "right interpreter."

11. CHARACTER AND ACTOR

The script carefully studied and the characters "felt" in all their ramifications, in the course of the fifteen or twenty reading rehearsals, the director begins the bland work of blocking, completes it, and finds himself at once in a renewed struggle with those slippery monsters, the characters. The actors know it well, for character and actor are two separate entities. For long days, the first eludes the second with infernal ease. The worst thing to do at this stage is to try to fight the demon, to force him to your will. If you wish him to come and meekly enter into your body and soul, forget him. The director's role, as expert observer of this pursuit by osmosis, is to inspire the actor with confidence, to convince him that he has, in the very expressive phrase, "found" or "rediscovered" his character. It is by no means naive to state that at a certain point in the development of a character, this confidence is all. It is by non-violence, by confidence in his ultimate conquest of the elusive monster, that the actor finally triumphs.

12

The scenic artist must realize the designer's sketches. Alternatively, there should be a designer-carpenter, right hand of the director, with full powers over the stage: a man of taste, devoted to his work and cultured. A hard trade.

13. OF COSTUME

In theatre, the hood sometimes makes the monk.

14. WHAT MUST BE DONE?

The work of production must include a written analysis of the play. The director must write it, and not despise the thankless job. The drafting of such an analysis compels the director to a clear and exhaustive knowledge of the play.

15

Question: Can one interpret something one doesn't understand?

16. CODA TO "WHAT MUST BE DONE?"

How may playwrights would be incapable of giving you a precise analysis of their play! of its plot, even!

17

A director who cannot detach himself from his work during the final rehearsals is only a mediocre craftsman, however much it might seem that this is the very point at which he should be most intensely involved in it. Failing this detachment, the director blinds himself—the worst possible error. Such poor fools forget that the theatre is play, in which inspiration and child-like wonder are more important than sweat and tantrums.

It is true that such detachment is so difficult to achieve at the right time that it is not surprising to find that few directors either desire or achieve it.

18

A quality fully as important to the actor in the right practice of his art as sensitivity and instinct, is the spirit of *finesse* (for a definition, see Pascal, who opposes it to the spirit of geometry). Without this quality, his work will only present a riot of anarchic expressions.

19

The actor is not a machine. This is a truism that needs to be shouted in people's ears. The actor is neither pawn nor robot. The director must assume from the start that his players have all the necessary talent.

20. INTERMISSION

"The idleness of an artist is work, and his work, repose." Signed, Balzac.

21

There is no technique of interpretation, but only practices, *techniques* (plural). Personal experience is all, and personal empiricism.

22

For the director, every actor is a special case. From this follows the requirement that he know every member of his cast well. Know his work, of course, but even more his *person*, up to the threshold of his inner life, and perhaps even beyond.

23. DIRECTOR AND ACTOR

Where the actor is concerned, the director's art is one of suggestion. He does not impose, he suggests. Above all, he must not be brutal. The "soul of an actor" is not an idle phrase: even more than the "soul of a poet," it is a continuing necessity. One does not win a creature's soul by brutalising it, and the actor's soul is more necessary to the work of theatre than his sensitivity.

24. OF SIMPLICITY

Three references:

a. Shakespeare-Hamlet: "Speak the speech, I pray you, as I pronounced it to you, trippingly on the tongue; but if you mouth it . . . I had as lief the town-crier spoke my lines . . . Be not too tame neither, but let your own discretion be your tutor . . . etc.", and all the rest of this famous passage.

b. Molière: *The Versailles Impromptu.*

c. Talmá-Lekain: "Lekain guarded against that hunger for applause that torments most actors and leads them into frequent error; he wished to please only the discriminating members of the audience. He rejected all theatrical fakery, aiming to produce a genuine effect by avoiding all "effects" . . . He *practiced a right economy of movement and gesture, deeming this an essential part of the art, since their multiplication detracts from dignity of bearing."* (Talma)

25

A production must be reduced to its simplest—and most difficult—expression: the stage action or, more precisely, the acting. Hence, the stage must not be turned into a crossroads of all the arts, major and minor (painting, architecture, electro-mania, musicomania, mechanics, etc.).

The designer must be put in his place, which is to solve the sightline problems of masking and teasers and to see to the construction of such set and hand properties as are strictly necessary to the action on stage.[1]

The immoderate use of projectors, floodlights and arc lamps should be left to the music-hall and the circus.

Music should be used only for overtures and scene bridges, and otherwise only when the script explicitly calls for music off, a song, or a musical interlude.

In short, all effects should be eliminated which are extraneous to the pure and Spartan laws of the stage, and the production reduced to the physical and moral action of the players.

---

[1] His chief task being to find the single *keynote of the set,* if set there must be. (J. V.)

[*Translated by Christopher Kotschnig*]

PART FOUR

THE DESIGNER

ROBERT EDMOND JONES

TO A YOUNG STAGE DESIGNER

SEAN O'CASEY

PRO-PER PROSCENIUM

To a Young Stage Designer

ROBERT EDMOND JONES

Beauty is the purgation of superfluities.—Michelangelo

Behind the words and movements, imperturbable, withdrawn, slumbered a strange smoldering power.—Henry Brocken

A stage designer is, in a very real sense, a jack-of-all trades. He can make blueprints and murals and patterns and light-plots. He can design fireplaces and bodices and bridges and wigs. He understands architecture, but is not an architect: can paint a portrait, but is not a painter: creates costumes, but is not a couturier. Although he is able to call upon any or all of these varied gifts at will, he is not concerned with any one of them to the exclusion of the others, nor is he interested in any one of them for its own sake. These talents are only the tools of his trade. His real calling is something quite different. He is *an artist of occasions.*

Every play—or rather, every performance of a play—is an occasion, and this occasion has its own characteristic quality, its own atmosphere, so to speak. It is the task of the stage designer to enhance and intensify this characteristic quality by every means in his power. The mastery of this special art demands not only a mastery of many diverse techniques but a temperament that is peculiarly sensitive to the atmosphere of a given occasion, just as the temperament of a musician is peculiarly sensitive to the characteristic qualities of a musical composition. Stage designers, like musicians, are born and not made. One is aware of atmospheres or one isn't, just as one has a musical ear or one hasn't.

A stage setting has no independent life of its own. Its emphasis is directed toward the performance. In the absence of the actor it does not exist. Strange as it may seem, this simple and fundamental principle of stage design still seems to be widely misunderstood. How often in critics' reviews one comes upon the phrase "the settings were gorgeous!" Such a statement, of course, can mean only one thing, that no one concerned with producing the drama has thought of it as an organic whole. I quote from a review recently published in one of our leading newspapers, "Of all the sets of the season, the only true scenic surprise was . . ." The only true scenic surprise, indeed! Every stage designer worth his salt outgrew the idea of scenic surprises years ago. If the critics only knew how easy it is to make a scenic surprise in the theatre! Take two turntables, a great deal of —But no. Why give away the formula? It is not surprise that is wanted from the audience; it is delighted and trusting acceptance. The surprise inherent in a stage setting is only a part of the greater surprise inherent in the event itself.

And yet a stage setting holds a curious kind of suspense. Go, for instance, into an ordinary empty drawing-room as it exists normally. There is no particular suspense about this room. It is just—empty. Now imagine the same drawing-room arranged and decorated for a particular function—a Christmas party for children, let us say. It is not completed as a room, now, until the children are in it. And if we wish to visualize for ourselves how important a part the sense of expectancy plays in such a room, let us imagine that there is a storm and that the children cannot come. A scene on the stage is filled with the same feeling of expectancy. It is like a mixture of chemical elements held in solution. The actor adds the one element that releases the hidden energy of the whole. Meanwhile, wanting the actor, the various elements which go to make up the setting remain suspended, as it were, in an indefinable tension. To create this suspense, this tension, is the essence of the problem of stage designing.

The designer must strive to achieve in his settings what I can only call a high potential. The walls, the furniture, the properties are only the facts of a setting, only the outline. The truth is in everything but these objects, in the space they enclose, in the intense vibration they create. They are fused into a kind of embodied impulse. When the curtain rises we feel a frenzy of excitement focused like a burning-glass upon the stage. Everything on the stage becomes a part of the life of the instant. The play becomes a part of the life of the instant. The terrible and wonderful dynamic of the theatre pours over the footlights.

A strange, paradoxical calling, to work always behind and around, to bring into being a powerful non-being. How far removed it all is from the sense of display! One is reminded of the portraits of the Spanish noblemen painted by El Greco in the Prado in Madrid, whose faces, as Arthur Symons said, are all nerves, distinguished nerves, quieted by an effort. What a phrase for stage designers to remember! *Quieted by an effort....*

It is to the credit of our designers that they have almost made a fetish of abnegation. But let me remark parenthetically that it is sometimes difficult to go into the background when there is nothing in front of you. These pages are hardly the place in which to perpetuate the centuries-old squabble between playwrights and stage designers begun by peevish old Ben Jonson, who scolded Inigo Jones so roundly for daring to make his productions beautiful and exciting to look at. This kind of petty jealousy makes sorry reading even when recorded in verse by the great Ben himself. It is enough to say that the jealousy still persists and is as corroding in the twentieth century as it was in the seventeenth. The error lies in our conception of the theatre as something set aside for talents that are purely literary. As if the experience of the theatre had only to do with words! Our playwrights need to learn that plays are wrought, not written.

There is something to be said in the theatre in terms of form and color and light that can be said in no other way.

The designer must learn to sense the atmosphere of a play with unusual clearness and exactness. He must actually live in it for a time, immerse himself in it, be baptized by it. This process is by no means so easy as it seems. We are all too apt to substitute ingenuity for clairvoyance. The temptation to invent is always present. I was once asked to be one of the judges of a competition of stage designs held by the Department of Drama of one of our well-known universities. All the designers had made sketches for the same play. The setting was the interior of a peasant hut on the west coast of Ireland. It turned out that these twenty or thirty young designers had mastered the technique of using dimmers and sliding stages and projected scenery. They had also acquired a considerable amount of information concerning the latest European developments of stagecraft. Their drawings were full of constructivism from Russia, every kind of modernism. They were compilations of everything that had been said and done in the world of scenery in the last twenty years. But not one of the designers had sensed the atmosphere of the particular play in question.

I recalled for them my memory of the setting for the same play as produced by the Abbey Theatre on its first visit to America. This setting was very simple, far simpler and far less self-conscious than any of their designs. Neutral-tinted walls, a fireplace, a door, a window, a table, a few chairs, the red homespun skirts and bare feet of the peasant girls. A fisher's net, perhaps. Nothing more. But through the little window at the back one saw a sky of enchantment. All the poetry of Ireland shone in that little square of light, moody, haunting, full of dreams, calling us to follow on. . . . By this one gesture of excelling simplicity the setting was enlarged into the region of great theatre art.

Now here is a strange thing, I said to the designers. If we can succeed in seeing the essential quality of a play others will see it, too. We know the truth when we see it, Emerson said, from opinion, as we know that we are awake when we are awake. For example: you have never been in Heaven, and you have never seen an angel. But if someone produces a play about angels whose scenes are laid in Heaven you will know at a glance whether his work is right or wrong. Some curious intuition will tell you. The sense of recognition is the highest experience the theatre can give. As we work we must seek not for self-expression or for performance for its own sake, but only to establish the dramatist's intention, knowing that when we have succeeded in doing so audiences will say to themselves, not, This is beautiful, This is charming, This is splendid, but— This is true. This is the way it is. So it is, and not otherwise. . . . There is nothing esoteric in the search for truth in the theatre. On the contrary, it is a part of the honest everyday life of the theatre.

The energy of a particular play, its emotional content, its aura, so to speak, has its own definite physical dimensions. It extends just so far in space and no farther. The walls of the setting must be placed at precisely this point. If the setting is larger than it should be, the audience gets a feeling of meagerness and hollowness; if smaller, a feeling of confusion and pressure. It is often very difficult to adjust the physical limits of a setting to its emotional limitations. But great plays exist outside the categories of dimension. Their bounty is as boundless as the air. Accordingly we need not think of a stage-setting, in a larger sense, as a matter of establishing space relations. Great plays have nothing to do with space. The setting for a great play is no more subject to the laws of space composition than music is. We may put aside once and for all the idea of a stage-setting as a glorified show-window in which actors are to be exhibited and think of it instead as a kind of symphonic accompaniment or obbligato to the play, as evocative and intangible as music itself. Indeed, music may play a more important role than we now realize in the scenic evocations of the future.

In the last analysis the designing of stage scenery is not the

problem of an architect or a painter or a sculptor or even a
musician, but of a poet. By a poet I do not mean, of course, an
artist who is concerned only with the writing of verse. I am
speaking of the poetic attitude. The recognized poet, Stedman
says, is one who gives voice in expressive language to the common thought and feeling which lie deeper than ordinary speech.
I will give you a very simple illustration. Here is a fragment of
ordinary speech, a paraphrase of part of Hamlet's soliloquy,
To be or not to be: I wish I were dead! I wish I could go to
sleep and never wake up! But I'm afraid of what might happen
afterward. Do people dream after they are dead? . . . But
Hamlet does not express himself in this way. He says, *To die,
to sleep; to sleep, perchance to dream: ay, there's the rub; for
in that sleep of death what dreams may come,* . . . Here are two
ways of saying the same thing. The first is prose. The second
is poetry. Both of them are true. But Shakespeare's way—the
poetic way—is somehow deeper and higher and truer and more
universal. In this sense we may fairly speak of the art of stage
designing as poetic, in that it seeks to give expression to the
essential quality of a play rather than to its outward characteristics.

Some time ago one of the younger stage designers was working with me on the scenes of an historical play. In the course of
the production we had to design a tapestry, which was to be decorated with figures of heraldic lions. I sent him to the library to
hunt up old documents. He came back presently with many
sketches, copies of originals. They were all interesting enough,
but somehow they were not right. They lacked something
that professionals call "good theatre." They were not *theatrical*.
They were accurate and—lifeless. I said as much to the designer.
"Well, what shall we do about it?" he asked me. "We have got
to stop copying," I said. "We must try something else. We must
put our imaginations to work. Let us think now. Not about what
this heraldic lion ought to look like, but what the design meant
in the past, in the Middle Ages.

"Perhaps Richard, the Lion-Heart, carried this very device emblazoned on his banner, as he marched across Europe on his way to the Holy Land. Richard, the Lion-Heart, *Coeur de Lion* . . . what memories of childhood this name conjures up, what images of chivalry! Knights in armor, enchanted castles, magic casements, perilous seas, oriflammes, gonfalons. Hear the great battle-cries! See the banners floating through the smoke! *Coeur de Lion, the Crusader, with his singing page Blondel.* . . . *Do* you remember Blondel's song, the song he sang for three long years while he sought his master in prison? 'O Richard, O mon Roi! L'univers t'abandonne! . . .'

"And now your imagination is free to wander, if you will allow it to do so, among the great names of romance. Richard, the Lion-Heart, King Arthur, Sir Percival and the mystery of the Holy Grail, the Song of Roland, the magic sword, Durandal, Tristan and Isolde, the love-potion, the chant of the Cornish sailors, the ship with the black sail; the Lady Nicolette of whom Aucassin said, *Beau venir et bel aller,* lovely when you come, lovely when you go; the demoiselle Aude, who died for love; the Lady Christabel; the Ancient Mariner with the Albatross hung about his neck; the Cid, Charlemagne, Barbarossa, the Tartar, Kubla Khan, who decreed the pleasure-dome in Xanadu, in the poem Coleridge heard in a dream. . . . And there are the legendary cities, too, Carcassonne, Granada, Torcello; Samarkand, the Blue City, with its façades of turquoise and lapis lazuli; Carthage, Isfahan, Trebizond; and there are the places which have never existed outside a poet's imagination—Hy Brasil, Brocéliande, the Land of Luthany, the region Elenore, the Isle of Avalon, *where falls not hail, or rain, or any snow, where ever King Arthur lyeth sleeping as in peace.* . . . And there is the winged Lion of St. Mark in Venice with the device set forth fairly beneath it, *Pax Tibi, Marce, Evangelista Meus;* and there are the mounted knights in the windows of Chartres, riding on, riding on toward Our Lady as she bends above the high altar in her glory of rose.

"These images of romance have come to our minds—all of them —out of this one little symbol of the heraldic lion. They are dear to us. They can never fade from our hearts.

"Let your fancy dwell and move among them in a kind of revery. Now in this mood, with these images bright in your mind, draw your figure of the lion once more.

"This new drawing is different. Instead of imitating, describing what the artists of the Middle Ages thought a lion looked like, it summons up an image of medieval romance. Perhaps without knowing it I have stumbled on a definition of art in the theatre; all art in the theatre should be, not descriptive, but evocative. Not a description, but an evocation. A bad actor describes a character; he explains it. He expounds it. A good actor evokes a character. He summons it up. He reveals it to us. . . . This drawing is evocative. Something about it brings back memories of medieval love-songs and crusades and high adventures. People will look at it without knowing why. In this drawing of a lion— only a detail in a magnificent, elaborate setting—there will be a quality which will attract them and disturb them and haunt them and make them dream. Your feeling is in it. Your interest is in it. You have triumphed over the mechanics of the theatre and for the time being you have become a poet."

The poetic conception of stage design bears little relation to the accepted convention of realistic scenery in the theatre. As a matter of fact it is quite the opposite. Truth in the theatre, as the masters of the theatre have always known, stands above and beyond mere accuracy to fact. In the theatre the actual thing is never the exciting thing. Unless life is turned into art on the stage it stops being alive and goes dead.

So much for the realistic theatre. *The artist should omit the details, the prose of nature and give us only the spirit and splendor.* When we put a star in a sky, for example, it is not just a star in a sky, but a "supernal messenger, excellently bright." This is purely a question of our point of view. A star is, after all, only an electric light. The point is, how the audience will see it, what images it will call to mind. We read of Madame Pitoeff's Ophelia that in the Mad Scene she handled the roses and the rosemary and the rue as if she were in a Paradise of flowers. We must bring into the immediate life of the theatre—"the two hours' traffic of our stage"—images of a larger life. The stage we inhabit is a chamber of the House of Dreams. Our work on this stage is to suggest the immanence of a visionary world all about us. In this world Hamlet dwells, and Oedipus, and great Juno, known by her immortal gait, and the three witches on the blasted heath. We must learn by a deliberate effort of the will to walk in these enchanted regions. We must imagine ourselves into their vastness.

Here is the secret of the flame that burns in the work of the great artists of the theatre. They seem so much more aware than we are, and so much more awake, and so much more alive that they make us feel that what we call living is not living at all, but a kind of sleep. Their knowledge, their wealth of emotion, their wonder, their elation, their swift clear seeing surrounds every occasion with a crowd of values that enriches it beyond anything which we, in our happy satisfaction, had ever imagined. In their hands it becomes not only a thing of beauty but a thing of power. And we see it all—beauty and power alike—as part of the life of the theatre.

Pro-Per Proscenium

SEAN O'CASEY

Naturalism, or the exact imitation of life, or the cult of real plays for real people, has brought the theater down very low in the plane of imagination. A playwright now is something of a real-estate agent. We can't pile the Tyrolean Hills on the stage, but fresh autumn crocuses will be planted for every performance. The pure stand-fast-to-truth minds want illusion before everything else, and must have it. Only today—the 4th of October, 1936—a critic writing in one of the greater London weeklies about the performance of *Oedipus Rex* tells us that "When I go to the theater I want illusion, and whether the Greeks wanted it or not, I just don't care." You see this great critic doesn't care a damn about what the Greeks wanted. He knows what he wants, and what he wants is a Watney. And yet this same critic twenty-nine years ago wrote this: "If you insist upon intellectual plays you must equally insist upon an audience trained to think. If you are a Shakespeare or writer of universal plays—this class of author is not so small as you would imagine if you go back far enough to include the Greeks—any audience how ordinary so-ever will do." Buzz, buzz!

This play evidently made this particular critic go all whoopee and hot all over, for he goes on: "Oedipus putting out his eyes that they may no longer be offended is like a man with a cold cutting off his nose so that it may no longer be blown." (If thy right eye offend thee, pluck it out, and cast it from thee.) "The final exit through the audience is one of those colossal mistakes of which only your highbrow producer is capable. Keep Oedipus within his frame and he remains Oedipus. Send him among us, and those bleeding sockets are merely red paint on the countenance of a delightful actor with whom you remember chatting at the last Test Match. The Reinhardt gang has never realized that to venture one inch beyond the proscenium arch destroys the whole illusion so laboriously created. This is the age of the picture stage, and even if you are twelve German producers rolled into one, you cannot put the clock back. You may put something in illusion's place, but that isn't what I want."

Let us duly think deeply and try to get at what is in these great thoughts of the critic. How can it be said that the clock can't be put back when it has been put back right under the critic's nose? He saw Oedipus actually step outside of the picture-frame and go his way. In this way I myself have seen the poor clock put back in the Abbey Theater, in Sir Barry Jackson's production of *The Marvellous History of St. Bernard,* in the performance of *Murder in the Cathedral* in the Century Theater, and at several crazy-week performances in the Palladium. Hundreds and hundreds of other instances have taken place in the theater generally, and many theatrical hands have been busy putting the hands of the clock back. This unhappy critic will have to organize a corps of shock guards to keep Oedipus within the picture-frame, and "thou shalt not pass" shall be their slogan. And isn't the "this is the age of the picture stage" a funny thing to say? One could say that this is the age of the aeroplane, the motor car, of concrete and steel, and of poison gas; but the age of the picture stage (maybe he means the films) is a funny, very funny thing to say. But let us be fair, and realize that the critic means, of course, the term in reference to the mechanical technique of the theater.

Twenty golden years ago the same critic received his first com-

munion in the faith of the picture-frame stage, for he tells us in
Buzz, Buzz that "All stage plays are pictures of a world removed
from the spectator, cut off from and presented to his consciousness by the gilt and molding of the proscenium." (Just imagine
any play being presented to any consciousness by the gilt and
molding of any proscenium!) "It is vital to the art of the actor
that he shall keep his frame, and that there shall be no point of
contact between him and the spectator." (This isolation and set-
ting-back of the player is admirably insisted upon by the use of
a gauze for the production of fairy plays.) "A hair's-breadth advance by an actor into the breathing world is utter annihilation."
Shakespeare knew better when he annihilated the theater, and
made the world a stage and all the men and women merely
players. He came out a little beyond the picture-frame. But the
best thing is to leave these sayings as they stand, the consciousness awakened by the gilt and molding, the no point of contact
between actor and spectator, the hair's-breadth advance, the
frame, and the fairy dance behind the gauze curtain—all wonderful things from the mouth of a Buzz-Buzz Boy.

But is he certain that the age of the picture-frame is not passing away? Does he think that this age will last for ever? For
ever and for aye. Ages may come and ages may go, the picture-frame will stay! When this critic says that "The Reinhardt
gang has never realized that to venture one inch beyond the
proscenium arch destroys the whole illusion so laboriously created," what does the fellow mean? The whole play, or only just
the character of Oedipus? Or does he mean that at no time, in
no theater, must any character in any play take a step that will
land him as much as an inch outside the proscenium arch? Is
there something sacred about the borderline of the picture-frame?
Is the picture-frame to come before the play? Is the picture-
frame to become the *ne plus ultra* of the drama? Are not the
intervals when many of the audience and some of the critics
hurry out to the forum to smoke, or into the bar to have a drink,
more likely to interfere with the keeping up of an illusion in

a play than any little step made by a character over the border
of the picture-frame? Surely an illusion must be loosely held for
a vision to fall and break when a character ventures to step an
inch beyond the borderline of the picture-frame. A critic is no
critic who makes the frame more important than the picture.
And when this critic says "keep Oedipus within his frame and he
remains Oedipus. Send him among us and he becomes an actor
with whom you remember chatting at the last Test Match,"
how does he know that within his frame he remains Oedipus?
Will this not depend on the acting of the part? He probably
means that, no matter how splendidly the part may be acted,
the moment a step is taken outside the proscenium arch the
illusion of the character as that particular character is broken
or altogether lost. But isn't he here describing his own personal,
one-man reaction to the stepping of the character over the proscenium arch? What right has he to say that the rest of the audience lost the illusion with him—unless he stopped and took a vote
man for man and woman for woman as the audience were hurry-
ing off to their homes. It is a cheeky thing to think that because
this critic reacted in a certain way to an action in a play the reaction of all the other (or any) members of the audience must
have been identical with his own. But in implication, a cheekier
statement follows. The critic tells us that "Production may put
something in illusion's place, but that isn't what I want. When I
go to the theater I want illusion, and whether the Greeks wanted
it or not I just don't care. Perhaps they were too High-Minded.
So be it." Perhaps to this critic the highest form of dramatic art
is the "Maskelyne Mysteries," the shutting-up of a woman in a
wooden case, the piercing of the case with many sharp swords,
the opening of the case showing the sight of the sharp swords
piercing it in every direction, and the woman gone! For if "illusion" be good, then the greater the illusion the greater the
play. And as the "Maskelyne Mysteries" are all illusion, then they
must be the greatest plays we have—which is hardly true. The
illusion that is anyway worth-while must be in the imaginative-

ness of the drama first, and this power of imagination in the play must be accepted by the imaginativeness of the audience assembled to see it. The imaginative power and emotion in a fine play will force itself out to the audience even through the obstacles of bad acting and poor production. And it is just as easy for the imaginative power in a play to climb or creep out over the footlights to an audience as it is for the imaginative power of an audience to climb or creep over the footlights on to the stage. Unfortunately, at least on first nights, the imagination in a play, as well as getting over the footlights, has to clamber over a sandbag barricade of critics. But the picture-framed stage is precisely the stage of the time of the sedan chair, the stagecoach, the candle, the linkman, the silk- and satin-clad ladies and gents that had become wholly separate from the people. In aristocratic Greece the theater was the theater of the people, high-minded and low-minded; in Shakespeare's time the theater was the theater of the people, high-minded and low-minded; but when the picture-frame was lifted on to the stage the theater crept away from the people, and became the theater of the dandies—very clever dandies (some of them, at least), to be sure, but dandies that made it impossible for the play to serve any entertaining interest but their own. The dandies are here still, to be sure, but few of them are clever. And now the stage has become a picture-frame, a fourth wall, a lighted box in which the actors and actresses hide themselves as much as possible from the people. (All except the stars, who, most of them ignorant of acting, are always anxious to throw themselves on the bosoms of their admirers inside and outside of the theater. If they can't get a name through their acting, they get it through their dogs, their dresses, and their divorces.) Again, the picture-frame stage has driven speech from the stage, and the next step will bring the actors to the playing of a play in dumbshow. Already they are among the whisper-and-I-shall-hear boys. They have lost the power to raise their voices, and indeed, taking most of the plays we have on the stage now, it is just as well that the dialogue should be reduced to a mutter. But it is strange that man should be allowed to raise his voice, and should feel no self-consciousness when he does so at a street corner, on a public platform, in the solemn House of Parliament, or even in the House of God; but no man must be allowed to raise his voice on the stage. The picture-frame stage of the naturalist has frightened the actors almost into silence. The critics have said *ipso facto* that all on the stage must be an exact imitation of life, and so nothing spoken there must dare to be above a whisper. (As if there were no shouting in real life.) And most of the dialogue used isn't worth even a whisper; but when every word shall be heard, and passion raises her voice again on the stage, when a shout in its proper place shall have the importance of a silence in its proper place, then the dramatist will have to think more about the words he gives his characters to say, and more still about the way in which the actors say them.

In a book written by Mr. Frank Vernon and published thirteen years ago, the sword is drawn for the protection of the proscenium arch. We are told here that "modern plays have retreated definitely behind the proscenium arch; and the attempts to bring the play amongst the audience have the effectiveness only of freakiness." The play, proscenium arch or no proscenium arch, *must* come amongst the audience to be effective. Again: "The apron stage does not bring the play nearer to the audience. It only brings nearer an actor whose make-up is increasingly obvious the nearer he comes to the audience. At close quarters he is no longer Antony, but a man with a painted face." He never could have been Antony, and always was a man with a painted face. He is a symbol, and as such is accepted by the audience just as a tin soldier, a metal cannon, and a cardboard fort is accepted by a boy, and a painted doll becomes the child of a little girl. Again: "My actor shall soliloquize behind the proscenium arch, where he looks like Hamlet or Macbeth, and not in front of it, showing the wrinkles in his tights and other aids to disillusionment." First it was paint on the face, now it is wrinkles in the tights. As if there weren't wrinkles in trousers in real life. The eye that fails to see Hamlet because there is a wrinkle in his tights is blind. This author suggests that the best way to overcome the need for an apron stage is to have a false proscenium behind the real one! He goes on: "I am for keeping the play where the play belongs—on the stage; and the stage is bounded by the proscenium arch. The theater is a box of tricks, and let us beware of the exposure of our tricks." (Another vote for Maskelyne.) Now the play does not "belong to the stage," for the stage is not the theater, and a play belongs to the theater; and the audience is as important a part of the theater as the stage or the actors on the stage. A theater cannot be divided up into parts —it is a unified whole, and what takes place on the stage must also take place in the minds of the audience, or, if not, then the unity is broken. And this author must forgive us if we refuse to accept the theater as "a box of tricks." The great men who have written for the theater were more than a pack of conjurers.

When the critic quoted at the outset of this article tells us that "when Oedipus stepped over the boundary of the proscenium, the whole illusion so laboriously created was destroyed," I wonder does he mean that the illusion so laboriously created had to be created by the actors and producer or by Sophocles, or if it had to be created by the waking up of his own mind? Possibly his own mind had to labor, for he tells us that "To pretend that the concatenation of miracles which is this play moves the modern mind to anything other than a purely poetical emotion is the rankest hypocrisy. It may interest or even excite. . . . Surely the fellow [he means Oedipus] must begin to see. . . . Surely after this he can't go on not knowing . . . and so the play gets hotter and hotter, as the children say," as if Sophocles had written the newest murdher mystery or a Shaftesbury Avenue detective puzzle-play. So it seems that this critic, from all his plaintive mutterings about the concatenations in the play, the Oracle, the Sphinx, the many innuendoes, the failure of Oedipus to see what fate had in store for him, lost the illusion of the play long before Oedipus ventured to put a foot across the proscenium arch. But what are we to think of the alarmed bluster in the statement that because an illusion is lost to a critic when a character in a play "ventures an inch beyond the proscenium arch," the illusion must necessarily be lost to every other member of the audience? There is no reason to believe that we all feel as the critics feel about this play or that play.

Commenting on the production of the same play, Mr. Ivor Brown says that "Today we are accustomed to the break-up of theatrical barriers and the irruption of actors from the back of the auditorium. Any young producer of a Left Wing Theater knows all these tricks now, a fact that proves Reinhardt to have been . . . a creator of tradition that has become part of our routine." Some critics evidently haven't got accustomed to it yet. Why is the bringing of the action of a play nearer to the audience emphasized as a "trick," while all the thousand and one tricks carried out in plays hiding behind the proscenium arch are looked upon (by the critics) as clever craftsmanship? And there is only one barrier in a theater, and that is the barrier of a bad play, though the terrible, vulgar, gaudily gilded thing called a proscenium arch is, in most of the theaters, the biggest barrier a play could have, and in the theater of the future will, in my opinion, have to be demolished. "This production," goes on Mr. Ivor Brown, "conforms to the Greek rather than to the English conception of theater." Well, the play was a Greek play anyhow. But what exactly is "the English conception of theater"? Are the ugly buildings strewn about Shaftesbury Avenue an English conception of theater? or the present mouse-like acting that goes on in naturalistic plays? or the frantic effort to make a building look like a law court when a trial-scene play was produced there? Or is the English conception of theater chained fast to the proscenium arch? There is no absolute English conception of theater, for the theater, like music, sculpture, or painting, is international, and when a great play is written, it belongs to all men.

The truth seems to be, nay, madam, it is, that the critics are still in the picture-frame age; they have lived all their life there, and they want to die on the old doorstep. But they mustn't object if we refuse to lie down and die with them. Perhaps some kindly manager will in some theater electrify the proscenium border so that any actor that steps over it will be immediately electrocuted; or, better still, put a sheet of Vita-glass into the picture-frame stage so that, to these poor people, all things done behind it may have a look of unalloyed illusion.

Sculpture, architecture, literature, poetry, and the domestic arts are actively walking about in new ways, and drama isn't going to stay quietly in her picture-frame gazing coyly out at changing life around her, like a languid invalid woman looking pensively out of a window in the fourth wall.

PART FIVE

THE CRITIC

Theatre Criticism

GEORGE BERNARD SHAW

REVIEWS OF HAMLET *[1897]*

STARK YOUNG

REVIEW OF HAMLET *[1922]*

KENNETH TYNAN

REVIEW OF HAMLET *[1958]*

Dramatic Criticism

MELVIN ASKEW

DUERRENMATT'S THE VISIT OF THE OLD LADY

GORDON ROGOFF

MR. DUERRENMATT BUYS NEW SHOES

Hamlet—2 *October 1897*

GEORGE BERNARD SHAW

The Forbes-Robertson Hamlet at the Lyceum is, very unexpectedly at that address, really not at all unlike Shakespear's play of the same name. I am quite certain I saw Reynaldo in it for a moment; and possibly I may have seen Voltimand and Cornelius; but just as the time for their scene arrived, my eye fell on the word "Fortinbras" in the program, which so amazed me that I hardly know what I saw for the next ten minutes. Ophelia, instead of being a strenuously earnest and self-possessed young lady giving a concert and recitation for all she was worth, was mad—actually mad. The story of the play was perfectly intelligible, and quite took the attention of the audience off the principal actor at moments. What is the Lyceum coming to? Is it for this that Sir Henry Irving has invented a whole series of original romantic dramas, and given the credit of them without a murmur to the immortal bard whose profundity (as exemplified in the remark that good and evil are mingled in our natures) he has just been pointing out to the inhabitants of Cardiff, and whose works have been no more to him than the word-quarry from which he has hewn and blasted the lines and titles of masterpieces which are really all his own? And now, when he has created by these means a reputation for Shakespear, he no sooner turns his back on London than Mr. Forbes-

Robertson competes with him on the boards of his own theatre by actually playing off against him the authentic Swan of Avon. Now if the result had been the utter exposure and collapse of that impostor, poetic justice must have proclaimed that it served Mr. Forbes-Robertson right. But alas! The wily William, by literary tricks which our simple Sir Henry has never quite understood, has played into Mr. Forbes-Robertson's hands so artfully that the scheme is a prodigious success. The effect of this success, coming after that of Mr. Alexander's experiment with a Shakespearean version of *As You Like It,* makes it almost probable that we shall presently find managers vying with each other in offering the public as much of the original Shakespearean stuff as possible, instead of, as heretofore, doing their utmost to reassure us that everything that the most modern resources can do to relieve the irreducible minimum of tedium inseparable from even the most heavily cut acting version will be lavished on their revivals. It is true that Mr. Beerbohm Tree still holds to the old scepticism, and calmly proposes to insult us by offering us Garrick's puerile and horribly caddish knockabout farce of Katherine and Petruchio for Shakespear's *Taming of the Shrew;* but Mr. Tree, like all romantic actors, is incorrigible on the subject of Shakespear.

Mr. Forbes-Robertson is essentially a classical actor, the only one, with the exception of Mr. Alexander, now established in London management. What I mean by classical is that he can present a dramatic hero as a man whose passions are those which have produced the philosophy, the poetry, the art, and the statecraft of the world, and not merely those which have produced its weddings, coroners' inquests, and executions. And that is just the sort of actor that Hamlet requires. A Hamlet who only understands his love for Ophelia, his grief for his father, his vindictive hatred of his uncle, his fear of ghosts, his impulse to snub Rosencrantz and Guildenstern, and the sportsman's excitement with which he lays the "mousetrap" for Claudius, can, with sufficient force or virtuosity of execution, get a great reputation in the part, even though the very intensity of his obsession by these sentiments (which are common not only to all men but to many animals) shews that the characteristic side of Hamlet, the side that differentiates him from Fortinbras, is absolutely outside the actor's consciousness. Such a reputation is the actor's, not Hamlet's. Hamlet is not a man in whom "common humanity" is raised by great vital energy to a heroic pitch, like Coriolanus or Othello. On the contrary, he is a man in whom the common personal passions are so superseded by wider and rarer interests, and so discouraged by a degree of critical self-consciousness which makes the practical efficiency of the instinctive man on the lower plane impossible to him, that he finds the duties dictated by conventional revenge and ambition as disagreeable a burden as commerce is to a poet. Even his instinctive sexual impulses offend his intellect; so that when he meets the woman who excites them he invites her to join him in a bitter and scornful criticism of their joint absurdity, demanding "What should such fellows as I do crawling between heaven and earth?" "Why wouldst thou be a breeder of sinners?" and so forth, all of which is so completely beyond the poor girl that she naturally thinks him mad. And indeed, there is a sense in which Hamlet is insane; for he trips over the mistake which lies on the threshold of intellectual self-conscousness: that of bringing life to utilitarian or Hedonistic tests, thus treating it as a means instead of an end. Because Polonius is "a foolish prating knave," because Rosencrantz and Guildenstern are snobs, he kills them as remorselessly as he might kill a flea, shewing that he has no real belief in the superstitious reason which he gives for not killing himself, and in fact anticipating exactly the whole course of the intellectual history of Western Europe until Schopenhauer found the clue that Shakespear missed. But to call Hamlet mad because he did not anticipate Schopenhauer is like calling Marcellus mad because he did not refer the Ghost to the Psychical Society. It is in fact not possible for any actor to represent Hamlet as mad. He may (and generally does) combine some notion of his own of a man who is the creature of affectionate sentiment with the figure drawn by the lines of Shakespear; but the result is not a madman, but simply one of those monsters produced by the imaginary combination of two normal species, such as sphinxes, mermaids, or centaurs. And this is the invariable resource of the instinctive, imaginative, romantic actor. You will see him weeping bucketsful of tears over Ophelia, and treating the players, the gravedigger, Horatio, Rosencrantz, and Guildenstern as if they were mutes at his own funeral. But go and watch Mr. Forbes-Robertson's Hamlet seizing delightedly on every opportunity for a bit of philosophic discussion or artistic recreation to escape from the "cursed spite" of revenge and love and other common troubles; see how he brightens up when the players come; how he tries to talk philosophy with Rosencrantz and Guildenstern the moment they come into the room; how he stops on his country walk with Horatio to lean over the churchyard wall and draw out the gravedigger whom he sees singing at his trade; how even his fits of excitement find expression in declaiming scraps of poetry; how the shock of Ophelia's death relieves itself in the fiercest intellectual contempt for Laertes's ranting, whilst an hour afterwards, when Laertes stabs him, he bears no malice for that at all, but embraces him gallantly and comradely; and how he dies as we forgive everything to Charles II for dying, and makes "the rest is silence" a touchingly humourous apology for not being able to finish his business. See all that; and you have seen a true classical Hamlet. Nothing half so charming has been seen by this generation. It will bear seeing again and again.

And please observe that this is not a cold Hamlet. He is none of your logicians who reason their way through the world because they cannot feel their way through it: his eternal self-criticism is as alive and thrilling as it can possibly be. The great soliloquy—no: I do NOT meant "To be or not to be": I mean the dramatic one, "O what a rogue and peasant slave am I!"—is as passionate in its scorn of brute passion as the most bull-necked affirmation or sentimental dilution of it could be. It comes out so without violence: Mr. Forbes-Robertson takes the part quite easily and spontaneously. There is none of that strange Lyceum intensity which comes from the perpetual struggle between Sir Henry Irving and Shakespear. The lines help Mr. Forbes-Robertson instead of getting in his way at every turn, because he wants to play Hamlet, and not to slip into his inky cloak a changeling of quite another race. We may miss the craft, the skill double-distilled by constant peril, the subtlety, the dark rays of heat generated by intense friction, the relentless parental tenacity and cunning with which Sir Henry nurses his own pet creations on Shakespearean food like a fox rearing its litter in the den of a lioness; but we get light, freedom, naturalness, credibility, and Shakespear. It is wonderful how easily everything comes right when you have the right man with the right mind for it—how the story tells itself, how the characters come to life, how even the failures in the cast cannot confuse you, though they may disappoint you. And Mr. Forbes-Robertson has certainly not escaped such failures, even in his own family. I strongly urge him to take a hint from Claudius and make a real ghost of Mr. Ian Robertson at once; for there is no sort of use going through that scene night after night with a Ghost so solidly, comfortable, and dogmatically alive as his brother. The voice is not a bad voice; but it is the voice of a man who does not believe in ghosts. Moreover, it is a hungry voice, not that of one who is past eating. There is an indescribable little complacent drop at the end of every line which no sooner calls up the image of purgatory by its words than by its smug elocution it convinces us that this particular penitent is cosily warming his shins and toasting his muffin at the flames instead of expiating his bad acting in the midst of them. His aspect and bearing are worse than his recitations. He beckons Hamlet away like a beadle summoning a timid candidate for the post of junior footman to the presence of the Lord Mayor. If I were Mr. Forbes-Robertson I would not stand that from any brother; I would cleave the general ear with horrid speech at him first. It is a pity; for the Ghost's part is one of the wonders of the play. And yet, until Mr. Courtenay Thorpe divined it the other day, nobody seems to have had a glimpse of the reason why Shakespear would not trust anyone else with it, and played it himself. The weird music of that long speech which should be the spectral wail of a soul's bitter wrong crying from one world to another in the extremity of its torment, is invariably handed over to the most squaretoed member of the company, who makes it sound, not like Rossetti's Sister Helen, or even, to suggest a possible heavy treatment, like Mozart's statue-ghost, but like Chambers's Information for the People.

Still, I can understand Mr. Ian Robertson, by sheer force of a certain quality of sententiousness in him, overbearing the management into casting him for the Ghost. What I cannot understand is why Miss Granville was cast for the Queen. It is like setting a fashionable modern mandolinist to play Haydn's sonatas. She does her best under the circumstances; but she would have been more fortunate had she been in a position to refuse the part.

On the other hand, several of the impersonations are conspicuously successful. Mrs. Patrick Campbell's Ophelia is a surprise. This part is one which has hitherto seemed incapable of progress. From generation to generation actresses have, in the mad scene, exhausted their musical skill, their ingenuity in devising fantasias in the language of flowers, and their intensest powers of portraying anxiously earnest sanity. Mrs. Patrick Campbell, with that complacent audacity of hers which is so exasperating when she is doing the wrong thing, this time does the right thing by making Ophelia really mad. The resentment of the audience at this outrage is hardly to be described. They long for the strenuous mental grasp and attentive coherence of Miss Lily Hanbury's conception of maiden lunacy; and this wandering, silly, vague Ophelia, who no sooner catches an emotional impulse than it drifts away from her again, emptying her voice of its tone in a way that makes one shiver, makes them horribly uncomfortable. But the effect on the play is conclusive. The shrinking discomfort of the King and Queen, the rankling grief of Laertes, are created by it at once; and the scene, instead of being a pretty interlude coming in just when a little relief from the inky cloak is welcome, touches us with a chill of the blood that gives it its right tragic power and dramatic sigrificance. Playgoers naturally murmur when something that has always been pretty becomes painful; but the pain is good for them, good for the theatre, and good for the play. I doubt whether Mrs. Patrick Campbell fully appreciates the dramatic value of her quite simple and original sketch—it is only a sketch—of the part; but in spite of the occasional triviality of its execution and the petulance with which it has been received, it seems to me to settle finally in her favor the question of her right to the very important place which Mr. Forbes-Robertson has assigned to her in his enterprises.

I did not see Mr. Bernard Gould play Laertes: he was indisposed when I returned to town and hastened to the Lyceum; but he was replaced very creditably by Mr. Frank Dyall. Mr. Martin Harvey is the best Osric I have seen: he plays Osric from Osric's own point of view, which is, that Osric is a gallant and distinguished courtier, and not, as usual, from Hamlet's, which is that Osric is "a waterfly." Mr. Harrison Hunter hits off the modest, honest Horatio capitally; and Mr. Willes is so good a Gravedigger that I venture to suggest to him that he should carry his work a little further, and not virtually cease to concern himself with the play when he has spoken his last line and handed Hamlet the skull. Mr. Cooper Cliffe is not exactly a subtle Claudius; but he looks as if he had stepped out of a picture by Madox Brown, and plays straightforwardly on his very successful appearance. Mr. Barnes makes Polonius robust and elderly instead of aged and garrulous. He is good in the scenes where Polonius appears as a man of character and experience; but the senile exhibitions of courtierly tact do not match these, and so seem forced and farcical.

Mr. Forbes-Robertson's own performance has a continuous

charm, interest, and variety which are the result not only of his well-known grace and accomplishment as an actor, but of a genuine delight—the rarest thing on our stage—in Shakespear's art, and a natural familiarity with the plane of his imagination. He does not superstitiously worship William: he enjoys him and understands his methods of expression. Instead of cutting every line that can possibly be spared, he retains every gem, in his own part or anyone else's, that he can make time for in a spiritedly brisk performance lasting three hours and a half with very short intervals. He does not utter half a line; then stop to act; then go on with another half line; then stop to act again, with the clock running away with Shakespear's chances all the time. He plays as Shakespear should be played on the line and to the line, with the utterance and acting simultaneous, inseparable and in fact identical. Not for a moment is he solemnly conscious of Shakespear's reputation or of Hamlet's momentousness in literary history: on the contrary, he delivers us from all these boredoms instead of heaping them on us. We forgive him the platitudes, so engagingly are they delivered. His novel and astonishingly effective and touching treatment of the final scene is an inspiration, from the fencing match onward. If only Fortinbras could be inspired with sufficient force and brilliancy to rise to the warlike splendor of his helmet, and make straight for that throne like a man who intended to keep it against all comers, he would leave nothing to be desired. How many generations of Hamlets, all thirsting to outshine their competitors in effect and originality, have regarded Fortinbras, and the clue he gives to this kingly death for Hamlet, as a wildly unpresentable blunder of the poor foolish old Swan, than whom they all knew so much better! How sweetly they have died in that faith to slow music, like Little Nell in *The Old Curiosity Shop!* And now how completely Mr. Forbes-Robertson has bowled them all out by being clever enough to be simple.

By the way, talking of slow music, the sooner Mr. Hamilton Clark's romantic Irving music is stopped, the better. Its effect in this Shakespearean version of the play is absurd. The four Offenbachian young women in tights should also be abolished, and the part of the player-queen given to a man. The courtiers should be taught how flatteringly courtiers listen when a king shews off his wisdom in wise speeches to his nephew. And the nice wooden beach on which the ghost walks would be the better for a seaweedy looking cloth on it, with a handful of shrimps and a pennorth of silver sand.

Hamlet Revisited—
18 December 1897

Public feeling has been much harrowed this week by the accounts from America of the 144 hours' bicycle race; but what are the horrors of such an exhibition compared to those of the hundred-nights run of *Hamlet!* On Monday last I went, in my private capacity, to witness the last lap but five of the Lyceum trial of endurance. The performers had passed through the stage of acute mania, and were for the most part sleep-walking in a sort of dazed blank-verse dream. Mr. Barnes raved of some New England maiden named Affection Poo; the subtle distinctions made by Mrs. Patrick Campbell between madness and sanity had blurred off into a placid idiocy turned to favor and to prettiness; Mr. Forbes-Robertson, his lightness of heart all gone, wandered into another play at the words "Sleep? No more!" which he delivered as, "Sleep no more." Fortunately before he could add "Macbeth does murder sleep," he relapsed into Hamlet and saved the situation. And yet some of the company seemed all the better for their unnatural exercise. The King was in uproarious spirits: and the Ghost, always comfortable, was now positively pampered, his indifference to the inconveniences of purgatory having developed into a bean-fed enjoyment of them. Fortinbras, as I judged, had sought consolation in religion: he was anxious concerning Hamlet's eternal welfare; but his general health seemed excellent. As Mr. Gould did not play on the occasion of my first visit, I could not compare him with his former self; but his condition was sufficiently grave. His attitude was that of a castaway mariner who has no longer hope enough to scan the horizon for a sail; yet even in this extremity his unconquerable generosity of temperament had not deserted him. When his cue came, he would jump up and lend a hand with all his old alacrity and resolution. Naturally the players of the shorter parts had suffered least: Rosencrantz and Guildenstern were only beginning to enjoy themselves; and Bernardo (or was it Marcellus?) was still eagerly working up his part to concert pitch. But there could be no mistake as to the general effect. Mr. Forbes-Robertson's exhausting part had been growing longer and heavier on his hands; whilst the support of the others had been falling off; so that he was keeping up the charm of the representation almost single-handed just when the torturing fatigue and monotony of nightly repetition had made the task most difficult. To the public, no doubt, the justification of the effort is its success. There was no act which did not contain at least one scene finely and movingly played; indeed some of the troubled passages gained in verisimilitude by the tormented condition of the actor. But *Hamlet* is a very long play; and it only seems a short one when the high-mettled comedy with which it is interpenetrated from beginning to end leaps out with all the lightness and spring of its wonderful loftiness of temper. This was the secret of the delighted surprise with which the public, when the run began, found that *Hamlet*, far from being a funereally classical bore, was full of a celestial gaiety and fascination. It is this rare vein that gives out first when the exigencies of theatrical commerce force an actor to abuse it. A sentimental *Hamlet* can go on for two years, or ten for the matter of that, without much essential depreciation of the performance; but the actor who sounds Hamlet from the lowest note to the top of his compass very soon finds that compass contracting at the top. On Monday night the first act, the third act, and the fifth act from the entrance of Laertes onward, had lost little more than they had gained as far as Mr. Forbes-Robertson was concerned; but the second act, and the colloquy with the grave-digger, which were the triumphs of the representation in its fresher stages, were pathetically dulled, with the result that it could no longer be said that the length of the play was forgotten.

The worst of the application of the long-run system to heroic plays is that, instead of killing the actor, it drives him to limit himself to such effects as he can repeat to infinity without committing suicide. The opposite system, in its extreme form of the old stock company playing two or three different pieces every night, led to the same evasion in a more offensive form. The recent correspondence in the *Morning Post* on The Stage as a Profession, to which I have myself luminously contributed, has produced the usual fallacious eulogies of the old stock company as a school of acting. You can no more prevent contributors to public correspondences falling into this twenty-times exploded error than from declaring that duelling was a school of good manners, that the lash suppressed garotting, or any other gratuitous ignorances of the amateur sociologist. The truth is, it is just as impossible for a human being to study and perform a new part of any magnitude every day as to play Hamlet for a hundred consecutive nights. Nevertheless, if an actor is required to do these things, he will find some way out of the difficulty without refusing. The stock actor solved the problem by adopting a "line": for example, if his "line" was old age, he acquired a trick of doddering and speaking in a cracked voice: if juvenility, he swaggered and effervesced. With these accomplishments, eked out by a few rules of thumb as to wigs and face-painting, one deplorable step dance, and still more deplorable "combat," he "swallowed" every part given to him in a couple of hours, and regurgitated it in the evening over the footlights, always in the same manner, however finely the dramatist might have individualized it. His infamous incompetence at last swept him from the reputable theatres into the barns and booths; and it was then that he became canonized, in the imagination of a posterity that had never suffered from him, as the incarnation of the one quality in which he was quite damnably deficient: to wit, versatility. His great contribution to dramatic art was the knack of earning a living for fifty years on the stage without ever really acting, or either knowing or caring for the difference between the *Comedy of Errors* and *Box and Cox*.

A moment's consideration will shew that the results of the long-run system at its worst are more bearable than the horrors of the past. Also, that even in point of giving the actor some chance of varying his work, the long-run system is superior, since the modern actor may at all events exhaust the possibilities of his part before it exhausts him, whereas the stock actor, having barely time to apply his bag of tricks to his daily task, never varies his treatment by a hair's breadth from one half century to another. The best system, of course, lies between these extremes. Take the case of the great Italian actors who have visited us, and whose acting is of an excellence apparently quite beyond the reach of our best English performers. We find them extremely chary of playing every night. They have a repertory containing plays which count as resting places for them. For example, Duse relieves Magda with Mirandolina just as our own Shakespearean star actors used to relieve Richard the Third and Othello with Charles Surface and Don Felix. But even with this mitigation no actor can possibly play leading parts of the first order six nights a week all the year round unless he underplays them, or routines them mechanically in the old stock manner, or faces a terrible risk of disablement by paralysis, or, finally, resorts to alcohol or morphia, with the usual penalties. What we want in order to get the best work is a repertory theatre with alternative casts. If, for instance, we could have *Hamlet* running at the Lyceum with Sir Henry Irving and Miss Ellen Terry on Thursdays and Saturdays, Mr. Forbes-Robertson and Mrs. Patrick Campbell on Wednesdays and Fridays, and the other two days devoted to comedies in which all four could occasionally appear, with such comedians as Mr. Charles Wyndham, Mr. Weedon Grossmith, Mr. Bourchier, Mr. Cyril Maude, and Mr. Hawtrey, then we should have a theatre which we could invite serious people to attend without positively insulting them. I am aware that the precise combination which I have named is not altogether a probable one at present; but there is no reason why we should not at least turn our faces in that direction. The actor-manager system, which has hitherto meant the star system carried to its utmost possible extreme, has made the theatre so insufferable that, now that its monopoly has been broken up by the rise of the surburban theatres, there is a distinct weakening of the jealous and shameless individualism of the last twenty years, and a movement towards combination and cooperation.

By the way, is it quite prudent to start a public correspondence on The Stage as a Profession? Suppose someone were to tell the truth about it!

Hamlet—*Sam H. Harris Theatre, November 20, 1922*

STARK YOUNG

Mr. John Barrymore seemed to gather together in himself all the Hamlets of his generation, to simplify and direct everyone's theory of the part. To me his Hamlet was the most satisfying that I have seen, not yet as a finished creation, but a foundation, a continuous outline. Mounet-Sully's Hamlet was richer and more sonorous; Forbes-Robertson's at times more sublimated; Irving's more sharply devised; and Sothern's, so far as we are concerned strictly with the verse pattern, was more securely read. But there is nothing in Mr. Barrymore's Hamlet to get in the way of these accomplishments also, with time and study. And in what he has done there is no inherent quality that need prevent his achieving the thing most needed to perfect, in its own kind, his Hamlet; I mean a certain dilation and abundance in all his reactions. This Hamlet of Mr. Barrymore's must give us—and already promises—the sense of a larger inner tumult and indeed of a certain cerebral and passionate ecstasy, pressing against the external restraint of him. He needs the suggestion of more vitality, ungovernable and deep, of more complex suffering, of not only intellectual subtlety but in-

422

tellectual power as well, all this added to the continuity of distinction that he already has, the shy and humorous mystery, the proud irony, the terrible storms of pain. Mr. Barrymore brings to the part what is ultimately as necessary to a fine actor as to a fine singer, the physical gifts that enable him to express his idea. He has a beautiful presence, a profound magnetism. His English, much of which is but recently acquired through the teaching of the remarkable Mrs. Margaret Carrington, is almost wholly reborn from what it once was, and is now almost pure, even and exact, though not wholly flexible. His voice, also to a considerable extent Mrs. Carrington's production, is not supreme. It is not a rich and sonorous volume such as Mansfield had, but it is capable of high, intelligent training, and is already in the middle tones highly admirable.

With such an artist as Mr. Barrymore has risen to be, one cannot escape the matter of the technical means by which he fills out and develops the kind of truth that he sees in his role, or confuses and prevents its realization. His chief technical triumph, I think, lies in the absence from his work of all essentially theatrical faults. There are no idle tricks of the voice, no empty display of actor vanity and professional virtuosity, no foolish strutting, none of the actor's idol's way of feeling his oats. There is no egotistical intrusion on the play, no capricious distortion of the truth in the service of histrionic exhibitionism. Throughout the performance the technical method is invariably derived from the conception of the part and never allowed to run ahead of it.

Mr. Barrymore's important technical limitations at this stage of his achievement seem to me to be two. The first concerns the verse. The "resistant flexibility," to use an old phrase, that is the soul of fine reading, he has not yet completely acquired. Much of his reading is excellent; but now and again in his effort to keep the verse true to its inner meaning and to the spiritual naturalness that underlies it—and because, too, of a

lack of concentration on his projection at times—Mr. Barrymore seems to be afraid to admit the line for what it is, verse.
Sometimes he allows the phrases to fall apart in such a way that
the essential musical pattern of the verse—which is a portion of
the idea itself—is lost. In the line—to take an example—

> Why, she would hang on him,

he put heavy stress on the word "hang" and almost let the "him"
disappear; a useless naturalism, for the same effect of sense
emphasis can be secured and yet the verse pattern of the lines
preserved, by sustaining the nasals in "on" and "him" with no
more actual stress on them than Mr. Barrymore used.

For one more instance out of a good many, take the line

> Must, like a whore, unpack my heart with words.

Mr. Barrymore let the phrase "like a whore" fall out solid from
the verse, which then began anew with "unpack." But there
is a certain sustained unity to the line; "must" and "unpack"
have a resistant connection together—to be secured by the
tone—which the intervening phrase does not break off. And,
as a matter of fact, everywhere in Shakespeare the long, difficult, elaborate and complex passages depend above everything
on their musical unity to recreate out of their many details that
first profound unity of emotion from which they sprang. Without this unity these details appear to be—as in fact they often
are, in the earlier plays especially—mere images and ornaments
thrown in, whose artificiality is only embarrassing.

The other technical limitation that I feel in Mr. Barrymore
is in his rendering of decreasing emotion. To be able to rise successfully to emotional heights is one measure of an actor's art;
but this declining gradation is a no less sure test of it. For an
illustration of what I mean, take the passage in the closet scene
where the Ghost vanishes.

> HAMLET: Why, look you there! look how it steals away!
>   My father in his habit as he lived!
>   Look, where he goes, even now, out at the portal!

> QUEEN: This is the very coinage of your brain;
> This bodily creation ecstasy
> Is very cunning in.

> HAMLET: Ecstasy!
> My pulse as yours doth temperately keep time,—

Mr. Barrymore repeats the word and goes on with the speech in a reasonable and almost even tone. But in such places a part of the effect of preceding emotion appears in the gradual lessening of it in the actor's manner and voice. This speech of Hamlet's is reasonable, yes, but the calm in the thought precedes the calm in the state of emotion; the will and the idea are to rule but only after conflict with the emotion.

I cannot admire too much Mr. Barrymore's tact in the scenes with Polonius. Most actors for the applause they get play up for all it is worth Hamlet's seemingly rude wit at the old man's expense. But Mr. Barrymore gave you only Hamlet's sense of the world grown empty and life turned to rubbish in this old counselor. And, without seeming to do so, he made you feel that Polonius stood for the kind of thing in life that had taken Ophelia from him. How finely—even in that last entreaty to Laertes for fair usage—Mr. Barrymore maintained an absence of self-pity in Hamlet, and thus enlarged the tragic pity of the play! What a fine vocal economy he exercised in the scene where Horatio tells him of his father's Ghost! And what a stroke of genius it was, when by Ophelia's grave Hamlet had rushed through those mad lines, piling one wild image on another, and comes to the

> Nay, an thou'lt mouth,
> I'll rant as well as thou

to drop on that last, on the "I'll rant as well as thou," into an aspirate tone, hoarse, broken with grief and with the consciousness of his words' excess and the excess of irony in all things!

And I must admire the economy of business—not all Mr. Barrymore but partly due to Mr. Arthur Hopkins, Mrs. Carrington and Mr. Jones—all through the part. The nunnery scene with Ophelia was done with a reaching out of the hands almost; the relation of Hamlet to his mother and through her to the Ghost was achieved by his moving toward the Ghost on his knees and being caught in his mother's arms, weaving together the bodies of those two, who, whatever their sins might be, must belong to each other at such terrible cost. There were no portraits on the wall with a Ghost stepping out, as Hackett used to do it in the sixties. There was no crawling forward on the floor to watch the King during the play, as so many actors have done; and none of Ophelia's peacock fan for Hamlet to tap his breast with and fling into the air, as Irving used to do. About all this production there were none of those accessories in invented business; there was for the most part, and always in intention, only that action proceeding from the inner necessity of the moment and leaning on life, not on the stage expedients. The inner limitations of Mr. John Barrymore's Hamlet are both less tangible and less amendable perhaps. They are in the direction of the poetic and human. With time, meditation and repetition it will gain in these respects no doubt; but it needs now more warmth, more abundance in all the reactions, more dilation of spirit. It takes too much for granted, makes Hamlet too easy to understand, and so lacks mystery and scope. It needs a larger inner tumult, more of a cerebral and passionate ecstasy pressing against the outward restraint of the whole pattern. It needs more of the sense of an ungovernable vitality, more complex subtlety and power. It needs more tenderness and, above all, more, if you like, generosity.

Miss Fuller's Ophelia could not dominate the longer speeches in her first scenes. But in the mad scenes she sang her ballads with unheard-of-poignancy; and the mere slip of her white, flitting body was itself the image of pathos. Miss Fuller sharpened the effect of madness by putting into it a hint of that last betrayal that insanity brings to Ophelia: indecency. Miss Yurka, though she subsided at times out of the part when she had nothing to do, read her lines admirably; and contrived to suggest without overstating it the loose quality in this woman that subjected her to the King. Mr. O'Brien's Polonius was good, simplified rather far, perhaps, but with a certain force of truth that rendered what Polonius, despite his fatuity, has: a kind of grotesque distinction. Mr. Reginald Pole brought to the Ghost's lines a fine ear and an exact method of reading the verse that you gratefully detect before he is three lines under way. The Laertes of Mr. Sidney Mather is the only very bad performance in the company. The role is extra difficult because of its Renaissance approach, through character and reality, to the flowery gallantry and lyric expedition required; though the bases of Laertes' feelings and actions seem to me fresh, accessible and human. The fact remains, nevertheless, that unless the actor gets the manner and flourish of Laertes, the expression of his vivid, poignant and decorative meaning cannot find its due outlet. Mr. Tyrone Power's King—superb in voice and meter—was admirable. He suggested not mere villainy but rather a tragic figure of force and heavy will. Mr. Power's King gave us also the sense of great charm exerted upon those around him that is attributed to the character in the play.

It is in the scene where Hamlet catches the King praying and does not kill him—the climax of the play—that the method of production employed by Mr. Hopkins and Mr. Jones is reduced, it seemed to me, to its most characteristic terms. The King enters through the curtain, already used a number of times, with the saints on it. He kneels, facing the audience. He lifts his hands and speaks to heaven. Hamlet enters through the same curtain. He debates the fitness of the time for the King's murder, decides against it, withdraws. The King says

> My words fly up, my thoughts remain below;
> Words without thoughts never to heaven go.

and rises and goes out. One man is here, one is there. Here are the uplifted hands, there the sword drawn. Here, sick conscience, power, and tormented ambition; there, the torture of conflicting thoughts, the irony, the resolution. Two bodies and their relation to each other, the words, the essential drama, the eternal content of the scene. No tricks, no plausible business, no palace chapel. And no tradition.

Tradition of conception there is now and again, of course; but throughout the entire production there is very little concern about external tradition. And what of it? If we had some kind of Théâtre Français, a conservatory where a classic like *Hamlet* would be seen from time to time as a star returns on its course; or if in our theatre we had a succession of rival Hamlets, as was once the case, the question of tradition would be more important. Under such conditions a certain symbolism of stage business might develop, full of deep significance, familiar and accepted, and not to be abandoned too readily. But in the American theatre today the disregard of Shakespearean tradition is easy and commendable. To pursue it doggedly is to block the way with dead husks of forms once full of meaning. It only thwarts the audience and Shakespeare's living matter with a kind of academic archaism and, even, with a certain fanaticism; which consists, as Santayana says, in redoubling your effort when you have forgotten your aim. Messrs. Hopkins and Jones and Barrymore have, for the most part, let sleeping dogs lie. Nothing could be easier than not to do so; hence their eminence.

Mr. Robert Edmond Jones has created a permanent setting of architectural forms and spaces, bounded across the stage, and down two-thirds to the front line of it, with a play of steps. Within this, easy variations are possible to indicate the changes of scene. The design of the setting cannot be conveyed in words, of course, but it is princely, austere and monumental. It has no clutter of costumes or elaborate variations in apartments, but instead a central rhythm of images, of light and shade innate to the dramatic moment. The shortcoming of this bold and eloquent setting is that it either goes too far or does not go far enough. In this respect the limit was reached when the time came for the scene of Ophelia's burial, where the setting was at least enough like a palace to make the grave toward the front of the stage— and therefore the whole scene—appear incongruous if not absurd. A greater vastness of imagination was thus required of the designer. In his defense it should be said, however, that our theatre does not easily allow for repeated experiment, with the discarding and choosing and the expense involved.

This production of *Hamlet* is important and is out of class with Shakespeare production from other sources. This is not through any perfection in the field of the Shakespearean so called; but because it works toward the discovery of the essential and dramatic elements that from the day it was written have underlain this play. The usual Shakespearean production, however eminent, goes in precisely the opposite direction. It does not reveal the essential so much as it dresses up the scene at every conceivable angle, with trappings, research, scenery, business.

Such a production as this of Hamlet could not hope to be uniformly successful. But in its best passages, without any affectation of the primitive or archaic, it achieved what primitive art can achieve: a fundamental pattern so simple and so revealing that it appeared to be mystical; and so direct and strong that it restored to the dramatic scene its primary truth and magnificence. For a long time to come this *Hamlet* will be remembered as one of the glories of our theatre.

Hamlet—
Stratford-on-Avon, 1958

KENNETH TYNAN

The case of Michael Redgrave is perennially absorbing, even to those who deny that he is a great actor. On he plunges, struggling and climbing and stumbling, bursting with will and intelligence, and seeking always to widen the range of his remarkable physical and vocal equipment. Never, to my knowledge, has he run away from an acting problem: he'll wrestle with them all. A serious actor, in short.

Yet something is missing. We admire, but are not involved. "I wish thar was winders to my Sole," said Artemus Ward, "so that you could see some of my feelins." Mr. Redgrave's trouble is that his windows are opaque—one might even say frosted. Sir Laurence Olivier once said he would rather lose his voice or his arms than his eyes. Watch Mr. Redgrave's: no matter how he rolls and darts them about, they remain somehow glazed and distant. We know from the evidence of our own that he has two of them yet something about him persistently suggests the Cyclops. When he looks at other people, either actors or audience, it is as if he saw them only in two dimensions. They are simply "things in his dream." Try as he may (and God knows he tries), he cannot establish contact with them as human beings. Just as we think he is about to break through to us, something within him shies and bolts. He withdraws into his solitude, and when next we look, the windows are shuttered again.

Now the business of "connecting," of getting into emotional touch with others, is at the heart of all acting. It is the very touchstone of the craft. And that is Mr. Redgrave's paradox. He has in abundance all the attributes of a great actor, without the basic quality necessary to be a good one.

Even so, he is always fascinating to watch. His present *Hamlet* is a packed, compendious affair, much richer in detail than the one he gave us eight years ago at the Vic. At fifty, Mr. Redgrave is the oldest Hamlet to have been seen in England since 1938, when Esme Beringer struck a glancing blow for feminism by playing the part in her sixty-fourth summer; and it must be conceded that the actor sometimes resembles less a youth approaching murder for the first time than a seasoned Commando colonel suffering from battle fatigue. Nor is the illusion helped by a Gertrude who looks even younger than Googie Withers—a surprising achievement, considering that Miss Withers herself plays the part. Sheer intellectual agility, of which he has plenty, is what Mr. Redgrave relies on. He knows the text inside out, and when he offers new readings (such as "Nilus" for "eisel" in the grave scene), we trust him as we would trust a walking Variorum Edition of the play. No subtlety of inflexion or punctuation escapes him; at times, indeed, he seems to be giving us three different interpretations of the same line *simultaneously,* which is a bit flustering.

In terms of character, Mr. Redgrave presents a man fearful of rousing the sleeping demon within him. Cocteau described the artist as a kind of prison from which works of art escape. This Hamlet is a prison from which fury escapes, in wild frustrated spasms. His lips quake with the effort of containing it. Bottled hysteria is this actor's specialty, as the cellarage scene brilliantly proves. Mr. Redgrave's Hamlet, like his Lear, is most convincing when closest to madness. It is, however, entirely, un-moving, for the reason mentioned above.

Dorothy Tutin's Ophelia, a mouse on the rack, makes some il-luminating minor points, chief among them her horrified reac-tion, in the play scene, to the mimic death of the Player King. I liked Edward Woodward's Laertes, Paul Hardwick's Rosen-crantz (a nervous hearty), and the notion of playing the Second Gravedigger as a supercilious bureaucrat. Almost everything else in Glen Byam Shaw's production is dismal. The courtiers line up like mechanical waxworks, raising their hands in polite em-barrassment when the royal family is exterminated before their eyes. The music is Victorian, the costumes are fussy, and the setting, an arrangement of shiny hexagonal pillars, appears to have been inspired by the foyer of the old Paramount Cinema in Birmingham. The best piece of business (Claudius slapping the face of the Player Murderer) comes from Hugh Hunt's 1950 production. About two of the major performances my feelings are neutral: Cyril Luckham's sane, plodding Polonius and Mark Dignam's Claudius, which very nearly makes up in practical shrewdness what it lacks in dignity and sensuality.

Duerrenmatt's
The Visit of the Old Lady

MELVIN W. ASKEW

I. THE MYTH AND THE RITUAL

In his presentation of the twentieth-century world and Every-man, Duerrenmatt uses a form as old as Greek tragedy and a staging method as modern as surrealism; he uses characters as old as the Sphinx in combination with our contemporaries, Eisen-hower and Nehru; and in his stage business, he uses motifs as old as Oedipal inspired fears of castration, dark, mysterious, and frighteningly uncontrollable, and motifs as new, as light, as ex-plicable as the operation of The-Place-in-the-Sun Foundry and the economics of a simple local grocery store. This total presen-tation he makes with an artistry before which the imagination, even of an imaginative critic, boggles; for with a gorgeously sim-ple style and technique, Duerrenmatt's dramatic lines achieve the stylization of poetry, and move from poetry to myth, where the complex of thought, passion, and affect become infinitely ex-pansible, indefinitely relevant, and meaningful without appar-ent limit.

One's impulse is obviously to speak only in the language of superlatives in an attempt to catch the quality of Duerrenmatt's

Der Besuch in the web of critical language, but faced with the apparently endless ramifications of thematic suggestions and with the dramatic power of the play itself, one's critical language fails woefully to communicate what one knows it ought. Nevertheless, it is the purpose of this essay to study the play from two distinct but obviously related points of view: first, to trace the principal sources of the tremendous (I use the word with its full etymological sense) effects of the play and to describe the world view it mythicizes by analyzing at least four levels of its theme, the psychological, religious, economic, and political: second, to trace in terms of the Aristotelian dialectic of tragedy, the structure and form of the play and the human experience which they embody.

The power of *Der Besuch*, like the power of *Oedipus Rex* or *Oedipus at Colonnus*, derives in great part from its reduction of life to ritual, but the most astonishing and the most profound effect of the play derives—unlike the effect of *Oedipus Rex*—almost exclusively from its successful ritualization and confirmation of some of the deepest, blackest, and perhaps most intolerable suspicions of modern man, as well as by its presentation of an almost hopelessly complex and ambiguous moral issue, one, in fact, which makes those same qualities in Hawthorne and Melville seem almost innocent and secure. The central figure by which this artistic compression and ideological and emotional ritualization occurs is, of course, Madame Zachanassian and especially by her association with the Sphinx; for it is through this sphinx-like figure that all the major themes of the play are introduced: The Sphinx immediately recalls the young ambitious Oedipus, and remembrance of Oedipus recalls immediately the legendary account of his guilt and suggests instantly the psychological theme and the sources of the castration complex which figures largely in this play. Moreover, the Sphinx suggests indirectly the selection of a king, for it is through the medium of her that Oedipus rises to assume command of his kingdom just as Alfred Ill intends to rise to his mayorship (the political theme), but finally rises or falls to greater glory or disrepute. Finally, the Sphinx figure suggests the political situation of the state and re-calls that she was directly responsible for the miserable economic and social conditions in Thebes when Oedipus first arrived, just as Madame Zachanassian is directly responsible for the eco-nomic and social plight of the Gülleners when *Der Besuch* opens, and except for the ravaging plague, the situation of the classi-cal Thebans and the contemporary Gülleners is the same. Thus the major themes of *Der Besuch* emerge from the nexus of the Madame Zachanassian-Sphinx combination and are worked out in the dramatic terms of the Oedipus-Alfred Ill-Clara-Jocasta com-bination, and therefore it occurs that the Oedipus-Ill who meets his sometime lover at the beginning of the play in the figure of Madame Zachanassian, discovers at the end of the play, when he is safely castrated and dead, his Jocasta-Mother-Lover-Sphinx, who will take his body to a shrine in Capri, bedeck his bier faithfully, and preserve and care for his corpse forever.

The hovering and pervasive ritual of *Der Besuch* is first intro-duced ideologically by the appearance of Madame Zachanassian, who, like the Sphinx with whom she is associated, broods from her balcony over the destitution and ruin of the city of Güllen, and this ritual is sustained by Alfred Ill, the "hero" of the play, who, ironically, is not obliged to answer the riddle itself, but rather to answer *to* it. Actually, and to one's dismay, the riddle (in *Der Besuch* concerning among other things Justice) is an-swered by Ill's wife, his church, his contemporaries, and his po-litical officers; and they apparently prosper. But in his answering to the riddle, Ill is sacrificed as the riddle itself demands, and he is sacrificed in an elaborately ritualistic scape-goat form, for as the play progresses, he is delegated progressively more and more of the sinful responsibility of the citizens of his town. And even his execution is ritualized: when he is strangled, he marches between two lines of men who, when the strangulation occurs, form about him an unbroken circle.

Now, in addition to the ritualization of the action of the play, the language and dialogue of the drama are with perfect propriety and decorum the language of ritual. Note, for example the following opening lines which are as highly stylized as the language in the complaint at the opening of *Oedipus* or *Agamemnon* and which deal with subjects not vastly different in tone and import:

THE FIRST: The "Gudrun," Hamburg to Naples.

THE SECOND: At 11:27 comes the "Orlando Furioso," Venice to Stockholm.

THE THIRD: The only pleasure we have left: watching the trains go by.

THE FOURTH: Five years ago the "Gudrun" and the "Orlando Furioso" stopped in Güllen. Also the "Diplomat" and the "Lorelei"—all famous express trains.

THE FIRST: World-famous.

THE SECOND: Not even the passenger trains. Only two locals from Kaffigen and the 1:13 from Kalberstadt.

THE THIRD: Ruination.

THE FOURTH: The wagon-works shut down.

THE FIRST: Bockmann bankrupt.

THE SECOND: The Place-in-the-Sun Foundry washed up.

THE THIRD: Life on the dole.

THE FOURTH: The soup kitchen.

THE FIRST: Life?

THE SECOND: Vegetation.

THE THIRD: Slow death.

THE FOURTH: The whole town.[1]

Here is the language of ritual, spoken by the faceless and representative characters, the dévotée or the priest, and here too is language as highly stylized and as ritualistic as the stychomythia of Greek tragedy. But consider also the following:

THE MAYOR: The bequest of Claire Zachanassian is accepted. Unanimously. Not for the love of money.

THE CROWD: Not for the love of money.

[1] For this and the following quotations, I am indebted to Professor James L. Rosenberg, Carnegie Institute of Technology, not only for his poetic and accurate translation of Duerrenmatt's entire *Der Besuch der Alten Dame*, but also for his description and explanation of the significance of certain words and phrases to those who know German intimately.

THE MAYOR: But rather for the love of justice.
THE CROWD: But rather for the love of justice.
THE MAYOR: And out of the promptings of conscience.
THE CROWD: And out of the promptings of conscience.
THE MAYOR: For we cannot live and yet suffer a criminal among us.
THE CROWD: For we cannot live and yet suffer a criminal among us.
THE MAYOR: A weed which must be uprooted.
THE CROWD: A weed which must be uprooted.

Here, again, is language, style, and action as suggestively ritualized as the responsive reading between cleric and layman, between oracle and supplicant. In the language, then, and in the rhythms of speech familiar to rituals, in the patterns of ritualistic action which have time out of mind given the imagination of man a secure embodiment, a stylized, integral, and imaginatively reassuring representation of his value in the scheme of things, his dignity, and his nobility in the face of inscrutable gods—in this credible and classical medium and in this language, the action and the thematic material of *Der Besuch* is embodied and communicated. But the profoundly disturbing power of the play occurs when the traditional human values ordinarily embodied in ritual are supplanted by materialistic and nonhuman values, when the inscrutable gods become a sphinx-like but real sixty-three-year-old female billionaire with a false hand and a false leg and a history of eight husbands, when her riddle becomes a scheme of vengeance coiled malignantly in the shadows of the language of justice, and when her object becomes the punishment of Everyman, Alfred Ill, who sinned—the primal sin, adultery—with her in his youth. And herein lie some of the sources of the terror, the ambiguity, and the profound effect of the play, and herein too lies the representation of a wholly new mythic Nature, one which can accommodate such actions and themes as Duerrenmatt envisions.

The mythic Nature which Duerrenmatt creates in *Der Besuch* is constructed in the image of the values of the collective rather than in the image of the values of the community. It is a world in which blood and flesh, love and fidelity, dignity and intrinsic human value have *only* cash value, one in which soul and spirit are manipulated by the power of money and the largesse of material wealth which money promises. Indeed, God is replaced by the international exchange and His vicars on earth are fairly obviously those with the greatest riches: these establish ethics, determine the fate and directions of nations, control the movements and the voice of the church, and make (still on the basis of cash values) fine philosophical distinctions, as, for example, the relationship or difference between revenge and justice. Or, slightly differently, this is the materialistic world which we experience daily and know to be true, but the one which we deny vigorously with all the illogical beauty and all the reassurance available in common and classic myth. And the power and the devastating emotional force of the world view and the new mythic Nature created in *Der Besuch* by Duerrenmatt is generated in direct proportion to his success in mythicizing and ritualizing this world of false collective values: thus the forms of reassurance are turned against the auditor and his investment of faith in ritual is returned, when false values are ritualized, with a compounded interest of disillusionment.

If, however, this world and this view of Nature are to be convincing and if they are to retain their *affectiveness*, they must remain unchallenged within the confines of their artistic embodiment. Not only, then, is this view unchallenged in *Der Besuch*, but it is deliberately and exclusively structured. When Madame Zachanassian arrives at Güllen, she arrives on the "Orlando Furioso," instead of the local train, the "12:40 local from Kalberstadt," which ordinarily stops at Güllen, as the "Orlando Furioso" distinctly does not. In order to stop the train, she pulls the emergency cord (which "no one *ever* pulls . . . even in an emergency"). When the train stops and stands hissing and steaming beside the station, the astounded and incredulous Railway Director cries:

The Laws of Nature have been repealed. The "Orlando Furioso" has always emerged from the Leuthenau curve, raced by, and disappeared —a black dot—across the Pückenried Valley.

It scarcely needs to be remarked that the regular, inevitable, and presumably irrevocable movements of the sun and moon have been equated with the movement of the train, but it is much to the point that a change in the motions of the train constitutes a repeal of the laws of Nature, for this is to identify Nature with money, property, material. This indicates that the citizens of Güllen (the citizens representatively of the world) along with the Station Director, have equated the laws of Nature with technology, travel, materialistic enterprise, wealth, the inevitability of "progress," with the world of commerce and industry, the world of supply and demand, the world of cash and carry. In short, the laws of Nature have been entirely divorced from the life and aims of the community and humanity and God, and are now embodied in the aims and enterprise of the collective, the group of insignificant people working toward significant ends, those ends to be realized in the amassing of material wealth and products.

In this new mythic Nature Madame Zachanassian, owner of the Armenian Oil Company, The North Broadcasting Company, the Western Railways, and the entire Hong Kong red-light district (and, as it is revealed, owner of Güllen itself), is the inscrutable God; her money is Providence; and her absolute control of the world and of natural law becomes indisputable as the new myth of Nature grows. She says:

Humanity, gentlemen, is made to be bought and sold by the millionaires of this world. My millions do not obey moral laws; they *create* them. The world made me into a whore, now I make it into a bordello!

Now obviously the entrance of Madame Zachanassian into the world of Güllen establishes a break from the old order of traditional values and establishes a new order of materialistic values and laws. And curiously her entrance into Güllen, her stopping the train, appears to be an interruption, a repeal of natural law, but this is more apparent than real: her stopping the train, far from being a repeal of the laws of Nature, becomes actually a confirmation of those laws of Nature intuited by the

Gülleners and stated by Madame Zachanassian. Note in this regard the following dialogue. The stupefied Conductor asks:

You have stopped the "Orlando Furioso" simply because you wanted to visit Güllen?

Madame Zachanassian replies simply but significantly: *"Naturally."* And with equal significance, after the Conductor discovers who she is, he apologizes by saying:

Oh, pardon, Madame. *Naturally,* that's another matter. We would of course have stopped in Güllen, if we had the slightest hint. . . .

What this dialogue recognizes and states is essentially this: Madame Zachanassian's will and desire can metaphorically change the course of the sun and the moon; the power represented by her money did not repeal the laws of Nature when she pulled the emergency cord, because her power *could not* repeal the laws of Nature: her power *is* (naturally!) the law of Nature. Thus there emerges the new ritualized mythic world with a strange mutilated god, Madame Zachanassian, and a new Providence, the power of her money, and the ironic action which establishes this new Nature (apparently abrogated but actually confirmed by Madame Zachanassian's curious arrival) is sustained by the sustaining irony of the remainder of the play.

After the establishment of this new mythic Nature, indeed, in the first few lines of the play, the drama subsequently becomes a study of the dissolution of the ideas and institutions humanity has clung to for reassurance and support, and a study of disillusionment in the fear, attempted flight, and the fate of Alfred Ill, the Everyman hero. The dissolution begins with religion, with the church, and with the institutionalized promises of meaningful human existence: the holiness of an individual soul, the security of spirit, and the dignity which is lent to humanity by its faith in an intimate relationship with a personal God. This theme is introduced in the following dialogue, early in the drama:

THE MAYOR: Gentlemen, the millionairess is our only hope.
THE PASTOR: Except for God.

THE MAYOR: Except, of course, for God.
THE TEACHER: But He doesn't pay off.

Obviously the Teacher speaks here for Man in the collective and Man with the values of the collective, and no further hope in God is expressed. The pastor does not reply to the Teacher's final statement of meaningful action and meaningful recompense: to pay off!: for he cannot concoct a suitable rebuttal. If, in short, then, an activity does not pay off, and pay off in negotiables, it is no longer good—even if the denial of its goodness is tantamount to a denial of the goodness of God and His Providence. Now the pastor, and through him the church, is not only drawn into this heretical dialectic by his silent acquiescence to this premise, but also he later takes up a rifle to hunt Madame Zachanassian's black panther which at one level is equated to Ill himself. Furthermore, when Ill seeks the succor of the church, the minister, preparing all the while to perform a baptismal service, casually and carelessly puts him off with the easiest, most complacent platitudes. Moreover, while he, in conjunction with the remainder of the town, is planning the death of Ill in order to receive the bequest of Madame Zachanassian, a bequest which will give to the town a half billion dollars and distribute a half billion among all the citizens, the minister with his incredible duplicity or ignorance preaches a sermon based on I Corinthians: 13, the beautiful, and, in the context of the play, the devastatingly ironic verses on charity. Finally, this same man, the agent and instrument of the church, agrees to what is tantamount to the sale of Ill's corpse to Madame Zachanassian for one billion dollars. The power, then, the authority, the beauty, and the security of the church dissolve before masses of money and before the millionaires who create morality and who usurp the position of God's providence in the hearts and imaginations of men.

But what is perhaps even more significant in this theme of the dissolution of religion is one of the symbolic roles of Madame Zachanassian herself, Madame Zachanassian, née Clara Wäscher. Her very name, which means illustrious, bright, or clear washer, is suggestive of at least one of the offices of the church, baptism, the sacrament which purifies the soul and grants rebirth. This office is usurped by Clara. With her arrival she brings an inundating deluge of money, a deluge which clearly washes away what she does not want and clearly sanctifies what she does want. And, ironically, after she has controlled the morality of the citizens of Güllen, after she has contrived their murder of Ill, the city and the people are "saved" economically; they are reborn in her materialistic image, and art, beauty, learning, industry, and enterprise emerge and flourish anew: the city and its people are reborn, suffer a rebirth of material wealth and grandeur just as holy baptism is supposed to inspire a rebirth of the spirit.

The second point of religious dissolution, the dissolution of the sacrament of marriage, is vitally and complexly involved with castration fears, which psychoanalysts contend arise from early Oedipal situations, feelings, and guilts, as well as with the quality of love, simply as a human phenomenon and experience. Now the only indication that love ever existed in Güllen is the story of the youthful love affair between Clara Wäscher and Alfred Ill; but this love was betrayed when Clara brought a suit against Ill to force his acknowledgement of his illegitimate child; when he bribed two witnesses (with schnapps) to testify that they had also slept with Clara; and when the judge delivered an unjust verdict. After this, Ill married his present wife, presumably because she had a modest sum of money from hardware and they could establish their small grocery business. Clara, in her own words, became a whore. Now, during the separation of Clara and Alfred, the pestilence and sterility of absolute and abject poverty descended on the city, but, as one learns later in the play, by the intentional financial designs and manipulations of Clara, subsequently become Madame Zachanassian. When Madame Zachanassian returns—in her role precisely identical to that of the Sphinx at the Gates of Thebes—Alfred Ill assumes the role of Oedipus, who must be the deliverer of the city; hence, the Oedipal feelings are symbolized in the actual Oedipus-role which Alfred plays. Thus the drama opens with the chorus of pain and disenchantment and sterility from the four men; it is agreed that Alfred Ill is the only man to save them, to deal with Madame Zachanassian, and to become the Mayor of the city (the municipal substitute for the king of the city-state), and when he discovers at what terrible price he will save the city, he performs his passive and pathetically weak agon, a half-hearted but nonetheless nightmarish attempt to escape. He then yields to his fate (the fate controlled by the laws of Nature, the money and will of Madame Zachanassian, now in the role of the gods), and to his banishment (he cannot be made mayor), and finally to his death. Güllen is saved as was Thebes.

With perfect consistency with the psychological implications of the entire Oedipus myth and the guilt feelings and castration terrors to which it gives rise—as well as, indeed, with perfect consistency with the sexual implications of the figure of the Sphinx (the half-woman who "eats up" the men who try her riddle)— Madame Zachanassian plays the role of the castrating female, and, insofar as the sphinx-half-woman concept is concerned, it is significant here that Madame Zachanassian is perhaps one-half prosthetic, for she has, among other things, a prosthetic leg and an ivory hand. Thus she returns to Güllen to go into competition with Alfred Ill, to wage her billion dollars against his lifetime spent in his village—a battle which she is obviously confident of winning because she brings his coffin along with her. But her will, her means, and her ends are set diametrically against his, and Alfred Ill is left defeated, passive, and completely helpless, completely castrated after her overpowering and insidious onslaught. And partially symbolic of her role as the castrating female is the black panther which she brings along in her retinue. This panther, which is ambiguously symbolic of Alfred Ill too, since she once called him her black panther, is symbolic of the darkness and destructiveness of her love, and yet of its power, and even perhaps of its grace. But also, in terms of the phantasy life, it is horribly and viciously toothed, to rend, to mutilate, and to emasculate.

But symbols are scarcely needed in view of Madame Zachanassian's history and her actions in Güllen. She brings with her two eunuchs, Koby and Loby, the castrated and blinded (like Oedipus), the false witnesses whom Alfred Ill had mustered before the court years before. These two eunuchs are portrayed as having no ability to think, as having no aggressiveness, indeed, as being unable to do anything but take orders, answer simple questions, and repeat endlessly and doubly their replies. Note the following passage:

POLICEMAN: Who are you?
THE TWO: We belong to the old lady, we belong to the old lady. She calls us Koby and Loby.
POLICEMAN: Madame Zachanassian is staying at the "Golden Apostle."
THE TWO: We're blind, we're blind.
POLICEMAN: Blind? Then I'll take the two of you there.
THE TWO: Thank you, Mr. Policeman, thank you very kindly.

This early passage sets the pattern of the double reply for castrati, of a double reply delivered in this same sing-song fashion. Note, then, that according to the patterns of speech established here, Madame Zachanassian ultimately castrates the entire community as symbolized in the following dialogue in which "All" represents the townspeople who have decided to kill Alfred Ill in order to get the billion dollar bequest.

POLICEMAN (*to* ILL): You're much safer here.
ALL: Much safer, much safer. . . .
THE MAYOR: No one wants to kill you.
ALL: No one, no one. . . .
THE TEACHER: A man of honor!
ALL: A man of honor! a man of honor!

The suggestion, then, is clearly that Madame Zachanassian has not only successfully castrated the two false witnesses, to date eight husbands, but also that she has castrated the entire community.

Alfred Ill's castration occurs not only in his accumulating passivity, in his total loss of masculine aggressiveness and strength, in a weakness which leads him ultimately to kneel passively before the murderous "manhood" represented by a muscle-man (himself castrated along with the rest), but also in the deterioration of his marital relationship and his loss of control or even relationship with his children. To both his wife and his children, Alfred Ill ceases to be husband and father: he is a thing, he is an object worth one billion dollars, and as a matter of fact, his life, his being are already given up—for them he is already dead—in lieu of the wealth that will come to them through his death. His daughter begins taking expensive lessons in literature, art, and French; his son buys a new car; and his wife buys a new mink coat—all on credit, all on time, against the time when the citizens will kill him and money will be abundant.

It is here that the decay of the sacrament of marriage fades into the theme of the castration complex born of Oedipal guilts, and that both point to a distinctly human problem which brings with it eventually not simply a human truth but a socio-economic truth as well. The human truth is, of course, by now painfully obvious: that no loving relationship can exist between the woman who must castrate and the male who will eventually renounce his manhood; that no love is aroused and sustained in a family where the nominal head no longer represents authority and strength and endurance; that the tenderest as well as the strongest feelings of love are contingent upon the responsible fulfillment of these roles with both the biological and the metaphorical heart, and to renounce the responsibility is to renounce the humanity, and to renounce the humanity is to renounce the reward of the relationship, the love.

It must be remembered, however, that the ultimate figure in the entire complex of this massive castration is Madame Zachanassian herself, and that the agent and instrument of her craft is money, wealth, and materialism; thus, the human truth of the situation fades into a socio-economic truth: in a totally materialistic world, like Güllen, where all relationships are figured on a cash and carry basis, where all symbiosis has as its sole medium money and credit, there can be no love in the humanistic sense of the word —no more than there can be individual love as in marriage. But there is a way in which money itself symbolically castrates or mutilates the possessors of it (if money itself and materialism represent their total life drive), and leaves them totally incompetent to recognize the soul, self-stuff, or identity of another person, leaves them totally unable to sympathize, respect, admire, or even to respond to the human *figure* as a human *being*. In such a system the identity of each figure is based on the function of the figure, and the person *is* what the person *does*, and the value of what the person does is measured entirely on the basis of the profit (the commodity) his activity yields: thus, if one ceases to yield profit, one ceases to be and/or to be important; or, if one source is more lucrative than another source, the more lucrative is obviously the better, and with a system such as this, distressingly close to the system of the world as well as of Güllen, humanity is indeed intended to be bought and sold, and the masses of money and the millionaires create and direct morals, morality, and relationships between semi-human functionaries. And it is through this system of developments from the original impulse of Madame Zachanassian that the entire world, based on a false system of values, becomes desexed, demoralized, and dehumanized, and the values of human love and respect, religious awe and reverence crumble, and the institutions built to preserve these values decay under the blight and defacement of humanity by money and money-ethic.

Carrying his audience upon the turgid and frightening flow of castration anxieties which are actualized in the drama itself, Duerrenmatt shows, then, the devastating effect of sheer and unalleviated materialism upon the institutions of one's own manhood and self-integrity, upon the church, upon the institutions of social intercourse, mutual respect, dignity, and humanistic love; and finally, in his ever-broadening sphere of relevance, he shows the extension of this same impulse into every modern political institution and completes his new mythic world and the new modern mythic Nature with its laws.

In Act II of *Der Besuch*, Madame Zachanassian assumes most distinctly her role of Sphinx and of the surrogate materialistic God. Most of the action of this section occurs in Alfred Ill's grocery, but it is witnessed by Madame Zachanassian and her intended ninth husband from the balcony of the hotel. She hovers, then, over the entire action, and her billions control it. But the extension of her materialistic, castrating, and dehumanizing force into the political institutions of the world occurs in this act when she casually remarks the names of those who are "on her side," who wish her well, and who are vitally involved in her welfare, since, the implication clearly is, her welfare is intimately related to their own. In this regard she gets notes of congratulation from Ike (Eisenhower) and Nehru; she reveals that she has been intimate with Count Holk and The Foreign Minister (generic, it seems, for them all); she gives instructions that the "Russians" be called and informed that she is "in agreement with their proposition"; she seduced one of her husbands in Buckingham Palace and kissed Lord Ismael in the shadow of the Sphinx; she indicates that Winston (Churchill) and The Duke and Duchess send their regards, and that (Aristotle) Onassis and the Aga Khan intend to attend her ninth wedding; finally, she indicates that the sedan chair which takes her every place (literally) was a gift from the President of France.

That this chair is carried by two criminals who were reprieved at the request of her one-million dollar payment indicates simply further the symbolic significance of her mode of movement on criminal energies, the pernicious results of her progress through the world, and the way in which the captains and leaders of the world as well as the small folk of Güllen have identified with her pestilential force and worship and pay homage to it. It also marks the last piece in the mythic pattern of the new mythic world and the new mythic Nature presented in the language and the forms of ritual, the new mythos which Duerrenmatt creates in *Der Besuch*. It is a world, needless to say, not unlike the world figured forth in *Brave New World* or in *Animal Farm:* but it is a new world with a difference. It is a world which is cast into some of the most famous legends and stories of Western civilization; a world recreated in the rhythms of the chant and the song, in the rhythms and the language of ritual; a world in which the modern forces and the modern ethics are embodied in the ancient figure of the Sphinx, the Sphinx who squats malignantly by the gates of all our cities; a world in which Everyman, as Alfred Ill or Oedipus, follows the patterns of his destruction, patterns of destruction wrought beyond, perhaps, his individual control: a world faced with an old figure with a new riddle, a riddle that must be solved by the warm passions of the blood and the fever of the brain.

II. THE MAN AND THE PASSION

The tragedy of Alfred Ill is that body and soul he becomes a commodity, both on the world market as represented by Madame Zachanassian and on the local market as represented by the citizens of Güllen. The bargain which Madame Zachanassian brings with her is the purchase of Justice, just as years before Alfred Ill, with a couple of bottles of schnapps had purchased injustice: for the corpse of Alfred Ill she will pay one billion dollars; for her, Ill has ceased to exist—as witnessed by the coffin she brings for him; and, for the citizens of Güllen he—as human—ceases to exist—he is commodity. And the tragic passions—pity and fear—are dramatized as a result of our knowing and intimate understanding of the feelings, the fear, the terror, and the hope of this *man,* which are set off in relief against the impassive and immutable backdrop of the monolithic attitude of the people of his city, the people who can no longer conceptualize him or sympathize with him as person or man but only see him as thing, only evaluate him as a commodity.

Quite correctly Alfred Ill recognizes that his situation is of his own creation, that he has spun out of his own motives and values the forces which destroy him. In the third act, he states in a moment of truth his astonishing comprehension of his position:

I made Clara what she is, just as I made myself what I am—a greasy old bag of wind running a broken-down shop. What should I do, teacher of Güllen? Play innocent? They're all my creations—the eunuchs, the butler, the coffin, the billions. I can no longer help myself—nor you.

And his point is absolutely correct. He—as Everyman in the modern world—established the set of values which destroys him. Years before he sold out his young spontaneous love of Clara Wäscher and abandoned his "love child" so that he might have material comfort. In order to marry a woman who had a little money and who could help him start a "secure" and "respectable" business, he literally sold the truths of the heart and repudiated them. Now he is faced with the magnified mirror image of his own doings in the figure of Madame Zachanassian, who has sold out an astonishing succession of lovers, who has, as a partial human being, operated almost solely on a cash and carry basis, and who now returns to buy Alfred Ill as he once sold her: to buy justice for her money as he, ironically, bought injustice with his —terrible confirmation of her statement that humanity is bought and sold and that money dictates institutional morality.

In this regard, then, Alfred Ill is a tragic hero in the classic sense: he is finally undone by a weakness of his own heart and mind and values; he detaches from himself a motive embodied in his action before the judge, and that motive grows to grotesque and almost absurd proportions in the figure of Madame Zachanassian, and it returns to destroy him. The act, then, which resulted from his shirking the responsibility of his original sin— adultery—and from his advocation of the totally materialistic values at the complete expense of the heart, weaves about him an iron tissue of necessity which finally strangles him in the figure of the athlete. And one of the deeply disturbing riddles of the drama is answered: How can man live with the values of the collective? How can man live when his entire being is evaluated as commodity, as thing to be bought and sold in the market-place? How can man live in a completely materialistic world where the individual is submerged beneath the group, where the good life is the "rich" life, where independence, distinction, and the needs of the heart atrophy away? And the play, *Der Besuch,* supplies the terrifying answer: He cannot.

The anagogical meaning of the play, then, becomes perfectly clear: Man has established an arbitrary set of values in a monetary system, and these values are achieved in the market-place by the process of buying and selling and storing. But finally the system of monetary valuation becomes so strong that is is obedient *only* to the *laws* which promoted it; it becomes autonomous and no longer controllable—just as Madame Zachanassian is. When it becomes autonomous and stronger than any individual man, it reflects upon its creator and re-creates him in its own image, and thus man himself becomes a commodity on the market, and his humanity disappears. Even his life, his very innermost and human existence is threatened, the play indicates, and Man needs no longer, the admonition is, to wait for germ-warfare, the atom bomb, or the hydrogen bomb to destroy him: he is progressively destroying himself with the values of the collective, the values that raise the worth of commodities with the defacement of the human and dignified life.

The terrible unrestrained progression of this kind of human destruction forms the inevitability of the plot, and the agents of destruction are created by geometric progression. In the city of Güllen one man, Alfred Ill, sinned against the heart for the sake of the money that his new fiancée might bring to him, and as we have seen, he is destroyed by the magnified mirror image of this gesture. But, now, and in the course of the play, *all* the citizens of Güllen are sinning against the human heart in order to get the money which the corpse of Ill will bring: they too are entering the process of creating the eunuchs, the butlers, and the Clara

Zachanassians, and they too, in poetic justice, will sometime be faced with the gigantic image of their sin, and will, presumably, be destroyed by it. Thus, the plot operates on the absolute classical lines of necessity and probability: each action is poetically and rationally necessary after the original sin of Alfred Ill; the plot structure is absolutely integral, and, through the figure of Ill-Everyman, the significance of the action is projected into universal relevance.

Clearly *Der Besuch* is tragic in intent and accomplishment: it employs classical myth, ritual, and language; it is obviously modeled in part at least upon the *Oedipus Rex;* Alfred Ill is a tragic hero in the classic sense; and the plot structure follows upon inevitable lines of necessity. Moreover, the tragic passions, pity and fear, are distinctly aroused; but with equal distinctness, these passions are *not* purged by aesthetic catharsis. The final form of the play is "open"; in the sense used by Robert M. Adams in *Strains of Discord;* that is to say that the tensions aroused in the play are finally not completely composed, and, like the *Hippolytus* of Euripides, *Der Besuch* ends by posing an apparent problem, an apparent dilemma, a new and unanswered riddle, as it were, of the speechless Sphinx.

This "openness" is the culmination of a series of apparent opposites melded in the play, a rhythmic composition of such objects as the realistic and common setting with which the play opens, that is, the run-down railway station and the four loafers, with the contrasting and phantasylike appearance of Clara Zachanassian, borne in a sedan chair by two gum-chewing and monstrous ex-criminals and followed by two castrati, her eighth husband, a black panther, a stone idol and a coffin; or by the rhythmic composition of the attitudes of the people of Güllen toward Alfred Ill: at the first of the play they revere him and look to him for the salvation of their city; at the end of the play they malign him and heartlessly sacrifice him for the billion dollar bequest; or by the juxtaposition and rhythm between such scenes as those that occur in the grocery store where citizens come in to buy bread and beer and sausages with such scenes as the one in the forest where the trees are played by the four loafers, while the sound of a woodpecker is imitated by beating a tobacco can with a key.

The problem and the enigma of the play is posed by the following contrast: How can the heartless and inhuman murder of the scape-goat, Ill, actually result in the accomplishment indicated in the final choral songs of the play which indicate that art flourishes in Güllen, that the cathedral is full to bursting at Christmastime, Easter and Whitsuntide, that the people drive new cars and limousines, that there is a new amphitheatre where interns are taught surgery, that learning blooms and industry expands. How, in short, can such apparently good things be purchased at the price of Alfred Ill's blood? And the answer is not, avowedly, an easy one.

First of all, it must go without saying that art and learning flourish and blossom during a time of comparative material wealth and comfort: scholarship—indeed as the word etymologically states—and art must be provided first of all with leisure, and it is not without significance that all the Miltons who followed the plow remain "unsung." But it certainly cannot be overlooked that the principal emphasis placed upon the "good times" in Güllen is embodied pre-eminently in material terms: the cars, the buildings, the dresses, and it cannot be overlooked either that the church—which Duerrenmatt is careful to point out has "The *Last* Judgment" on the door—is crowded, like our own, only during special observances. In view of this, the last choral song sung by all the citizens of Güllen can be read as pure, stupid credulity on their part, pure irony on the dramatist's part.

It reads as follows:

> May God yet protect us
> In the perilous days
> Of pounding prosperity;
> Protect our holy and sacred purity;
> Preserve our peace, preserve our freedom;
> Night, remain distant!

Nevermore darken the streets of our town.
Protect, O God, the newly established
Splendor of life
Wherewith we happy ones nourish our happiness.

The stage directions and the context of this choral ode indicate
the mediocrity of its spirituality and its validity as a commentary
on the entire action of the play. In the first place, the stage directions given before the choral parts indicate "the Gülleners,
men and women in evening clothes and tail-coats, are gathered.
They form into two choruses, similar to the chorus of Greek tragedy, the voice of the community. It [the voice of the community]
is like a sinking ship sending out a last signal as it goes slowly
down." This falling and sinking note is grim enough and augurs
no good, it seems, for the Gülleners. But notice again the introduction to this final choral ode. Madame Zachanassian approaches the train station with the corpse of Ill, and when she
appears the Mayor says:

> THE MAYOR: Here she comes—
> ALL: The bringer of blessings!
> THE DAUGHTER (*of* ILL): The giver of good!
> ALL: Accompanied by her rich entourage!
> THE MAYOR: Long live the lady!
> ALL: Long live her goodness!
> RAILWAY STATION DIRECTOR: *All* aboard!

Indeed, the final impact of the play occurs in the horrible implications of the Railroad Station Director's speech. The bringer
of all blessings and the giver of all good is God, and the god of
the Gülleners is Madame Zachanassian, and the people of Güllen have been baptized in the flow of her materialistic values
and reborn in her own image: they are all aboard—all aboard the
sinking ship—but more importantly, all aboard the train which
in the first few lines of the play indicated the new mythic Nature
and the new set of collective values which destroys and de-
humanizes man. Hence, their voices sound like the last wail of a
sinking ship, and their joy, like the joy of the Thebans after the
departure of the Sphinx, will be short-lived, and they will all in-

evitably be faced with the embodiment of their own guilt just as Alfred Ill—the Everyman—was, and like him too, they will be destroyed.

But in spite of the clarity of the significance of these last few choric lines, which bring the play to its conclusion and assert its complete artistic integrity, the effect which it leaves is nonetheless deeply disturbing, and the implications and the assertions of *Der Besuch* haunt one's associations and raise gaunt and phantasmal spectres in the bright secure world of neon lights, automobiles, and television sets; but it stands as a beautiful artistic medium through which one may see at what expense of spirit and humanity the goods of the world are purchased and how disastrous are the consequences of Everyman's total commitment to the Madame Zachanassians of the world.

Mr. Duerrenmatt Buys New Shoes

GORDON ROGOFF

The returns are in. A Swiss playwright has been "discovered." A year ago the name of Friedrich Duerrenmatt suddenly studded the hopeful theatrical gossip of the alert drinkers in the Salisbury, Cranborne, and Arts Theatre. No director worthy of the name "Peter" was without curiosity. To acquire the production rights for *The Visit of the Old Lady* would be considered a virtual *coup d'état* for any ambitious directorial career. Travelers from the continent regaled us with stories: one had seen the play in Munich with Therese Giehse, a famous Mother Courage seen here in Benedek's film *Kinder, Mutter, und Ein General;* another had seen the great Käthe Dorsch as the Old Lady; yet another the Paris production (not a notable success) with that delicate, withered little bundle remembered from many French films, Mme. Sylvie. Copies of the French version were floating mysteriously from hand to hand in the back rooms of the West End; the big question, Which Peter would win? The answer was predictable though in the nature of an anti-climax. Peter the First had won because in his endless travels abroad he had been the first to make the discovery; three months before the talk he had quietly secured the rights.

455

What had we learned about Duerrenmatt and his play during all that chat and maneuvering? Some of the facts handed to us might have been half-fact, but from the weight of the evidence, we could at least deduce that Duerrenmatt was a relatively young Swiss with at least four major plays in his drawer, that *The Visit* was the most theatrically spectacular, that it was a magnificent vehicle for one of the Dames if she would be willing to place herself in a play where the real star was a town and where she herself would be required to act her age. No one was willing to give anything more than a brief summary of the story line which sounded simple and direct, yet left many questions of possible allegory and parable unanswered. That was fair enough, we felt, since we would eventually be treated to Mr. Brook's production in which all the continental enthusiasm would be clarified. Most reassuring of all, we were solemnly informed that Mr. Duerrenmatt was a man of unyielding integrity, was refusing permission to many European bidders because he felt that some of the productions had already distorted his play beyond his own recognition. Naively, perhaps, we forgot the natural impurity of our commercial theatre and assumed that such continental success would undoubtedly be repeated—free of distortion—in England and America. After all, why should our theatre tamper with what had already proved a good selling item elsewhere? With Brook offstage and a Dame on stage, Mr. Duerrenmatt couldn't miss.

The rest of the history is more publicly familiar. At each new turn our initial elation and eagerness to see the play had to wage a losing war of attrition. Not a suitably aging Dame giving way to a town, but the Lunts would star in the play. Mixed feelings here. On the one hand, how splendid that they should come out of hiding from the harmless and genteel Coward-Lindsay-Crouse mausoleums. On the other, what would their undeniable talent, yet equally unavoidable glamour do to this sacredly profane and serious play about which we had heard so much? We had heard little of the man's role in the drama and

we couldn't help regretting that the more accomplished member
of the team should be once again playing *mezza-voce* to the ageless prima donna. Still . . . with Mr. Brook in command, the town
seemed a safe, if unsung, star.

Once again we were conveniently forgetful. The commercial
dike had already sprung too many ominous leaks and there were
more to come. To be sure, the English-language version appeared to be in reliable hands. Mr. Maurice Valency was best
known for his adaptations from the French, particularly Giraudoux' *The Madwoman of Chaillot, The Enchanted* (*Intermezzo*
in the original) and *Ondine.* The history here was respectable. If
we troubled to think about it, we could bring several doubts to
mind, though we preferred to suppress them. For instance, that
word *adaptation.* Why? Why not *translation?* Were we not entitled to *echt* Duerrenmatt? The argument that natural teutonic
loquacity made the play too long for the average Anglo-American sitting powers didn't really convince; the truly Wagnerian
heavenly lengths of the two latest Eugene O'Neill successes made
something of a lie out of that. The hint that original Duerrenmatt was unmercifully nasty and unpleasant might be true, but
what of it? Were not the stars insurance enough? Furthermore,
imagine John Osborne *adapted* into German or French, not simply translated, but adapted with the nastiness, scathing sar-
casm, and seediness of Jimmy Porter and Archie Rice removed
or softened at the harsh outer edges. Would we consider that fair
representation? Still . . . why be fearful and presumptuous? The
Giraudoux-Valency "collaborations" were written in clear, cool
prose that was accessible to actors and therefore stage worthy.
True, lurking in the background was the awful memory of Mr.
Lunt's production of *Ondine* with Audrey Hepburn and Mel Fer-
rer, a dismal *meringue glacé,* baronial, inflated, and largely un-
intelligible. There however we had good reason to lay blame
squarely at the leaden feet of the incompetent stars. Mr. Lunt,
up against unmanageable acting material and the management's
obvious fears about selling French confectionery to the Broadway

blue-haired dowagers, couldn't be held unforgiveably responsible; and Mr. Valency seemed to do his work in a straightforward, craftsmanlike way. Once more we could comfort ourselves: at least the management that now owned the Duerrenmatt play didn't suddenly come up with the bright idea of asking Audrey Hepburn to play the Old Lady.

Next chapter. As Lynn Fontanne moved in, the Old Lady moved out. Even the *"Visit"* was temporarily removed from the title, and for a time the British provinces knew the play in a vague, amorphous, what-does-it-mean title, *Time and Again.* Castillo was designing Miss Fontanne's costumes, we heard reports of a glorious red wig, we felt alternately assured and amused when we heard of the retention of the original Old Lady's cigars; but of course we knew it all along: no former Mother Courage was playing Claire Zachanassian. We could only continue to hope; if compromises were to be made, they would be made by Miss Fontanne in the direction of honest, true-to-text, serious acting.

Meanwhile back in the unglamorous lower regions of New York, in a confining and unsuitable off-Broadway theatre, we had an opportunity to see one of the other Duerrenmatt plays, his first European theatrical success (in 1952), *The Marriage of Mississippi,* given under the title *Fools Are Passing Through,* presumably to avoid confusion with the American state and river. Once again the play was listed in the program as an adaptation, this time by Mr. Maximilian Slater who also directed it. Mr. Slater's previous work was a relatively unknown quantity in New York, although his Viennese background appeared distinguished: a pupil of Max Reinhardt, he was for six years a Director of the Theatre in "der Josefstadt." Without both texts before us we could never be certain how much Duerrenmatt and how much Slater we were seeing and hearing. Mr. Slater's English often sounded very German, but the impression was unmistakable that the real Duerrenmatt was being set before us. Here indeed was a man of prodigious gifts. His theatrical inventions were bold, and in the midst of a bitter and sardonic drama, audaciously punctuated with sharp wit and cutting satire. Unlike what we knew of *The Visit*, the plot was virtually beyond summary. The play literally began with its final scene, the murder of a man who, white tie and tails notwithstanding, turned out to be an opportunistic Communist rebel leader; after his murder he gets up to tell us that we have just witnessed the last scene. (Brecht influence do you think? With Duerrenmatt we soon learn not to jump to such clear conclusions.) Impossible to grasp a story line here, we happily settled for the exhilarating quick changes in development, the totally unpredictable exchanges between one character and another, the sense we were getting of a brilliant private world, cruel, brutally and honestly observed, mushroom cloud perhaps hovering overhead, amoral to a man and woman. Yet even in its amorality, just when we were being led to believe that all human beings and all human institutions are doomed to inevitable corruption, one character was permitted to stretch feeble arms above the cloud. The fool: a comic and undeniably pathetic figure always on the fringe of the play's intrigue, he is presented to us first in his plot role, the dubious heroine's ex-lover, a true romantic Count, now destitute because in his jungle missionary work he was continually rebuffed and robbed by his patients and disciples; no longer useful to his whore, or to anybody else for that matter, he spends the rest of the play talking to himself and to the audience, and is finally presented in his true role. The play's final image is of the Count, lance in hand and helmet on head, acting the noblest fool of all, Don Quixote. It is a startling image, making one feel that to understand Duerrenmatt we shall have to return to Cervantes. Yet this too may be a leap into a dark alley.

What now could we say we know of Duerrenmatt? At once original and eclectic, he seemed a writer who saw the world in disorder and wrote of it in a disorderly manner. Influences seemed abundant: certainly German expressionism in his stage freedom; writers such as Cervantes, Brecht, Pirandello, even Shaw if one considers some of the twists and shifts during ideological and moral arguments between a public prosecutor and a prime minister. Unafraid to tackle enormous worldly concepts, Duerrenmatt seemed a playwright more interested in ideas than characters. Although more puppets than people, his characters almost always come to life theatrically. Their behaviour was logical if one could find logic in the life of a snake pit, yet accepting the mental writhings of this unique world, we were almost prepared to accept it as a painfully accurate reflection of our own world. If we could scarcely ever identify with Duerrenmatt's people, we could easily identify with his atmosphere. The thickly textured chaos of his amoral world had a strange clarity and credibility.

One thing was now certain. On his own terms he could be no more popular a playwright than Beckett or Brecht. The critics were, as always, condescending in the face of their confusion. The production was unavoidably cramped; the acting bordered on distinction only in the case of the Count-Quixote figure, Mr. Martin Waldron, but the rest ran the gamut from sincere to indifferent to mediocre. Only on the strength of building an audience out of people curious about the Lunts' new playwright could *Fools Are Passing Through* hope for success. Predictably, people curious about the Lunts were not curious about their taste; the production closed after twenty-four performances.

Our first live encounter with Duerrenmatt had now aroused an insatiable curiosity. We felt we were at last to make the discovery for ourselves already made by our continental back room colleagues and friends. We felt definite confidence in the new playwright; a man of strong mind and daring technique, he wouldn't fail to clarify himself soon, particularly in what we understood to be a better play. Forgive us our trespasses, but we were also curious now about his various commitments, literary, theatrical, social, and political. Was he forging his own style in the theatre? Was his view comic? Or was he seeking a particularly contemporary approach to tragedy? We didn't want to snare him and lock him in any one familiar compartment, but we desired more clues about his direction. Unfortunately with each new clue the confusions and apparent contradictions were as maddening as . . . as a Duerrenmatt character.

First Mr. Duerrenmatt on what (we thought) could be fairly described as his theatrical and social commitment: in his essay "Problems of the Theatre" we are told that he argues that the time for writing tragedies has passed; that for tragedies we need a well organized world, with established standards of guilt and personal responsibilities; our disorganized world, in which we live "like Gulliver among the Giants" (yet another literary influence, Swiftian satire), powerless to resist the course of events bigger than ourselves, calls for comedy, not born of despair but of courage. "The World for me," says Mr. Duerrenmatt, "stands as something monstrous, an enigma of calamity that has to be accepted but to which there must be no surrender." We are naively informed by the writer of the program note for *Fools Are Passing Through* that "this is the message of Friedrich Duerrenmatt."

Second, Mr. Duerrenmatt on messages. In an interview published in the *New York Times* (May 25, 1958) he is represented as saying that the first maxim of playwriting is that the theatre is no place for maxims. "When you write a play you don't do it to teach a lesson or prove a point or build a philosophy because you can never force art to prove anything." The evidence of *Fools Are Passing Through*, particularly the lack of independent life in the characters, proved that the playwright and thinker were not practicing in agreement.

Now we were coming closer to the arrival of *The Visit*, and we braced ourselves for new assaults on Duerrenmatt-analysis, *ergo* new confusions. Duerrenmatt had said that ours was not a time for tragedy. Mr. Valency writing in the *New York Times* (May 4, 1958) and the May issue of *Theatre Arts Magazine* called *The Visit* a "modern tragedy" or "a tragedy played by comic characters," not "eine tragische Komödie" as Duerrenmatt had originally dubbed it. Thoroughly unenlightened, we could only conclude that semantics can be stupefying. We would call the play a "play" and leave it at that.

At last the play. Or rather . . . the adaptation. We were warned by Mr. Valency in his *Times* article not to take *The Visit* as a modern morality play. "It has no allegory. Its doctrine has nothing to do with contemporary ideology." The theme is simply that money is the root of all evil. Economic necessity is our culture's substitute for Greek fate. We could be forgiven if we felt the hot breath of one particular contemporary ideology in the Duerrenmatt background. At least we had good reason to suspect that he had read one or two famous nineteenth- and twentieth-century philosophers, even if nobody connected with the play or production was about to admit such a possibility. But once again it seemed best not to be overwhelmed by all the hedging, the gentle apologies, the subtle contradictions: so the play is not a modern morality, yet it is a modern tragedy (no, no tragedy says Duerrenmatt), it has no allegory, yet (says Mr. Valency in *Theatre Arts*) "it is a hard contemporary reality" that it depicts. We couldn't help remembering those reports from Germany last year when it was suggested that the Old Lady was America making her post-war visit to Germany on her own economic terms: sell out everything and you will buy recovery, stability, and power. It had even been suggested in more general terms that the play was founded on the notion of the inevitable corruption that follows when any society is based on the profit motive. We could easily surmise that Duerrenmatt was no formal modern Communist, but wasn't it just barely possible that the impulse for his play was not primarily Greek, medieval, Christian and timeless, but rather a bitter observation—and criticism—of the entire structure of capitalist society? However, we had been asked to enter the theatre with no such dangerous and direct thoughts stimulating our minds. To each his own.

What did we finally see in the theatre? A thoroughly professional and often impressive theatrical collaboration. The Valency version, taken (as it had to be) strictly on its own, was a clean, spare conception written in much plainer English than Mr. Slater's *Fools Are Passing Through*. The story line could scarcely have been clearer; the inexorable drive to the cruel, unsparing trial and murder scene was handled with swiftness and unyielding directness. The thick texture of Mr. Slater's Duerrenmatt was totally absent. Even while surrendering to the stunning visceral impact of the play we couldn't help thinking that a fine cutting comb had been working on Duerrenmatt. Arguments seemed to be missing; credible reasons for individual behavior didn't seem to be there (the Anton Schill we see seems so utterly incapable of the youthful act of callous cruelty or the present act of heroic resignation); the second-act desertion of Schill by the town occurred too quickly. We realized that we were being asked to accept certain motivations and behavior almost by definition. A barber had been thinning hair: the impression of a full head of hair remained, but important strands were missing.

Mr. Brook's production had considerable surface brilliance. As usual the stage pictures were models of design, color, and light. Often we felt the stealthy ritual hands of the Andronicii; fortunately the "Titus" mood was not inappropriate to the play: Grand Guignol with a velvet touch. Presumably Mr. Theo Otto had as much to do with the deceptive Brechtian atmosphere as Mr. Brook. The simplicity and grandeur of his backdrop, cut-out sets, moving furniture, and flying lights helped to make this one of the least heavy and most fluid productions seen on our customarily overloaded stage. Thanks to Mr. Brook's and Mr. Otto's keen visual sense the production always gave an illusion of single-mindedness, clarity, and even style.

The atmosphere of compromise and confusion surrounding this production couldn't be so easily escaped, however. In the end, any play depends upon its direct interpretation, which means its acting. Here—despite individual brilliance—is where too much of *The Visit* broke down. Just as we couldn't fail to question the intelligibility of the Valency version, we had to question its interpretation. Mr. Brook has always been more an incomparable choreographer and oratorio conductor than an actor's director. Here too he couldn't hammer his individual actors into a unified style; perhaps that is too much to ask in our theatre with its current lack of rehearsal time and lack of traditions. Miss Fontanne, technically able, splendid as always to the eye (unlike Duerrenmatt's Old Lady), strayed in from the world of high comedy; we were forced to accept the menace of Claire Zachanassian again by definition. Mr. Lunt, working against the sudden shifts of the given text, set a standard that might well have been followed by all—if they had his unique talent. Cautious, delicate, stepping on horror with the tips of his toes, he presented a moving, muted figure drawn from the outer spaces of a naturalistic style. Nobody else was given much chance to make a vivid impression, although Mr. Peter Woodthorpe tried a few sharp, boyish uppercuts on his role of the teacher who tries not to sell out; and Mr. Eric Porter gruffly set about making the Burgomaster into the one authentic mittel-European character in the production. Accents clashed and traditions rubbed noses. In yet another aspect of the Duerrenmatt saga . . . to each his own.

The cycle now completed—Duerrenmatt rumors to Duerrenmatt reality—we could only feel that somewhere along the commercial line we had been let down, if not precisely sold out like Schill. Upon post-production investigation, we learned that not only was half the title given to us in the Anglo-American production, only half the play was used. The greatest excision came in that swift and puzzling second act. The sell-out of Schill was a slower, more insidious process in Duerrenmatt's text; therefore it must have been more credible. The citizens of the town begin to buy on credit from Schill's shop, and from scene to scene we apparently learn that yet another man or woman has bought a fancy new pair of shoes (altogether they never have cash on hand for Schill); in this version, the shoes have been bought by the citizens, the new bells by the church, almost before we have time to digest the fact that they have considerably reversed their position. The new shoes too must be accepted by definition.

It is a cynical and morbid reflection of our world, this Duerrenmatt play, no matter which version is presented. We are told reliably that Mr. Duerrenmatt agreed to all the changes suggested by his Anglo-American collaborators. It is certainly true that this version works in the theatre on a far higher level of endeavor and achievement than most of the plays we see. Yet we can't help feeling cheated. Perhaps if the playwright honestly observes the world around him and sees nothing but corruption and compromise, he feels no particular twinge of pain when his own work is sold to the bourgeois, materialist public he is criticizing so that much of his harsh criticism is stifled, though not entirely snuffed out. Perhaps he is what is quaintly known these days as a "realist." His *Fools Are Passing Through*, more translated than adapted, was a failure. By selling his *Old Lady* to the people who were best qualified to sell it to an unserious public, he has bought himself a hit.

We can almost visualize the business transaction as directed by Mr. Brook. The lights are dim, only shafts of sharp light piercing the gray atmosphere. Flash bulbs blind our eyes. A mass of extras hover in the shady background, occasionally bringing on materials needed for the action: a pair of scissors, a cheque book, pens and pencils. The script of the play is down stage centre, limp if not quite lifeless. On one side stand the management and assorted realistic Americans and Britishers; on the other the huge imposing figure of the Swiss playwright, now wearing dark glasses. A faint echo of Beethoven's setting of Schiller's "Ode to Joy" can be heard on the off-stage tape recorder. The management hands a cheque over the script to the playwright. The playwright, never looking down at the script, gently takes the cheque, places it in his pocket, nods, clicks his heels, and begins to move away into the crowd. If we look closely when he clicks his heels, we suddenly notice that he is wearing a sleek, black, shiny pair of new shoes. The lights fade. Beethoven can't be heard any more. Curtain.